ARNOLD BENNETT

ARNOLD BENNETT

a biography by

Margaret Drabble

Weidenfeld and Nicolson
London

for Barley Alison

ISBN 0 297 76733 X

Printed in Great Britain by
Redwood Burn Limited
Trowbridge & Esher

Contents

List of Illustrations

Introduction

My first reason for wanting to write this book was that I very much admired Arnold Bennett as a writer. I can't remember when I first read his novels but I liked them from the beginning. I started with the usual ones – *The Old Wives' Tale*, *Clayhanger* – and then moved on to his lesser known, and finally to his most frivolous books. And somewhat to my surprise, I liked them all. I'd been brought up to believe that even his best books weren't very good – Leavis dismisses him in a sentence or two, and not many people seemed to take him as seriously as I did. The best books I think are very fine indeed, on the highest level, deeply moving, original, and dealing with material that I had never before encountered in fiction, but only in life: I feel they have been underrated, and my response to them is so constant, even after years of work on them, and constant rereadings, that I want to communicate my enthusiasm. The fact that I enjoy even his minor works and his popular journalism – and he was a notoriously prolific writer – gave me an added confidence in his achievement. I don't expect everybody will share my affection for some of his fantasies, though plenty did in the past, but I've found it to be undiminished by familiarity. Some of his silliest jokes make me laugh, and his manuals on self-improvement still make me want to improve myself. I find his impact completely undiminished by time.

So I wrote the biography in a partisan spirit, as an act of appreciation. And as I wrote it, I found my admiration for Bennett as a man, and not only as a writer, was also considerable. It, too, has grown with knowledge. He was an exceptionally kind, good and generous man, who triumphed over considerable difficulties in his personal life; he was the kind of reliable, sensitive and tactful person who would make an ideal friend. Perhaps some would call his life dull, as it was not marked by any spectacular scandals, and goodness has always been thought to be less interesting than vice. I don't think this is so, and one of the things I like most about his books, his letters, his journals and journalism, is the sense they give that life is extraordinarily varied and interesting. He was the least bored and the least boring of people. He was often depressed – it would be a mistake to think he was constantly cheerful – but he was never dull. He always leaves me with a sense that life is full of possibility.

I haven't found it possible, in the scope of this book, to deal with anything like the whole of his output. He wrote an enormous number of words in his lifetime, as he himself was fond of pointing out, and nobody could hope to cover them all. I've had to leave out, for reasons of space, most of his popular handbooks, and haven't even bothered to describe when they were written or published, as otherwise this book would have become a mere list of publications. But I'd like to say here that I've enjoyed them – he liked, as he put it himself, 'a big public and plain subjects' and he was exceptionally good with them. But he certainly wouldn't have objected to their omission, for he believed that most English biographies are far too long.

He doesn't make the task of writing a short biography easy. In a way he wrote his own, in millions of words, in his *Journals*. His letters are also voluminous. So I have had to select, somewhat arbitrarily, the points about him that most interested me. This does not aim, in other words, to be a complete scholarly account of his life and work, listing every article he ever wrote and every meal he ever ate. He did a great deal of listing himself, and there seemed little point in duplicating some of it. There are several other books about Bennett (though surprisingly few), the most complete of which is Reginald Pound's *Arnold Bennett*, first published in 1952; I owe it a great debt, though I've tried not to rely on it too much. Mr Pound knew Bennett as a journalist when Bennett was a famous public man, and I haven't tried to portray that section of his life very fully: Mr Pound has done it better than I ever could. What interests me more is Bennett's background, his childhood and origins, for they are very similar to my own. My mother's family came from the Potteries, and the Bennett novels seem to me to portray a way of life that still existed when I was a child, and indeed persists in certain areas. My own attitudes to life and work were coloured by many of the same beliefs and rituals, though they were further in the past for me, but as Bennett knew all too well they are attitudes that die hard. He might have been surprised to find how closely I identify with them, after two or three generations of startling change. So, like all books, this has been partly an act of self-exploration.

There are many people I should like to thank for helping me with this work. First of all, I should like to thank Dorothy Cheston Bennett, for all the time she spared me; I enjoyed our conversations greatly, and am much in her debt for many incidents and touches of perspective which she gave me but most of all for her overall picture of Bennett as a man. It was a pleasure and a privilege to be able to talk about him with her. I've also talked to several other members of the family, all of whom were most helpful – his daughter Virginia, his nieces Margaret Shingler and Margaret Kennerley, and I have the kind permission of his nephew Richard Bennett to quote from his letters. Ruth Bennett, another neice, kindly wrote to me with help. I've met and talked to several friends of his who remembered him well – Violet Wyndham and Lady Diana Cooper brought him very much to life.

I also owe a very great debt to Professor James Hepburn, whose excellent editions of Bennett's letters have been extremely useful. His notes have been invaluable, and I have made much use of them. My thanks also to Bennett's agents, A.P.Watt, and to Methuen and Chatto and Windus (particularly Mrs Norah Smallwood) for helpful information. Useful suggestions came from many friends and acquaintances, particularly Anthony Curtis, Tim Hilton, and Ian Dunlop.

Thanks for permission to quote are also due to the Oxford University Press and Michael Holroyd.

I should like to thank Peter and Joyce Cheeseman for talking to me about Bennett's reputation in the Potteries today, and for letting me use photographs of their Bennett productions at the Victoria Theatre, Stoke-on-Trent; John Ford and Derek Beard of the Stoke Public Library for their help in locating Bennett's settings; Manny Rühl for his photographs of the district.

I should like to thank Barley Alison for encouraging me to start the project, and Tony Godwin for seeing it through, and Joan Duerdoth, who most efficiently typed out and tidied up my extremely untidy typescript. My family have patiently accompanied me on some strange excursions in pursuit of Bennett and listened to my problems with sympathy.

Lastly, I should like to thank Harold Landry for his help, and for finding me, over the years, many items of Bennett's ephemera that would not otherwise have come my way.

Postscript: In the very first paragraph of this book, I describe the Potteries as depressing. I wrote that some time ago, and I've let it stand, because it was true when I wrote it. But I must in fairness add that the reclamation schemes, then only just under way, are now flourishing, and the slag heaps are green with clover and wild flowers. In another few years, the district will have improved beyond all recognition. There are still some who don't want it improved, and who liked it as it was, dirty but distinctive, but even they must appreciate the imagination that has gone into the new landscapes. As Mr Beard said to me, it's possible now to imagine Stoke as a garden city. Five years ago such a suggestion would have seemed laughable.

I

The Five Towns

Arnold Bennett was born in a street called Hope Street. A street less hopeful
it would be hard to imagine. The house where he was born, on 27 May 1867,
has since been destroyed, but from the surrounding district one can imagine
that it is no great loss. A café now stands on the corner site, and on the wall
of the café there is a bronze commemorative plaque. As Bennett himself was
no great defender of his home towns, there is no need to protect them on his
behalf. It can be said, plainly, that there are few regions more depressing to
the eye than the Potteries today, and they must look considerably better now
than they did a hundred years ago, before the concept of clean air had been
dreamed of. The landscape lacks the scale which makes some of the industrial North (from a passing train) picturesque and dramatic, but it bears the
same scars. There are the same neglected industrial sites, the same rows of
terraced workmen's cottages, the long high brick walls, the desolate patches
of muddy grass. In 1971 the City of Stoke-on-Trent (a conurbation formed
in 1925 of the six Five Towns) boasted more derelict land within its boun-
daries than any other county borough in England. Almost a twelfth of the
city's area is officially derelict. The coal mines and the clay marl pits defy the
schemes for improvement. Trees are planted, pits are filled with slag heaps,
disused railways tracks are adorned with shrubs and used for cycling, but
it is slow work. There are grants now for reclamation, prize-winning schemes
are made, plans are being put into action. Trees will be planted on the largest
spoil heap, the one that elegantly shades Burslem Cemetery. The public
were asked if they wanted the slag heap flattened. No, they said. They liked
their slag heap. They didn't mind its being landscaped, but they didn't
want it taken away.[1] Bennett would have liked that.

Of course the squalor is not unrelieved. The flights of architectural fancy
are few, but they exist. The golden angel weather vane on the Town Hall

and the dirty but ornate façade of the Swan Bank Methodist Chapel (demolished since I began writing this) are among the rare attempts at decorative beauty, and feature as such in Bennett's books. It is not surprising that Bennett became interested in the idea of architect as hero. Beauty, in such a region, does not meet the eye: it has to be looked for; and when we find Orgreaves explaining to the young Clayhanger the virtues of the Sytch Pottery, we sense the author's relief at finding that even in such unpromising places there are, to the trained eye, points that can be admired. Edwin, having been told that the window of the Pottery is 'the most beautiful window in Bursley, and perhaps in the Five Towns' finds that he has to think again, for 'it had never occurred to him to search for anything fine in Bursley. The fact was, he had never opened his eyes at Bursley. Dozens of times he must have passed the Sytch Pottery, and yet not noticed, not suspected, that it differed from any other pot-works: he, who had dreamed of being an architect!'[2] One cannot really blame the young Clayhanger or the young Bennett for their lack of perception; although Edwin immediately decided to place the Sytch Pottery on a plane with the edifices of the capitals of Europe, a feast for discerning eyes, not many of the inhabitants can have so regarded it. And it is significant that the beautiful window, as pointed out by Mr Orgreaves, was in fact in the process of being boarded up.

It wasn't until he had left the Potteries that Bennett even thought of them as material for fiction. Having left them for London, he never went back to live there, though he visited friends and family. He could appreciate their virtues only from a distance. Indeed he claimed that he had not thought of using them as fiction until he read another man's work of fiction, George Moore's *A Mummer's Wife*; he wrote to Moore on 24 December 1920, 'I wish also to tell you that it was the first chapters of *A Mummer's Wife* which opened my eyes to the romantic nature of the district I had blindly inhabited for over twenty years. You are indeed the father of all my Five Town books.'[3] Among the passages which must have aroused his admiration in *A Mummer's Wife* are those which describe the landscapes – passages like these:

'Below her in the dazzling morning light lay a valley miles upon miles in length. It was one of those terrible cauldrons in which man melts and moulds this huge age of iron. And of what did this valley consist? Of black plains that the sunlight could not change in colour; of patches of grass, hard and metallic in hue; of tanks of water glittering like blades of steel . . . sharp as the teeth of a double saw were the interminable gables, and not a ray of light glinted against the black windows. . . . There behind Bucknell were more desolate plains full of pits, brick and smoke; and then for miles rose up against the sky, with a roll oceanic in grandeur, the interminable hills'. . . . 'No spray of green relieved the implacable perspectives, no aesthetic intention broke the frigidity of the remorseless angles. Wide widths of walls, bald rotundities of pottery ovens, reigned supreme; before them nature had disappeared, and the shrill scream of the steam tram as it rolled solemnly up the incline seemed man's cry of triumph over vanquished nature[4] [chapter 4].'

It's easy to see what Bennett saw in this: he saw scale, and dignity, and importance given to what he had thought mean and dirty and insignificant. Once a writer like Moore uses the phrase 'aesthetic intention', even if only to deny its existence, the reader enters the realm of art. And Bennett needed the distance of art to make the reality tolerable and malleable. One of the experiences he describes frequently is the experience of being aroused to aesthetic appreciation by things read or said, a very real and common experience, which many writers are too vain to admit. Bennett admits it openly. He was an insatiably self-educating man, and one of his great charms was his eagerness to learn, to be informed, to extend his appreciation; but that's not the whole clue to his admission of his dependence on Moore. (One must allow for the fact that his letter to Moore may have been in part a polite gesture towards a writer whom he genuinely admired, but I think there was at least some truth in it.) He needed Moore, because the material he grew up in, the Five Towns material, was intractable. As a fact, it was so. It was harsh, difficult, unattractive. Bennett needed a guide when he travelled abroad – and his *Florentine Journal* is touchingly full of his delightful efforts to see and understand all, through his Baedeker; but even more he needed a guide to his home town. Not because there was so much to see, as in Italy, but because there was so little. He doesn't in any way slavishly follow Moore's outlines; on the contrary he reacts against them, he is mock-heroic rather than heroic, he writes with wry human insight rather than with the visitor's eye of Moore, who saw nothing but the grandiose in the landscape. But Bennett needed the reassurance that the grandiose was there, behind it all, as a backcloth.

Bennett created the Five Towns. Once he had seen how to do it, he went ahead and made them. The reality of his creation is at times confusing; many people think not of the Potteries as they were, but of the Potteries as he described them. Even the names get mixed up. There were in fact six towns, not five, but even serious newspaper articles have to explain this,

3

because for many readers Bennett's phrase, the Five Towns, has stuck so firmly that it has more meaning than the places themselves. This is partly the fault of his own method of providing pseudonyms: he stuck so close to the original that he forgot which was which. Tunstall became Turnhill, Burslem became Bursley, Hanley became Hanbridge, Stoke became Knype, Longton became Longshaw, and Fenton he missed out altogether. On a similar scheme he converts Waterloo Road into Trafalgar Road, Swan Bank into Duck Bank – this last a highly characteristic and suitable piece of bathos. But he was not wholly bathetic or comic in his choice of names: there operated in him something of the spirit of defiance, the spirit which led to the real-life naming of the suburbs of Florence and Etruria, and it must surely have been some frolic of aspiration, some kick at the face of dreary destiny, that led him to christen his heroines by such names as Leonora and Annunciata? Harold Owen, another local man, writing in 1901 in *The Staffordshire Potter*, makes it clear that he at least considers that the naming of Etruria was ironic; he writes that the Potteries are 'unutterably unlovely', that even Birmingham has its Edgbaston but the Potteries is all Soho, and 'as for the classic suburbs of "Florence" and "Etruria", vassals to Longton and Hanley – or even the more modern if equally modest claim of Dresden – they are merely sly and deliberate examples of the irony of nomenclature.'[5] And in a way Owen may be right – which of us, familiar with the industrial North or the wastes of London, does not know some Violet Bank where surely violets never blossomed, some Primrose Road deep in soot, some Endymion Way where no goddess would ever risk her bare feet? And how can one not speculate at the motives of the council which deliberated over such a name?

The Potteries have their Paradise Street and their Paragon Road, their Pleasant Row and their Sun Street, as well as several Cemetery Roads. Perhaps it is aspiration, not irony, that inspires the choice. Bennett wanted there to be a Leonora and an Annunciata, realist though he was. Duck Bank was there, yes indeed, but why not imagine better?

One of the most appreciative visual descriptions that Bennett wrote of the Potteries was written in 1897, in his journal, when he was thirty, and long free of the place; and it too, like Edwin's appreciation of the window, bears the marks of intention and goodwill and curiosity, as much as of a natural response. He writes:

'Friday, September 10, 1897
'During this week, when I have been taking early morning walks with

Tertia and when I have been traversing the district after dark, the grim and original beauty of certain aspects of the Potteries to which I have referred in the introduction to "Anna Tellwright" has fully revealed itself for the first time. Before breakfast, on the heights of Sneyd Green, where the air blows as fresh and pure (seemingly) as at the seaside, one gets glimpses of Burslem and of the lands between Burslem and Norton, which have the very strangest charm. The stretch of road on which one stands, used by young men and women on their way to work, is sufficiently rural and untouched to be intrinsically attractive. It winds through pretty curves and undulations; it is of a good earthy colour and its borders are green and lush. Down below is Burslem, nestling in the hollow between several hills, and showing a vague picturesque mass of bricks through its heavy pall of smoke. If it were an old Flemish town, beautiful in detail and antiquely interesting, one would say its situation was ideal. It is *not* beautiful in detail, but the smoke transforms its ugliness into a beauty transcending the work of architects and of time. Though a very old town, it bears no sign of great age – the eye is never reminded of its romance and history – but instead it thrills and reverberates with the romance of machinery and manufacture. . . .'[6]

(I had a startlingly similar experience when writing *Jerusalem the Golden*, which I had based on my childhood memories of Sheffield. I wrote the book from memory, and then decided I'd better go back and check up that I'd remembered right, so I went up for a night, arriving after dark and staying in the Station Hotel. In the morning I was expecting to look out of the window and see those soul-destroying grim industrial perspectives, but in fact I looked out, the sun was shining, the hillsides were glittering, green fields fringed the horizon, it was all bright and sparkling and beautiful. I felt as though I had maligned the place completely in my memory. After the flat dull overbuilt sprawl of London, it was Sheffield that looked like Jerusalem. Of course, clean air may have had something to do with this impression. Sheffield is a different city now, since the Clean Air Act of 1956: the creation of Smoke Control areas, in 1959 and 1972, has transformed its views and its atmosphere. A similar change has of course overtaken Stoke-on-Trent; Burslem no longer appears from the heights of Sneyd Green to lie 'in a heavy pall of smoke', as Sheffield used to lie in my memories of the 1940s and 1950s, when one returned to it from the hillsides of Derbyshire.)

Bennett's admiration of the views of the Potteries is perhaps somewhat constrained, as was and is mine of Sheffield: no amount of goodwill can transform Sheffield into Rome, or Burslem into an old Flemish town, however much one may wish to try. It is not wholly complimentary to one's birthplace to return to it after years of exile and find it not as bad as one remembered. It's typical of Bennett that he had to make the reference to the old Flemish town, just as Edwin Clayhanger had to see the Sytch Pottery as an edifice on a plane with the capitals of Europe. The Five Towns have their virtues, but only retrospectively, when gilded by a superior and wider knowledge. Bennett must have been describing his own feelings in *Leonora*, when the hero, a businessman made good, returns to his home town from America, and reflects: 'And during all those racing years of clangour and success in New York, the life of Bursley, self-sufficient and self-contained, had preserved its monotonous and slow stolidity. Bursley had become a museum to him; he entered it as he might have entered the Middle Ages. Some of the streets seemed like a monument of the past, a picturesque survival; the crate-floats, drawn by swift, shaggy ponies . . . struck him as the quaintest thing in the world' [chapter 2].[7]

These are indeed the sentiments of the returning conqueror. As Harold Owen said, 'The greatest advantage incidental to living in the Potteries is the hope of being able to make enough money to live out of it.'[8] And when you're out, you can look back with pleasure. You can enjoy, then, the quaintness of the old names – the Sytch, the Hadderage, the Jenkins, Hole House – without having to live with them. Burslem isn't Bruges. It takes will-power even to see a whisper of the past, and it takes an iron will to see beauty in the smoke that shrouds the present, and romance in manufacture. But then, an iron will was what the Bennett family had. They made themselves, they made life, out of poor materials; they transformed, through the effort of the will, the little that they were given.

Will-power was a Wesleyan inheritance. The community as a whole was deeply imbued with a faith in the virtues of hard work, discipline and self-help, and regarded poverty as a moral failing. Bennett, an extremely hard-working, productive and industrious man, continued to the end of his life to describe himself as naturally lazy, partly because the standards of effort set for him were so high. H.G.Wells claimed that one cause of Bennett's enormous output was the ingrained belief that idleness was somehow wicked, a loophole for sin. This is no doubt what the Methodist community believed, and Bennett himself had an added incentive to effort in the example of his own father, who was a man of dogged, dogmatic, inbred perseverance. Enoch Bennett, Arnold's father, had left school at the age of twelve to become a potter like his own father, returned to school as an apprentice pupil teacher

6

a couple of years later, went back to the potbanks and became a partner in a firm which failed, took up pawn-broking – the house in Hope Street where Arnold was born was a pawnbroker's and small-draper's shop – and finally became a solicitor at the age of thirty-four. With an example like that behind him, indeed constantly before him, it's not surprising that Arnold felt driven. He was driven. His father did not leave his example to speak for itself, he constantly sang the praises of endeavour, he would not let the children play on the streets, he insisted that they should study and work hard, and make 'sustained efforts'. Although brought up in comparative affluence, Arnold must have felt the breath of poverty and disgrace behind him. He claims that he could remember the shaming black bundles of clothes in the hall of the house in Hope Street. His was the first member of the family to rise to the professional classes, and it was up to Arnold, as the eldest son, to maintain progress.

It would be a mistake, however, though a natural one, to imagine that Bennett's family had experienced, in living memory, the spectacular hardships which he describes so movingly in *Clayhanger*. Darius Clayhanger, who started work at the age of seven in the potbanks, and was rescued from the Poorhouse by Mr Shushions the Sunday School teacher, went through worse than Enoch Bennett knew, though in many ways he is modelled on Enoch: he had his bad temper, his indigestion, his discipline, his ambition. The descriptions of his labours as a child, and his days in the workhouse, are not drawn from Enoch's own past, but largely from a book by William Shaw published in 1903, called *When I was a Child, Recollections of an Old Potter*. But Arnold Bennett's knowledge of such matters cannot have been gleaned wholly from books. It must have been in the air. The Bennetts had been potters for generations, probably since the industry developed towards the end of the seventeenth century; in 1786 John Bennett, potter, was sufficiently educated to sign his own name in the marriage register at Norton-in-the-Moors, and he was Arnold's great-great-grandfather. Conditions changed during the nineteenth century, but they were still, in Bennett's father's youth, appalling. In 1843, the year of Enoch Bennett's birth, the report on the Staffordshire Potteries compiled by Samuel Scriven gives a horrifying picture of child labour, of 'jiggers and mould-runners, who by the very nature of their work are rendered pale, weak, diminutive and unhealthy. . . . During this inclement season I have seen these boys running to and fro on errands, or to their dinners, without stockings, shoes or jackets, and with perspiration standing on their foreheads, after labouring like little slaves, with the mercury 20 degrees below freezing . . . many die of consumption, asthma and acute inflammations.'[9] This picture is all the more horrible because Scriven does not seem to realize what he is saying, and continues to describe the employers as men of 'warm-hearted sympathy'.

Although Enoch himself never worked on the potbank as a child of seven, he must have known plenty who had or did. Many of them, like Darius in *Clayhanger*, were stoics: Jacob Ball, twelve-year-old runner of dish moulds, is quoted by Scriven as saying he would like a chance to 'play me a bit. I should like to go to school, evenings; I should do that too. . . .'[10] It was a hard-working inheritance, without self-pity. Conditions gradually improved, with Factory Acts restricting and finally forbidding child labour, but pottery remained a dangerous industry. In 1860, six years before Bennett was born, a typical obituary in *The Potter* (18 August 1860) reads: 'For a flat presser, he exceeded the average age, the years of his life numbering fifty.' In 1891 the Factory and Workshop Bill reformed sanitary conditions in the work-shops, but it wasn't until seven years later that there was a Home Office inquiry into lead poisoning, which resulted, the following year, in a notifica-tion from Whitehall that the use of raw lead must be discontinued entirely. The number of cases of lead poisoning dropped, but even so as late as 1905 seventy-five cases were recorded, twenty-nine of them women and girls. The past died slowly, and Bennett, sitting in Paris or London or on his yacht, never forgot that but for his own labours and those of his father before him he might well have been suffering from lead poisoning himself. Nor did he ever, like so many self-made men, turn against the working man with self-righteous indignation; he never scorned the failure to rise, he sometimes disagreed with but never sneered at the unions, he never regarded poverty as a crime. In fact he completely lacked the censorious side of Methodism, its judging, its sniffing and sneering, its righteous scorn for others; he kept his high standards to himself and didn't try to impose them on others.

If potting was the industry of the district, Methodism was its religion, and the two together formed the Bennett inheritance. By the time Bennett was born, religion was a more potent force than potting in the family. The first member of the Bennett family to take the significant step of becoming a Wesleyan Methodist was Sampson, son of John the potter; he joined the Methodist faith round about the year 1816, by which time Methodism was flourishing all over the Potteries. It was a religion ideally suited to the district, as Wesley found when he visited Burslem: his first visit, in 1760, was rather a wash-out because, as he crossly remarked in his *Journal*, 'the cold con-siderably lessened the congregation. Such is human wisdom! So small are the things which divert mankind from what might be the means of their eternal salvation!' But the word did not fall on deaf ears, for he made converts; when he went back three years later he found 'a large congregation at Burslem; these poor potters four years ago were as wild and ignorant as any of the colliers in Kingswood. Lord' [he says, enigmatically, possibly intending a pun?], 'thou hast power over thine own clay!'[11] After this, Methodism spread rapidly, and chapels sprang up all over the Five Towns: the first was built in 1766, and chapel-building went on right through the decline of the congregations at the end of the nineteenth century, for, as Bennett cynically observes in *These Twain*, the response of the Wesleyan community to a falling attendance and shortage of ministers was to 'prove that Wesleyanism was spiritually vigorous by the odd method of building more chapels'.[12]

At the beginning, however, Wesleyanism was truly a religion of the people and for the people. It was a genuine working-class movement, which offered spiritual hope and material improvement to its followers. It offered education, betterment, a brighter future in material terms, and an emotional release from the grim realities of the present. It preached thrift, discipline and frugality. Unfortunately these very virtues were to become weapons in the hands of the employers, and created the ambiguous attitudes to wealth and self-help and industry that were almost to ruin the religion's spiritual power. The Methodist was the ideal workman, as the employers were quick to realize: Robert Peel, writing in 1787, says: 'I have left most of my works in Lancashire in the management of Methodists, and they have served me excellently well.'[13] The improved Methodist, with honestly saved money in his pocket, became just as repressive and worldly as the churchmen he had despised. Wesley himself foresaw this dilemma, when he wrote:

'... religion must necessarily produce both industry and frugality, and these cannot but produce riches. But as riches increase, so will anger and pride and love of the world. ... How then is it possible that Methodism, that is, a religion of the heart, though it now flourishes as a green bay tree, should continue in this state? For the Methodists in every place grow diligent and frugal; consequently they increase in goods. Hence they disproportionately increase in pride, in anger, in the desire of the flesh, the desire of the eyes, and the pride of life.'[14]

He might have been foreseeing the exact combination of frugality and wealth that produced Auntie Hamps, in *Clayhanger*, lavish in her black ribbons, bestowing golden sovereigns on nephews and great nephews, feeding her servant on dripping, and dying proudly in an unheated bedroom, considering herself a thoroughly religious woman, while her nephew considered her a thorough hypocrite. It was the double-thinking of Methodism that annoyed Bennett most profoundly, as a child and as an adult, and his rebellion against it lies behind many of his absurd extravagances – those frilly expensive shirts, those fictitious scenes in which people impulsively buy expensive bags and cars, or burn up pound notes. He sensed from the beginning that parents and aunts and uncles imposed religion on children not because they themselves truly believed in it, but because, like employers with workmen, they thought it was good for them; in *My Religious Experience*, he writes: 'We children felt that religion was imposed upon us not for religious but for disciplinary reasons.' Similar suspicions were voiced by my mother, who was brought up in a similar chapel-going district in South Yorkshire; she recalls even now the indignation with which she realized that Chapel and Sunday School were being used as ways of keeping children quiet while adults slept after Sunday lunch. The good workman, like the good child, does what he is told, is clean and quiet, does not play marbles, saves his money (the poor Clayhanger children, like the wretched children in *Bleak House*, are forced to save up their birthday money), does not drink, does not waste time on pleasure.

The two tendencies of Methodism, the popular and the respectably repressive, caused several schisms in the Movement, one of which originated in the Potteries: two Staffordshire men, deciding that Methodism was getting too dull and unspiritual, began to hold open-air meetings on the hill of Mow Cop. They were accused of encouraging wild, over-excited gatherings and were expelled. They formed a breakaway group, the Society of Primitive Methodists. In 1836 there was another schism in the district, which directly involved Bennett's own family and which also involved that extremely significant institution, the Sunday School, which played so large a part in the novels of Bennett and the lives of millions. The particular incident was the breakaway in Burslem of a group of Sunday School teachers, who were expelled from Swan Bank Methodist Church.

The reason why they were expelled was extremely interesting. They were expelled because they refused to stop teaching. One might have innocently supposed that the purpose of a Sunday School was to teach, but it was not as simple as that. The early Sunday Schools – by no means all of them Wesleyan, though Wesley thoroughly approved of them – did indeed have in mind the purpose of teaching; they sprang up all over the country in the eighteenth and nineteenth centuries, and they offered opportunities of education to children who worked a six-day week, and worked the incredibly long hours that were then permitted. Children who started full-time work at school age had nowhere else to go to learn, and those who wished to learn to read and write loved their Sunday School with a touching passion. Some of the early descriptions of these schools are amazing, to those accustomed to think of the Sunday School as a dumping ground: William Shaw, the author of *When I was a Child*, writes: 'What shall I say of the benefit I got from the Sunday School? To speak of the benefit it has been to this nation would be a joy, and all I could say would fail to tell the measure of its beneficence and inspiration, especially to the children of the poor in those days. To me, very soon, it was a life within my life.... Sunday was verily an oasis in the desert to me.'[15] In these schools children not only found peace and quiet after the muck and grind of the factory; they found dedicated men and women, willing to spend time trying to teach them all the things of which their social class had deprived them. They offered a chance to catch up, to make good: they offered the only chance, before compulsory primary education, for the working-class child.

Unfortunately, the powers above soon noticed that although thrift and frugality were good for workmen, education was not necessarily at all to the employer's advantage, and a distinct change of policy emerged. It was decided that, after all, it was wicked to teach poor children to write: a pamphlet by Robert Martin called *The Impropriety and Sinfulness of teaching children to write on the Lord's Day* shows clearly enough what kind of excuses were thought up to cover this essentially political decision. The teaching of writing was prohibited by the Methodist Conference: Jabez Bunting, one of the most powerful Methodist ministers in the first half of the nineteenth century, was determined to put an end to what he called 'this secular art', and he succeeded. Reading was still allowed, because after all the poor had to be able to read the Holy Scriptures. It's hard now to picture the pious Sunday Schools as hot-beds of Jacobinism and dissent and radicalism, but that's how they were regarded. The poor, of course, were quite well aware of the reasons why they were being deprived of their education: Shaw, the Old Potter, says, 'I remember hearing a clergyman oppose educating the people on the grounds that they would write nasty things on the walls',[16] a fair description of the first level of political consciousness. Samuel Bamford, the distinguished Lancashire radical, learned to write at the Methodist Sunday School of Middleton – he gives a good description in his autobiography of the difference between the old style and the new:

'I soon mastered the rudimentary lines, and quitting "pothooks and ladles," as they were called, I commenced writing largehand. For the real old Armenian Methodists . . . thought it no desecration to enable the rising generation, on that day [i.e. Sunday] to write the Word of God as well as to read it. Had the views and very commendable practice of these old fathers been continued in the Sunday School generally, the reproach would not have been cast upon our labouring population, as it was in the publication of the census of 1841, that a greater proportion of the working classes of Lancashire were unable to write their names, than were to be found in several counties less favoured by means of instruction. The modern Methodists may boast this feat as their especial work. The Church party never undertook to instruct in writing on Sundays; the old Armenian Wesleyans did undertake it, and succeeded wonderfully, but the Conferential Methodists put a stop to it.'[17]

In fact, it was in order to put a stop to just such men as Samuel Bamford that the Methodist Conference of 1814 did vote as it did, in favour of no writing in schools. Bamford learned far more than to write his name on the wall; he became a reformer, an agitator, and an author – altogether a bad influence, from the employers' point of view.

It wasn't only the pupils who objected to the new reactionary school of thought on education; some of the teachers objected too. To return to the Bennett family – when a group of Sunday School teachers at the big Chapel at Swan Bank in Burslem were told to stop teaching, they refused. The orthodox Wesleyans were so incensed that they not only expelled them, they actually locked them out. Undaunted, and convinced of their social mission, the teachers went off with most of their pupils and founded Hill Top Chapel, which opened in 1837. Its inscription read, defiantly, Burslem Sunday School. The Bennett family became members of this chapel and John Bennett, Arnold's grandfather, was a trustee and superintendent. Hill Top had a Benevolent Fund, a Clothing Fund and a library, but it was by no means altogether progressive – 'a Minister was asked not to play cricket, a local preacher was reprimanded for attending the theatre, and Sunday school teachers were reported for skating on Sunday'.[18]

But by the time Arnold Bennett himself came to Sunday School age, the dramas of schism and lock-outs were little more than a backcloth. Indeed the Bennett family had moved back to Swan Bank, which now taught reading and writing not on Sundays, but on Monday evenings. Sunday School was now a dreary obligation to those who could get their education in greater comfort during the week; the old imposed it on the young as a matter of form. The heroic days were over. It is not surprising that what Bennett emphasizes most in his own religious background is its hypocrisy. Methodism was an extraordinarily double-edged affair. One of its most puzzling features, to those not reared under its shadow, was (and perhaps still is) its strange combination of emotionalism, enthusiasm, even fervour, and extreme dourness and repression: and this was, at heart, evidence of its greatest hypocrisy, its most profound double-thinking. For Methodism really was, in a sense, the opium of the people. It was masochistic, submissive, debasing. It gave the people a sense of release, of emotional indulgence, while at the same time vigorously repressing all disturbing manifestations of energy: sexual, social or political. All the latent emotionalism of hard-working people was channelled off into Chapel, and even Bennett, rationalist as he was, felt at times its surreptitious pull. Christianity has often been called a slave religion, and the Methodists, singing of bleeding wounds and fountains of blood and loads of sin, and wallowing in their abasement, must certainly invite the accusation. And of course this religion could easily be turned, as we have seen, to the employer's advantage; it suited him well to have a work force crushed with guilt, conscious of its own shortcomings, eager to find salvation through labour, keen to eschew the diversions of drink, games, cricket, skating, fives, marbles. In Dr Andrew Ure's alarming work *Philosophy of Manufacture* (1835) this view is seen in its true colours: he urges the utility of moral discipline, praises Sunday Schools as 'fortresses against vice', and persuades mill-owners that if they 'organise their moral machinery on equally sound principles with their mechanical' they will find the truth of the Gospel saying, that 'Godliness is great gain'. This was the Dr Ure who saw, in the miserable Darius Clayhanger and Jacob Ball, 'lively elves', 'always cheerful and alert, taking pleasure in the light play of their muscles – enjoying the mobility natural to their age. . . . As to exhaustion by the day's work, they show no trace of it.'[19] The moral, to Dr Ure, is clear: people love work, and there is no better workman than a Methodist, thoroughly convinced that idleness is wicked and drinking a vice, whose libido is harmlessly fulfilled in metaphors of blood and sin.

The people were not, of course, completely crushed. They continued to try to organize themselves in unions, to fight back politically, to assert their rights. But for some reason the potters were not very good at political action; most of their efforts petered out and came to nothing. The one thing they would not relinquish was the Wakes, which was their annual festivity, at which they let off steam. Various attempts were made to stop them (by employers and ministers combined) but the men always won: Josiah Wedgwood wrote plaintively that however he tried to persuade his employees to work through the Wakes, by promising them a longer Christmas, 'I know it is all in vain, for Wakes must be observed though the world was to end with them.'[20] The Wakes were a huge orgy of festivity in the drab lives of the people; and as such they fitted in peculiarly well with the emotional rhythms of Methodism itself. The early Methodists had been emotional enough, but as the religion had become more and more respectable displays of feeling had become less and less acceptable; by the middle and late nineteenth century all that was permitted was the odd emotional binge, in the form of a revival meeting or a procession. E.P.Thompson, in *The Making of the English Working Class*, describes this peculiar rhythm. He says:

> 'But what must be stressed is the *intermittent character* of Wesleyan emotionalism. Nothing was more remarked by contemporaries of the workaday Methodist character or of Methodist home life, than its methodical, disciplined and repressed disposition. It is the paradox of a "religion of the heart" that it should be notorious for the inhibition of all spontaneity. Methodism sanctioned "workings of the heart" only upon occasions of the Church; Methodists wrote hymns but no secular poetry of note; the idea of a passionate Methodist lover in these years is ludicrous.'[21]

This account is extremely relevant to Bennett's own development as a man, and to the background of his novels. He was without doubt sexually inhibited by his repressive background, and he knew it; this was one of the reasons why he loathed the 'pietistic religious humbug' of his home town. It had maimed him, and he never forgave it. Unlike many youthful materialists and radicals, he never softened into respectable middle-aged religiosity and public church- or chapel-going: he maintained his anti-religious position till the end, writing very near the end of his life a pamphlet called *The Religious Interregnum*, in which he stresses the cruelty committed by organized faiths, their intolerance, their bigotry: 'Religious propaganda,' he says, 'has always been marked by desperate cruelty . . . narrow-mindedness, injustice and tyranny', and he also comments that 'most religious people spend their time vilifying the views of others'.[22] He was not perhaps the thorough-going materialist he declared himself to be; few are. There are signs in his later life and novels of an interest in the less organized forms of religion – he attended a spiritualist seance with Roger Fry and Yeats, he read a little of Mrs Besant, he pondered on the life of the spirit and the power of dreams. But Methodism was a dead letter to him; he took as his own creed the verse that the Methodists most signally ignored: 'Judge not, that ye be not judged.'

In *The Religious Interregnum* he states that he himself had never 'felt within [him] the operation of a religious instinct. Even as a schoolboy . . . I never felt anything but a cautious disdain for the impassioned beliefs surrounding me.'[23] And this was doubtless true. Nevertheless, it was impossible wholly to resist the weight of feeling in the Wesleyan community, however insincere one might feel it to be. In his Five Towns novels Bennett gives a fine description of a certain phase of historical and religious development; the phase towards the end of the century, when Methodists were wealthy, respectable, no longer embodying dissent but spokesmen of conformity – indeed it was said 'you were no good in Burslem unless you were a Wesleyan'[24] and the Methodist chapels greatly outnumbered the Church of England establishments. (According to the Victoria County History, there were forty-six Methodist chapels in the Potteries by 1851, twenty-three other Nonconformist places of worship, and only seventeen churches; there was a great spate of chapel building in the 1890s, as well.)

Bennett found the weight of respectability stifling. In later years he was to love casual social life, bohemian behaviour, eccentricity. Nevertheless, the Methodists had not managed to wipe out all feeling from their lives; they were still, even in Bennett's day, given to great emotional outbursts on approved occasions. Such an upbringing cannot be shaken off entirely, and Bennett reports upon its exact historical phase with objectivity, with feeling, but without sourness – a rare enough feat when one remembers how crippling such a background might have been. He forgave it, as he forgave his father, and one of the finest descriptions in *Clayhanger* is of the Sunday School Centenary, which Edwin Clayhanger and his contemporaries attend in a spirit of superiority, contempt and patronage, only to find themselves moved, despite all. Here is Edwin, in the Square, listening to the huge inter-denominational gathering singing that Freudian piece (deeply disapproved, as I remember, by the Quakers):

> 'Rock of Ages, cleft for me,
> Let me hide myself in Thee;
> Let the water and the blood,
> From thy riven side which flowed,
> Be of sin the double cure:
> Cleanse me from its guilt and power.

'The volume of sound was overwhelming. Its crashing force was enough to sweep people from barrels. Edwin could feel moisture in his eyes, and he dared not look at Hilda. "Why the deuce do I want to cry?" he asked himself angrily, and was ashamed. And at the beginning of the second verse, when the glittering instruments blared forth anew, and the innumerable voices, high and loud, infantile and aged, flooded swiftly over their brassy notes, subduing them, the effect on Edwin was the same again: a tightening of the throat, and a squeezing down of the eyelids. Why was it? Through a mist he read the words "The Blood of the Lamb", and he could picture the riven trunk of a man dying, and a torrent of blood flowing therefrom, and people like his Auntie Clara and his brother-in-law Albert plunging ecstatically into the liquid in order to be white. The picture came again in the third verse – the red fountains and the frantic bathers.'

Later, a preacher appeals to the crowds, announcing that 'even for the veriest infant on a lorry, there was no escape from the eternal fires save by a complete immersion in the blood. And he was so convinced and convincing that an imaginative nose could have detected the odour of burnt flesh.' After a little more of this, Edwin has suddenly had enough. The mist before his eyes clears, and he turns to his companion, Hilda Lessways, and whispers: "More blood!"

' "What?" she harshly questioned. But he knew that she understood.
' "Well," he said, audaciously, "look at it! It only wants the Ganges at the bottom of the square – " '[25]

Hilda implores him not to make fun, even though, as she says 'we don't believe'. And a few minutes later she is passionately defending 'When I Survey the Wondrous Cross' as the most splendid religious verse ever written. And Edwin thinks, fancy exciting herself over a hymn, forgetful that he himself, a few minutes earlier, was on the verge of tears over the 'Rock of Ages'. Here, in passages like this, Bennett perfectly catches the death-throes of the old passion, and the mingled awe and scorn of the younger generation who dare to defy it.

There is another beautiful expression of the difference between the old and the new Methodists in the same book – the old and the new, as described by Samuel Bamford. It is embodied, suitably enough, in the character of a Sunday School teacher, old Mr Shushions, who had once, long ago, saved Edwin's father, Darius Clayhanger, from the workhouse. When Edwin first sees Shushions talking to his father he regards the old man 'impatiently, as an aged simpleton, probably over pious, certainly connected with the Primitive Methodists'. Mr Shushions's credentials are presented partly by the services he has rendered in the past to Darius, which Edwin never learns, and partly by his present contempt for a hilarious notion called the 'Prayer Gauge', devised by Sir Henry Thompson – 'The scheme was to take certain hospitals and to pray for the patients in particular wards, leaving the other wards unprayed for, and then to tabulate and issue the results.' (There is another fascinating dissertation on the same theme in *These Twain*, where the children decide to test the efficacy of prayer by praying for a penknife, and are somewhat frightened when a concealed adult, overhearing their prayer, throws a penknife into the garden where they are gathered. Their shock almost outweighs their delight, but they decide nevertheless to push their luck and try for a bicycle, though, as one of them says, 'We'd better all stand as close as we can to the wall, under the spouting, in case.') Mr Shushions is entirely opposed to such irreverent trials of God's powers: 'I've preached in the pulpits o' our Connexion for over fifty years ... but I'd ne'er gi' out another text if Primitives had ought to do wi' such a flouting o' th' Almighty.' He turns up again later in the book, at the Sunday School Centenary, old, toothless, doddering, to be mocked by all around, and refused his rightful place on the platform, mumbling in a senile fashion of the past – 'Aye,' the old man droned, 'I was Super when we had to teach 'em their alphabet and give 'em a crust to start with. Many's the man walking about these towns i' purple and fine raiment as I taught his letters to, and his spelling, aye, and his multiplication table – in them days!'[26] There indeed is a description of the old style, completely rejected by the new, and it's much to Bennett's credit that he could see the difference, although much nearer to both than we are now. Bennett is one of the greatest writers of the passage of time in the English language. Here he is at his best, in his epitaph on Shushions, which serves also as an epitaph for the Primitive faith itself.

'Thus was the doddering old fool who had given his youth to Sunday schools when Sunday schools were not patronized by princes, archbishops and lord mayors, when Sunday schools were the scorn of the intelligent, and had sometimes to be held in public-houses for lack of better accommodation – thus was he taken off for a show and a museum curiosity by indulgent and shallow Samaritans who had not even the wit to guess that he had sown what they were reaping.... And Darius Clayhanger stood oblivious at a high window of the sacred Bank. And Edwin, who, all unconscious, owed the very fact of his existence to the doting imbecile, regarded him chiefly as a figure in a tableau, as the chance instrument of a woman's beautiful revelation. Mr Shushions's sole crime against society was that he had forgotten to die.'

If Shushions represents the old school, the new is represented by the parson Abel Peartree, in Bennett's real life a Mr Appleby – another example of the subtle system on which Bennett invented his pseudonyms. It is Peartree who, in *Clayhanger*, is so loathed by Edwin for his introduction of Saturday Afternoon Bible Classes for schoolboys, and who turns up again twenty years later in *These Twain* to try to persuade Edwin to act as district treasurer for the Macclesfield District Additional Chapels Fund, a fate from which he is saved only by the bravery of his wife Hilda, who has the audacity to declare that she and Edwin are no great chapel-goers. And it's interesting to note that Peartree and Auntie Hamps were the couple responsible for converting Darius from Primitive Methodism to Wesleyan Methodism. In the same way, Bennett describes the congregation in the chapel in Duck Bank in *The Old Wives' Tale* as 'influential', a 'magnificent and proud majority', and comments on Mr Povey, sitting there quietly, 'a recent convert from Primitive Methodism in King Street to Wesleyan Methodism on Duck Bank, dwelling upon window tickets and the injustice of women. . . .'[27] Evidently, the journey from King Street to Duck Bank, from Primitive to Wesleyan, was a journey up the social ladder. Edwin, in King Street – William Clowes Street – where Auntie Hamps lies dying, is shocked by its squalor – 'suddenly thrown back into it at its most lugubrious and ignoble, after years of the amenities of Trafalgar Road, he was somehow surprised that that sort of thing still continued to exist. . . .'[28] Is it possible to detect in Bennett's attitude to the old and the new a slight shame at the family's social climbing? Are there any memories of old John Bennett, Super at Hill Top, woven into the portrait of Shushions, Super for so many years in the Connexion?

The Wesleyan Methodists, then, are seen through Bennett's eyes as hypocrites and conformists, with what justice we must judge for ourselves. His moments of sympathy for the faith are rare. Anna, in *Anna of the Five Towns*, is certainly a sincere believer and a Sunday School teacher at that, but even she has difficulties in feeling the true movements of grace. She tries desperately, at a revival meeting, to be saved and converted; like Edwin, she falls partly under the spell of the emotional, hypnotic force of the revivalist, but like Edwin she cannot fully submit, she is filled, even in the midst of her efforts, by 'a vague sensation which was partly sorrow and partly an inexplicable dull anger – anger at her own penitence'. She is full of shame and discomfort, and as she emerges from chapel 'a doubt whether the whole affair was not after all absurd flashed through her, and was gone'.[29] She is a sincere, religious young woman, but the point Bennett makes is that she is atypical – much more typical is her old father the miser, who had inherited a small fortune from his father, a Wesleyan Methodist, and who, himself an ardent Methodist, was much less smitten with the doctrine and spirit than with 'those fiscal schemes of organization without whose aid no religious propaganda can possibly succeed. It was in the finance of salvation that he rose supreme – the interminable alternation of debt-raising and new liability which provides a lasting excitement for Nonconformists. In the negotiation of mortgages, the artful arrangement of appeals, the planning of anniversaries and of mighty revivals, he was an undisputed leader. To him the circuit was "a going concern". . . .'[30] One could not hope for a clearer description of the connection between religious and financial enthusiasm. The old miser represents spiritual thrift and meanness to a grotesque degree. But, as Bennett suggests, there were many like him, dating from those industrious factory managers of the eighteenth century described by Robert Peel. The endless round of appeals, disputes, prayer meetings, sewing meetings, chapel-building and anniversaries was a whole way of life. For many it was the only social life of the district.

There is no doubt that one of the things Bennett most resented about Methodism was its effect on social life, and its contribution to the peculiar joylessness of provincial towns in his day. His emphasis on this joylessness strikes us strangely, at times, today, for one of the features of his novels that delights most is his ability to convey the variety and charm of daily existence, even when far removed from organized entertainment. But perhaps, after all, it is the irreligious families in his novels that enjoy themselves most. Certainly Bennett himself became an ardent believer in enjoyment. He liked theatres, music, art, parties. Writing in *Our Women* in 1920 he says: 'To my mind the tragedy of existence – provincial existence in particular – fifty years ago lay in the failure of communities to organize themselves for pleasure',[31] a sentiment which is reinforced with a different emphasis by the Old Potter, writing in 1903, who says: 'It was my misfortune to live in a town where there was not then one public institution to help those who had either taste or ambition to rise above their environments.'[32]

Of course the Potteries were not completely devoid of entertainments – there was singing, clog dancing, the circus, the football club, a music-hall. And there were the Wakes, for a week every year, in June, a week of 'orgiastic carnival'.[33] These popular delights, however, were frowned upon by the religious and the respectable. Although there were theatres, such as the Blood Tub (properly known as the Wedgwood Theatre, and so-called because of the bloody melodramas it put on), in Burslem, and the theatre in Hanley which George Moore describes in *A Mummer's Wife*, it was considered slightly risqué to go to them: the audience for the amateur production of *Patience* in *Leonora* consisted of both those who 'had never been in a theatre, either from lack of opportunity or from a moral objection to theatres', and others who avoided opera but 'seldom missed a melodrama at the Hanbridge Theatre Royal'.[34] Characteristic of the general attitude towards the drama is Bennett's mother's comment, recorded by him in his *Journal* on 18 July 1910: 'Tertia said that the mater said, on seeing *Carmen* at Hanley Theatre, "I don't like that woman at all." '[35] But at least she went. The Bennetts were, relatively, an enlightened family.

Culturally, the towns did improve as the century wore on. Libraries were opened, discussion groups sprang up. An art school was founded in Hanley, which also established itself as a musical centre; Elgar conducted the first performance of *King Olaf* there in 1896, in the fine Victoria Hall. In 1869 the Wedgwood Memorial Institute was opened in Burslem; this was an ambitious and remarkable building, with a very elaborate, highly decorated façade. It contained a museum, a picture gallery, lecture rooms, a reading room and a school of art. Increasingly prosperity enabled families to go for summer holidays to the fervently disputed rival delights of Llandudno or Blackpool. Bennett himself was keenly aware of the civilizing effect of a holiday, as he shows so poignantly in his description of Anna's trip to the Isle of Man (*Anna of the Five Towns*, chapter 10) and in his own constant delight in travel. Towards the end of the century and the beginning of the twentieth century new parks were opened in several of the towns, proving that some effort was being made to reclaim and make attractive the vast areas of wasteland that adorned and still adorn this rather disorganized group of districts. In the first chapter of *Helen with the High Hand* Bennett grows quite lyrical about the charms of the new Burslem town park, with its emblazoned gates, elegant railings, fountains, cascades, bowls, brass bands and wildfowl. He admits that 'in spite of the park's vaunted situation, nothing can be seen from it save the chimneys and kilns of earthenware manufactories, the scaffoldings of pitheads, the ample dome of the rate collector's office, the railway, the minarets of nonconformity . . . but I tell you, before the days of the park the lovers had no place to walk in but the cemetery. . . . That is the sufficient answer to any criticism of the park.'[36]

Finally, it would be ridiculous to speak of the culture of the Potteries without considering their most important contribution to the culture of the nation, the pots themselves. Despite the ruination of the landscape and the dangers and miseries of labour, the Five Towns did and still do produce some of the finest works of art in England, a fact of which the region is proud, although it is equally proud of the muckheaps which it votes to keep. But this local pride is curiously and characteristically uninvolved and un-expressed; people from the Five Towns do not boast about their products or their achievements. Bennett himself showed hardly any interest in the local industry and art when he was a child, despite the fact that his grand-father had 'the reputation of unsurpassed skill as a "turner" '. Perhaps the aspiring Bennett family thought of pottery as trade, something to be for-gotten outside work hours; a long history of labour lay behind them, pre-venting them from seeing the romance of industry. It took Bennett years to work up curiosity about his own potting inheritance; he says he began to make inquiries about it when he was '29 or 30' because he needed the infor-mation for a novel.[37] He does describe various aspects of the industry in some detail in various novels and stories, but the only occasion on which he shows any real artistic appreciation of the pots as works of art is in his short story, 'The Death of Simon Fuge'. The narrator, a ceramics expert from the British Museum, comes up to the Five Towns to inspect some slip-decorated dishes, and finds himself impressed not only by the dishes but also by the amount and intensity of the social and cultural activity that flourishes so far from London. It is perhaps Bennett's warmest picture of life in the Potteries – and yet even this picture is filtered through the lens of a de Maupassant short story. He saw the model, then rebuilt the memory. The cultured musical doctors, the witty museum keepers, the complicated barmaids seem more real to him when seen through the eyes of a French realist.

This chapter has been some attempt to describe the background, historical and physical, in which Bennett grew up, and of which he wrote with such mixed emotions. One of my favourite anecdotes from Bennett's journal perfectly expresses the character of a way of life, a way of life which amused, enraged and inspired him. It deals once again with a subject that clearly fascinated him, as a comic concept, if not as a theological one – the efficacy of prayer.

'Sunday, December 24, 1899
'Thomas Arrowsmith called on John Beardmore for a subscription to Burslem Wesleyan Chapel. Beardmore declined to contribute, and explained how he was losing money on all hands and had in fact had a very bad year. He went to such lengths of pessimism that Arrowsmith at last interrupted:
' "If things are as bad as that, Mr Beardmore," he said, "we'll have a

word of prayer," and without an instant's hesitation he fell on his knees.
'Beardmore began to stamp up and down the room.

' "None o' that nonsense," he shouted. "None o' that nonsense. Here's half a sovereign for ye." '[38]

Bennett makes no comment. There is no need for one.

2

Bennett's Childhood

There is not very much to be gained from tracing the Bennett family ancestry in detail. It was not distinguished – as in so many English families, the majority were hard-working unnoticeable people, in this case mostly potters, rent-collectors, shopkeepers. Some combined potting and shopkeeping. And again, like so many families, it had its claims to artistic talent – there was the musical aunt, the uncle who painted. There was also the notorious distant figure, James Brindley, whose importance in the story lies more in the interesting pride which Arnold felt in him than in the facts of the family tree, for the connection was merely rumoured, illegitimate, non-proven. James Brindley was a canal engineer (1716–72) and a man of genius. Encouraged by the Duke of Bridgewater, he designed and built 360 miles of canals in the north of England and the Midlands – he was responsible for the Grand Trunk Canal, the Staffordshire, Worcestershire, Coventry, Oxford, Chesterfield and Birmingham canals. He was a man of vision and also a man of great practical talent, a combination which Bennett particularly admired. Bennett says in his journal that it was his Uncle John, the uncle who painted, that told him of the connection – he says: 'The Bennetts . . . were descended illegitimately, as my Uncle John once told me, from Schemer Brindley the engineer.'[1] Later, he was to revive the same story in an article he wrote for the *Daily Express* in 1928 called 'The Making of Me', which begins: 'It is said locally, with what truth I know not, that my family is descended on the paternal side from James Brindley, the eighteenth-century canal engineer! . . . He was apparently a genius . . . he worked too hard and died young. Doubt has been cast on his morals.'[2] The message of this is clear – even if he wasn't descended from Brindley, Bennett liked to think that he was, and no wonder. The glamour of having an ancestor with doubtful morals, amongst all those Sunday School superintendents, must have cheered up the ambitious youth enormously. Perhaps there is no truth in the story at all – it is a well-known habit of ordinary families to lay claim to distinguished and raffish predecessors, especially when they are too far removed to cast any real shame on existing members. One gets the piquancy without the embarrassment. And there weren't many notorious characters around for the Bennetts to claim.

I should note at this point that my original interest in Bennett himself sprang from a similar source. My maternal great-grandmother was a Bennett, and the family were potters from Hanley: my great-grandfather Bloor worked at the Bloor Derby works. It is widely believed in the family that there is a close family connection with Arnold Bennett; I have not set about verifying it at Somerset House, partly through laziness, partly because I would like to believe it to be true, just as Bennett liked to believe he was connected with Brindley. It was natural enough for the family to wish to claim the connection, for Bennett was a great local man, even though his reputation locally was slightly ambiguous – he was, after all, very rude about the district that produced him. But so are many of those who lived there, not least my own relations. I never lived in the Potteries myself; we were brought up in Yorkshire, as were both my parents. Most of the family has now moved away. Like Bennett himself, they didn't like it much. But many of the things he described – the meat teas, the winding of the grandfather clocks, the kitchen dressers, the stone steps, even the pots on the mantel-piece – are part of my own memories. My mother struggled through the same disdain for conventional Sunday School religion. His need to escape was felt throughout our family. It was natural to hope there was a real connection, as well as a connection of sympathy.

Arnold Bennett didn't want to be an engineer, but he did want to be a genius. There wasn't much trace of it in the rest of the family, who didn't live up to Brindley's glamorous example. Arnold's great-great-grandfather was a John Bennett, born in 1760, and as he was illegitimate he may well have been Brindley's son. His elder surviving son, Sampson, produced eight sons and four daughters, the eldest of whom was another John, prob-ably born in 1810. This John was Bennett's grandfather, the breakaway Sunday School superintendent of Burslem. He and his father Sampson were probably both potters, as well as shopkeepers – both had shops and both lived in Pitt Street, according to the 1851 directory. In 1834 John married Mary Vernon, Arnold's grandmother, and in 1843, in Pitt Street, Enoch, Arnold's father, was born, the second son of the marriage. There were five children altogether, a Sampson who died in infancy of whooping cough, an

Emily who died of phthisis, John, who went to America, Enoch and Sarah, the musical aunt, who became Mrs Samuel Barlow. The Vernon side of the family didn't make much impression on the family identity, for Arnold writes, again in his journal, of the Vernons 'of whom several I believe are living now in Burslem ignored by my father and us'.[3] But there were signs of talent in the offspring of grandfather John. Uncle John was a pottery painter; Arnold says of him, with evident pride and perhaps a little exaggeration, 'The Potteries being too small for him, he went to London, to a cottage in Lambeth. He exhibited a pottery-painting in his parlour window. Sir Henry Doulton, strolling that way, saw it and engaged the artist for his Lambeth works. Then, Doulton's being too small for him, my uncle emigrated to America where he succeeded and made money.'[4]

Enoch too was an ambitious child, but he had a rougher time getting where he wanted. He was intelligent, in Arnold's phrase 'highly precocious', and by the age of eight (in his view) and ten to twelve (in Arnold's) was earning 2*d.* an hour teaching in 'a sort of night school'. Was this one of those Monday evening schools that taught writing, thus avoiding the sin of teaching writing on the Sabbath? We are not told. Anyway, Enoch was not able to pursue an academic or legal career; although he didn't become a potter at seven, like Darius Clayhanger, he took up the job at an early age. Not much is known about his days as a potter. He probably kept it dark in later years, as Darius kept his own past. At the age of twenty-two he was a master potter, and probably worked with a partner, Thomas Hurd, at the Eagle Pottery, Nile Street. But the business failed, and in 1866 he married and set up as a draper and pawnbroker in Hope Street, in the house where Arnold Bennett was born. He struggled on there, in poverty, producing children, until his father John died in 1870, leaving him some money – the Sneyd Pottery, part of the estate, went to his sister Sarah, but there must have been a fair amount left for Enoch and Uncle John. It was at this point that Uncle John took off for London, but Enoch took advantage of his portion by attempting to fulfil his ambition to become a solicitor. He gave the Hope Street shop to his sister Sarah, 'a tall, slim, auburn-haired, refined and yet forceful woman',[5] who ran the business successfully for many years, and he articled himself as solicitor's clerk to Brabazon Wood Ellis. He was now twenty-nine. In November 1876, at the age of thirty-four, he qualified as a solicitor.

Those years, the formative years of Arnold Bennett's infancy, must have been grim by any standards, as hard for Arnold's mother, struggling to rear her family – three of whom died as babies, as was common in those days – as they were for Enoch, struggling with financial anxieties, law examinations, and his own ambition. Mrs Enoch Bennett was by all accounts a pleasant, hard-working, unassertive woman, much dominated by her husband – her own character does not emerge at all clearly from any of the family records or reminiscences. She must, like most wives in this district at this time, have been much subdued; certainly she had none of the troublesome 'superior' qualities which Lawrence's mother possessed, and which produced many of the conflicts which turned him into a writer. Bennett owes to her no such doubtful debt. She may have been ambitious for him, but she didn't show it. Arnold was to remain an attentive and affectionate son – for years he wrote to her every day and sent a constant flow of postcards, on one occasion (31 August 1904) sending as many as seven postcards on the same day. No wonder he criticizes the neglect of the feckless Cyril Povey, in *The Old Wives' Tale*, who forgets to write home.

Mrs Bennett's maiden name was Sarah Ann Longson, and her background, though of the same class, was different from the Bennetts'. Her grandfather had been a farmer at Mellor, Glossop – in his journal Bennett notes:

'We were talking of the neighbourhood of Macclesfield. . . . My mother said: "We" (that is, herself, sister and brother) "were all baptized at Mellor Church, near Marple. Grandfather had a farm there. Father and his three brothers were all born there, and he brought us over from Glossop to be baptized at the church. There were four Longson brothers, James, John, Robert and Henry."

' "All dead, I suppose?" I said.

' "Eh, bless ye yes. Long and long ago." '[6]

The Longsons had never had anything to do with potting. Sarah's father Robert, who started life as a weaver, moved from Glossop to Burslem in 1860, when Sarah was twenty, and opened a tailor's shop in St John's Square. Six years later she married Enoch. But the life in the shop in the Square, immortalized in *The Old Wives' Tale*, was one of the most interesting parts of Arnold Bennett's background. There Sarah and her sister Frances must have spent years plotting their future, as do Sophia and Constance. Arnold spent a great deal of time there as a child, and one of his sisters, Emily, was virtually brought up there by Aunt Frances. Sarah must have been relieved to have a little help with the children; her own house was crowded enough. Aunt Frances Longson (later Mrs Ezra Bourne) was the more spirited of the two sisters, and described by her nephew as 'one of the most powerful, attractive and formidable characters I have ever encountered'[7] – he wreaked his revenge on her for her power in his glorious portrait of Auntie Hamps, surely one of the most vital, dreadful, awe-inspiring women in English fiction. Sarah, the elder sister, was more gentle-natured; or perhaps she was made so by constant childbirth and by her dominating husband. For Enoch was an autocrat. Arnold wrote ('The Making of Me'): 'Napoleon of the Tuileries was not more of an autocrat, nor better served. It was beneath his dignity to carry a latchkey. Arriving home he would rap with his wedding ring on the glass of the front door, and somebody scampered to open it, at no matter what hour.'[8] He was exacting with his wife, and severe with his children, who were not allowed out to play as other children were. Perhaps Aunt Frances, dismayed by her sister's subjugation, very reasonably decided that she would not be made a doormat in the same way. She married Ezra Bourne, Master Potter of Messrs Bourne and Leigh, and ran him very efficiently. In fact, the two sisters represent very clearly two types of working-class wife – the quiet, well-disciplined wife who never asks what her husband is earning, and the one who demands the whole pay packet and lets the husband have a little pocket money.

Mrs Bennett's early married life was extremely hard work. She was twenty-six when she married in 1866. The first child, Arnold, was born in 1867 in the wedge-shaped corner shop in Hope Street, to be followed a year later by Frank, then Fanny Gertrude (Sissie) then Emily and Tertia, then Septimus, with three intervening children dying in infancy. The Longson shop must have been a refuge, for the mother as well as for the children, for she used to go there from time to time to serve behind the counter, and would also make hats at home. Her mother wasn't much use to her, as she was crippled with arthritis and died blind, but her father and sister offered not only refuge, but also financial assistance – the family lived rent-free at one point in a house that belonged to Mr Longson in Newport Lane. (This is the house that Hilda Lessways lived in.) For they didn't stay in Hope Street – they left when Arnold was five, and moved from one dingy rented cottage to another. It is not surprising that Arnold was to write with such passionate enthusiasm about bathrooms, windows, plumbing, heating. The only comfortable place of his early childhood was indeed the shop, described again and again, in different guises: Adeline Aked, the heroine of his first novel, *A Man from the North*, is brought up in just such a shop, by her maternal grandparents and two uncles, and her joy at watching the stalls go up in the Square outside, her pleasure at 'the immense proportions' of the house, its profusion of staircases (for it was three houses knocked into one), its variety of cellars, its mysterious shuttered look on Sunday afternoons, is clearly a description of Arnold's own pleasure in his grandparents' interesting home.

The shop was, and still is, in the centre of Burslem, in an important and busy site, in marked contrast to the drab terraces of Dale Hall, Newport Lane, and Hope Street where the young Bennetts lived. It stands at the bottom end of St John's Square and now houses a bookmaker, but the building itself is largely unchanged; it has three storeys and a basement, with a front entrance on to the Square and a side entrance on to what was then King Street (now William Clowes Street), a road which descends sharply to the amazingly drab and neglected church and cemetery at the bottom. There is a mysterious bricked-up window, and the roof has a pleasantly ancient irregularity. Thanks to the redevelopment of Hanley as the main shopping centre, Burslem itself is very little changed from Bennett's day, and all its principal buildings are within two minutes' walk from the Longson shop; the Square itself has most of its original buildings, and a Saturday morning market, as well as Swan Bank with the George Hotel, the Wedgwood Institute, the handsome Big House (built by the Wedgwoods in the eighteenth century, and now the Midland Bank), and the Old Town Hall with its golden angel, which are all within easy reach. The Town Hall has recently been cleaned, and looks surprisingly attractive. Unfortunately, the Meat Market, which lay just to one side of it, has been demolished. Bennett admired it, and ironically its empty site now supports a curious brick wall with a plaque to Bennett on one side of it, and a plaque to another quite disconnected Alderman Bennett on the other – a fine example of local economy in monuments. Also within a minute's walk of the Square is the site of the Hill Pottery, which too has disappeared. Bennett called it the Sytch Pottery, and the hill which descends beyond it is still known as the Sytch, though not on the street maps. In the Longson shop Bennett, like the Baines girls in *The Old Wives' Tale*, must have felt himself at the hub of the town's activities; like them, he must have watched life going on under the windows and longed to get out into it.

One of the most curious features about the Potteries, and one that distinguishes them from other provincial industrial cities, is their smallness. Six local centres, each with its own Town Hall and its own character, create a very different atmosphere from one large city with endless undifferentiated suburbs and back-to-back housing. It is true that there is little sense of planning, a lot of wasteground, and a weird higgledly-piggledy development of houses, shops, factories and public buildings all jumbled up together. But this had its advantages. A child like Bennett could, in a short walk, see all the main activities of Burslem in action. Potteries were not built in distant industrial estates; they were mingled with houses, and some of them had real architectural merit. Pot banks and chimneys still rise up oddly behind pubs and small shops. Most of the pottery-owners were small family business men, as Enoch Bennett would have been had he flourished. It was not a district of large monopolies, but of small firms. Clayhanger's printing works was right in the centre of town, like the Longsons' shop. This homely scale led to an intense civic pride (and an intense dislike of the idea of federation) and it also gave Bennett as a young boy the feeling that he could get to know and be concerned in all the affairs of his region. There was a lot of ugliness and poor housing; there are still derelict terraces and unlovely streets; there are still many families who feel they cannot begin to live until they get right outside into the country. But as a community, the town of Burslem was extremely interesting and intensely individual, where a small man could make a large impact, as Bennett was to demonstrate to the rest of the world in later years.

Enoch Bennett's ambition was to get out of dark rented houses and into something better. He did not like to depend on his wife's family. He worked away every evening, passed his Law Society examinations, and became a solicitor in November 1876. The strain had been dreadful, and the family believed that it caused his breakdown of health later. But for the time, at least, the long grind had paid off, and Enoch was able to enjoy a long stretch of hard-earned rising prosperity before he fell ill. The family moved into a bigger house in Waterloo Road in 1878. (Waterloo Road is the Trafalgar Road of the novels, and was to house many Bennett characters and connections – his brother Septimus was to live at no. 182, his uncle Barlow lived in 81, his brother Frank lived at the corner of Hill Street and Waterloo Road, while Dr Stirling and Mr Fearns the solicitor, both fictitious, inhabited the superior Bleak Hill house belonging in real life to Dr Russell.) In 1879, Enoch Bennett was able to buy a building site for £200 at the top of Waterloo Road, the best end, described many times as such by Arnold, with immense satisfaction.

Waterloo Road is a long thoroughfare which links Hanley and Burslem, replacing the older and more tortuous Nile Street; it was built after the Napoleonic Wars, to find labour for the returned and unemployed soldiers. It's a switchback of a road, and then as now it contains a great variety of housing – small shops, terraces, garages, hairdressers, old people's homes, factories, and grander detached and semi-detached residences.

On the site which Enoch Bennett bought, he built, for a further £900 (borrowed on mortgage) the house which is still preserved as a Bennett Museum, 205 Waterloo Road. Arnold was a young teenager when the house was being built, and he must be describing his own feelings when he describes Edwin Clayhanger, watching the building of his own family home:

> 'When the house began to "go up", Edwin lived in an ecstasy of contemplation . . . the measurements, the rulings, the plumbings, the checkings! He was humbled and he was enlightened. He saw a hole in the ground, with water at the bottom, and the next moment that hole was a cellar; not an amateur cellar, a hole that would do at a pinch for a cellar, but a professional cellar.'[9]

And Edwin, who unlike Arnold was destined to live his married life in this home, this analogy for 205 Waterloo Road, meets his wife-to-be in the empty, unfinished house, in the middle of the night – the romance of it is so strong that he is drawn towards it, and creeps in, and goes up to the room which is to be his, and plans where he will put his books . . . 'only now, he could not dream in the house as he had meant to dream; because beyond the open door was the empty landing and the well of the stairs and all the terror of the house. The terror came and mingled with all the delicious sensations. . . . No! Never had he been so intensely alive as then!'[10] The spaciousness of the house, the size of the rooms, the fact that the hall is square instead of long, cramped and narrow, its carpets, its offer of privacy, are all deeply felt in terms of someone who hadn't known such things. Only those who have endured the inconveniences of living in a dark row of terraced housing can fully appreciate the effects of lightness, the glories of having a detached house. It's not only a question of social standing, though that's involved too: what one feels coming through Bennett's descriptions is sheer physical relief.

The house wouldn't strike many as being particularly desirable today, though it does have a certain period charm; it's in red brick, with lavish use of terracotta in the decorations, a characteristic both of the district and the period. It is on three floors, with two huge cellars below: it has six bedrooms, and the two front bay-windowed rooms are large and light. The decorations are Victorian and ornate: stained glass with birds fills the tops of the windows, flowery tiles surround the fireplace. It was doubtless, in Bennett's day, over-furnished by our standards, and although Bennett refers to its *Clayhanger* equivalent several times as 'palatial', it hardly justifies the adjective. But in terms of what they had left behind, it was a palace, and the features which to us look quaint and dated (however charming) were to them the height of modernity.

And of course the house was not simply a house. It was a symbol of the ascent of the Bennett family into the middle classes. Enoch was now a professional man, and his neighbours therefore should be doctors, solicitors and aldermen. 205 Waterloo Road was in the right part of Waterloo Road, on the ridge known as Cobridge, and as Bennett says in *Anna of the Five Towns*, to reside there 'was still the final ambition of many citizens, though the natural growth of the town had robbed Bleakridge [Cobridge] of some of that exclusive distinction which it once possessed'.[11] Bennett was deeply affected by the move, and it must have been during this period that he developed his extreme interest in property, bricks, rents and mortgages; many of his novels give extremely detailed descriptions of the buildings as well as of characters, a fact which was to annoy Virginia Woolf greatly. She thought it was not spiritual to be so interested in bricks and mortar. But Bennett, who had been brought up the hard way, knew exactly what the power of bricks and mortar was. Later, he was to work as a rent-collector for his father's firm, a job which he did not care for, and he came to know the housing conditions of the district well. Family conversations at home must have been full of talk about property, which is reflected in the novels: Alderman Sutton in *These Twain* deplores the fact that there is 'jerry-building' even in Trafalgar Road; Hilda Lessways and her mother own and worry about property, so does Anna, and the Card is a rent-collector. To Virginia Woolf such details were dull externals; she did not want to know about houses, she wanted to know about souls. To Bennett, as to Lawrence, houses expressed souls. People were not disembodied spirits, and the houses that they built were as much a part of them as their bodies. And in 205 Waterloo Road Bennett found for the first time what Virginia Woolf herself demanded as the right of every writer: a room of his own.

But it was not to writing that Arnold's mind turned when the desire for self-improvement and achievement first gripped him. He didn't turn his mind to writing for many years, and then only in an apparently most casual, almost accidental manner. He was not one of those children who consider themselves born poets and novelists, and at one point he suggests that he wrote his first novel because a friend suggested to him that it would be a good idea. (This is not as unusual a starting point as it might seem: Angus Wilson says that it was his psychoanalyst who suggested to him that he might start writing fiction.)[12] In fact one of the enduring oddities of Bennett was an inability to judge the possibilities of his own talent; quite late in life he started to write poetry, some of which was published in the *New Age*. He devoted considerable time and thought to it, and it was not at all good, though astonishingly enough Philip Larkin has included an appalling example of it in the *Oxford Book of Twentieth Century English Verse* – perhaps an example of one provincial sticking to another. Larkin's poetry does have some of the qualities of Bennett's prose, but Bennett's poetry has nothing to recommend it. Similarly, as a child, he decided like Edwin Clayhanger that he would be an artist, inspired by the gift of an excellent box of watercolours, and he went on painting throughout his life. His sketches and watercolours are much better than his poems, and gave him and his friends a great deal of pleasure, but they are nevertheless amateur. It's odd that he doesn't seem to have recognized the enormous difference in quality between his sketches and his novels; at times, reading his journals and letters, one gets the impression that he was faintly surprised that one talent should have been so fully recognized, the other not at all.

Clearly, then, he was an artistic child, with no strong sense of direction. He recounts his first encounters with literature and education in his book *The Truth about an Author*, which he wrote in his middle thirties. It's a lighthearted book, but nevertheless interesting, partly because it contains his only reminiscence of the thoroughly repressed days in Hope Street – he is in the kitchen, a very small child unable to read, but staring virtuously at a piece of paper which he is holding in his hand, being 'good' (very like the young Sartre in his autobiography *Words*), while his younger brother, baby Frank, is bellowing in the pawn shop ('full of black bundles') which lies at the end of 'a very long and mysterious passage'. This, he says, is how 'we came together, literature and I'. The first story that he remembers reading is, significantly enough, 'The Ugly Duckling', which he found when he was six or so: doubtless he realized the significance of the way in which it struck him, for he says:

> 'When the ugly duckling at last flew away on his strong pinions, and when he met the swans and was accepted as an equal, then I felt sorrowful, agreeably sorrowful. It seemed to me that nothing could undo, atone for, the grief and humiliations of the false duckling's early youth. I brooded over the injustice of his misfortunes for days, and the swans who welcomed him struck me as proud, cold, and supercilious in their politeness. I have never read The Ugly Duckling since those days. It survives in my memory as a long and complex narrative, crowded with vague and mysterious allusions. . . .'[13]

There is a fine bit of literary criticism, and its relevance to Bennett's own struggles is obvious enough; one wonders how much he had read back into his original reading.

He wasn't exactly an ugly duckling in his childhood, because after all there was no reason why he should think himself cut out for better things. But he had his problems. He developed in infancy a stammer which he never overcame, and which prevented (or saved) him from undertaking lectures, public speaking, and after-dinner speaking in his later life. It is the kind of affliction that can make a child's life a misery, and though there's no evidence that Arnold was bullied or victimized, he must have felt set apart. Various school friends remember him as being 'moody' or 'not particularly happy'. It's impossible to know what caused his stammer, because it is more or less impossible to diagnose the reasons for any stammer. I personally feel that a stammer that begins for one reason may accrue around it all sorts of other personality difficulties, so that it changes during its owner's lifetime, becoming a safety valve first for one set of anxieties, then for another. Mrs Bennett thought that it was caused because he fell out of his high chair on to his head on the floor when he was three (the age when speech begins to produce problems), and was scolded by his father for doing so. Other suggestions are obviously possible. H.G.Wells, backed by Bennett's other biographers, thought it might be connected with some sexual shock in infancy, and when one thinks that Mrs Bennett had nine children, of whom three died, all in rather close quarters, it does seem likely that Arnold may have seen something that the Victorians and Dr Spock think he ought not to have seen. Such a theory would account for his later sexual development and its difficulties, but I think it far more likely that Arnold was a classic case of a child nervous before an over-dominating father with far too high expectations of his children. This is a situation in which stammers commonly develop. Often the stammer is induced by the excessive anxiety of the parents, who insist that the child should speak clearly and not hesitate at an age when it is hardly capable of doing so; there is an analogy with over-rigorous pot-training, which Arnold like all his generation probably suffered from, and which is thought to produce many of the Victorian-Wesleyan qualities of thrift, neurotic cleanliness, bowel fixation, interest in figures and statistics and hypochondria. Nobody could say that Arnold grew up mean, for he was the most generous of men, but he was certainly unusually interested in and proud of his money-earning capacity, and he was also certainly a hypochondriac.

Be all this as it may, and none of it can ever be proven, it can be proved that Arnold had an exacting father, who expected a great deal of him, and that he worked hard to try to placate him. He was always a responsible and conscientious child, with a strong desire to please and a need to be liked. His sense of responsibility sprang partly, perhaps, from the fact that he was the eldest of six, and no doubt had to do his share of amusing and controlling the little ones. Throughout his life he was to take his duties to his siblings seriously, stepping in to help with money, illnesses, holidays, nephews and nieces. He and his brother Frank, the two eldest, were the natural leaders of the family; there was only a year in age between them. Mrs Beardmore (Fanny Gertrude, known as Sissie) recalled in an article in the *Sunday Chronicle* (22 December 1929) that the rest of the family always had to do what Frank and Arnold decided. But the little ones seem to have been willing victims, for Arnold, even when young, was full of schemes and ideas.

Mrs Beardmore recalls in particular the family Christmas, a ritual which bears a strong resemblance to the one handed down in my own family, and still largely extant. Preparations would take weeks – the children would plan surprise presents for their parents, usually home-made, as they had little pocket money. Frank was good at carpentry, Arnold at fretwork, and the girls were rather reluctantly bullied into sewing. They would make their own Christmas decorations – Chinese lanterns and ornaments from decorated hoops. On Christmas morning there would be hymns at the piano, then at twelve o'clock the distribution of presents; Enoch Bennett, always keen on self-improvement, always gave books. At one o'clock there was dinner, followed by quiet reading of the books, then in the evening there would be a party with charades, songs and dances. Arnold organized the charades efficiently; even at this age he was a keen organizer. It was at one of these Christmas evenings that Sissie remembers first hearing him sing his party piece, with which he was to amuse sophisticated audiences at *soirées* in Paris, and a whole theatre-full of distinguished guests in London: 'Sucking Cider Through A Straw' was the song. When he sang Bennett's stammer left him, and he was able to sing confidently in public, though he always loathed making public speeches.[14]

Bennett seems to have got on well with his brothers and sisters throughout childhood, though difficulties were to arise later. He was close to Frank, but his favourite was his sister Tertia, a handsome, intelligent girl with whom he always stayed closely in touch. She too had literary aspirations as a child, according to a school friend, H.K.Hales, and she did in later life publish children's stories. Septimus was also to prove artistic, though he was several years younger than Arnold, and can't have had much effect on him as a child. Sissie was to grow up into a strong-minded woman of public affairs, a strict teetotaller, with little feeling for books. Emily grew up eccentric, but we don't know what she was like as a child; she was less a part of the Bennett family, having spent much of her childhood with her grandparents. It was a

34

lively household, despite Enoch's strictness – the children made their own amusements, went swimming, had family jokes, kept a dog called Spot ('Out, damned Spot,' said a witty friend to the dog when telling it to leave the room, thereby earning Arnold's admiration and envy) and in fact behaved much like other nice, well-brought-up children in the Five Towns. (They didn't play on the street. It wasn't respectable to play on the street, it was dirty and one might meet nasty neighbours.) Bennett catches the feeling of his childhood in many of his novels – a curious mixture of freedom and circumspection, in which children had to watch adults carefully but could get away with a great deal if they set about it subversively enough.

Bennett's education started at the Infants' Wesleyan School in Swan Square, which he attended in the Newport Lane days, walking past the Longsons' shop to get there, and often dropping in on the way home for a meal. The year after he left, the school's headmaster committed suicide, a fact which he stored up for future use. In 1877, when he was ten, he started to attend the Endowed School, in the Wedgwood Institute, Queen Street, Burslem, a school halfway between Swan Square and the shop and a minute's walk from both. The Wedgwood Institute, covered in ceramic decorations bearing witness to the man it commemorates, now houses the public library downstairs and an annexe to the college of further education upstairs. It is an astonishingly ornate building; the façade presents not only many reliefs of the potter's trade but also, in twelve arches that were originally intended as windows, terracotta reliefs of the twelve seasons. Apparently the original design was considered not to demonstrate the Wedgwood theme clearly enough; certainly there is now no mistaking it. Rarely can a building have been so covered with monuments to the art of ceramics.

The school, however, was not as distinguished as its building, for Sissie Beardmore claimed that in those days the books were so dirty that the Bennett children were 'discouraged from borrowing them', a phrase which shows that even in those far-off days, the days of Newport Lane, the Bennetts still felt themselves to be better than their neighbours. This relentless superiority and keeping up of appearances was an exhausting business and it was common among a certain social class. It's the kind of striving that marks one for life. My mother recalls the Whitsun Outing, which all the Sunday Schools joined in, and says that she hated the teas because the mugs were of thick pottery, and because the cakes had coloured icing, and she had been told that coloured icing was 'dangerous' and 'vulgar'. The sense of moral confusion must have been acute: the outing was in a pious cause, therefore must be good, but the cakes were vulgar, therefore must be bad.

Similarly, in *A Man from the North*, little Adeline Aked's religious upbringing is marred by social doubts – she was not allowed to go to Sunday School: 'Although Uncle Mark and Uncle Luke taught there, and grandpa had once actually been superintendent, she was not allowed to go there, simply because the children were rude and dirty.'[15] (Remember Mr Shushions, and the old days when children came to school and had to be given a crust of bread to keep going, and old John Bennett, who insisted on being allowed to teach them to read.)

When Bennett was at the Endowed School the headmaster was Horace Byatt, who apparently raised the school from a very low ebb, but dissipated his energies by teaching evening classes. In 1880, oddly enough, he moved to Midhurst Grammar School, Sussex, where he became H.G.Wells's headmaster. Byatt was succeeded by a Mr Stanton Russ, under whose rule the school was transferred from Queen Street to an attractive large mid-Victorian house, Longport Hall. Bennett was lucky in the locations of his schools. Two years after the removal to Longport Hall, in 1882, he left the Endowed School to go to Newcastle Middle School. This was a superior school; for the Bennetts were by now in their 205 Waterloo Road, holiday-taking, middle-class years. It had been known since 1705 as Orme's School, after one of its charitable founders, the Reverend Edward Orme, and the School as such had opened in 1872 with forty-two pupils. By the time Arnold and his brother Frank got there it was flourishing. Arnold and Frank, and their two second cousins Alan and Jim Bennett, used to walk daily across the Grange and across Wolstanton Marsh from Cobridge to Newcastle, a walk which Bennett describes in *Clayhanger* and a walk which, more than any other, gives one the feel of the Potteries and a sense of what it must have been like to live there.

As we have seen, there is a great deal of wasteground in the Potteries, and much of it lies between Cobridge and Newcastle. The landscape is extra-ordinary: hilly, marked with slag heaps, mines and chemical works, and full of surprises. Flowers flourish in disused workings; pink smoke rises from a waste dump. It must have been more rural in Bennett's day, as some of the housing estates are new, but on the other hand the air is cleaner now, and reclamation schemes are well under way. Grass is growing, small trees are planted, slag heaps have been transformed into small green mountains. Odd bits of industrial machinery have been left, deliberately, both as a reminder of the past and because, when surrounded by greenery, they are curiously beautiful. The strange, haphazard development of the region is nowhere more marked than in these patches of no-man's-land between town centres.

Drawing of 205 Waterloo Road, *c.* 1925

An invitation to a Christmas party at Hatfield House, designed by Septimus Bennett, with pictures by A.B.'s eldest nephew and niece

FATHER CHRISTMAS
HAS PROMISED TO CALL
AT
HATFIELD HOUSE
STOKE UPON TRENT
ON
SATURDAY 23RD DEC. 1905
FROM 3 TO 7 O'CLOCK
WHEN
&
WILL BE PLEASED
IF YOU WILL COME
TO THEIR PARTY
TO GREET HIM
"OH SAY WILL YOU COME"

above Enoch Bennett *(back left)* with a group of friends, September 1886. Left to right: Tom Bennett (no relation), Arthur Wilkinson, Absalom Wood, T.F. Wood (seated) and John Beardmore

below Family group taken at 205 Waterloo Road, *c.* 1883

Burslem Town Hall

View of the Potteries today

The young Arnold Bennett, *c*. 1905

In many ways they are a paradise for children, though they may have been ugly to adult eyes; derelict ground is ideal for playing on, and in this the children of the Potteries were luckier than their counterparts in Sheffield or Manchester. The Bennetts used to play football on their way home.

They also used to play on the canal banks, another delightful and distinctive feature of the district. Canals feature largely in Bennett's Five Towns novels. Bennett and his friend Frank Beardmore, like Clayhanger and his friend the Sunday, were familiar with the grassy banks, deep in yellow weeds, that line the Trent and Mersey Canals and go right through the city centres, taking their own silent and mysterious route. They are extraordinarily romantic; the contrast of the harsh architecture, the high dark-red blank walls of potteries and warehouses, with the little locks, the triumphant vegetation and the small boys fishing is very striking. Boys fish, lovers walk with each other and old men walk with their dogs, just as they did in Bennett's day. There is here a mixture of dereliction and beauty that must be unchanged. As I write these words I am staying in the North Stafford Hotel, which Bennett knew well, and which now boasts a Clayhanger Bar in his memory; it is just opposite the railway station, in a central and highly convenient position. Last night I went for a little walk at about nine o'clock in the evening, thinking of Bennett. I turned left, along Station Road, and within three minutes I was in the middle of the strangest landscape. I was on a canal bank, with nothing but a green hill ahead. To reach it I had walked down a back street such as one might find in the slums of Glasgow. There was the water, smelling faintly but pleasantly of detergent. There was new green grass. There was a swan floating about idly. And there was a group of Indian women in long silk trousers, enjoying the warm evening with their children and grandchildren. The mothers asked me questions in their own language; the children interpreted. I wondered what Bennett would have made of this scene, which struck me as the essence of a certain type of provincial life today. Children on bicycles, mothers on doorsteps and canal banks, young men roving bored and idle. In his day the women on the doorsteps were 'sundry experienced and fat old women, standing or sitting at their cottage doors, some of them smoking cutties',[16] and they stared at the young Bennett–Clayhanger as he walked back with his satchel on the way home from school. The first two chapters of *Clayhanger* are devoted to this walk, and to an evocation of the district – it is all there, the canal, the brickworks, the astonishing lone surviving grange farm, the flowing scarves of smoke. As Bennett says: 'Beauty was achieved, and none saw it.'[17] The walk affected him profoundly, and he was able to recall it in every detail years later. Indeed,

37

as he points out in *Clayhanger*, it was probably more educational than much of what he learned at school.

He did quite well at school, however, despite his protestations of knowing nothing whatsoever about geography, recent history or anything to do with the potting industry. He wasn't intellectually precocious, but he was always at or near the top of the class. In a piece called 'My Education' he recalls the three schools he attended and says: 'The first is not worth mentioning. The second is hardly worth mentioning. I despised the third for a strange reason: namely, because, well aware that I knew nothing, I nevertheless rose with extraordinary rapidity to be top of the school!'[18] He was at the Middle School for only a year, but he underestimates the effect it had on him. Its headmaster, D.B.Hurley (who was head from 1879 to 1906), was responsible for introducing Bennett to the delights of the French language, thus providing him with a lasting enthusiasm. Enlightened French teaching was rare in those days, and Bennett was lucky to find such encouragement. It has often been said that Bennett never learned to speak French properly, however hard he tried, but then by public schoolboy standards he never learned to speak English properly either, which reflects only on his accent, not on his grammar or his feeling for literature. He never lost his Burslem accent, and grew to be proud of it.

There was, perhaps, an irritating element of Five Towns one-up-man-ship in his acquisition of French, for he did tend to see the cultural world as a competitive place – requiring strategy for success – a tendency illustrated by a piece he wrote for his old school magazine when he was turned forty. In it he describes a visit that D.B.Hurley paid him in France. He was living at the time with his wife at Fontainebleau. Hurley arrived on a bicycle, and found himself in a household ideally suited to challenge his reputation as a linguist – Bennett's wife was 'a southern Frenchwoman of the purest extraction', and the other guests included a German, the music critic Calvacoressi and his Greek mother. And Bennett says:

'Into such company came the linguist from North Staffordshire. I said to myself, "We shall see whether Mr Hurley is really equal to his immense local reputation."

'He was. He was far more than equal to it. He shone, and I was extremely proud of him.'[19]

He was also, clearly, extremely proud of the cosmopolitan nature of his own establishment, and had fulfilled every schoolboy's dream of impressing the headmaster. Honour was satisfied on all sides; no wonder he reports the encounter, and the discussions of French idioms, Greek roots and German classics, with such satisfaction.

While at the Middle School, the school magazine from which the Hurley extract is taken reports that he became head boy, and also that (more oddly) he played for the football first eleven. He had been top of the form, too, at the Endowed School in 1879, with full marks in several subjects – his worst subject was reading, presumably because of his stammer. He was top again, in 1880 and 1881. Yet a school friend of his, H.K.Hales, recalls:

'Bennett did not shine in the school room. Even in English composition I do not recall that he excelled to any really noticeable degree. . . . I can see him now as he was in those days. He sat to my left and slightly in front of me. In his hands he held his wooden-framed slate complete with pencil and sponge. "Spit" was our watchword as we laboured at our slates, for the unaided sponges were of little use in erasing the hard pressed lines of our slate pencils. Poor Bennett hated spitting, yet he was forced to spit again and again to remove the fine neat writing. . . .'[20]

Evidently he was already a fastidious boy, and warnings about dirty books and dirty behaviour had left their mark on him.

He was also a hard worker, and in December 1882 he passed the Cambridge Junior Local Examination, alone in his class. He would therefore have been qualified to go on to the Newcastle High School, and thence to university – as did a second cousin, Stephen Allen Bennett. Had he done so his life would have been very different. But he didn't. He left school at the end of 1883, at the age of sixteen.

It's surprising, in a way, that his ambitious father didn't press for him to go to university. Instead he took him into his office in Piccadilly, Hanley, where Arnold began work (and where he gained much experience of life and property through rent-collecting and other humble tasks). At the same time he studied for his matriculation, both with his father and at the night-school at the Wedgwood Institute. Perhaps his father thought that university would have been too soft an option. He certainly didn't discourage his children in their intellectual and artistic interests – on the contrary, he encouraged them to read. As soon as he had any money he began to buy books, and one of the features of the house in Waterloo Road was its 'Book Room'. Arnold recalls: 'His library was the largest in my youthful experience. I estimate it at one thousand volumes – mostly dull and worthless, but all dignified. He had a passion for filling his offspring with information, at small trouble to himself. When any point of dispute arose he would say "look it up". We looked it up!'[21] One can imagine more sophisticated forms of encouragement, but even so much was remarkable. The Bennetts clearly regarded themselves as a cultured and rather remarkable family – the relics left at the museum in Waterloo Road bring back a nostalgic sense of their Christmas charades, pedantic jokes, home-made entertainments. The whole family had a passion for one of the quiz games of the period which penny papers like *Pearson's Weekly* used to run; they took it so seriously that they and their friends formed a syndicate and pooled their intellectual resources. The excitement generated by such games was tremendous, as Bennett recalls in his description of Missing Words in *These Twain*. They were hardly very highbrow, being designed to meet the needs of amusement plus self-improvement of the new mass readership, but they must have helped Bennett with his vocabulary, if with nothing else. The Missing Word game itself consisted simply of guessing the correct word to fill in a gap in the text of a paragraph of the magazine, but there were other more difficult verbal puzzles such as anagrams and acrostics. (*Pearson's* magazine was later to invent the cross-word, as yet unknown.) The papers offered cash prizes as incentives, and aimed at large audiences, but nevertheless such games doubtless had a genuine educational value. As recent surveys have shown, children who are deprived of comics and their puzzles show up less well in intelligence tests than those reared on a strong diet of *Dandy* and *Beano*. And word games, unlike comic strips, had respectability. They were hardly the kind of amusement that an illiterate or philistine family would find amusing.

The children were also artistic. Recalling his early passion for watercolours Arnold goes on to say:

'From fine I turned to applied art, diverted by a periodical called *The Girl's Own Paper*. For a long period this monthly, which I now regard as quaint, but which I shall never despise, was my principal instrument of culture. It alone blew upon the spark of artistic feeling and kept it alive. I derived from it my first ideals of aesthetic and of etiquette. Under its influence my brother and myself started on a revolutionary campaign against all the accepted canons of house decoration. We invented friezes, dadoes, and panels; we cut stencils; and we carried out our bright designs through half a house. It was magnificent, glaring, and immense; it fore-shadowed the modern music hall. Visitors were shown through our rooms by parents who tried in vain to hide from us their parental complacency.'[22]

And this passage is as revealing about the parents as it is about the children – they actually allowed their children to do all these things, they were proud of them, instead of repressing and discouraging them. It was even more common to discourage children in those days. The Bennetts rightly considered themselves an unusual household.

And of course their friends, the visitors who would have been called upon to admire the friezes and stencils of Arnold and Frank, were a self-elected cultural élite of the district; they were a group such as can be found in many such a town today. It's not surprising that one of Arnold's favourite themes was to be the distinction of provincial culture; he is perpetually teasing his metropolitan audience with little snippets about the superiority of provincial amateur pianists, of provincial bookbinders, etc. and he handles the subject with a profound insight in his masterly short story, 'The Death of Simon Fugue', where the limitations and achievements of such a culture are beautifully captured. Enoch's friends, like the characters in Simon Fugue, were cultured – they included Joseph Dawson, son of a Wesleyan minister, who was a printer and bookseller, Absalom Wood, the architect, William Owen (a descendant of the Christian socialist Robert Owen) and John Beardmore, the solicitor.

They were not only cultured; they were also active in the community. The social organization of the Five Towns was such that it was easy for a small group of energetic people to make their presence felt, and Bennett's father's friends were all well-known local characters. Their activity expressed itself at one point in the ambitious project of founding a local newspaper, the *Staffordshire Knot*, which began life as a weekly in 1882, became a daily in 1885 and perished in 1892, subsumed, though far from ignominiously, by the larger and well-established *Sentinel*. William Owen was editor, Dawson was sub-editor and Enoch Bennett and others of the group were shareholders. It must have been an exciting enterprise, much discussed at home when Bennett was a teenager; he took it all in, remembered it and used it for background for the journalistic exploits of George Cannon and Hilda Lessways, for the details about printing in *Clayhanger*, and for the legal wrangles of 'The Great Newspaper War' in *The Card*. Doubtless, involvement in the paper also gave Bennett a taste for journalism as a career; although the *Staffordshire Knot* rejected his first offering, the *Sentinel* later accepted several articles by him.

So the family atmosphere was far from being dour, anti-intellectual, anti-social. Thomas R. Roberts, in his booklet *Arnold Bennett's Five Towns Origins*, rightly criticizes the tendency to see Arnold's family in terms of Clayhanger's family – the similarities are there, and they are striking, but so are the differences. The Bennetts' house was not cold, empty and silent, like the Clayhangers' – 'When the family were growing up, they were encouraged to bring their friends, and the house rang with laughter, music and singing. Half a dozen young friends might stay and sleep in the roomy house overnight. The atmosphere resembled that of the Orgreave household more than the Clayhangers. Holiday times at Llandudno, the Isle of Man and elsewhere were occasions for large seaside parties for many young men asked permission to take their holidays wherever the Bennett daughters were going.'[23]

Why, then, did Enoch Bennett expect Arnold to settle down so quietly upon leaving school and become an unpaid lawyer's clerk? For that is what he did expect, and it took Arnold years to shake himself free. And it is in this region, perhaps, that the facts of the fiction are more revealing than the facts of biography. For although, as has been said, Enoch was a much less difficult and despotic character than old Darius Clayhanger, he did have some of his qualities – and a determination to have his own way was one of them. He refused to consider that Arnold was not suited for a career in law, just as Darius Clayhanger refuses to consider Edwin's desire to be an architect. Edwin slowly and moderately abandons his aspirations, and takes over his father's printing business: his father declines, he ascends. But Arnold quit. Perhaps he would not have done so had he been successful in his law examinations, but, somewhat to his own surprise, he failed them. He passed the London matriculation examinations but he never managed to obtain a law degree. The first time he received news of his failure he could only say to himself, as he waited for his father's wrath: 'There must be some mistake, there must be some mistake.' But it wasn't a mistake, and he never qualified. Perhaps he simply lacked motivation, though it's odd that his very considerable gifts of perseverance and application didn't make up for such a lack.

These must have been dreary years for him, with little hope of better things to come. During the day he worked, at fairly dull and menial jobs, and in the evenings he had to study. His portrait of Leonora's daughter, Rose, studying for her matriculation in chemistry at London University, betrays a certain sympathy: she is tall and pale, she is 'dowdy', she is 'deficient in style', she is the 'serious member of the family',[24] but nevertheless she is not mocked for these things, as most masculine writers of the time would have mocked her. He knew what it was like. It was difficult for him to protest about the long hours his father expected him to work, because after all his father had done the same, and supported a family while doing it.

Some of the jobs which Bennett did at the office he must have found distasteful. The office itself was in Piccadilly, Hanley, now unrecognizably redeveloped as part of the new shopping centre. In Bennett's day it was the Lincoln's Inn Fields of the district, less respectfully known as Rogue's Alley. Bennett describes it years later in *Whom God hath Joined*, a novel which is in part an act of revenge on those wasted years. The road is a sinister little street, he says, with houses converted into offices, the front doors kept invitingly open, and drab panels lettered in black proclaiming the names of the solicitors within. The offices themselves were deliberately drab – 'You cross ragged mats, and climb sombre, narrow, naked, soiled stairs, and push tremblingly against portals of ground glass. . . .'[25] The most established solicitors, Bennett says, were so conservative and professional that they did not even boast bells or typewriters, thinking them new-fangled and somehow unrespectable, though one gay adventurer had gone so far as to install a Turkish carpet. The setting was gloomy, and the jobs were dull. Bennett must have particularly disliked the task of rent-collecting; he was a shy young man with a stammer, and approaching truculent or impoverished strangers cannot have been very agreeable. He describes some typical tenants in his novels – an 'old, bent, bareheaded woman . . . with a filthy rent book, and with it a greasy half-crown that was offensive even to the touch',[26] in *Whom God hath Joined*, and Widow Hullins in *The Card*: 'Mrs Hullins was one of the last old women in Bursley to smoke a cutty . . . she smoked her pipe and thought about nothing in particular. Occasionally some vision of the past floated through her drowsy brain. She had lived in that residence for over forty years. She had brought up eleven children and two husbands there . . . now she was alone in it. She never left it, except to fetch water from the pump in the square.'[27] The Card himself has an easy, friendly, joking relationship with such old ladies, for he is one of them by birth, with a seamstress as a mother, but Bennett may well have been more constrained. After all, he was now a middle-class boy, no longer one of the people; one wonders if he felt all the more embarrassed in such situations because of his own family's recent pretensions. There are few who lack the common touch more conspicuously than Grammar School children of aspiring working or lower middle-class parents, who have been made deeply aware of the barriers that divide them from their own origins – dirty books, greasy half-crowns, spitting, bad language, roughness.

It's tempting to imagine that in the Card's easiness Bennett is projecting an image of what he would have liked to be, in those distant rent-collecting days. The Card is gay, benevolent, curt, kind and ruthless all in one; he greets Mrs Hullins cheerfully as 'Mother', and sits down to chat with her and to cajole her. Bennett would have liked to be like that, but at that age he certainly wasn't. More likely he was tormented with nervousness, and already unhappily aware of life's injustice.

He, too, was a victim of injustice. One of the most trying aspects of his role as student worker was the lack of pay. Enoch Bennett, like Darius Clayhanger, was mean, and would not pay his son for the work he was doing. There is no record of any struggles between Enoch and Arnold over the question of money, but Arnold's emotions at least are surely implied in the scene between Edwin and Darius in which Edwin, at the age of twenty-five, earning seventeen shillings and sixpence for a sixty-five-hour week, and paying his sister ten shillings a week for board, has the audacity to ask for a rise, because he is contemplating marriage. (Arnold is speculating here; he left home when he was twenty-one and didn't marry until he was forty-one.) Darius refuses at first, but then consents to a rise of a pound a week. His consent, however, is given in a manner so insulting that Edwin is not grateful but outraged, and as his father departs calmly from the scene he stands in the hall 'furious and impotent' and says to himself: 'When you're old, and I've *got* you ... when I've *got* you and you can't help yourself, by God it'll be my turn!'[28] Such a reaction was natural enough. And it's greatly to Arnold's credit that when Enoch did, years later, fall dramatically and finally helpless, Arnold behaved towards him with exemplary kindness.

In these last years in the Five Towns, before he left for London, Bennett claims to have done little reading, apart from work for his law examinations; though he admits to *Ouida* and Vizetelly's translations of *Zola* (*The Truth about an Author*). Nor did his thoughts turn towards writing, except, interestingly enough, when inspired to do so by the lure of a guinea, offered by the local paper for suitable short stories from local people. The odd guinea would have been a welcome supplement to his miserable income, but his first effort, which contained an actress heroine called Leonora, a favourite name of his, was declined. Later he was more successful with articles on tramlines and coffee houses for the *Staffordshire Sentinel*. It would have been hard to guess at the future novelist from the rather frustrated young journalist – far more likely, one would have said, that his mind had turned to the newspaper world because it offered a bit of excitement and a bit of action, rather than through any real talent for writing. There is a little anecdote in *The Truth about an Author* about his struggles to write a piece about an election of a county councillor while his grandfather lies dying. He says he was 'absolutely obsessed by the delicious feeling of the tyranny of the press. ... "I must write these facetious comments while my grandfather is dying upstairs!" This thought filled my brain. It seemed to me fine, splendid. I was intensely proud of being laid under a compulsion so startlingly dramatic. Could I manufacture jokes while my grandfather expired? Certainly: I was a journalist.'[29] This episode was clearly the origin of the scene in *Hilda Lessways*, where Hilda, although she has been summoned by telegram to London to the sickbed of her mother, remains to see to press the first edition of the Five Towns' *Chronicle*. Her feelings about the paper are mingled with her feelings for George Cannon, the editor, but it is the drama that she enjoys most:

> 'Her joy became intense . . . her life became grand to her. She was known in the town as "the girl who could write shorthand". Her situation was not ordinary; it was unique. Again, the irregularity of the hours, and the fact that the work never commenced until the afternoon, seemed to her romantic and beautiful. . . . All the activities of newspaper production were poetised by her fervour. The Chronicle was not a poor little weekly sheet, struggling into existence anyhow, at haphazard, dependent on other newspapers for all except purely local items of news. It was an organ! One day it would trample on the Signal!'*[30]

Hilda's mother subsequently dies, though not precisely of neglect. Arnold's grandfather, however, lived to survive, as he nonchalantly puts it, 'a few more fatal attacks'.

Arnold, like Hilda Lessways, could write shorthand. He was first introduced to it at school, when he was fourteen, by a lecture on Speech Day given by the first assistant master, Mr Legg, and the subject must have attracted him. He studied Pitman's shorthand, still a relatively new accomplishment, and it proved his passport to the world. He started to apply for situations in London, and in 1889 he was offered a job as shorthand clerk with a firm of solicitors called Le Brasseur and Oakley, of Lincoln's Inn Fields. His salary was to be twenty-five shillings a week. And in March 1889, having borrowed the train fare from his mother, and having received (from Beardmore, his father's friend) the moral advice which his father shirked, he set off for London. He was only twenty-one. The years between leaving school and leaving home must have seemed long to him, but in fact he hadn't wasted much time. Enoch couldn't prevent his departure but nor, evidently, did he condone it, at this stage. The moral courage involved in making such a break is really very considerable: millions stay at home in jobs they detest, going into family businesses which they hate, rather than assert themselves

---

* The *Signal* was the fictional counterpart of the *Staffordshire Sentinel*; the *Chronicle*, clearly, of the *Staffordshire Knot*.

against the wrath of a dominating father. Enoch must have been an alarming man, who found the small change of family conversation difficult, and who found it difficult to express his emotions – it's significant that he couldn't bring himself to tell his son the facts of life. Not all the family remembered him as being dominating; he was strict but not unreasonable, they said. But it seems likely that Arnold, the eldest, bore the brunt of his obstinacy. Luckily, Enoch had transmitted some of his own will-power to his son; without it, Arnold would certainly have lingered on at home. That he dwelled constantly upon what would have happened to him if he had done so is proved at length in the *Clayhanger* trilogy. One wonders if perhaps Arnold kept failing his law examinations on purpose – not, of course, consciously on purpose, but through a very deep psychological sense of resistance to his father's will. He identified law with his father, and therefore could not do it. It's hard to think of any other reasonable explanation for his failure; he never failed at anything else in his life. If he really put his mind to something, he could do it. He was able and persevering. When he picked up his law books, did he go blind with fear of failure? Or did he maybe realize, on some deeper level, that if he passed his examinations he would be chained for life, with no reasonable excuse for escape?

As it was, he got away, and he put his father out of his mind. (He continued to sign himself with his father's initials, until some time after his father's death, and then dropped the 'Enoch' entirely.) There was no dramatic permanent break, as there might have been; Enoch did not cut him off or cast him out of his mind for his defection. In fact, once he had accepted his son's independence, he became more helpful than he had ever been; and Arnold, feeling himself to be free, became more responsive. This is quite a common story. But even commoner is the story of the son who is too frightened to move. Arnold must often have wondered if, had he stayed at home, he would have gone the way of his brother Frank, who did stay and become a solicitor, and who failed badly. On the other hand, it seems that Arnold's escape made the future of some of the other Bennett children easier – as so often happens, the eldest had the hardest time. Sissie was allowed to go to London to study as a nurse, an unusual step in those days; Tertia studied singing; Septimus won a scholarship and went off to London. Arnold had put his father to the test and won a victory on behalf of all of them.

3
London

The yearning of the provincial for the capital is a quite exceptional passion. It sets in early, and until it is satisfied it does not let go. It draws its subjects into a strange world where trains and hotels take on an exceptional significance. Many suffering from it become travellers, but perhaps they are aware that travel is simply an extension of that first uprooting, a desire to repeat that first incomparable shock. Bennett must have been gripped by it from an early age, like the hero of his first novel, *A Man from the North*; he was one of those young men born to be a Londoner, who, long before school days are over, 'learns to take a doleful pleasure in watching the exit of the London train from the railway station. He stands by the hot engine and envies the very stoker.'[1] There are traces of this early fixation in many of the novels; for instance, in *Whom God hath Joined* there's a description of the up-platform and down-platform at Knype Station, where the up-platform is described as being the 'modish' one, for though the main down-platform 'pointed at Manchester, Liverpool and Scotland, and though the greatest expresses halted their magnificence before it, it could never – no, not on the morning of the Grand National! – compete in social distinction with its rival'.[2] And in the same way, King's Cross remains for me the really serious station in London, for it was the first place in London that I ever saw, and at the age of nine its promise was enormous. The other termini never take on quite the same momentous significance, though they establish their own charms. There's a fine description at the beginning of *Clayhanger* of Victoria, which in contrast with the busy harshness of the Northern and Midland stations is 'unstrenuous, soft', it speaks of relaxation and pleasure, the passengers that frequent it are well-dressed, wear furs, have expensive and delicate dogs, and have 'an assured air of wealth and of dominion.'[3]

I should acknowledge at this point my own debt to Bennett, in my novel

47

Jerusalem the Golden, which was profoundly affected by his attitudes, though as they are of course also a part of my own background I can't quite distinguish what came from where. The girl in *Jerusalem the Golden,* like Bennett's first hero, is obsessed with escape, and she too is enraptured by trains and hotels and travelling: she feels she has 'a rightful place upon the departure platform' of her home town. There is a good deal of Hilda Lessways in her too, for like Hilda she relished adventure and irregularity, and like Hilda she is summoned to her mother's death bed by telegram and does not respond in quite the right spirit. Perhaps it is irrelevant to mention these matters, but to me they are so much bound up together that my novel is almost as much an appreciation of Bennett as this book is meant to be. I don't think I read any of Bennett's novels when I was a small child, so I must have formed my attitudes before I came to him, but I do remember that reading him was a kind of revelation. He was not, of course, the only Northerner or Midlander to feel these emotions; they still attract thousands to London every year. Some were even more obsessed. Branwell Brontë is said to have learned off the names of streets and to have familiarized himself with London maps to such an extent that he could give detailed directions to obscure places in a city in which he had never set foot. Tragically, his first visit to the city of his dreams was a disaster: Winifred Gerin reports (*Evolution of Genius*) that 'the magnitude of London seemed to crush his spirits so that, "little squibs of rum" aiding, he went about in a daze, understanding nothing of what he saw. . . . When, after days of desultory wandering, he eventually visited the National Gallery and saw the works of the great masters after which he had yearned all his life, his reaction was one of despair. He saw their perfection and realised his own incapacity. . . .'[4]

Such a dismay, such a collapse, must be a common enough occurrence. But Arnold Bennett, unlike Branwell Brontë, was a man of character, and survived the initial depressions that beset lonely young clerks in London. Perhaps his expectations were not so high; he did not at this stage consider himself a genius, as Branwell did, though he says, perhaps with hindsight, that 'some achievement of literature certainly lay in the abyss of my desires, but I allowed it to remain there, vague and almost unnoticed'. Meanwhile, he got on with settling down, getting to work, getting a rise, and looking around. He arrived in London on 2 March 1889, and took lodgings in Hornsey, at 46 Alexandria Road. It is a district he describes with little affection in *Hilda Lessways* – it strikes Hilda at first sight as consisting of 'the longest street she had ever seen', ten thousand small new houses, all alike, and vistas of 'endless, endless railway arches'. There is also a grim description of the trains in rush hour and the 'dark torrents of human beings ... covering the platforms with tramping feet'.[5] This was not the London he wanted; this was the suburbs. He stayed there, in a bedsitting room, for a year or so, and then moved south-west, first to Raphael Street, Knightsbridge, and then to Victoria Grove, Chelsea. True to his principle of economy in the invention of names, he makes the hero of his first novel, *A Man from the North*, Richard Larch, live in lodgings in Raphael Street, whereas Cyril Povey from *The Old Wives' Tale* leaves the Five Towns for Victoria Grove. It's interesting that the first novel doesn't tackle Hornsey, though it tackles loneliness bravely enough, and the portrait of Richard, wandering alone to the theatre, eating alone, longing for society, certainly reflects those first months. The life of the solicitor's office is to be found in the novel, too, down to the exact salary of twenty-five shillings; Le Brasseur and Oakley are transformed into Curpet and Smythe, and Bennett's first London friend, John Eland, appears as Mr Aked.

This first friend was also a shorthand clerk, and he was only a few years older than Bennett (according to Arthur Coveney, another colleague, in a letter to Louis Tillier,[6]) whereas the Mr Aked of the novel is of an older generation. Eland was a Francophile and bibliophile, and he encouraged Bennett in the interests that had been aroused by Mr Hurley, the headmaster, and Joseph Dawson, the bookseller of Burslem. They would talk French, eat in French restaurants, read French newspapers and visit the British Museum together. John Eland was, Bennett says, 'acquainted with every second-hand book stall in the metropolis', and he inspired his friend with an interest in bindings and collector's items that lasted all his life. Together they decided upon a scheme which Bennett has the grace to call 'farcical': they decided to compile 'a bibliographical dictionary of rare and expensive books in all European languages'. They got two-thirds of the way through the letter A, working before breakfast, and spending every lunch hour in the Reading Room – 'and then suddenly, irrationally, without warning, we dropped it. The mere conception of this dictionary was so splendid that there was a grandeur even in dropping it.'[7]

This, then, was his life, during his first year or two in London. He was quite comfortably off; he was soon given a rise, to £200 a year, which went a long way in those days when board and lodging could be got for about fifteen shillings a week. He was able to go to theatres, to buy a book a day, to visit the music halls. He went swimming frequently in the Endell Street baths and, like his first hero, he sampled vegetarian restaurants. He might have gone on like that for ever, as a loyal clerk growing older with the same firm. His work consisted of preparing bills of cost for taxation, and he claims to have been talented at it, but one imagines that he cannot have found it very stimulating; life surely held more in store than an escape from one lawyer's office to another, even though the new one was in the relatively distinguished setting of New Court, Lincoln's Inn. (The firm of Le Brasseur and Oakley, still flourishing, is now in Great Russell Street.) A fellow clerk who remembered him from those early days told Reginald Pound, Bennett's biographer, that he was not popular with most people in the office. He was 'too temperamental for the law and often gloomy; not easy to get on with'.[8] It's not surprising that he was often gloomy; on many occasions the wonderful metropolis must have seemed almost as dreary as Burslem and Hanley, and the freedom Bennett had hoped to find must have resolved itself into loneliness. Bennett was to stay in the same office for nearly five years, a long stretch for an ambitious young man with no solid prospects, a dislike of the law and no clear vision of what to do next.

His social contacts in London were few, and his most serious problem was that he couldn't get to know any girls – a problem which haunted him, as it did his hero Richard Larch, who would grow quite faint at the sight of the arms and petticoats of totally strange and unattainable women. He was not the kind of cheerful, confident young man who can dispense with introductions and chat up casual acquaintances, and the longer he remained on his own the more acute the problem must have become. Like the characters in early novels by Wells – shop assistants, clerks, teachers, students, all far too poor and too young to marry – he must have suffered acutely from sexual frustration. Luckily or unluckily, he did not rush in, as Wells and Mr Lewisham and Mr Polly did, and find himself trapped, for the sake of sex, in a hopeless marriage. But he did try to make contacts. Only a couple of months after his arrival, he was writing from his first lodgings to Douglas Baddeley, a nephew of his father's partner, requesting introductions to 'feminine cousins'; a second letter asks for 'introductions to *families* not odd members. Twig?' and states further on, in a fit of bravado: 'I have met only one decent girl since I came up. She can talk, play, sing, dance, and looks immense, both face and figure. She is engaged at the Alhambra, one of the *coryphées*. Perhaps it would be as well not to blab this all over the place. It might get me talked about.'[9] One can well imagine that this was not an intimate relationship, and did not prosper, though it does show the birth of his interest in the world of music hall, theatre, promenade concerts; also his curiosity about actresses and courtesans, which he found easier to satisfy in later years in Paris. Meanwhile, unsupplied with girls, he swam, played tennis, hunted books. And gradually he began to find his way around, and to meet the kind of people he wanted to know, who could help him to shake off the 'irksome' intellectual and artistic standards of Burslem. As so often happens, it was a Burslem contact that introduced him to this more congenial circle, which was to do so much to encourage him to become a writer. This contact was a man called Joseph Hill, a friend of Bennett's father. He was the director of the Blackheath School of Art, and also art director at Goldsmith's College. Bennett met him in his father's company in the summer of 1889 and describes him as 'a spiffing fellow'.[10] Hill obviously tried to befriend Bennett, who may well at this time have been a shy and difficult guest, despite his good cheer in letters home; and he succeeded. (The kindness was to be repaid, to Hill's son Gregory.) Bennett would go to Blackheath for musical *soirées*, and in the autumn of 1890 he met there Frederic Marriott, another art teacher from Goldsmith's, who was to be a lifelong friend. The Marriotts lived in Victoria Grove, Chelsea, and they needed a lodger, so Bennett moved in with the family from his Raphael Street lodging as a paying guest.

It was a move of great significance, and in the right direction. Fred Marriott was six years older than Bennett – old enough to guide, but young enough for intimacy. He had been born in Stoke-on-Trent, but had no contacts with the Potteries. With the Marriotts, Bennett found himself among friends. This was a cultured household, with musical evenings, improvised theatricals and constant talk of art. It was also informal. Marriott recalls that Bennett used to read at meals. 6 Victoria Grove (now Netherton Grove) was a fairly large attractive double-fronted house in a leafy cul-de-sac off the Fulham Road. Many of the houses have artistic touches, in the form of ornamental pre-Raphaelite plaques over doors, ornate knockers, *art nouveau* glass panels, and the Marriotts' house had a studio in the garden. After a life of bedsitters and landladies it was a great improvement. Victoria Grove was not in the most fashionable part of Chelsea, but it was near enough, and Chelsea was in those days enjoying a fine reputation for artistic life. The Carlyles and the Rossettis had graced Cheyne Walk a generation earlier, but there were still plenty of working artists around: Sargent, Whistler and Wilde all lived there, and so did William de Morgan, Sickert and Wilson Steer. The Chelsea Arts Club was founded in 1891, the year after Bennett moved into the district, and was responsible for the celebrated institution of the Chelsea Arts Ball, which Bennett was to attend as a distinguished guest in the years of his fame.

In the 1890s, however, Bennett was merely a modest and highly

impressionable observer, a young clerk from the provinces. He was passionately eager to learn. Marriott used to take him around and show him the
sights. On Sunday afternoons they would visit the studios of G.F.Watts and
Edward Burne-Jones. This was more like life than Le Brasseur and Oakley.
Bennett immensely enjoyed the contrast in manners between the life in
Chelsea, and life as it had been in the Five Towns, a contrast which was to
produce some of his best writing. He says:

> 'I began to revolve, dazzled, in a circle of painters and musicians who,
> without the least affectation, spelt Art with the majuscule. . . . I had lived
> in a world where beauty was not mentioned, seldom thought of. I believe
> I had scarcely heard the adjective "beautiful" applied to anything what-
> ever, except confections like Gounod's "There is a green hill far away".
> Modern oak sideboards were called handsome, and Christmas cards were
> called pretty; and that was about all. But now I found myself among souls
> that talked of beauty openly and unashamed.'[11]

He describes his arrival at the house in Chelsea, and the pattern of the frieze
of the newly papered wall: the frieze itself astonishes him, but more so the
artist, who describes his frieze as 'charming' and 'beautiful'. He can hardly
believe that a grown man can take such an interest in the appearance of his
wallpaper. The recollection recalls the passage in *Clayhanger*, where Mr
Orgreave describes the window of the Sytch Pottery as beautiful, and Edwin
is shocked, for he 'had never heard the word "beautiful" uttered in quite
that tone, except by women, such as Auntie Hamps, about a baby or a valen-
tine or a sermon. But Mr Orgreave was not a woman; he was a man of the
world, he was almost *the* man of the world; and the subject of his adjective
was a window!'[12] There's another similar piece in *The Old Wives' Tale*,
which marvellously illustrates the ironies of taste – young Cyril Povey, the
sophisticated dilettante art student, the pride of the Potteries, demands that
his mother make him a smock, and she makes him one from an old model
of a genuine smock, obtained from a country woman who sells butter and
eggs in the covered market. She embroiders it with fancy stitching, taken
from an old book of embroidery. When she shows it to him, 'he examined it
intently; then exclaimed with an air of surprise: "By Jove! That's beautiful!
Where did you get this pattern?" ' He turns over the pages of her embroidery
book with a 'naive, charmed astonishment' – but for her 'the epithet "beautiful" seemed a strange epithet to apply to a mere piece of honest stitchery
done in a pattern, and a stitch with which she had been familiar all her
life'.[13]

Bennett quickly learned the ways of this new world, for in a sense he had been looking for it for years. In some respects it was not so very different from his own home circle. Marriott, who went to stay with the Bennett family in Burslem for Christmas, found the Christmas festivities and musical entertainments there very congenial, and records that Frank, Arnold's brother, played the piano brilliantly. But in Chelsea there was more freedom, more excitement, more talented friends, no watchful parents. Arnold began to practise the piano again seriously himself, probably with the encouragement of the pianist and musician Herbert Sharpe, who was one of the circle, and to whom he later dedicated *Anna of the Five Towns*. He also helped to organize the musical evenings, insisting on printed programmes and evening dress. Marriott recalls, with a probably unintentional note of sadness, that when the evenings 'came under the efficient directional influence of Arnold Bennett the character of the programmes improved very much and developed into thoroughly well organised entertainments which were both instructive and agreeable'.[14] Perhaps Bennett was indirectly apologizing for his neurotic insistence on printed programmes years later, in *These Twain*, when Edwin and his wife Hilda become involved in a ridiculous row about the same subject, Hilda insisting passionately on 'gilt-edged cards', and Edwin reluctant to trouble his stubborn old printer, Big James.[15] They also have a row about the arrangement of the chairs and the piano, but whether Bennett was recalling some similar *contretemps* with the Marriotts about such matters cannot be known; more likely that he was trying to exorcise similar struggles with his own wife Marguerite.

It was natural that in such an atmosphere his mind should turn to writing. Everybody else he met was busily engaged on some kind of creative or intellectual work, and he had to keep his end up. Doubtless he had told his friends of the pieces he had written for the *Staffordshire Knot*, and of his second-hand book catalogue, *A Century of Books for Bibliophiles*, which he had issued early in 1891. He recalls that Marriott was critical of his connoisseur attitude to rare books, for when he once showed him a very rare illustrated copy of Manon Lescaut, all that Marriott would say was that it was one of the ugliest books he had ever seen. In vain did Bennett protest its rarity and its value. Though in fact a contemporary antiquarian bookseller would regard Bennett's trade in books with some surprise, as books in those days were amazingly cheap; none of the items on Bennett's catalogue was priced at more than ten shillings. What lawyer's clerk today could indulge in a passion for expensive bindings?

Clearly the second-hand book trade and the provincial papers were not enough to give Bennett status. He decided to attempt literature. He began modestly enough; warmly encouraged by his friends, he entered a competition held by *Tit-Bits*. The prize money was twenty guineas, and it was offered for a 'humorous condensation' of a sensational serial which the paper had been running. The serial was called *What's Bred in the Bone*, and it was by Grant Allen, a scientist-turned-novelist like Wells, now chiefly remembered for the title of his novel *The Woman Who Did*. Bennett's parody was successful: he won the twenty guineas and his piece was published on 19 December. He was twenty-four years old. He says: 'This was my first pen-money, earned within two months of my change of air'[16] – thereby giving credit where credit was due. He had proved himself. And he had also, perhaps by this venture, gained a knack of writing sensational fiction himself that was to bring him a good deal of money over the next few years.

The money didn't come at once, however. He now began on what he describes as 'the humiliating part of my literary career, the period of . . . free-lancing'.[17] He describes the miseries of this very vividly in *A Man from the North*, where Richard Larch also tries to write for *Tit-Bits* (disguised as *The Trifler*). The rejection slips, the lack of ideas, the despondent study of those great models de Maupassant, the Goncourts, Turgenev, the abortive novel – they are all there. Richard's little essays were more fanciful than Arnold's. His first attempt is a piece called 'Memories of a City of Sleep', whereas Bennett earned his first ten shillings after the prize money with an article of three hundred words under the gripping title, 'How a Case is Prepared for Trial'. He followed this with 'Lawyers and their costs', and found the vein exhausted. However, he also managed to get a short story published, again in *Tit-Bits*, for a guinea. It was not much to build on, but it was enough. For a year or two he wrote bits and pieces, short stories for the cheaper evening papers, political skits for the more expensive ones. Stories have been traced in the *Sun* and the *Star*, but his friends, ever sympathetic, inquired of him, 'Why don't you write a novel on Sundays?' He protested that he was too busy, that he had no vocation, but the idea stuck. He still thought of himself as an aspiring journalist, not as a serious writer; he could not connect his passion for the French realists with any possible talent of his own. And then, in 1893, at the age of twenty-six, he suddenly, and one would think almost to his own surprise, wrote a good story. He says that he was 'visited' with it – the phrase shows the surprised humility and pride of a writer who knows he has written something good. That he knew it was good is shown by the fact that when it had been rejected by a popular weekly because its style was below standard, he sent it straight off to the *Yellow Book*.

He would not have dared to send his first *Tit-Bits* story, 'The Artist's Model', to the *Yellow Book*, but this time he knew he'd made it.

The *Yellow Book* was a new periodical, at this time at the height of intellectual fashion. Founded in 1894, it ran for four years only, but in these years it made a lasting impact. It was beautifully printed and illustrated and its editors, Aubrey Beardsley and Henry Harland, published a provocative and brilliant mixture of work by such highbrow and fashionable contributors as Henry James, Max Beerbohm, Ernest Dowson, George Gissing and William Watson. Bennett was aiming high, as a more or less unpublished and certainly unrecognized author, but he'd done the right thing. His story was called 'A Letter Home', and it appeared in July 1895, some time after he had written it. It is good, it is recognizably Bennett, and it was favourably received. Its subject is the death of a young man in a London hospital. He is from the Five Towns (and, like the Bennett family, his family had a dog called Spot). Here, in this story, Bennett begins his re-creation of the Five Towns: Stoke becomes Knype, for the first time. But it is not a Five Towns story. Its main point is a somewhat unlikely tragic irony, and the victim's origins are more or less incidental. The irony, a mislaid letter from a death-bed, recalls Hardy, whom Bennett much admired. His friends liked it; George Sturt, one of his new literary friends, with whom he kept up a long correspondence, wrote after its publication 'it *is* distinctly pleasant, after doggedly slating a man, to be able at last to say honestly, Bravo!'[18] And the confidence which came from having it accepted by the *Yellow Book* must have been great. He was moving into a new realm of aspiration.

He was also moving out of the lawyer's office. He had never seen the law as anything other than a means of earning his living; few of the portraits of lawyers in his novels show any affection, and his picture of office life is drawn with positive dislike. So he was glad to get out, and had probably been wondering for some time whether he dare risk doing so. His earnings from his freelance journalism must have been encouraging, if not substantial. During 1893 he was told that the assistant editorship of a weekly magazine called *Woman* was available, and he obtained the position. In order to do so he had to buy shares in the firm, and his father put up the money. Enoch must have been impressed by his son's London progress. Arnold impressed the editor, Fitzroy Gardner, too, by showing him a list of all the periodicals and papers to which he had contributed, and some samples of his work. Gardner liked the work; he found it 'smart'. And he offered Bennett the position, at £150 a year, £50 less than he was earning at Le Brasseur and Oakley. Bennett accepted, not without misgiving. But, as he said to himself.

the job left him with much more free time; it would give him an opportunity to write his novel. He left the lawyers at the end of 1893, with great satisfaction, telling them that he was going 'on the staff of a paper'. He records, 'My pride must have been disgusting.'[19] He also points out that they were losing in him an excellent costs clerk with a hundred and thirty words a minute of shorthand.

Their loss was *Woman*'s gain. He started work on New Year's Day 1894. *Woman* was a weekly that had been going for five years. One of Bennett's early realistic fears was that it would fold, as so many other papers did. It cost a penny, and it was about twenty-six pages long. Its motto was 'Forward but not too fast', which caused some mirth in the Bennett circle. This was the age of rising militant feminism, but the pages of *Woman* remained womanly, though not uncultured. There were extensive social gossip columns each week, and articles on fashion, the theatre, books, gardens, cycling, cookery, etc. It produced fashion supplements, and Christmas supplements of children's poetry. After Bennett himself became editor in 1896 the character changes slightly, in that there are less purely domestic pieces and more short fiction and features. It is not easy to see exactly which articles Bennett wrote, in his first three years as assistant editor and his subsequent years as editor, for many of them were signed with composite 'office signatures', such as Gwendolen, Barbara, Ada and Cecile. He did a bit of everything. He learned about recipes and layettes, about making-up, making-ready and running-round. He reviewed plays and books, principally in a weekly paragraph called 'Music and Mummery'. He acquainted himself with hundreds of subjects that would never have come his way otherwise: features speculated about 'Do rich women quarrel more frequently than poor', 'The professional girl at home', 'School for novel-writing', and 'Women under Victoria', whereas the domestic column told one 'How to train a Cook', 'How to keep parsley fresh', 'How to make money at home', 'How to bath the baby (Part One)'. The knowledge was not wasted, for Bennett is one of the few novelists who can write with sympathy and detail about the domestic preoccupations of women – poor Constance Povey's worries about servants and bricklayers, her fingers roughened with cloth, her love for her furniture, her appreciation of 'good' clothes and umbrellas, all these details surely owe something to *Woman*, as well as to memory. It must have been at this time, too, that Bennett acquired his unusual knowledge of the behaviour of babies, for he had none himself till he was very much older; also the information about central heating and other labour-saving devices which embellish the Card's home.

56

He was a born journalist, as his editor said on his first day at work. He took to it naturally. He liked the life, for it was smart and informal. The office was in the West End – first of all in Shaftesbury Avenue, and then later in Cecil's Court, in Saint Martin's Lane. He was in the middle of everything. There were well-dressed women everywhere and they were no longer inaccessible: they were colleagues, he could have easy friendships with them without the strain of expectations. He became interested in journalism for and by women, and was shortly to write a very readable little handbook on the subject. He relates with relish the pleasure of choosing a sub-editor from the 'world of struggling lady-journalists': the lady, summoned to his office, asks him 'Who recommended me to you?' – and he replies, grandly, 'No one. I liked your stuff.'[20] The role amused and satisfied him. He also, through this job, became acquainted with the less smart working women, the single women who were so marked a sociological feature of the time, and whose discontent fed the suffragette movement: the typists, the secretaries, the failed Ann Veronicas who had broken away from middle-class homes, the overworked shorthand girls who had worked their way up out of the shirt factories. It was the time when office life as we know it began to be organized; and it was a system that required a vast amount of cheap female labour. The single working girl in the big city was a new phenomenon. In many ways the economic system itself brought her into existence. It found her employment, it conceded her right to work, and then it exploited her. She appears again and again in Bennett's novels, usually in the background but once, in *Lilian*, playing a main part. He had great sympathy with her. He makes jokes about the middle-class militants, it is true, but the pallid typists and efficient middle-aged spinsters are treated with respect.

They feature in many other novels of the period, notably in the work of the novelist George Paston, who was a niece of John Addington Symonds, whom Bennett got to know, and about whom he writes with enthusiasm to his friends; she was exactly the kind of young woman to whom his new job would provide an easy introduction. He reviewed her novels, discussed fiction with her, admired her intellectual fearlessness, dined with her and her mother, enjoyed her company, and maybe hoped for more. She was a feminist, she voiced the view that women should marry men ten years their senior, and was an upholder of the rights of the down-trodden woman journalist and office worker: her novel, *A Modern Amazon*, which was published in 1894, is a good picture of the kind of Fleet Street world Bennett worked in. Its heroine works on a magazine called *Men and Women*, is young and beautiful, lives on buns, and is loved by her editor. Her story is romantic and ends with a sell-out, but the minor characters – the governess living alone in a bedsitter on bread and butter, the dismissed office worker with her shabby dress, scanty hair, and pink swollen eyes – are well done, and the author's attitude towards their circumstances is militant. Women, she says, work harder than men for less money, which is why men try to keep them out of the professions; men feel chivalrous about 'young and beautiful girls' who find themselves struggling in offices, but are not at all troubled by the fate of the elderly and the infirm who work in the same conditions, though much less fitted to survive them. This is how she describes the situation in which she as a writer and Bennett as employer found themselves:

> 'Of late years employers have made the startling discovery that women of birth and education may be adapted for other uses than those of household ornament and domestic pet; that they may be converted, in fact, to sober industrious and very useful drudges, who will work quickly, carefully and thankfully for half the salary that would be required by a man of equal qualifications. Hence the sudden demand for female clerks, secretaries, typewriters and journalists. Poor ladies, charmed at the prospect of independence and release from the necessity of becoming governesses without a gift for teaching, or companions without the requisite cheerfulness or domesticity, or wives without love or respect, flock to the City and pick up the crumbs that fall from the business men's tables.'[21]

Not all of Bennett's readers of *Woman* would have held such advanced views, and as editor he had to provide them with what they wanted. Journalism for women, he says, was something of a specialized trade, and inevitably most of his magazine was domestic, as most such magazines still are. But he also gave them what he wanted to give them, whether they asked for it or not. It was during his years on *Woman* that he learned the trade of book reviewing, which he was to keep up, with great *éclat* and influence, for the rest of his life. He had done a little freelance reviewing – his first published review was probably one which appeared in the *Illustrated London News* in November 1893, over the initials A.B., for which he says he was 'handsomely' paid. His weekly stint for *Woman* appeared under the name of Barbara. He says that the stuff he wrote was 'entirely unsuited to the taste of our public', but he enjoyed writing it, and perhaps his readers enjoyed it too. Like most reviewers with a regular column, he had a good deal of choice – indeed he complains in a letter (December 1895) of being bombarded with books.[22]

Bennett selected the things that interested him – notably novelists such as Henry James, Thomas Hardy, and his friend George Paston. It was through a review of a book by H.G.Wells that the two men first became friends, Bennett taking the initiative and writing to Wells in September 1897 to say how much he liked his work, and to ask him how well he knew the Potteries, which Wells had mentioned in several of his stories. (By this time, having finished *A Man from the North*, he was well into his first Five Towns novel, *Anna of the Five Towns*.) Wells responded, and after desultory correspondence over a couple of years, the two men met and remained friends for the rest of their lives, exchanging letters, encouragement, literary and practical advice and praise. There is no doubt that they genuinely admired each other's work immensely; Bennett in later years was to defend Wells from the attacks of younger critics, and Wells was one of the first to recognize the stature of *The Old Wives' Tale*. They had much in common. Both came from the same social class, both had sharp family memories of poverty and failure, both were ambitious. They were both socialists, and remained socialists, in their different ways. They were the same age (within months); they lived through the same patch of history. Both were to experience marital and sexual difficulties, through which they tolerantly supported each other. The accident of their acquaintance, through *Woman*, was one for which both were grateful, for they gave a great deal to each other even on a practical level: many years later, we find Wells asking Bennett where to find a secretary, Bennett asking Wells where to send his nephew to school.

Such introductions were among the perks of his position. *Woman* might not be the most eminent of periodicals, but it was a useful centre for operations and Bennett boasted that his reviews, even if they were over the heads of most of his readers, attracted the attention of the literary world. He was not exaggerating. In 1897, when he was thirty, he was invited to write regularly for *Hearth and Home*, a weekly which later merged with *Vanity Fair*. He wrote for them under the pen name of Sal Volatile. A year later he received a more serious proposition. Lewis Hind invited him to contribute to the *Academy*. This was distinction, for the *Academy*, founded in 1869, was a serious review of the arts and sciences and at this stage, in the 1890s, its prestige and literary influence were at their highest. Its contributors were distinguished – Matthew Arnold, Mark Pattison and Andrew Lang had written for it in the 1880s, and its current writers included Lionel Johnson, Maurice Hewlett and William Sharp. Here, in this context, Bennett was able to indulge his enthusiasm for more serious writers such as Turgenev, George Moore and Gissing, though he also chose to devote a good many articles to an inquiry into the popularity of certain very successful writers and genres of popular fiction – several of these essays were gathered together and published later in 1901 under the title *Fame and Fiction*. Some of these pieces show Bennett at his best, in his role of mediator between the popular and the highbrow: his understanding of the average lazy reader, his fine grasp of the tone of provocation which never degenerates into abuse, his insistence on the highest standards cunningly concealed beneath an analysis of and, in some cases, a real affection for the crudely successful, are joined together in a fine display of ingenuity, tact and attack. He informs without offending, a rare enough gift. Some of his subjects are extremely unusual – he devotes a whole serious and excellent essay to an exploration of the fame of Silas Hocking, who wrote novels calculated to please 'the taste of the Methodist million', who sold by the million, who was unheard of in Knightsbridge but wildly popular in the dissenting provinces. Apart from any other interest, this essay throws light on Bennett's own reading background; he discusses the debate between Puritanism and the arts, describes the deep suspicion with which all fiction was regarded in Hocking circles, and says: 'How often have I heard the impatient words: "This is too exciting for me; if I went on I shouldn't be able to leave it." '[23] It must have been up in Burslem, where reading had recently been regarded as a wicked sin, that he heard such remarks. He was ideally placed to see both Hocking's appeal and his faults. The vast provincial public was on the whole ignored by the highbrow periodicals, and flattered by the lowbrow: Bennett's special talent was to take it seriously, criticize it, encourage it, be at times rude to it, and in a very real sense to educate it. No wonder his work was in demand – it's a rare author who can write on three levels for three different periodicals, write light short stories, and work on serious fiction all at the same time.

As one can see from his essays on the realists, his mind was at this point greatly preoccupied with thoughts about the art of fiction. Many of his reflections on the subject at this stage, when he was formulating his own artistic principles, can be found in his lengthy correspondence with his friend George Sturt. George Sturt was a writer and a wheelwright: he lived in Farnham, where he kept his father's shop, and has recorded the dying life of the craftsman in several books, now highly regarded by the Cambridge school, such as *Change in the Village* and *The Wheelwright's Shop*. He and Arnold Bennett met in the home of James Conway Brown, in Richmond, Surrey; Jim Brown was a professional musician, and Bennett may have met him through another young man from Burslem, a civil servant, W.W. Kennerley, who was later to marry Bennett's sister Tertia. Kennerley, Sturt and Bennett became good friends, and saw a good deal of each other – or as much as Sturt's ill health and reluctance to leave Farnham would permit.

In many ways the Sturt–Bennett friendship is an unlikely one, for they were very dissimilar, and in reading their correspondence and Sturt's *Journals* one is struck by the contrasts. Many of Sturt's literary observations seem extremely banal – one wonders why he bothered to make some of the notes in his journal.* Long passages, interspersed with dissertations, equally unstimulating, about Art and Nature and Instinct and Literary Style and Dialogue (all with majuscules) make Sturt's *Journals* heavy reading: the interesting details of country life, the affairs of the Grovers and the Goatchers, seem to have crept in almost against his will, and even then he tries to tidy them up a little.

It is not surprising to find Bennett writing back, however light-heartedly, on one occasion:

'28 January 1896

'Dearest Sturt

'Six weeks since I received your letter! If intention, the best, could hold a pen and write, what letters you would have had from me in that space! Your agile disquisitions upon fiction as an exercise for the intellect and fiction as the presentment of feeling for the appreciation of feeling, make clear to me one great and lovely fact: I have no real interest in the theory of our sacred art. I don't give a DAM for it. Guided by an instinct which I cannot explain and on which I rely without knowing why, I seek to write down a story which I have imagined with only fitfully clear vision. Why I select certain scenes, why I make a beginning of a chapter at this point, and end a chapter at the other point, why I go into minute detail here and slur over whole months there – God only knows. The only vital part of any art can never be learned and certainly cannot be talked about with the slightest advantage. And yet one likes to talk about, and hear it talked about.'[25]

And perhaps that was the point. Bennett liked to talk about what he was doing, and Sturt and he were both working on novels at the same time, so it

---

* Take, at random, these entries:

25 November 1892

I suspect that the frequency of strained situations in modern fiction indicates a consciousness in the writers of some weakness of imagination, or of insufficient skill in character drawing. It is needful to attribute some great deed to the hero, before he is recognised as differing from the ordinary folk who surround him....

And

28 December 1904

Beauty is not inherent in things; but it is the glimpse we get of the coherence or 'fit' of things one with another. Thus it is a sort of elixir of philosophy....[24]

was natural for them to compare notes and difficulties. Bennett takes a pleasure in recommending to Sturt books that his friend finds distasteful; perhaps it was Bennett's fervent advocacy of de Maupassant and Flaubert and Turgenev that led Sturt, later, to rate them irritably below Scott and Hugo. One cannot help the suspicion that, unknown to himself, Bennett enjoyed the association because of his own superior vigour: he loved to try his ideas out on somebody who could not challenge them. There is no question of his real affection for Sturt; his letters are extremely friendly, his admiration of Sturt's work is either genuine or affectionate or both, and he published one of his stories in *Woman* (1 May 1895) – years later he was to write a foreword for *A Small Boy in the Sixties*. They were loyal to each other, and affected each other considerably – it was Bennett who encouraged Sturt to start keeping a journal, on the principle that all successful authors kept journals. So they were able to compare notes about their journals and how they were keeping up with them, as well as about the progress of their novels. Bennett was tireless in his promotion of Sturt's work. He energetically promoted his novel, *A Year's Exile*, negotiating with Lane and with Chapman, and did his best for the *Bettesworth Book*, which was even more uncommercial. In return, Sturt was remorselessly critical of Bennett's popular writing; Bennett writes to him 'I get no encouragement to be deliberately and exclusively artistic – except perhaps from you and Ken sometimes.'[26] Later in the same letter he announces 'I started a novel the beginning of the month – not a conscientious novel, now, but a glittering, topical, meretricious business' – as though fully aware that Sturt would not approve such an undertaking, but defying him to disapprove. A few letters later he says that Kennerley dislikes his book reviews and 'pooh poohs them en bloc', and then goes on, 'I wrote a topical story for the St James last week, and got slated all round for it. Kennerley said it merely bored him; Chapman was "disgusted," but he added his opinion that only E.A.Bennett could have done it. And yet the St James put it on their placards, an honour not given to a story by the daily press once in a twelve month. What the devil is a fellow to do? Am I to sit still and see other fellows pocketing two guineas apiece for stories which I can do better myself? Not me. If anyone imagines my sole aim is art for art's sake, they are cruelly deceived.'[27]

Most writers would recognize the Sturt–Kennerley type of friendship, and Bennett's increasingly self-assertive response to it. He wanted to be a serious writer, he wanted his intellectual friends to respect him and take him seriously, but at the same time he could not live in their rarefied, watery, critical, artistic atmosphere. He wanted to be a man of the world; his letters are comic, practical, aggressive, disorganized. One wonders how Sturt took Bennett's assertion that 'I believe I could fart sensational fiction now'.[28] For Sturt was not remarkable for his sense of humour, nor for his self-criticism. The impression that Bennett is doing all the work in the relation-ship, and dragging a rather querulous, difficult, self-satisfied Sturt behind him may come from the fact that Bennett lived in London and had journalistic contacts and was better placed to harry publishers and their readers than Sturt was. There is a revealing little interchange about Sturt's desire to publish pseudonymously, which reveals the difference between the two men. Sturt did in fact publish under the name of George Bourne, and in May 1896 Bennett takes him up on this intention. He writes: 'Why the Hades call yourself George Bourne? Why not George Sturt? If my name were Ebenenezer Spoopendyke, Ebenenezer Spoopendyke I would call myself, and dare anyone to laugh. And the reality of Sturt is distinguished, Bourne atrociously commonplace.'[29] Sturt replies, reasonably enough, that he is not changing his name because he thinks it a slightly ridiculous one, or an undignified one (which is Bennett's implication): he writes, 'It's wholly because of the blasted business [i.e. the wheelwright's business] that I want my book to go under a pseudonym. Consider, sir: in a little town like Farnham, a man's private affairs are regarded as public property. Now, my best customers are either non-conformists who read Henry Drummond, or mere bourgeois capitalists who despise art and dislike the artists. I can fancy 'em saying of me, "If he's writing novels, he isn't attending to his business." Quite true: but I don't wish it to be formulated. I'm already suspected of being an atheist and a socialist.'[30]

And that is the difference between the two – Bennett couldn't have cared less about being accused of atheism and socialism, and indeed rather enjoyed shocking the people of Burslem. He would have given short shrift, moreover, to anyone who suggested that he couldn't be an efficient editor, novelist and journalist simultaneously. But then he wasn't trying to run a respectable family business. He might have viewed the matter of pseudonyms dif-ferently had he still been a lawyer's clerk for Bennett and Baddeley. The truth is that he could not possibly have flourished in the small, quiet, gossipy, self-satisfied village world that Sturt would not leave. He did not like the country: his novels are remarkable for their lack of rural landscape. Urban landscapes abound, but there is hardly a phrase descriptive of the beauties of nature without man. Even the local scenic beauty spots such as the Peak District are described in terms of the fittings of their hotels. Despite his periods of taking country cottages and living in the country as a country gentleman, he never got to know much about country life – thanking a friend for a 'horticultural' box, he says 'damned if I should have known differently had it contained but potato roots and turnip blossom. However, I shall be aware of the flowers when they sprout. . . .'[31] He writes in 1900 from his first country home, Trinity Hall Farm, again to John Rickard, who evidently had an interest in gardening – 'I want a nice garden (and shall have one) and a horse that will go (and have got one) but I don't want to be troubled with the details. I am now reconciled to this. I have no real interest in anything except eating, writing, music, and the graphic arts. . . . I would sooner play a piano duet than understand about inflorescences, and I would sooner write about digging than dig.' He adds as a postscript – 'Yet I am passionately in love with rusticity and the country. I gathered blackberries Sunday morn and ate 'em Sunday night.'[32]

Such a dilettante, townsman's attitude to Nature could not be more different from Sturt's. Sturt wrote well about what he knew well – the processes and labour of country life. His work is narrow, and his larger speculations are almost always marked by a kind of earnest banality, which is truly provincial, for it comes from an ignorance of the fact that what is being said is not new or interesting. This is not to underrate the *Bettesworth Book*; it has its place, it is authentic, it is real. What is surprising is that Bennett admired it so much, and persevered in Sturt's cause so long. It is amusing to find him writing to Sturt, in 1900, to persuade him that it would be a good idea to try to sell *Bettesworth* to Pearson's (a firm for which he was now a reader and adviser) – he suggests that he himself write a preface for it, and that it be published under the title *Talks With My Gardener: a study of the English peasant*. As though well aware that Sturt would not approve of this kind of salesmanship and dressing up, he says that Sturt couldn't write the right kind of preface 'not being a hack journalist. Once the book was accepted, we could calmly strike out my preface and substitute anything you wanted.'[33]

His postscript to this letter is 'If I could get Bettesworth published I should be a proud man the day.' His loyalty and stubbornness were, one can see, extremely useful to his friends: once he had taken up a cause, pride did not let him relinquish it. Sturt could count himself lucky to have such a champion, though one wonders if he quite appreciated his luck; he seems at times to criticize Bennett's practical attitude, while hoping to profit from it himself.

Bennett, however, enjoyed haggling with publishers, and was extremely good at it; his dealings with agents and publishers set a fine example for timid and easily exploited authors. He probably enjoyed chivying Sturt along. But this was not the only basis of their friendship. Bennett was not only a businessman and a hack journalist; he was also at this time, despite his denials, deeply preoccupied with artistic theory, and so was Sturt. They were both, as described, working on novels at the same time; they were both struggling under the shadows of Turgenev, Tolstoy, de Maupassant, eagerly discussing how much and how little detail to use, how to make their scenes more visual, whether a novel should have a purpose. Bennett's first title for his novel was *In the Shadow*, and his book is certainly not the bright, light, meretricious thing he had thought of writing; it is heavily overcast by fears of failure. It is also a book of remarkable integrity, quite unmarked by the commercial dazzle of his short stories and journalism – thus demonstrating early enough, as did the *Tit-Bits/Yellow Book* double, his capacity for work on different levels. That he reached the deeper, unshowy level must surely be in part due to the influence and friendship of men like Sturt, Marriott and Kennerley, who kept him up to the mark all the time, and who continued to expect of him more than he thought was in him. He began his first novel in April 1895, when he was twenty-eight, a year after becoming assistant editor of *Woman*; he finished it in May of the next year. But he did not find it easy going. In a long letter to Sturt, written in November 1895, he says:

'I find a novel the damnedest, nerve shattering experience as ever was. Nothing but my strong aversion to being beaten by anything on God's earth that I set myself out to whip, prevents me from throwing up the present one. And this, mind you, in spite of the facts that I have all my material in hand, and the whole thing mapped out in detail, and that I am not short of inspiration – as I believe they call it! It is the *arrangement* that kills one, the mere arrangement of "sensation and event"....'[34]

This does not read, like some of his remarks, as a comic exaggeration: it sounds like the truth. Again, in *The Truth about an Author*, which is a book deliberately flippant and provocative, there is a description of the effort involved in finishing his first novel – he says he had written thirty thousand words in six months, and felt as though he had been on a treadmill. Then, one day, things began to pick up, and he found the courage to reread what he had written. He says: 'It was bad, but viewed in the mass it produced in me a sort of culminating effect which I had not anticipated. Conceive the poor Usual at the bottom of a flight of stairs, and the region of the Sublime at the top: it seemed to me that I had dragged the haggard thing halfway up, and that it lay there, inert but safe, awaiting my second effort.'[35] This has always seemed to me a very striking description of what many writers experience halfway through a book: the image of the burden being carried up a flight of stairs may not be romantic; it intentionally evades any suggestion of joy or enthusiasm. But it is true. One knows what he means. And the second half, as he says, is easier.

His second effort was successful. He finished writing *A Man from the North* in the May of 1896. He writes in his journal for 15 May: 'At noon precisely I finished my first novel . . . yesterday, I sat down at 3 p.m. to write, and, with slight interruptions for meals etc., kept at it till 1 a.m. this morning. The concluding chapter was written between 9 and 12 today.'[36] He must have known already what he was going to do with it, for he sent it off promptly to John Lane, who also published the *Yellow Book*, and by 28 May (the day after his twenty-ninth birthday) he had seen the reader's report. Such speed is, to say the least, unusual in publishing; Bennett was profiting from his contacts, for John Lane was a personal acquaintance. Like Bennett, he was a provincial (though from Devon, a farmer's son) and like Bennett he was a bibliophile. With Elkin Matthews, he had founded The Bodley Head, but at this stage the two had split up, and John Lane was on his own, with a good list of authors, including Richard le Gallienne, Gosse, Grant Allen (whose work Bennett had parodied) and William Watson. Lane's reader was John Buchan, who read *A Man from the North* and liked it, although he said it would probably not be popular. To Sturt, Bennett writes that the report was 'very laudatory'[37] but to his journal he confides that it was not 'critically appreciative'.[38] In any case, Lane accepted the novel, offering a 5 per cent royalty. Bennett took this triumph calmly enough, outwardly, and his journal shows no outbursts of excitement, but he writes to Sturt of his success – 'I sort of feel that I ought to feel myself a devilish lucky fellow; also that I owe you an apology for marching ahead with my book while permitting yours, which should have had precedence, being finished first, to linger by the wayside.'[39] Such consideration and generosity are characteristic.

The novel came out in 1898, two years later: a long delay in view of the speed of Lane's decision. It is a sober book; Bennett himself at one point describes it as 'grey, sinister and melancholy', like life itself. Later he began to think it might be 'hysterical' or 'exotic', but perhaps these doubts were partly aroused by contact with Buchan, young, fair, Scottish, for whom the adjectives 'clean and wholesome' were highest praise. Certainly, compared with some of its French models, *A Man from the North* is clean and wholesome enough, and it avoids the sensational almost too scrupulously. The man in question comes to London from the Potteries, works as a clerk in a lawyer's office, is befriended by an older clerk who has a daughter Adeline, tries to write articles and finally a novel, fails, fails to marry Adeline and marries the young girl Laura Roberts, a Wesleyan cashier from the vegetarian restaurant. In fact, he is a failed Arnold Bennett. There is, perhaps, a touch of melancholy hysteria in Richard Larch's lonely yearning for 'any living creature in petticoats', and in the deaths that mark the pages – Mr Aked's, his sister Mary's – but the tone on the whole is not (to use another of Bennett's own words) 'strained'. The conclusion is finely realistic: Richard, having lost the superior Adeline, having despaired of his novel, opts for the suburban life, which he knows will prevent him from attempting to write again. 'In future he would be simply the suburban husband – dutiful towards his employers, upon whose grace he would be doubly dependent; keeping his house in repair; pottering in the garden; taking his wife out for a walk, or occasionally to the theatre; and saving as much as he could.'[40] Bennett must have written these lines with mingled fear and confidence. He also describes with peculiar vividness Richard's experience when he too, like Bennett at the thirty-thousand mark, rereads his manuscript; whereas Bennett felt that his novel was there, 'inert but safe',[41] Richard is appalled: 'The lack of homogeneity, of sequence, of dramatic quality, of human interest; the loose syntax and the unrelieved mediocrity of it all, horrified him. The thing was dry bones, a fiasco. The certainty that he had once more failed swept over him like a cold green wave of the sea, and he had a physical feeling of sickness in his stomach. . . .'[42] The whole book, then, is a projecting of fears, a confronting of the worst. And by writing it, by finishing it and publishing it, Bennett ensured that the worst would never happen to him. For he had made it: he had become an author.

It had been a fairly long haul, and had required sustained effort, over a period of life – his late-twenties – when he was working full time simply to earn his living. Many aspiring writers in his situation would have given up at the first hint of difficulty, but Bennett was a man of perseverance, and he would not give up. There was a seven-year gap between the publication of his first piece in *Tit-Bits* and the publication of his novel, a gap which had been well filled by journalism of many kinds, as well as office work; he could easily have contented himself by becoming a successful journalist and editor. What made him aspire to the loftier role of novelist? It is impossible to decide how much came from his own innate desire to excel, his own private reading and feeling for literature, and how much he drew on the encouragement of a sympathetic circle of friends – a circle which Richard Larch lacked. He acknowledges his debt to the Marriotts again and again, and demonstrated his loyalty to the end of his life. The Chelsea air had been necessary for him.

He was, of course, a naturally hard worker, and remained one. It was in his nature to set himself more and more difficult tasks, more and more ambitious projects; he was incapable, even at the very end, of resting on his laurels. When one looks at these years of his life, the years he spent in Victoria Grove, one feels that he must have worked extremely long hours, with in a sense little permanent to show for it. One wonders if he knew his own aims and his own abilities. It's hard to tell. He knew that he had to keep writing, but at this stage even he probably did not realize how far he could go.

Although he worked hard, he was also well able to enjoy himself, and had now found congenial friends to share his pleasures, some of which were new to him. It was just after he finished his novel, in the summer of 1896, that he allowed himself his first trip abroad: he went with friends to Belgium in the third week of August. They arrived in Ostend, then went to Bruges and Brussels; his friend Brown sketched, and Bennett, watched, observed, and made notes. It was his first trip abroad, and for him it was a momentous experience – almost unexpectedly momentous, one gathers. He caught from it a passion for foreign travel that stayed with him for the rest of his life, and which gave him some of his greatest pleasures. There is a very moving description of this first visit to the Continent, printed in a volume called *King Albert's Book*, which was collected and sold in aid of the *Daily Telegraph* Belgian Fund during the First World War. Bennett describes how one day he 'learned by chance that the first-class return fare from London to Ostende by steamer was only half a guinea. I had imagined that "the Continent" could only be visited by rich people – certainly not by clerks. . . . The fact that the cost of reaching the Continent from London was much less than half the cost of reaching my own home in the Midlands struck me such a blow in the back as wakes up a man dozing on the highroad and sends him staggering forward on his way.'[43] He describes the outward journey, and the incomparable thrill of the first view of 'a lighthouse, a long line of pale hotels, and the grandiose outlines of the Kursaal' – and says that his emotion as he walked about in Ostend, for the first time on foreign soil, was 'one of the major formative emotions of my whole life'.[44] There speaks a true traveller, one of the band of addicts. Belgium showed him foreignness, it showed him cities of art where every street was a vision, it showed him for the first time a Continental capital, and filled him with aspirations. He always kept his affection for Belgium, partly for its own sake, partly because it initiated him in this way, so that he could repeat his original thrill whenever he stepped on to the quay at Ostend; when he lived in Paris, some years later, he used

above 6 Netherton Grove (Victoria Grove)
below 9 Fulham Park Gardens

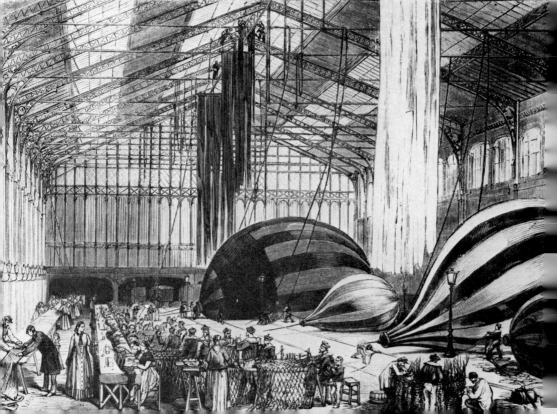

left Siege of Paris 1870
right Marguerite

left The Gare d'Orléans being used as a
workshop for the balloon post
right Drawing of Bennett at Les Sablons
by F. Marriott

above 'Les Néfliers', Bennett's French home

below Colchester Cycling Club, late nineteenth century

to go backward and forward by train from Paris to Brussels, just for the fun of it.

He returned home after three weeks, and settled down to a new, serious and extremely English novel, at this point called *Sis Marigold*, which he said was to be 'a study in paternal authority',[45] a subject on which he was well equipped to speak; this was the starting point of *Anna of the Five Towns*. He writes in his journal that 'all the old timidities, banished for a while by the prompt acceptance of my first book, have crept back again imperceptibly . . .',[46] and indeed this novel was to take him a long time to complete. But he had a busy life to distract him. Reviewing, concerts, theatres filled his time, and in November of 1896 he succeeded Fitzroy Gardner as editor of *Woman*. Gardner went off to become a theatrical manager and impresario, a risky venture which proved unsuccessful, but which interested Bennett greatly and gave him some tantalizing glimpses of the theatre from behind the scenes. As a full-time editor it's not surprising that he needed to organize his private writing time ruthlessly, but nevertheless there is something rather startling about the way he can write to Sturt: 'Tomorrow at 6 p.m. I begin my next novel.'[47] He did in fact have a little trouble getting started, but can't have been out by more than an hour or so, for at 10.30 that evening he writes in his journal that he has written nine hundred words and received a call from Kennerley. And yet the process is clearly not purely mechanical; he went to bed that night to read about the death of Jules from the Goncourt *Journals*, in order to put himself into the right artistic mood.

He managed to read a great deal, and not only for work, although he complains at one point that 'a list of the masterpieces I have *not* read would fill a volume. . . . I have been extremely fond of reading since I was 20, and since I was 20 I have read practically nothing (save professionally as a literary critic) but what was "right" . . . and yet in ten years I seem scarcely to have made an impression upon the intolerable multitude of volumes which "everybody is supposed to have read".'[48] But to the average reader his input and output, which included not only paid journalism, but also long letters and chunks of journalism, are most impressive.

His activities were not all intellectual. He enjoyed playing tennis, but his great passion seems to have been for the great new sport, bicycling. It is hard to realize now the importance of the bicycle, which liberated a whole generation of youths, did a great deal (indirectly, through the bloomers) for the emancipation of women, and changed the kinship structures of British village life, possibly saving many a pocket of rural England from genetic decay. Bennett succumbed wholeheartedly to this convenient new democratic pastime, sometimes taking solitary rides up to Tower Bridge to see the dawn, sometimes taking longer, more ambitious trips with such friends as Marriott, Sharpe and Alcock. He was undeterred by the inevitable accidents: in May 1897 he dislocated his elbow and had to use a sling for six weeks after an operation with chloroform, but he was off again to Ipswich and Felixstowe in June, and cycled all the way to Halifax at the end of July. He remained a bicycle enthusiast for years, until he could afford more ambitious forms of transport, such as yachts and Rolls-Royces. It suited his nature particularly well; he loved the feeling that he was overcoming obstacles, making progress over bad roads through bad weather, and bravely facing up to possible disaster. He liked 'the sense of deep satisfaction, the satisfaction of facing and overcoming difficulties, of slowly achieving a desired end'.[49] Riding a bicycle was not unlike writing a novel: both were good for exercising the will.

1897, however, was to prove for one member of the Bennett family a tragic year. In the summer, after his trip to Halifax, Bennett went off with friends to France, and while he was there he heard the news that his sister Tertia's fiancé had been drowned in a bathing accident at Barmouth. He received the news of the accident in a letter from his mother. His journal entry for 2 September 1897 includes the whole of her letter and her account. The two Boulton brothers, and Frank and Septimus Bennett, had gone bathing and been caught in a current; Enoch Bennett had run for a boat, but he was too late and Willie Boulton was drowned. The others only just escaped with their lives. Mrs Bennett writes: 'Tertia was hysterical after she came in from the beach: several times we have missed her from the room she has been found lying on Willie's bed hugging the clothes that he took off just before bathing; and the cap that he used to wear, a brown check one, never leaves her hands, she clasps it to her tightly and paces backwards and forwards in the room: scarcely any sleep for anybody. . . .'[50] This was not the expressionless, stoic behaviour of the Midlands, which Tertia was able to assume later. One of Bennett's holiday companions was Kennerley, who was later to marry Tertia. He too read the letter and asked Bennett if he would return home. 'What's the use?' said Bennett, but he caught the Newhaven steamer back that night, and was in Burslem the next day.

Tragedy, as so often happens, made him peculiarly receptive. The description in his journal of the parting of the steamer at night is unusually vivid, and he seems to have seen his home town with new eyes. There is also a narrative confidence, a quiet certainty, in the way he recalls his meeting with Tertia, which forecasts the simplicity of his later novels. He says: 'I went into the breakfast room at home, scene of a thousand love-makings. Tertia, dressed in black, sat in the easy chair in front of the fire. It was cold. She got up.

' "Poor old girl!" I said, as I kissed her. She cried a moment. Then we began to talk of common affairs. Tertia sat silent.'[51]

After the funeral, he notes that the Goncourts in his place would have 'noted every item', observing particularly themselves. But he did not do too badly.

Nor did he content himself with artistic observation. On 15 September, two days after the funeral, he brought Tertia to London with him, and she began to keep house for him, as she was to do for the next few years. Doubtless he thought the change would do her good; perhaps he already hoped for a marriage with Kennerley. They lived at first at the Marriotts' house, where Bennett had now been for six years. The Marriotts obligingly moved into the studio in the garden to make more room for the Bennetts. Bennett, who had started off as a humble lodger, was now doing well enough financially to take over the whole house. And in February next year, 1898, he moved to the first house of his own, and became a householder.

The new house was not far from Victoria Grove. It was further down off the Fulham road, in Fulham itself rather than in Chelsea. The road was Fulham Park Gardens, a road which had been developed between 1885 and 1887 in the massive building expansion that transformed Fulham, in the second half of the nineteenth century, from a rural area to a London borough. Bennett's house was number 9, a large semi-detached on three floors, in a grey-yellow brick, with a large bay on the ground floor and a curious attic gable on the top. The street, as its name implies, is wide and pleasant, and the houses are individual, not to say idiosyncratic. It was an area populated by the aspiring middle classes who couldn't afford larger rural houses or smarter, more central ones. It was convenient for good schools, tennis clubs, cricket. In Bennett's day, Fulham Park Gardens was new and smart, and the houses were well equipped with bathrooms, electricity and individual decorative plaster mouldings. Other residents included an architect, a chemical engineer, two teachers and a consulting electrician, while at number 10 there lived for many years an artist, Rinaldo Werner, who had been official artist to King William of Württemberg and whose works were owned by many royal patrons. It was a good district; not exactly the height of chic which he was eventually to achieve but good enough for the first house of a man of thirty. He celebrated his removal with a champagne house-warming. It was a week after his first novel, *A Man from the North*, had been published.

Houses were cheap in those days, and so were servants. The average price for a house in Fulham seems to have been £300–£400, and the average wage for a servant (yearly) from £12 to £14. On his wages as editor, pleasantly supplemented by freelance journalism, Bennett could live in some style. He had a large household to support. There was Tertia, who was housekeeping and studying singing. There was his younger brother Septimus, who like Cyril Povey had won a scholarship – in Septimus's case, the National Scholarship for Sculpture, at South Kensington. And there was also Mrs Hill, widow of Joseph Hill who had died three years earlier; she came from Blackheath with her son Gregory to join the Bennett household, and the fact that she also took on the role of housekeeper confirms the view that Tertia's work was largely therapeutic. Bennett's kindness to the bereaved extended to Gregory, who accompanied him on his holidays abroad, and who was given some little jobs of reporting to do for *Woman* while he was still in his teens.

Mrs Hill and Tertia cannot have found running a house for Bennett a particularly easy task. Despite his good nature he was very particular in his domestic habits, and insisted, for instance, on obsessively punctual meal times. He also had a passion for rice pudding which young Gregory did not share. The fastidiousness which grew from early years in a crowded, dark house was setting in quite firmly, and as he was a bachelor there was no wife or children to check or moderate it. He had manservants: the names of two, Fish and Pond, are recorded for their comedy value. He was always firm with his servants, or at least thought himself to be so; though Mrs Bennett later records that they often took advantage of him. He looked upon himself, no doubt, as a practical man, a benevolent despot, but there are hints that at times his rule was more despotic than benevolent; some of his father's domestic tyranny had made its way through to him.

He was also, by now, becoming a hypochondriac and an insomniac. His bachelor state, which gave him freedom to indulge and dwell on these problems, was maybe also partly the cause of them. At the age of thirty he had had no intimate relations with women: he had worked with them, he had employed them, he had written about them, and, if the evidence in *A Man from the North* is to be believed, he had yearned for them. But he had not got one. Nor could he any longer explain this lack in terms of finance: he had got a house of his own, he could well have afforded to marry. The average age for marriage was of course older then than it is now, and one of the striking features of novels of the period is the number of thirty-year-old (and older) bachelors who litter their pages: Ann Veronica, in Wells's novel, is pursued by a most eligible bachelor, and she herself remarks at one point that the cause of feminine unrest lies in those unoccupied years between school and the conventional age for marriage at twenty-eight or twenty-nine. Nevertheless, Bennett cannot have been wholly satisfied with his single life.

There are two interesting entries in his journal in the autumn of 1897: on 30 September he writes, of John Lane, 'Speaking of his approaching marriage, he said: "I want it to come; I want it to be soon; I must settle down; one needs a woman in the house. I am tired of my present life, have been tired of it for a long time." This from a bachelor aged circa 40.'[52]

Five days later he writes, vividly, of insomnia – 'To wake up at midnight, after an hour's sleep, with a headache, slight but certainly indicative of the coming attack; to hear the clock strike, every note drilling a separate hole into your skull' – etc. etc.[53] He is beginning to sound like a middle-aged man, though in fact he was only thirty. Did he envy John Lane, did he want to settle down too?

There was no obvious reason why he should not have married. During his nine years in London he had achieved a considerable amount, and he had a great deal to offer. He was a published author and an influential editor, he had a respectable income and lively friends. There must have been plenty of girls attracted by his power in the world of journalism; he was in a position to hand out employment and advice. He did in fact write a little book for such girls, called *Journalism for Women; a Practical Guide*, which, like all his popular books, is both readable and practical. John Lane, delighted with it, published it without losing any time, after meekly accepting Bennett's insistence on a higher royalty. Bennett remarks: 'How different the reception of this book from the frigid welcome given to A Man from the North! The latter, a serious and laborious work, has waited, after acceptance, nearly two years for publication. "Journalism for Women" thrown off in about eight weeks, is to be printed and published in less than a month.' There must have been plenty of readers of this book who would have welcomed an overture from Bennett. One cannot help but speculate as to whether he made the overtures and was declined, or whether he was too inhibited even to try.

He did still have certain difficulties. He was not a particularly handsome man, though he had learned to present himself with panache. He was shy, and he still stammered badly. The hesitance of his speech made him more direct and incisive in his prose, but women do not marry prose. He was very sensitive, and must have feared rejection. Perhaps through self-defence he surrounded himself with a large household, for it was not responsibility he feared, but intimacy. He had a large circle of friends, but underneath all his

73

social activities he remained curiously solitary. He remarked once that in all his years of theatre-going he made no friends among the other regular reviewers. Many writers are marked by this simultaneous need for company and an essential sense of loneliness; even when, in later life, he did form deep personal relationships with women, there were still things he would not share and he still clung to his privacy. It must, to a great extent, have been his family background and upbringing that formed his sexual inhibitions and there is evidence that he was perfectly well aware of this. After all, he was working during this period on the idea of a novel in which a child's spirit is crushed by a dominating father, and in his journal of December 1897 he recalls the way in which his grandfather had run after servant girls and the horror which this had caused in the family. He adds: 'It is curious that at such a time of life, the long-repressed instincts of a man who had lived as a strict Wesleyan Methodist, should at last have become unmanageable.'[54] Coming from such a background, it's not surprising that he had problems. It would have been more surprising if he hadn't. And one must remember, also, that the whole age he lived in was repressed. The Marriotts, the Hills, the Kennerleys, may have represented liberation of a kind, after the Five Towns, but they hardly formed an *avant-garde* or a permissive group; even art teachers and musicians led rigidly respectable lives in those days. No wonder most people married late. His friend Sturt was ultra-respectable, a quality which began to irritate Bennett in the end.

Luckily, he had at least one close friend who had a colourful personality, an independent style and views, and an ambition to be a man of the world. This was the architect, A.E.Rickards, whom he had met through the Marriotts at a musical evening. Rickards was four years younger than Bennett, but precocious. He had started life, like Wells, in a draper's shop and, like both Wells and Bennett, he had had to struggle for his education and professional training. Indeed, Bennett recalls that, despite his prodigious success, he never gained or attempted to gain any 'certificates, degrees or distinctions'.[55] When Bennett knew him he was working in partnership with the architect H.V.Lanchester. They were an enterprising firm and won the competition for a new City Hall in Cardiff, an event Bennett used in fiction at a later date.

Rickards's impact on Bennett was powerful, and can be traced in many of Bennett's novels, from little jokes in *Hugo* about an infant prodigy of an architect, to whole scenes and themes in larger novels. He opened Bennett's eyes to the world about him, and fostered his passion for construction, his fascination with the way things are done, which had already been aroused by the building of 205 Waterloo Road. Waterloo Road was exciting enough, but Rickards was a real architect, with public buildings to his credit, and a respect for art as well as business. His friendship provided intellectual companionship and information. He was also to prove an excellent companion on later holidays, for he was a talented painter and cartoonist as well, and he and Bennett were to combine their gifts on several volumes of travel recollections. Like Bennett, Rickards was something of a showman, and they were both fancy dressers, wearing flowing ties and strange shirts. They were both self-made men, and they kept up each other's confidence. Rickards was an immensely energetic man, and also a tremendous egoist: as Bennett was not exactly self-effacing with friends, it says much for his affection for Rickards that he let him get away with his flamboyance, though he does complain, sadly, in his journal, of a meeting in later years when 'he talked about himself the whole time, except when the curtain was up, from 6.40 to 12.15. Of course this exasperated egoism was painful as a disease to witness, but his talk was exceedingly good and original.'[56]

There are several architects in Bennett's work, and his knowledge of their ways was drawn considerably from Rickards. He writes to him in 1910, apropos of the *Clayhanger* trilogy, saying that he has made his first appearance 'in the last part of it, as an infant' and that he will be 'the hero of the fourth book, about London'.[57] This fourth book was to be *The Roll Call*, and the infant was of course George Cannon, Edwin's stepson; Edwin's own ambition was to be an architect, like Mr Orgreaves, but it is George who has to fulfil it.

The peculiar attraction which architects held in the Bennett world can be ascribed in part to the position which the architect holds, halfway between the world of the arts and the world of business. Architecture is a practical affair, an affair of bricks and mortar, which satisfied the Nonconformist passion for hard work and common sense, but it is also a profession which involves creativity, style, imagination. It is for these same reasons that the architect has now become the hero of so much of women's magazine fiction: he is the man of all worlds. Bennett records in his journal for 22 May 1901 a scene which recalls the young Clayhanger gazing at the foundations of his new house: he and Rickards had gone to the 'vast, unfinished Roman Catholic Cathedral in Victoria Street, and found it distinguished, impressive, a work of great and monumental art. Bentley, the architect, was wandering under the dome, and enjoying his mighty production, and the realisation of a conception which must live for many centuries. It was an impressive sight to see him, an impressive thought to think that one had seen him, so, this

magnificent artist, who started life as a stonemason, and is now slowly dying of cancer on the tongue.'[58] This scene was to reappear in *The Roll Call*; we have Rickards's informed guided tours to thank for such moments.

Evidently, they were companions with a great deal to share. They were both single: Rickards, like Bennett, did not marry until much later – he married, in November 1915, a girl twenty years younger than himself, whom Bennett appears to have met only at Rickards's funeral. It was Rickards who accompanied Bennett on his first trip to Paris. They went on 23 October 1897, only a month after the French trip from which he had been recalled by Tertia's loss. His descriptions of this trip, in his journal, are prefaced, characteristically, by a eulogy of the Continental train, 'the visible symbol of pleasure, adventure and romance',[59] and he recalls his emotion, in the drab days of Hornsey, when he used to see the Edinburgh Express pass by. But his comments on Paris itself have all the confusion and weariness of a traveller stunned by novelty and variety; he says glumly, after two days of sightseeing and the Opera, that he felt at times gloomy, worn out, worried that he wasn't seeing the right things, wishing he had more money, annoyed by his lack of command of the language he had been struggling with for so long. Perhaps it was at this time that he resolved to 'do' Paris more thoroughly one day, and master the elements in it that eluded him as a breathless and exhausted tourist.

Rickards had been to Paris several times before, and proved an excellent guide. He had acquired there his own un-English taste for the baroque, and he imparted it to Bennett, who was as usual an excellent listener, eager to learn. (Rickards's passion for the baroque expressed itself permanently in the Central Hall, Westminster, which he designed, and which is fairly described by Pevsner as displaying 'a surprisingly worldly and surprisingly French style'.[60]) Bennett much appreciated Rickards's enthusiasm and wrote years later, after his death: 'He was in fact the least prejudiced of observers, and his capacity for appreciation knew no fatigue. . . . He must have seen the Louvre dozens of times before we saw it together; yet I shall not easily forget his unspoilt enthusiasm on that occasion.'[61] At other times Rickards's 'lack of fatigue' proved less attractive. Bennett complains that he was 'wonderfully addicted to talking in the early hours of the morning',[62] and would deliver long monologues on modern art when his friend clearly needed his sleep.

They were there for only just over a week, but it was long enough to make a lasting impact. Bennett had been preparing for his visit for years. As a boy in Burslem he had longed for London, and as a young man he had been enraptured by a day trip to Ostend. He was thirty when he first saw Paris, the city of Zola, de Maupassant and the Goncourts. He had read about it, read its newspapers, studied its language. There was more in it than he could possibly see in a week, but he had seen enough to want to know more. And the next time he was to explore it not as a tourist, but as an inhabitant.

4

The Professional

It was in 1898, the year after his trip to Paris, that Arnold Bennett decided
to try to write fiction for his living. He was thirty-one years old. He did not
resign his editorship of *Woman* until 1900, but his thoughts had been moving
for some time towards the possibility of becoming a full-time writer. In
Paris, he had noted in his journal that his mind had 'gone forward to
speculate as to his future career, which seemed but of narrow possibilities'[1] –
and he had determined to widen them. It can hardly have been the success
of *A Man from the North* that led him towards writing more novels; it had
been a critical success, it had been well and widely reviewed, but his profits
from it, he says, 'exceeded the cost of having it typewritten by the sum of
one sovereign'.[2] Clearly, the writing of serious novels was not going to keep
him in comfort. But there were other kinds of novels. There were sensational
novels, a much more marketable commodity. These novels appeared in
serial form in various periodicals – Grant Allen's *What's Bred in the Bone*,
which appeared in *Tit-Bits*, was typical of the genre. Editing *Woman* had
kept Bennett in touch with popular taste, and he knew what was wanted.
So he set about producing it.

He had already, as noted, produced a good many short stories for the
popular press, and was to continue to do so. But they were not as lucrative
as serials. Writing serials seemed a logical step – and yet it was one that
caused him some slight artistic misgivings. He had said to himself that however mercenary he became in the realms of journalism, and however much he
pandered to the vulgar taste in articles and as an editor, he would never do
so in a real novel; he was going to keep the novel for art. But art, in the shape
of *A Man from the North*, didn't pay. So he took the first steps down what
should have been the slippery slope to commercial success and literary failure,
and began to write his first serial. He was well in, as a buyer, with one of the

78

large syndicates that bought and sold fiction 'like any other fancy goods';[3] he bought nearly all his fiction from the syndicate Tillotsons, which got him 'important names at a moderate price'.[4] So, when next the Tillotsons' representative called, Bennett sold him his first serial, then called *For Love and Life* but now known as *The Ghost*. He sold it for £75. He was quite carried away with the idea and he planned another, *The Grand Babylon Hotel*, which was to be not only sensational but sensationally successful. He worked out that if he could continue to turn out serials at the rate he planned, he could earn three guineas for half a day's work; and less than ten years before, at Le Brasseur and Oakley, he had been earning £2 10s. a week. The temptation was worth it. If he fell, he fell at a good price. He managed to quell the doubts he felt at the thought of Sturt and Flaubert; he tried to compromise, a little, by toying with the idea of publishing under a pseudonym, but such prevarication was against his nature. If he was going to be a sensation-monger, he would do it under his own name, and let everyone know. It is comic to think of Sturt, modestly hiding his extremely modest works under a false name, while Bennett let everybody know the worst. And it would have taken a great deal of foresight, at this stage, to guess that Bennett was not seduced away from serious writing for ever.

His move towards popular fiction was not, of course, unsupported by all his friends, and it was at this stage, and largely over this decision, that he became intimate with Eden Phillpotts, a writer who was to influence him, collaborate with him, form certain lasting professional habits in him, and finally to quarrel with him. Without the example of Phillpotts, it is unlikely that he would have struck out so boldly into the freelance world. He first met Phillpotts in May 1897, at the Press Club, and their professional friendship was cemented by a good review which Phillpotts gave *A Man from the North* in the periodical *Black and White* – Phillpotts was assistant editor of *Black and White* at the time. The two men both had aspirations towards wealth, as well as literary distinction, and Phillpotts persuaded Bennett that it was possible to get both at once but only, as it were, by cutting oneself in two, and letting one half make the money while the other half wrote the art. He had been doing this himself – he was five years older than Bennett – and had novels both frivolous and serious to his credit. His serious novels were mostly regional: he was a Devonshire man, and he wrote of country life in such early works as *Down Dartmoor Way* (1896) and *Children of the Mist* (1898), and subsequently in many volumes which probably still have some admirers. But it is hard to imagine that Bennett can have truly admired his serious stuff; one can hardly think that Bennett liked this kind of prose:

'Patches of August blue now lightened the aerial gray; then sunshine set a million gems twinkling in the great bejewelled bosom of the valley. Under this magic heat an almost instantaneous shadowy ghost of fresh vapour rose upon the riparian meadows . . .',[5] and so on, and so on. Still, friendship blinds one to many faults, and Phillpotts was certainly a professional, if not a great stylist. And it was the example of his sensational and commercial work that most inspired Bennett; he had little to learn from him as a writer, but he learned much from him as a well-organized and prosperous businessman.

Like Bennett, Phillpotts had made his way into journalism and literature from the dullness and poor pay of an office – not in his case a lawyer's office, but the office of the Sun Fire Insurance Company, where he had worked from 1880 to 1890. Like Bennett, he became an assistant editor, reviewer, novelist, man of letters: he also married, in 1892, at the age of thirty. From the first, his output was marked by versatility and volume, and during his extremely long literary career he was to try his hand at everything – plays, poems, essays, autobiography, novels, serials, detective fiction. He was so prolific that he had to adopt pseudonyms, through modesty, and many of his detective stories were published under the name of Harrington Hext. I recently saw a collection of Eden Phillpotts volumes in a West Country bookshop: there were over 120 titles, and that wasn't a complete collection. He was popular as well as productive, though it's hard now to assess how serious his reputation was; his Dartmoor novels still have their admirers, but he was never taken as seriously as Bennett. He was essentially a middle-brow writer, and an ephemeral one at that. The wonder is that Bennett didn't turn out more like him, for they had much in common, but Bennett was to achieve the higher flights that Phillpotts never even attempted.

His effect on Bennett, in these early years of their friendship, was very striking. It is from this period that many of Bennett's professional habits date, not least the habit of noting in his journal, in figures, the number of words written during the day. This was a Phillpotts habit. Eden Phillpotts kept a diary for sixty-five years, and one of the things he noted regularly was his output: he aimed at 600,000 words a year, and could write an eighty-thousand-word serial (i.e. a full-length novel, by modern standards) in thirty days. Bennett's journal had never been unwordly: like the Goncourts, on whom he modelled it, he had always recorded prosaic details of financial transactions, as well as impressions, incidents, overheard conversations. But his obsession with wordage began round about 1898, and never left him. He and Phillpotts used to encourage each other, to compare notes, to boast to one another about their prodigious facility. The influence was not all one way: it was Bennett who persuaded Phillpotts that it would be more lucrative in the long run to write serials rather than short stories, and the result of this persuasion was a work called *The Golden Fetish*, the writing of which Phillpotts described as 'disgustingly easy. . . . I've no trouble with plots, you know, and the rest is mere writing.'[6] But at the same time Bennett was writing to Sturt (having tried to enlist Phillpotts's support for the *Bettesworth* book, and hence Sturt's support for Phillpotts): 'I have no intention, nor does Phillpotts advise me, to write novels for money. But he points out that a few really serious novels give a man a standing that nothing else can, and thus indirectly pay very well by making a good market for ephemeral stuff. Thus Phillpotts himself now gets 8 guineas (5 here and 3 in America) per thousand for his pot-boiling short stories, chiefly on the strength of his serious work. So that serious work does actually pay.'[7] This contorted advice sounds highly dangerous; but it paid off.

It was not only Bennett's approach to work that Phillpotts affected: he also gave him an image of life, a new picture of what it was like to be a writer, as a public figure. It must be remembered that Phillpotts, being a few years older, was a few years ahead in the game; he had a house in Torquay, where Bennett visited him in February 1899, and he had there a wife and two children, and 'several rooms about 20 feet square' as Bennett notes with some envy. He says: 'I left Phillpotts full of a desire to live in the country in a large house with plenty of servants, as he does, not working too hard, but working when and how one likes, at good rates. It can only be done by means of fiction. Perhaps the sale of this my first serial may be considered as a step in the desired direction.'[8] And this, shortly, was what he was to do. He was already renting a country cottage at Witley in Surrey for weekend retreats; the next step was to move into the country. But, as we have already seen, he did not really ever care for the country; he could not, like Phillpotts, have got excited about whether or not a camellia was really only a rhododendron, nor would he have spent hours pottering around greenhouses, or crossly replanting uprooted primroses in hedge bottoms. Phillpotts's love of nature was genuine enough, whereas it was the image of being a writer living in the country, with dogs and a pony trap, that appealed to urban Bennett.

But before following him to his next stage of life, the life of a freelance, bravely unsalaried, living by his pen, it is worth looking briefly at the nature of the works that helped him on his way.

What were they like, these sensational serials? They do not exist, these days: their readership now applies itself to purer detective fiction or to the glossy television serials, those with an element of chic, mystery and romance. They were written for the many, but they were set in a glossy, superior world. The heroine of Grant Allen's *What's Bred in the Bone* was a Girton girl (all the Grant Allen works that I have seen have Girton girls as heroines). Bennett, in his first attempt, concentrated on London's fashionable West End – originally called *The Curse of Love*, then *For Love and Life*, this work was later published by Chatto and Windus in 1907 as *The Ghost, a fantasia on modern themes*. (Bennett was embarrassed about this publication, although he had done some rewriting in the interval, and was not at all pleased with its sales either. He even questioned the publisher's figures: concluding, in a letter to his agent, Pinker, 'Anyhow we have done with C and W.'[9]) The novel is full of theatrical clubs, drinks of gin and angostura, musical comedy actresses, crystal balls, divettes, titles, foreign names, jewels, and pen sketches of Bruges. (Bennett wasted nothing and his few trips to the Continent are made to work hard.) The dénouement, involving the defeat of the ghost of a former fiancé, takes place in Paris; the hero wins the lovely Rosetta Rosa of the Opera Comique, who says she will stop singing for a while to marry him, for 'Money doesn't matter, You have enough, and I – oh, Carl, I've got stacks and piles of it.' She doesn't say, though, that she will stop singing for ever, to be a good wife; she says to the narrator, 'You are my life, aren't you?', but adds in the next sentence, the penultimate sentence of the book, 'But perhaps singing is part of my life too. Yes, I shall sing.'[10] A little of George Paston had made its way through, even here. Bennett was no great feminist, but he always liked women who did things – writers, actresses, singers, journalists, secretaries – and both the women in his life were women of talent and independence. In fact, *The Ghost*, silly though it is, ends on a more positive note than many of the feminist propagandist novels of the times.

His next attempt at sensational fiction, *The Grand Babylon Hotel*, was such a success that it is still selling respectably in hardback (it was last reprinted in 1971). That he could not have predicted, or he would not have sold it so nonchalantly; it must have been affairs like this that so convinced him of the value of a good literary agent. He recounts his sale in *The Truth about an Author* – he says that the syndicate were willing to buy this serial, as they had bought the last, but offered him no higher rates; he declined to sell on the old terms, and the syndicate invited him to lunch. At lunch, he made 'one of the greatest financial mistakes' of his life: he named his price – 'it was a good price, for me, then; but the words were scarcely out of my mouth before I saw that I had blundered. Too late! My terms were quietly accepted. . . .' As he reflects: 'I ought to have known, with all my boasted knowledge of the world of business, that syndicates do not invite almost unknown authors to lunch without excellent reason.'[11] He had under-priced himself; but he had the sense to notice, immediately, with his acute business instinct, that he had done so, and he was careful not to do it again. Nor was he for much longer to refer to himself as 'an almost unknown author'.

The Grand Babylon Hotel was one of the books that made his name. He notes with satisfaction that it was the first of his works to be reviewed in *The Times*. It contains many of the ingredients of *The Ghost*, but also introduces the luxury-hotel motif, which runs through his life and writing, till its final culminating expression in *Imperial Palace*. (Hotel literature still preserves its appeal, as does the luxury hotel itself; the same people like to stay in hotels and read novels about hotels. There are plenty of them and they have a lot of money. Arthur Hailey, the best-selling novelist, claims to have studied Bennett and Vicki Baum and other successful hotel novelists, before producing his own well-appointed and luxurious work, *Hotel*.) The Grand Babylon is a splendid place; its guests wear faultless evening dress, and it contains oriental rugs, temperamental barmen and chefs, millionaire Americans, modern women, foreign royalty and corpses. It provides an excuse for loving descriptions of menus in French and cocktails in English. There is a mystery, and a certain amount of detection, though it is not a classic detective work.

There is also a romance, between Nelly Racksole, the proprietor's daughter, and Prince Aribert, reluctant heir to the throne of Posen. There is the comedy of English/American manners; there is even the comedy of Semitic manners, in the person of the wealthy Mr Sampson Levi. It is typical of Bennett that, despite the immense pressure of the snobbery of the genre, he allows Sampson Levi to resist and stand up for himself; compared, for instance, with a contemporary writer like John Buchan, Bennett's racial tolerance, even in his least serious fiction, is quite striking. It is true that Mr Levi is 'a prominent member of that part of the Stock Exchange familiarly called the Kaffir Circus'[12] and that he is 'very rich and very hospitable', but he is also made to manifest a business ethic at least as admirable as that of the prince, to whom he refuses, with some dignity, to lend a million pounds. After the refusal confrontation Bennett comments:

'It was a scene characteristic of the end of the nineteenth century – an overfed, commonplace, pursy little man who had been born in a Brixton semi-detached villa, and whose highest idea of pleasure was a Sunday up the river in an expensive electric launch, confronting and utterly routing, in a hotel belonging to an American millionaire, the representative of a race of men who had fingered every page of European history for centuries, and who still, in their native castles, were surrounded with every outward circumstance of pomp and power.'[13]

And it's clear that, although Bennett revels and expects his readers to revel in his glittering settings, he hasn't forgotten that there is a world elsewhere. The work was, in his own words, 'a boom': it sold over fifty thousand hardback copies in his lifetime and was translated into many languages – by 1904, when he was still comparatively young as a writer, it had appeared in French, German, Italian and Swedish. It remains the best known of his popular fiction. He was to write more such extravaganzas, but he worked on few with such enthusiasm, and finally he stopped altogether – though, as some would say, his serious work unfortunately took on the qualities of his popular work until the one had subsumed the other. Some of the other serials – *The Gates of Wrath*, *Hugo* – have a certain flair, but some of them, as he was the first to admit, were simply appalling: *Teresa of Watling Street*, for instance, is so pedestrian, dull and ridiculous that it's no wonder he wanted to disown it. Still, it was a good way of earning money, and it didn't stop him from doing other things he wanted to do (such as plodding on with his novel, *Anna Tellwright*, later *Anna of the Five Towns*) and it saved him from having to do things he didn't want to do, such as appearing at the office, even for several half days a week.

The chagrin which Bennett felt at failing to predict the financial success of *The Grand Babylon Hotel* is interesting, partly because it foreshadows his attitude towards the literary agent. He had, at this time, no regular literary agent, though some of his work from 1898 onwards was handled by William Morris Colles, who ran an agency called The Authors' Syndicate, founded under the auspices of the Society of Authors. Colles was also Eden Phillpotts's agent. But Bennett did not find Colles satisfactory; he was not as good at selling Bennett's stuff as Bennett was himself, and appears to have been less than energetic on his behalf. This experience might have led Bennett, so confident in handling his own affairs, to take the line so commonly taken by authors: that agents are parasites and useless middlemen, who do nothing for their 10 per cent that an astute author cannot do better. One can well imagine Bennett in such a role. But events turned out quite differently, and Bennett became one of the keenest defenders of the relatively new role of agent, and one of the sternest critics of the greed and incompetence of publishers; an attitude manifested by the fact that once he had found a good agent, he stuck to him for life, whereas he changed publishers with irritable frequency and seemed to enjoy a good row with Methuen or Chatto and Windus. He was, of course, precisely the kind of writer to need an agent; the stuff he wrote was so varied that it could never have sufficed him to have one continuous relationship with one loyal and friendly publishing house. Writers need agents for differing reasons – because they are so little known that they need help with obtaining decent terms and with the publicity and selling processes, or because they are so well known that they cannot cope with the detail and trivia and volume of their own contracts and negotiations and paper work. Bennett was to gain, very shortly, the second more satisfying position, and he was lucky enough, having disposed of Colles in an admirably terse letter – the last sentence runs 'I cannot agree to you being my agent at all'[14] – to find an agent who had faith in him, nurtured him, befriended him, and did very well through and for him – James Brand Pinker, who nursed him from relative obscurity to his role as the best-paid writer in the country.

5
Country Life

In 1900, at the age of thirty-three, Bennett went to live in the country. For so urban a man, and such an enthusiast about London, this was a strange step, but he had his reasons. One of his reasons, as we have seen, was the pursuit of the image of the successful freelance writer. Eden Phillpotts, with his nice house and large rooms and servants in Torquay, was an encouraging sight, and Fulham, though pleasant enough, was not quite as impressive as Cheyne Walk. Bennett had been practising country life for some time; in the autumn of 1898 he had begun to rent a country cottage at Witley in Surrey where he would go for weekend visits with friends. From there, he could visit George Sturt; he installed a piano and held musical evenings with friends from Chelsea. He shared the rent with Charles Young, a friend of the Kennerleys, and a publisher, who worked for and later bought up a small publishing firm called Lamley and Co., which published some of Bennett's early books and also some children's books by his sister Tertia.

Then as now it was a matter of status to have a weekend cottage, and Bennett was prepared to put up with cold baths under the pump in the garden. But he never cared much for the spiritually rustic life which was then in vogue. When he and Young took the cottage over it was occupied by an artist, an art journalist, a woman novelist and a woman art critic, who had altered its name from the somewhat earthy 'The Fowl House' (a name that intrigued Bennett so much that it crops up thirty years later in a short story) to the more elevated 'Godspeace', an alteration in keeping with the fact that all four were vegetarians, and all wore sandals. Bennett notes, after meeting them to negotiate the takeover: 'They have an air of living the higher life.' And the following day he writes in his journal: 'Last night I dreamed that I wore sandals and was ashamed.'[1]

Bennett himself certainly did not intend to lead that kind of higher life in the country. Although a socialist, he never approved of or indulged in the kind of high-minded, plain-living, faintly homosexual Fabianism which men like Edward Carpenter made so fashionable at that time, though he had dabbled experimentally with vegetarianism in his Lincolns Inn days. His idea of country life was more stylish, comfortable and grandiose. He can hardly have been said to have participated in the country-cottage cult, although he rented one. Of course, for some the cult was genuinely useful, for then at least cottages could be really cheap. The Lawrences and the Middleton Murrys were able to rent one in Cornwall in 1915 for £5 a year. But then as now there was a vogue for making the expensive appear cheap; Edith Nesbit, another early Fabian, writes an entertaining description of an ex-Girtonian friend, Charlotte Wilson, who was married to a stockbroker, and who 'at last declined to live any longer on his earnings . . . now they have taken a quiet little cottage where she means to keep herself by keeping fowls! It is a charming and quite idyllic little farm. . . . The kitchen is an *idealised* farm kitchen, where of course no cooking is done – but with a cushioned settee – open hearth, polished dresser and benches, and all the household glass and crockery displayed mixed up with aesthetic pots, pans, curtains, chairs and tables. . . .'[2] There is another description of one Harold Cox, a friend of G.B.Shaw's, who started up a co-operative farm in Surrey, with all the new scientific methods, and could produce nothing but radishes. Bennett had nothing as lofty or as bogus in his mind when he started to think of living in the country; he was no farmer and he liked the expensive to appear expensive, though it was some time before he could afford the kind of country house he really wanted.

It was in the autumn of 1900 that he made his move. In September he made his final break with *Woman*, and resigned his editorship, as he had been intending to do for some time. Nearly two years earlier, in January 1899, he had written to Mrs Penrose, the novelist, saying: 'It is not my intention to sit here all my life editing a miserable female paper, or any other paper. . . . My desire is to be moving on, and I shall not remain at *Woman* a moment longer than I can help.'[3] In December 1899 he writes to Thomas Humberstone: 'I swear I will get out of that damned office inside two years or shoot myself. . . . Not that I object to editing a woman's paper and looking after nursery notes. . . . but I can't tolerate working for a company unless I am managing director or God almighty or something of that kind.'[4]

So he left, and in October he went to live, permanently, at Trinity Hall Farm, Hockliffe, Bedfordshire, to try his hand at earning his living as a freelance. It must have been a relief to give up his editorship; the volume of his output, in reviews, short stories and serials, for the past two years had been quite enormous.

When he moved, he had been in London for just over ten years. (The anniversary had been celebrated, with music and pork pies, on 2 March 1899 in Fulham Park Gardens.) He had had Trinity Hall Farm lined up for some months before moving; in January 1900 we find him writing from the Farm to Mrs Phillpotts, that he is 'trying to get the garden respectable for Eden before he comes',[5] but he didn't move till October that year. In *The Truth about an Author* he gives a spirited and amusing account of his removal, and of the necessity of cutting a dash as a country author, with a Dalmatian and a dog cart. Doubtless he did like the idea of cutting a dash and playing at being a country gentleman – the Heir of Hockliffe, as his friends used to call him. But there was another reason for his removal, and a less cheerful one; characteristically, it was not one he boasted about.

He moved to Trinity Hall Farm, in part at least, in order to provide a home for his father and mother, a home where his father could spend his last months of life. He had taken in Tertia when she was in trouble; now he was to take in his parents. The kindness of this act, perhaps an ordinary one in itself, appears greater when one remembers that Bennett had little cause to feel affection or gratitude for his father; they had never been on intimate terms. Their relations had improved, possibly, after Arnold left home; his father's attitude to his successful literary career was manifested in the loan of money to buy his way into *Woman*, and by his flattering remark that the publication of *A Man from the North* was 'better than a poke in the eye with a burned stick'. But probably neither of them had envisaged the state of dependence to which Enoch Bennett was now reduced. In November of 1899 he had what Bennett describes as a 'very serious nervous breakdown',[6] and came to stay with Bennett in Fulham Park Gardens. The addition of his parents and one of their servants stretched Bennett's house to its limits; he had to turn them out or move, and so, when he could, he moved. He took the family with him to Hockliffe, and there, in January 1902, Enoch Bennett died.

Trinity Hall Farm is a large, square, pleasant house, built in much the same yellow-grey brick as the house in Fulham. It is a real farm, with its own grounds and outbuildings, standing on a slight ridge just outside the village off the main road. It looks south, over the fields, downs and white quarries of Bedfordshire, with an extensive view. The village of Hockliffe is really little more than a road junction, standing on the crossroads between the A6 going north, and the road going west to Leighton Buzzard; its several pubs must have done better business in Bennett's day, before much of the traffic was diverted on to the M1. The old Roman road of Watling Street, which passes Bennett's farm, is much less busy than it used to be. One of Bennett's reasons for choosing Hockliffe, he says, is that it was 'on a certain main-line at a certain minimum distance from London',[7] but there was not really very much else to recommend it. The house was large, the garden was pleasant, the view was wide (and doubtless also windy), but as far as scenery goes, he could have done much better. Bedfordshire is described by the *Blue Guide to England* as 'the least picturesque of English counties', and there's some truth in this. If Bennett had been looking for a scenic retreat he could surely have found something more attractive nearer home, but then, as we have seen, he was not very susceptible to fine scenery, at least in these years.

Perhaps he chose it in a hurry, pressed by the need to get his father out of London quickly. It can't have been easy house-hunting in those days; Bennett had to do it on his bicycle. He never grew as fond of the district as he was to become of the seascapes round his home in Essex, which he bought twelve years later, nor does he seem to have taken more than a perfunctory interest in local affairs. He did write one very bad novel, *Teresa of Watling Street*, using the farm as a background, and this novel is still well remembered by the family who bought the house when Bennett left. This family is still there, and the house looks much the same as it did in his day – a partition that Bennett put up has been taken down, but everything else is the same, down to the greenhouse where Enoch Bennett's corpse lay awaiting burial.

The truth is that these cannot have been very cheerful years for Bennett. His career was going reasonably well, it is true, but the effect upon him of his father's lingering illness and death was enormous. In the long term, Arnold was to be haunted for ever, particularly towards the end of his life, by the fear of going the same way. The illness which killed Enoch Bennett was variously known as softening of the brain and hardening of the arteries (cerebral arterio-sclerosis), but it was invariably ascribed, by the family, to the strain and overwork he had suffered as a younger man. He was not old when he died: he was fifty-eight. Arnold Bennett, a congenital overworker, might reasonably have worried about the same fate; he must also have worried about the possibility that it was a hereditary family disorder. It is not hereditary, in fact, but nevertheless other younger members of the family did develop it.

The effect of the illness was to render Enoch Bennett weak and senile; he who had once been a dominant, dictatorial figure was now reduced to pathetic helpless dependence, living on one son's kindness and leaving his business to another son and to his partner. Luckily, he had worked so hard and effectively in his middle years that he had no need to work any more. But the process of watching his slow decay, which is described so movingly in *Clayhanger*, must have been extremely painful. Bennett made good use of it as material, but the signs of pain are apparent. Senile decay was a subject which was to preoccupy him, as it preoccupied Balzac – one remembers his comments on his grandfather who ran after the serving girls, in true Balzac style; and interestingly he notes in his journal for 4 November 1899 (not mentioning his father's collapse, which may or may not have preceded this entry) that Phillpotts had told him a story about an old man of ninety – 'For thirty years one or other of his aged daughters had always been at the old man's side. He had never been left. One day both daughters happened, under very special circumstances, to be away together for a quarter of an hour. They left the old man apparently quite well, but he took advantage of their absence to die.'[8] This scene is clearly used in *The Old Wives' Tale*, which he wrote several years later – the young Sophia left her paralysed father's bedroom, to talk to her lover in the shop, and he too 'took advantage of her absence to die'.

The decay of Darius Clayhanger is documented with such fine attention and feeling that we can only assume it to be taken from life. The first intimation of Darius's illness is received when Edwin sees him hanging around in the garden, after midnight; he is standing there 'silent and apparently irresolute, with a mournful and even despairing face'. The word 'irresolute' is masterly; it tells the whole story. Clayhanger has just returned from burying Shushions, the Sunday School teacher (another senile old man), and his will to live has snapped. Edwin, quite unaware of Darius's feeling for Shushions, imagines that his father has had 'a drop too much, for once in a way', and tries to mother him into bed in his old-maidish fashion. But Darius is finished. He responds to questions 'with a most profound melancholy', he falls on the stairs and begins to weep, he sighs terrible sighs, his gestures are 'inexpressibly sad'.[9] Edwin gets him into bed safely, but Darius never recovers. He becomes infantile, he gives up business, he wants to grow mushrooms in the cellar, he cannot manage his knife and fork. And the family rejoice in his fall. This is the aspect of the case that could never be described save in fiction. Auntie Hamps arrives on the scene of the tragedy and, as Bennett brilliantly notes, she enjoys the domestic crisis 'with positive sensuality': 'the infernal woman,' he says, 'with her shaking plumes and her odour of black kid, was enjoying herself!'[10] Edwin himself (and no doubt Arnold is describing himself) was too tormented to rejoice, and too threatened, but he must have felt the sweetness of revenge; there is a scene of confrontation, when Darius has been swearing profanely at Edwin's sister Maggie, and Edwin yells at him 'You'll have no money, and you'll grow no mushrooms. . . . You've got to behave in this house!' The tables are turned, and Edwin sees his father in these terms, as he shouts at him: 'With his pimpled face and glaring eyes, his gleaming gold teeth, his frowziness of a difficult invalid, his grimaces and gesture which were the results of a lifetime devoted to gain, he made a loathesome object. Edwin hated him, and there was a bitter contempt in his hatred.'[11]

Some of this bitter contempt must have swept over Arnold during those months at Trinity Hall Farm, waiting for his father's death. We are not to know how close the portrait is of Enoch's illness or of Arnold's emotions. It feels close enough, and closely observed. But there was another, and more fruitful side, to this period of time. Enoch Bennett, like most old men, was given to reminiscence; now, prematurely aged, for the first time in his life he had nothing else to do. And Arnold Bennett was working on *Anna*, though his work was much disrupted by his father's illness, as was his journal – he gave up his journal completely from 10 April 1900 until the New Year's Day of the following year, a gap which covers his removal and the worst period of adjustment to his father's condition, and its implications for the future. But his work on *Anna*, and his attitude towards the Staffordshire material, received a tremendous strength from this new proximity to his father. Several of the entries in his journal for the period of his father's collapse, before the removal to Hockliffe, cover things his father had told him about the past: there is the episode when Enoch, as a pinafored boy of eight, had run off with another boy to buy a lop-eared rabbit at Stone with embezzled money – one remembers the young thief Cyril Povey. Arnold notes that his father's father, on catching him, 'thrashed the Pater with his braces till neither of them could very well stand'.[12] Another episode, recorded a week or two earlier (24 December 1899), probably came from the same source – this is the account of Arrowsmith's call on Beardmore, for chapel funds, quoted on page 21. And on 9 February we find Bennett recording: 'Last week I wrote my best short story up to now, "A Feud in the Five Towns: a Staffordshire story", and I propose to stick to Staffs, at the rate of one story per month.' The source of this renewed interest is acknowledged in a letter to Sturt. He writes: 'I am absorbed in the Potteries just now: a great place, sir, and full of plots. My father's reminiscences have livened me up considerable.'[13] 'The Feud' (republished in the collection, *Tales of the Five Towns*) is about a drapery establishment, and a dispute about property which took place between its owner, Ezra Brunt, and a man named Timmis, a preacher in the Wesleyan Methodist Connexion. It was not Bennett's first published work about the Five Towns: he had published an article on the Potteries in *Black and White* on 12 March 1898, and had written to Wells as early as September 1897 congratulating him on his use of the Potteries and declaring his own interest in it – 'I am quite sure there is an aspect of these industrial districts which is really *grandiose*, full of dark splendours, and which has been absolutely missed by all novelists up to date.'[14] But it is clear that renewed daily contact with his father, though it may have impeded his work in a practical sense for a while, was to remind him of anecdotes and events that he had forgotten, and we find his interest aroused to such an extent that he actually goes off to Burslem to observe 'the effect of the Wesleyan Methodist Conference on the community'.[15]

Not for nothing had he described *Anna of the Five Towns*, in a letter to Sturt, as 'a sermon against parental tyranny'. By the time his once tyrannical father arrived in Fulham Park Gardens, he had been toying with drafts of *Anna*, under different titles, for over three years. Perhaps his father's arrival brought the material back; perhaps it fortified him to continue with the book. It cannot be an accident that the writing of *Anna* and the dying of his father should so have coincided. On 14 May 1901 he wrote a letter to Humberstone in which the two strands are intermingled, two parts of the same preoccupation: the dying part and the living part. He writes first:

'My dear Humberstone,

'I should have answered your letter before, but I am so preoccupied with the serious, melancholy and fine novel of Staffordshire life which I am just finishing, that I have been letting all my correspondence slide. (I find that living in the country increases one's correspondence enormously.) I am now on the last 3 chapters, which will "write themselves," and D.V. the damn thing will be done by Sunday. . . .'

He then makes a few remarks about Humberstone's efforts at journalism, delivered in his man-of-the-world tone: 'It is very improbable that you will be able to keep yourself in London during August and September. The idea of getting a journalistic situation for those two months is one of those comic opera-bouffe ideas that only occur to men of large ideas' – and invites his friend to come and stay with him during those two dead months. Then he moves on to the subject of his father, after mentioning his own future plans for building a country mansion, before the age of forty, by the sea:

'I could be happy here, were there such a thing as happiness. Which there isn't. My father was glad to hear of your interest in him. He is not better, but worse. Nor is there the slightest hope for him. He is in every way feebler. My father has been rather an extraordinary man. His father was a working potter, and he too went into the potting industry. For some time he was a pawnbroker. Then, at the age of thirty, with four or five young infants, he set to work to matriculate (think of it!), did matriculate, and became a solicitor at 35. He lifted himself right above all his relatives (though his elder brother, an artist, was a much cleverer man, and made a pot of money in the States); he collected a library of 2,000 books; the best thing he ever did was to make me work at nights as well as in the day-time. It is peculiarly melancholy to see a man like this (full of force, once, though antagonistic to all forms of art) reduced to a mere Observer-of-Force by an obscure nervous disease which the doctors can scarcely even give a name to.'[16]

It is curious to see, in the same letter, the debt to his father, and the debt acknowledged: Arnold, declaring that 'This place is not heaven, but it is an appreciable step towards that country mansion which I am going to build (before I am forty) by the sea's margin' is very much the son of Enoch, who decided at the age of thirty to become a solicitor. Arnold was aware of how much of his father there was in him; he was aware, also, of the damage he had suffered, in psychological and sexual terms, as he makes perfectly clear in *Clayhanger*. Did he, like Edwin Clayhanger, have his moments of revenge? Did he too watch his father 'snoring under the twilight of the gas . . . like an unhappy child, who had found refuge in sleep from the enormous, infantile problems of his existence',[17] and find himself sobbing, too? Again and again, Bennett stresses the melancholy and profound sadness of old Clayhanger: 'The mere sight of a man so broken and so sad was humiliating to the humanity which Edwin shared with him.'[18] What was the cause of this terrible sadness, and did Bennett himself expect to suffer from it? It is the kind of hereditary doom which is often feared and so often, alas, fulfilled. I must admit that in my first readings of Bennett I did incline to see him as a melancholic, a stoic, even a depressive, deeply imbued with a sense of the inevitable dreariness of fate and pettiness of human effort; it is easy enough to interpret some at least of the books in this way, and such a view would certainly be supported by his accounts of and experiences of his father. But on balance I think it is wrong to stress such a view. It would be stretching the evidence to paint Bennett as a depressive, or even as a manic-depressive. He

93

managed, on the contrary, by what does seem to be a miraculous stroke of luck, to be a happy man. The pleasure he took in life was enormous, and the hard struggle to gain certain pleasures in no way prevented him from enjoying them. For a man with his background, and a man who remained a liberal, progressive socialist to the end of his life, his lack of guilt in enjoying what was available to him is astonishing. One thinks of Wells, who possibly gained more, at least in terms of sexual fulfilment, but who on balance maybe enjoyed life less. Wells's gloom, particularly towards the end of his life, was indeed profound; he never really liked humanity at all. There was in him a misanthropy so deeply rooted that he could not enjoy life, except in spasms. Whereas Bennett achieved a level of solid, reasonable, generous, outgoing happiness, despite his very obvious handicaps – his speech problems, his appearance, his sexual difficulties. He liked people; he liked the world. As his father died, slowly, at Trinity Hall Farm, he must have thought about these things, and wondered what the final reckoning with his father, in terms of his own temperament, would be. It would have been so easy for him to have been different; to have had the ambition, the industry, the hard work, the accompanying handicaps of diffidence and a stammer, to have had, even, genius, a real talent as a writer, and yet to have lacked the one thing that would make these things of value: the talent to enjoy them, the gift of happiness. Luckily for him, he had it, in such abundance that it balanced the score, and enabled him to say, with sincerity, that he was glad his father had made him into a hard worker. His father's shadow was large. But he did not have to live in the darkness of it, as so many do. He had his own light. Where it came from is anybody's guess.

The hero and heroine of his first two novels have a certain amount of light, too, but both succumb to darkness. Richard Larch in *A Man from the North* was a portrait of a failed Arnold Bennett; Anna Tellwright is another of the same breed, but she fails more heroically, against greater odds, and with fewer concessions. The ingredients that went into the making of Anna are several, and they have been bound together with a considerable skill and a new sense of power. As has been noted, the book took a long time to write; it was conceived by February 1896 ('I know a good lot about my second novel already – *moeurs de province* it will be, utterly unliterary'[19]), begun on 29 September 1896 and finished in May 1901. Its titles varied from *A Strange Woman* (March 1896) through *Sis Marigold* (September 1896), *Sis Tellwright* (November 1896), *Anna Tellwright* (January 1897) to the final version, *Anna of the Five Towns*, under which Chatto and Windus published it in September 1902. We don't know how much Bennett changed his attitude towards it during the process of writing it, but in view of the time span, and in view of his renewed close contact with his father towards the end of the composition, he probably developed his original conception considerably. And the claim that it is a novel 'utterly unliterary' could certainly not be upheld of the finished version; of all Bennett's novels, it manifests its debt to a parent novel most clearly.

The parent novel is Balzac's *Eugénie Grandet*, also a novel of provincial life. It's revealing that Bennett even used the French phrase, *moeurs de province*, in sketching out his intentions to Sturt. Both novels have young girls as their central characters, but both young girls are overshadowed by their miser fathers. Eugénie and Anna are both wooed for their wealth, and both fall in love unsuitably; both defy their fathers for their loved ones, and defy him in financial terms, the only terms he understands – Eugénie gives away her birthday gold (technically her own to do what she likes with) to her worthless cousin Charles, and Anna burns a bill of exchange to prevent prosecution of Willie Price, a defaulting tenant. (For other similarities, see Louis Tillier, *Studies in the Sources of Arnold Bennett's Novels*, 1949.) But Anna is not simply Eugénie rewritten in English terms – the debt is obvious, but in many ways Bennett has added to and altered his material. Indeed, much of the material in Anna is peculiarly Bennett's own: the Sunday School meetings, the Methodist preachers, the outings, the Methodist obsession with money and fiscal affairs – comparable, in terms of plot, to the French peasant Grandet's obsession, but quite different in origin and expression. The local politics, the descriptions of rent collecting and potbanks – all these are nothing to do with Balzac; they are first-hand accounts of an area of life which had hardly surfaced into literature at all. Bennett's experiences as dogsbody in his father's office are turned to good account at last, and revenge is wreaked upon all those compulsory chapel attendances. Anna, also, is a very different character from Eugénie; she is much more spirited, more modern, more subtle. In fact, she is much more real. Whereas Eugénie is motivated largely by a romantic passion for Charles, Anna is motivated by a whole complex of passions, of which (characteristically in Bennett) sexual love is far from dominant; her feeling for the simple Willie Price is one of a rather superior pity and concern, mingled with a deep financial guilt, which she mistakes for love. But she does not reveal herself to him; instead, she succumbs to the pressures of the society she lives in, and marries the man of business, Henry Mynors, whom she does not love, and who is 'astonished and enraptured beyond measure'[20] when he learns that his betrothed, who had always lived so simply and got into trouble with her father if she peeled

95

the potatoes too thick, was worth £50,000. Though, being a man of business, he must have expected something of the sort. And with Henry Mynors at her side, Anna faces the future 'calmly and genially'.[21]

Apart from the differences of character and place, there is also a large part of the plot of *Anna* which is entirely original, and which is rooted in various incidents in the history of the Five Towns and the Bennett family. This is the part relating to the suicide of Price's father, old Titus Price, the Duck Bank Sunday School superintendent, a part which gave Bennett his first opportunity to describe scenes at which he was to excel – the sense of the community, its outrage and delight, its greed for every detail, its hypocritical concern, are all brought out with an unindulgent clarity. How wise old Enoch had been to take his illness off to the wilds of Bedfordshire, out of sight of the friendly neighbours. Like the murder in *The Old Wives' Tale*, the suicide of Titus Price is clearly based on real local events; in this case, on an amalgam of three deaths which must have been widely discussed. The first was of Henry Wilkinson, who killed himself on 26 June 1878; he had been headmaster of the Swan Bank Wesleyan Day School, which Arnold and his brother Frank had both attended until 1877. The second was of a first cousin of Enoch's, Samson Bennett, who hanged himself on 13 December 1889 in one of his pottery shops (Titus Price hanged himself in the slip-house of his pottery works). The third death was of Councillor A.J. Wilkinson, a relative of Henry Wilkinson, who killed himself discreetly abroad on 12 May 1891; according to the état-civil register at Montreux the cause was melancholia. It is interesting to note that when Ephraim Tellwright is told of Titus Price's death, he says, 'I am na' surprised. Suicide's i' that blood. Titus's uncle 'Lijah tried to kill himself twice afore he died o' gravel.'[22] Titus, of course, kills himself for excellent reasons – because he is in grave financial and legal difficulties, and because he has embezzled £50 from the chapel-building fund. But it is revealing that Ephraim, no fine psychologist, accepts so easily that suicide is something 'in the blood'. The epitaph on Titus Price is a fine piece of analysis, both of the man and the society. Bennett writes:

'The town was profoundly moved by the spectacle of this abject yet heroic surrender of all those pretences by which society contrives to tolerate itself. Here was a man whom no one respected, but everyone pretended to respect – who knew that he was respected by none, but pretended that he was respected by all; whose whole career was made up of dissimulations: religious, moral, and social. If any man could have been trusted to continue

96

the decent sham to the end, and to preserve the general self-esteem, surely it was this man. But no! Suddenly abandoning all imposture, he transgresses openly, brazenly; and snatching a bit of hemp cries: "Behold me; this is real human nature. This is the truth: the rest was lies. I lied; you lied. I confess it, and you shall confess it." . . . The young folk in particular could with difficulty believe their ears. . . . They were dazed. The remembrance of his insincerity did nothing to mitigate the blow. In their view it was perhaps even worse that he had played false to his own falsity.'[23]

There are few better descriptions of such a type, such a situation, in English literature since George Eliot's description of that other Nonconformist, Bulstrode, in *Middlemarch*.

Bennett, then, in this novel, had found his serious speaking voice. One wonders what his father would have made of it, had he been well enough to read it. Would he have seen anything of himself in Ephraim Tellwright, who also used that famous phrase, 'It's better than a bat in the eye with a burnt stick'?[24] Would he have seen anything of Arnold in Anna? Would he have recalled the family holidays to the Isle of Man, here so lovingly evoked; or his cousin's suicide?

Probably not. Bennett was already skilful at rendering apparently objective, apparently documentary, events and emotions that were very much his own. The Tellwrights are not the Bennetts; nor are they the Grandets translated. The theme of domestic tyranny is carefully transposed. But it is nevertheless true that this is not the kind of book that Bennett could have written had he stayed at home in Burslem. One can see, already, why he was and is not more loved, as an author, by his own country. Some regional novelists, like Eden Phillpotts, stay on in their regions, usually sentimentalizing them more and more as time goes on, and become much loved local characters, and Free Men of their birthplaces – as Phillpotts was made of Torquay. Others move out, and tell the truth, and are not very often asked back. Bennett, like D.H. Lawrence, was one of these latter. One of his aunts, he says, burned his first novel in Wesleyan horror. A whole community must have shivered, slightly and prophetically, over *Anna of the Five Towns*.

Anna of the Five Towns was a very important step in Bennett's career. If he hadn't managed to write it – and he nearly didn't, so many domestic and professional interruptions intervened – he would probably never have tried another serious novel again, but would have gone on making a good living with journalism and popular serials. He had already for some time been dabbling in the theatre, and with the adaptation of plays, under the influence of the highly selective and dubious advice that plays make more money than novels. It is amusing to note that Sturt, Bennett's supposedly 'aesthetic' critic, was not particularly admiring of *Anna*; he writes complaining that Bennett makes 'an inventory of the furniture in Anna's kitchen', that his characters don't come alive in the detail but are 'studied as though they were animals in the Zoo' – criticisms which were to be echoed, more understandably but equally ineptly, by Virginia Woolf.[25] Bennett writes back staunchly, saying: 'Your explanations of the partial failure of my novel are all wrong. The partial failure is not in the novel but in yourself. . . . If the characters do not seem real to you, not intimate to you, they seem real and intimate to every other person, expert or inexpert, who has taken the trouble to say anything at all to me about the book. Nay, they seem intensely real . . . but what astounds me most is your remark that I refuse to be emotional, that I am unimpassioned. The book is impassioned and emotional from begining to end. . . . But you have not perceived the emotion. Your note on the description of Anna's dresser is a clear proof of this. The whole thing, for some reason or other, has gone right past you.'[26] No wonder the correspondence began shortly to cool off. Bennett had gained everything he could from Sturt; he no longer needed him, even as a sounding board. They remained friends, but the urgency was gone.

Bennett's interest in plays was a relatively new thing, again stimulated by Eden Phillpotts; he had been toying with the idea and had produced one or two pieces before moving to Hockliffe, and worked on several others while he was there. He had started off modestly, writing duologues for private entertainments – such little plays would fit easily into the Witley weekends, the Marriott musical evenings, the social gatherings. As is so often remarked, before the days of television people made their own amusements, and it was natural that the charade and the musical programme should extend themselves to contain the play – and that the idea of the play, under printed-programme-enthusiast Bennett, should quickly turn professional. He was already practised at writing songs for home amusement, and had written the words for an operetta, *Rosalyn*. It was in 1899 that he really got moving: he wrote a short piece called *The Music Lesson*, and then three little one-act plays which his friend Charles Young of Lamley's published in November of that year under the title *Polite Farces* – they are dedicated to his brother, and have received nothing (except for *A Good Woman*, which appeared as a curtain-raiser many years later) but drawing-room performances. The first,

The Stepmother, draws heavily on the woman's magazine world, and concerns a novelist named Cora Prout; the second, *A Good Woman*, contains remarks like:

> Rosamund: My excuse is that I am not up in these minute details of circumspection: you see, I have been married so seldom –[27]

and the third, *A Question of Sex*, has this interchange, between sisters-in-law Helen and May:

> Helen: I left my own little ones, and Ernest.
> May: I haven't any little ones, but if I had I should have left them, I'm sure I should. I left Jack and the two kittens, and there was nothing else to leave.[28]

Although not exactly brilliant, one can see the type of sophistication at which he was aiming, and no doubt he received enough encouragement from his friends to wish to continue. It was all very much a friendly affair. One notes that in the same year, 1899, Lamley also published a work by Tertia Bennett entitled *Tip Tail; or, the Adventures of a Black Kitten.*

But, as Bennett was to find, the world of the professional theatre was not as easily amused as the family circle. It held out bribes, it offered money and fame, but it was remarkably hard to get anyone actually to put anything on. The situation is exactly the same today, except that there are now the films to contend with as well. On Friday, 10 November 1899, the month his *Polite Farces* were published, we find Bennett recording in his journal a meeting with Cyril Maude at the Haymarket Theatre. He says:

> 'He was very kind and good-natured about my one-act play, The Stepmother, without overflowing into that gush which nearly all actors give off on all occasions of politeness. He said that he and Harrison would certainly consider seriously any 3 or 4 act play of mine. He advised me against doing any more curtain-raisers.
>
> 'Speaking of Phillpotts, he asked me if he was doing well.
>
> ' "Very well indeed for a novelist," I said, "but a novelist never makes much money compared with you folks."
>
> ' "Except," interrupted Maude, "when he writes a good play. I have a vivid recollection of sending Barrie a cheque for £1,000 for the first six weeks of the provincial tour of The Little Minister." '[29]

So that was it; Maude knew his man. And Bennett was to strive away at plays for some time before he finally hit the jackpot.

His next efforts were collaborations. With his friend Arthur Hooley he wrote in 1899 a melodrama, *The Chancellor*, and a year later a farce, *A Wayward Duchess*. Also in 1900 he worked with Eden Phillpotts on an adaptation of Phillpotts's novel, *Children of the Mist*. In 1902 he attempted, with an unknown collaborator, to dramatize Violet Tweedale's novel, *Her Grace's Secret*; and later in the same year worked with H. G. Wells on a play called 'The Crime', which they never finished. In January 1904 he worked with Phillpotts on a play called 'Christina'; in November of the same year they worked on a play called 'An Angel Unawares'. None of these plays was ever published or produced, and the uninitiated might well wonder why he bothered to persevere in so unrewarding a line of business. But of course, then as now, it was perfectly easy to pick up quite a nice bit of money on commissions for dud projects. In *The Truth about an Author* he says: 'My collaborator and I then wrote a farce. "We can't expect to sell everything," I said to him warningly, but I sold it quite easily. Indeed, I sold it, repurchased it, and sold it again, within a space of three months.'[30]

He had learned to play the option game, which has proved profitable to so many. He says, a little further on, 'Unsuccessful plays are decidedly more remunerative than many successful novels,' and he and Phillpotts evidently found the pickings well worth their while. His attitude towards writing plays was at this stage wholly commercial; he never expected any particular artistic success, and says that what he wanted from the plays was 'money in heaps, and advertisement for my books'. It is doubtful whether the public would get to know of his books through his unpublished plays, but there was one highly influential social group that did – the world of actors and theatrical managers got to know Bennett very well, and familiarity with them was to prove useful to him in many ways – socially, professionally, and as material. He had not known many theatrical people before his first meeting with Cyril Maude and Frederic Harrison at The Haymarket, though it must be recalled that he had been a dramatic critic for years – but as he admits (*The Truth about an Author*) that he had scarcely any friends in the theatre. 'After all those years of assiduous first-nighting,' he says, 'I was almost as solitary in the auditorium on the evening when I bade a blasé adieu to the critical bench as when I originally entered it.'[31]

Bennett was very much attracted towards the theatre, with its glamour and its high risks, and he enjoyed finding himself on good terms with famous actors and actresses; but he remained critical, noting that the theatrical manager is usually a failed actor, who 'conducts his affairs too self-consciously, with too much fuss and flourish, and too little precision'. Like

all gamblers, he says, 'They are prodigal of money when they have a lot.'
They are also, he says, ignorant: 'I have heard them again and again bravely
and cheerfully assert that ignorance was one of the necessary penalties of
their calling. They are too busy not to be ignorant. As a rule, they read
nothing but press notices.'[32] He was clearly drawn to this world of dramatic
businessmen; he was also drawn to the more rarefied literary avant-garde
of the theatre, which he mocks in *The Regent*. It amused him to be part of its
vicissitudes, to have plays accepted one week, rejected the next, to have
managerial conferences in dressing rooms, to see Maude with and without
his makeup. And, as has been said, it was not unprofitable. He notes on
27 January 1901: 'In the first year of our play-writing partnership Arthur
Hooley and I have got two plays accepted for production by first-class
managers, and have received £220 in actual cash.'[33] £220 for a couple of
plays was good money when one thinks of what he got for his novels, or
even for his deliberately commercial serials.

On the whole, then, his decision to become a freelance writer was paying
off, and the move to Hockliffe, though made principally for family reasons,
had proved a sound one. He had more time for his own affairs, and London
did not forget him: he received constant offers of work, and had forged
enough links to keep himself busy – indeed, by most people's standards, he
was more than busy. Short stories, plays, a serious novel, serials, reviews,
journal, letters – the words poured out of him. He even found time to read
for Pearson's, the publishing house, and his journal is full of comments on
novels he is enjoying. It is in a way rather a relief to find that he abandons
his journal for a couple of years in May 1901; it proves he was human after
all, though it is a pity that we do not have a more personal account of his
reaction to his father's death in January 1902. He had become a shrewd
businessman, a man who wasted nothing. In 1901 he managed to get his
essays for the *Academy* published in a bound volume under the title *Fame
and Fiction*, an act which, in terms of double payment, and in rendering
permanent the ephemeral, must have pleased him considerably. He also
started to publish in the *Academy*, in May 1902, instalments of the work
which finally appeared under the title *The Truth about an Author*, an intentionally provocative and worldly description of his own literary career to
date. (In handling quotations from this work, it's always necessary to remember that it was written to shock, and that it was meant to dispel the image of
the author as an unworldly soul waiting penniless and patiently for inspiration.) Nothing was wasted: every minute was used, and sometimes twice
over. And with all this, he did find some time for other pursuits: gardening,

as we have seen, did not interest him, but he appears to have enjoyed going for walks and talking to farmhands about cows and horses and snipe, and he thought nothing of cycling for long distances. He notes (May 1901) that after seventeen hours' work to finish *Anna*, he went to sleep for four hours, 'got up with a frightful headache, and cycled through Hemel Hempstead to St Albans, lunched at the George, and home – 42 miles.'[34]

So the country life suited him. But when his father died, one of the reasons for staying there died with him. Bennett had no intention of living for ever at Hockliffe, in a not particularly attractive rented house. His mother, some-what to his surprise, elected to return to Burslem, as did Constance Povey in *The Old Wives' Tale* – the pull was too strong, and after all most of her family was still there. She returned to Waterloo Road, to number 179, a few doors along from 205, and there she spent the rest of her life, living with her maid Annie, and surrounded by a dense network of friends and relatives. Sissie, Frank and Septimus were all living nearby, and grandchildren were on the way; the second eldest of these, Margaret Shingler, who was Sissie's eldest daughter, told me that she used to go and spend every Saturday with Granny Bennett, who taught her to play bezique, and who would read to her from Arnold's daily letter, a treat to which she never paid much attention. Ruth Bennett, another granddaughter who lived a few doors away, recalls that whenever they had a rabbit she was sent up to Granny Bennett with the head in a basin, because it was her favourite bit. It's not surprising that she preferred this familiar way of life to the more isolated grander style of her most successful son.

What is curious is that her personality doesn't emerge more strongly. One gets very little sense, from Bennett's letters and journals, of her presence at Hockliffe, whereas Enoch's shadow darkens all. I asked Margaret Shingler, who remembers her well, what kind of woman she was; she said she always enjoyed her Saturdays, that Granny Bennett was very close to all the family, that she called her close friend Mrs Beardmore Mrs Beardmore, and was in turn called Mrs Bennett by her, and that she was thin, not fat like Constance Povey. She was evidently a woman who existed as part of a family pattern, fulfilling herself in her role as grandmother and mother, unwilling to be cut off from her identity. She visited Arnold frequently in later years, and was visited by him; he paid for a nurse to accompany her on seaside holidays. We don't even know what she thought of his success. She must have been proud of him, but possibly she felt herself more at home with the others.

The Hockliffe household was disbanded. Mrs Bennett left, and shortly afterwards Tertia became engaged to William Kennerley. They had had a long friendship, and although there were those who said that she never cheered up after the death of her first fiancé, and remained rather serious and quiet, she and William were to have a long and happy marriage. She was to settle into her role as wife and mother, abandoning her artistic aspirations, singing only at family parties on Saturday evenings.

Bennett, suddenly, found himself with no more dependants. Interestingly, one of the points he makes when he writes to Kennerley to congratulate him on the engagement is that from now on 'I shall have about 5 times as much money as is good for me and no one to spend it on except your brother-in-law'.[35] So, doubtless, his mind turned to new schemes of expansion. He had already embarked on just about every literary enterprise possible, so there was only one way left to make a change, and to conquer new fields. He would go abroad.

6
Paris

He decided to go to France. We do not know how soon he made this decision; we do know that during the last few months of the lease of Trinity Hall Farm he spent less and less time there. He left Tertia to do the packing, and spent more of his time in London, where his friend Rickards let him a room in his flat in Red Lion Square. In January, when the lease expired and Tertia married, he went off on holiday for a month to Algeria, alone. On the way back he passed through Paris, and decided that he would live there for a while. Accordingly, in March he moved to the Hôtel du quai Voltaire, where he stayed (apart from visits home) until he found a more permanent home in the autumn.

What took him there? Boredom? Adventure? The fulfilling of some childhood brag? A desire to cut a new dash in the new world?

Perhaps, in moving away from England, he was hoping for some kind of liberation. He was thirty-five, and still unmarried – still, in many ways, inexperienced. He had found he could not form sexual relationships in England; perhaps it would be better abroad? And as far as abroad went, the obvious place was Paris. Paris represented a peculiarly appropriate combination of attractions – it was the city of Balzac, the Goncourts, Zola and de Maupassant, and therefore it was for him intellectually respectable, a place of inspiration. He knew working-class Paris through their writing – one of the reasons why he was so attracted to the French realists was that they could reveal the interesting in the dull, the beautiful in the squalid, the passionate in the daily, a revelation which he, as a boy from the Potteries, had so badly needed. (Quotidian is, interestingly, one of his favourite words.) They were not exclusive, upper class, and literary, at least in their artistic creed. So Paris, from that point of view, was a place of pilgrimage. He had been introduced to its architectural excitement by Rickards, and had been much impressed. He had studied the language for years: with John Eland, years earlier, he had learned to read French papers and visit French restaurants. And Paris, at this period, was a peculiarly glamorous place. It had always represented sophistication and sin to the Englishman, particularly to the Northerner, and it still does, though in those days it had more real claims to its reputation. The women of the Five Towns, as Bennett makes clear in his later novels, looked on Paris as a den of fashion and vice. Bennett doubtless hoped it was. It was also a bohemian, artistic city, at the height of its glory. Living in Paris would at least shock the relations in Burslem, and might also provide him with a more relaxed sexual atmosphere in which he could make a new start.

If one thinks in these terms, it is interesting to note that the first entry in his re-commenced journal, for Monday, 29 September 1903, is an anecdote featuring what he describes as the '*sans-gêne* of Montmartre': he is sitting at a café table, two men and *une petite amie* arrive at the next table, she shouts at the cab driver, the cab driver reads a coloured comic paper, a servant sits in the cab holding the *petite amie*'s dog and laughing with the cab driver.[1] It is nothing, just a trivial incident. But it is another world.

On the other hand, he was still an observer, not a participant. Like most English people in Paris, he must have found it difficult to get going. He brought a certain amount of distinction with him – he was well known in England, and *Anna* had been translated into French – but these things mean nothing to French literary society. He was too old to mix with younger people; and people of his own age there are settled and exclusive. He did find friends, eventually, in the literary world – Schwob the critic and his wife the actress Marguerite Moréno, Henri Davray the translator and publisher, Mrs Devereux, writer and contributor to *Woman* – but he must have felt the cold chill of loneliness and insignificance that he had felt fifteen years before in London, and had worked so hard to dispel. The echo of this is found in one honest little note in his journal, for December 1903 – after describing his dinner out and his visit to the theatre he says: 'I hate, now, having any evening quite free, with no society. It is on these evenings, although I amuse myself with writing letters and reading, that I feel "out of it".' And that phrase expresses the whole thing. ' "Out of *it*." What *it* is I don't exactly know.'[2]

It is in these months of his life that a character named 'C.' begins to feature in his journal. Reginald Pound tells us that she was a chorus girl, named Chichi, and that she was introduced to Bennett by a journalist friend. She seems to have spent a good deal of time with him, and to have told him many stories about life in Paris: about wages, fire precautions in theatres, the habits of chorus girls, *accouchements*, the verisimilitude of *Nana*, and the *demi-monde* in general. She may well have introduced him to aspects of sex that were not freely discussed in England, though what he actually did about them is another matter. His understanding of women – middle-class women, at least – was still incomplete, as his subsequent mistakes show. But what Paris, as well as Chichi, did provide was an atmosphere where sexual matters could be discussed in mixed company, where it could be calmly agreed at a polite dinner party that there was no reason why a man should not take money from his lover, just as a woman would, where Bennett could discuss, with Marguerite de Moréno, Rémy de Gourmont's new book on the sexual instinct – he said: 'She supposed she ought not to admit that she had read it, and she forebade me to read it. She said that all the pornography was interlarded with reflections in the style of Paul and Virginie.'³ And in Paris, wherever he went, the same scenes presented themselves: at the Casino he sees one of the most celebrated and expensive of cocottes, who used to take with her her young child aged seven or eight – a fact which would have thrown Dickens into a passion of moralizing, but which Bennett coolly notes down, saying 'the effect was certainly effective'.⁴ At the Duval, his local restaurant, where he used to eat regularly, he sees a fat middle-aged *maniaque* whore, and his mind starts to move in the direction of his original conception of *The Old Wives' Tale*:

> 'I immediately thought of a long 10 or 15 thousand words short story, The History of Two Old Women. I gave this woman a sister, fat as herself. And the first chapter would be in the restaurant (both sisters) something like tonight – and written rather cruelly. Then I would go back to the infancy of these two, and sketch it all. One should have lived ordinarily, married prosaically, and become a widow. The other should have become a whore and all that; "guilty splendour". Both are overtaken by fat. And they live together again in old age, not too rich, a nuisance to themselves and to others. Neither has any imagination.'⁵

It is easy to unravel, from this, various of the strands that end up in *The Old Wives' Tale*, and to note the most striking difference: Sophia, the daring sister, becomes neither fat nor a whore, and the fat whore role is taken over by a Frenchwoman, Madame Foucault. Sophia remains upright and dour to the end, though there are points in the plot when Bennett could have adhered to this original conception, and given her a little guilty splendour. But he couldn't imagine an Englishwoman doing it. The fat guilty women remain essentially foreign, characters seen across a restaurant, tragi-comic. Sophia, who is seen from within, is unbending Five Towns, and Bennett quite rightly judged that there was in her (as there was in him) a quality of irreducible, stubborn propriety, whose dictates could not be ignored. Frank Harris (naturally) was to regret the loss of the Sophia-courtesan, and to complain that Bennett's landlady Sophia had the soul of a muckrake. D.H. Lawrence, too, was to protest in the same way, and his novel *The Lost Girl* is a deliberate attempt to find some other sexual emancipation for the Sophia-type: his draper's daughter becomes neither a landlady nor a courtesan, but finds her sexual salvation, in true Lawrentian style, by running off to Italy with an Italian actor. He could not bear the rigid, confining, grim, stoic conception of character that made Sophia what she was. He could not accept what Bennett had to accept. But Bennett was aiming at realism in *The Old Wives' Tale*; unlike Lawrence, he was no prophet. And which portrait, that of Sophia Baines or that of Alvina, strikes one as more truthful?

Bennett had found a new world, a new society; he went constantly to the theatre, the ballet, the opera, the music hall, to exhibitions and concerts, to watch Isadora Duncan dance. Paris was, historically, at its most dazzling, at the height of *la belle époque*: restaurants, courtesans, art, adultery, all flourished. Bennett got close enough to it to know it intimately, but he was never a part of it. Perhaps significantly his closest friends remained those who spoke excellent English, and he mixed a great deal with the Americans in Paris. His French, though improving through practice and industry, was probably not good enough to make him feel entirely at home amongst the French, who are not renowned for their tolerance of foreigners. Marcel Schwob, a scholar and linguist, whose own English was excellent, became a close friend: Schwob was on friendly terms with many of the great names of his time – he was visited by Wilde, de Montesquieu, Henri de Régnier, Jarry, Jammes, Valéry, Colette, Gide, Claudel, Jules Romain, Mme de Noailles, Sacha Guitry, and had in his time visited the salon of Edmund de Goncourt. He was deeply admired by some of the younger generation: Apollinaire and Jarry, the *avant-garde*, saw him as a sympathetic precursor. Indeed, Jarry, whose usual costume was 'that of a bicycle racer: tight sweater, short coat, and old trousers tucked into his socks',[6] untucked his trousers at Schwob's funeral, as a symbol of great respect. (For Mallarmé's funeral he had worn a pair of Madame Rachilde's bright yellow shoes.) Schwob's own literary tastes were different from Bennett's: he was not in the tradition of the French realists, he admired Whitman, Poe, Twain, Stevenson, and had even travelled in Stevenson's steps to Samoa. He had translated Shakespeare:

Sarah Bernhardt triumphed in his version of *Hamlet*. He had many English friends, and indeed married in England; though his wife, Marguerite de Moréno, was far from English. She was a distinguished actress, a friend and correspondent of Colette's, and she was to outlive him by many years, playing in 1945, towards the end of her long career, the Madwoman in Giraudoux's *Madwoman of Chaillot*, a role created for her. Their household was informal and bohemian, and Bennett met there many well-known people, but the only ones with whom he seems to have made lasting contact were those who spoke English, such as Henri Davray.

Davray befriended Bennett, and took him around; he introduced him to a Pole named Kozakiewicz, who translated Wells, and took him to a party where he shook hands with Rodin. Gide, whom Bennett was later to know well, did not meet him until later in 1911, though he was a friend of Schwob's, and had first met Jarry there.

Apart from the French friends whom he met at Schwob's, Bennett got to know a considerable number of expatriates, many of them artists. Amongst these was J.W.Morrice, a Canadian impressionist, a friend of Matisse and a heavy drinker; Bennett learned a great deal from his work, admired it, and mentions him with respect in his novels. A close friend of Morrice's was an Irishman, Roderick O'Connor, and Clive Bell recalls that:

'Every now and then O'Conor, Morrice and I would meet by appointment in Arnold Bennett's flat, and take him to a triperie. That was a great treat for Arnold Bennett, so we thought at the Chat Blanc . . . We were giving Bennett a taste of real Parisian life; so we thought, and upon my word I believe he thought so too. For Arnold Bennett, about 1904, was an insignificant little man and ridiculous to boot. Unless I mistake he was writing the Savoir Vivre Papers for *T.P.'s Weekly*, and had written one or two trifling and ninetyish novels: above all he was learning French, and he took longer about it than anyone has ever taken before or since. There we found him, sitting in his little gimcrack apartment, amidst his Empire upholstery from Waring and Gillow, with a concise French dictionary on the table . . . he was the boy from Staffordshire who was making good and in his bowler hat and reach-me-downs he looked the part. He was at once pleased with himself and ashamed – we rather liked him, but we thought nothing of his writing.'[7]

This extraordinarily snobbish account is paralleled by a reminiscence of Sir Gerald Kelly, who claims that Morrice didn't care much for Bennett, that Bennett was a figure of fun whose front teeth stuck out, and who talked with 'a most appalling accent'. Morrice, according to Sir Gerald, saw so much of Bennett because he liked 'everything comic'.[8] Somerset Maugham also makes fun of the Empire furniture with which Bennett surrounded himself in his flat in the rue de Calais, whither he moved from the Hôtel du quai Voltaire: but, as Bennett himself pointed out years later, he didn't choose Empire furniture because of a real passion for it, but because 'the Empire style was the only style within the means of a man who had to earn his living by realistic fiction. Louis Quinze and Louis Seize were not for writers. . . .' His willingness to learn about painting and sculpture and modern music and French shows up the attitudes and manners of his so-called friends in a poor light. But they were young at the time, and some of them changed their minds about him later – Somerset Maugham, in a frank piece written just after Bennett's death, recalls these early days in Paris. He writes of the dinners in the Chat Blanc, the French mistresses, the acrimonious discussions about French poets, and says that Bennett:

'. . . was older than most of us. He was then a thin man, with dark hair very smoothly done . . . he was much more neatly dressed than we were, and more conventionally. He looked like a managing clerk in a city office . . . his Empire furniture . . . was certainly not genuine, but this he did not know, and he was exceedingly proud of it. Arnold was a very tidy man and his apartment was very neat . . . he was good company, and I always enjoyed spending an evening with him, but I didn't very much like him. He was cocksure and bumptious and he was rather common.'[9]

He also recounts a strange incident, with a somewhat apocryphal ring, in which Bennett offered him his mistress (an educated woman, 'she reads a great deal, Mme de Sévingné and all that') for two nights a week. Maugham refused. But in the same article, after painting this rather damning picture, Maugham goes on to say how his friendship with him prospered in later years, what a lovable man he was, and how great a novel *The Old Wives' Tale* was. He discusses his agonizing stammer at considerable length (Maugham himself suffered from the same impediment), speculates about whether it was this that forced Bennett into the introspection that made him a writer, and concludes: 'I remember that once, beating his knee with his clenched fist to force the words from his writhing lips, he said: "I am a nice man." He was.'[10]

Other expatriates whom he knew were Violet Hunt the writer, George Ullman, an American painter who married Bennett's friend Alice Woods, Mrs Devereux, whom he had known from the old days on *Woman*, and Mrs

Agnes Farley, a friend of Violet Hunt's and the wife of an American dentist in Paris. It was Somerset Maugham who introduced Bennett to Violet Hunt. She and Bennett used to see a good deal of one another, as she related in her reminiscences in the *American Bookman* (August 1932). She was a few years older than Bennett – she was born in 1862 – and was still remarkably handsome, an auburn-haired, large-eyed beauty, whose parents had moved in pre-Raphaelite circles in London. By the time she met Bennett, she had already been through several affairs and had indeed fled to Paris upon the collapse of her most recent passion for Oswald Crawfurd. She was an adventuress of the emotions, described by Arthur Mizener as 'a middle-class Moll Flanders or Molly Bloom'.[11] They would dine together frequently and exchange stories about life and sex, a subject on which she at least was well informed, and she comments that she suspected her interests were 'too purely sexual' for him. She had no designs on him herself, it would appear, though she had made approaches to and got off with many other literary figures of her time (and ended up, notoriously, with Ford Madox Ford, and the tertiary syphilis she had inherited from an earlier love). Bennett, however, was a useful friend. She used him, frankly, as an escort; she says in her reminiscences: 'When Maugham left Paris and I wanted somebody to go about with, I turned to Arnold Bennett. He was a charming, patient, erudite and sporting companion, and there was not a sight or sound of Paris with which he was not acquainted. . . .'[12]

They may also have talked about literature, for she was a professional writer, whose short stories had attracted the admiration of Henry James. She also wrote novels, some of them frankly autobiographical, and reviewed frequently in various papers and periodicals.

Most of this circle, in fact, dabbled in either art or literature, some more seriously than others. Alice Woods wrote a novel, Mrs Devereux wrote novels and journalism, Agnes Farley edited an edition of Casanova's *Memoirs* with Violet Hunt, and also wrote a novel and a book about country life in France, to which Bennett contributed a preface, expressing the wish that Mrs Farley, who was an expert gossip, matchmaker and hostess, would also write about life in Paris. (This was particularly generous of him in view of the fact that her matchmaking on his behalf had turned out disastrously.) One gets a fairly clear picture of the kind of society he moved in – social, journalistic, with some friends (like Morrice and O'Conor) faintly raffish, and others bohemian but respectable. At times, inevitably, he felt lonely, for there was much from which he was excluded, and he was living completely alone for the first time for some years, but his energy carried him forward. He saw as much as possible, ate alone at his local Duval or out with friends, began slowly to embark on entertaining people for himself, visited the Chat Blanc, learned to give afternoon teas 'with immense effect', reread Balzac and de Maupassant and wondered whether he would be accused of plagiarism – and, of course, he worked. His journalism was fairly regular: he had stopped writing for the *Academy*, and was now doing a less highbrow and literary series for *T.P's Weekly*. The series was called, to begin with, the Savoir Faire Papers, and it began in November 1902; a year later it changed its name to *The Novelist's Log Book*, but it continued to cover much the same kind of middle-brow topics: train travel, ABC lunches, how to keep one's house warm, how to live alone in London. Although a few articles are Continental and man-of-the-world in flavour, most of them are aimed at the ordinary English reader, and show clearly the journalistic skill he picked up on *Woman*. The articles on living alone in London are a rather sad and depressing reminder of the old days of *A Man from the North*. Was he cheering himself up, alone in Paris, by remembering how much worse things had been ten years earlier? And is there an element of sour grapes in his two articles on marriage, in which he seriously inquires of the married man, after a very gloomy description of marriage: 'Do you not wish violently, at least once a week, that you had never married?'[13] He was also, as well as his regular column, writing a good deal of light fiction at this period – several stories appeared in *The Queen*, *The Sphere* and in *T.P.'s Weekly* itself, and six were written for *The Windsor* and finally collected under the title *The Loot of Cities*. These were all fairly light-weight enterprises – 'good on their plane', as he himself described some of them. With such a large output, it is not surprising that inspiration occasionally runs a little dry: there is a Savoir Faire Paper on the noble animal, the horse, a subject which interested Bennett little and about which he knew less. But he was a professional, and prided himself on being able to turn his hand to anything. His diverse productions were by this time being handled by the efficient Pinker, who had been introduced to Bennett in 1901; he could hardly have managed the negotiations and the composition of so much work by this stage, especially over such a distance: though the post between Paris and London was remarkably good.

He was not writing only journalism. Another serious novel, *Leonora*, appeared in October of 1903, and shortly after that he began to work on a fourth novel, *A Great Man*, which was to be neither serious nor sensational. *Leonora* is cast in the same mould as *Anna of the Five Towns*, but it did not take him nearly as long to write it; it seems that he had started it towards the end of 1902 and had finished it by June 1903. (One must admire the expedition with which books were published in those days.) In his journal (8 January 1904) he records retrospectively that 'between April 1st and June 30th I wrote nearly all "Leonora" '. He must have worked very hard on it during those few months. He remembers later that while he was writing the book he used to leave the Hôtel du quai Voltaire where he was living, and go out for a walk along the rue de Rivoli, 'with a sensation as if the top of my head would come off. But I did not recognise it as fatigue, simply as the result of worry, a nuisance.'[14]

Leonora is not as good a book as *Anna*, though it uses much of the same material and background; at times one feels that it contains many of the observations and ideas that were left over from his lengthy work and research on *Anna*, which would explain why he was able to write it so quickly. It is clear that he himself took it seriously, however. Writing to Pinker, he says at one point, in a familiar vein: 'You know I would write books like Leonora for pleasure and nothing else; but I don't precisely write serials for fun, and when I do them I want to get the last penny out of them.'[15] A little later he writes again, more emphatically still, of a later collection of stories: 'I regard it as very important that the book of Five Towns stories should appear in the autumn, because they are serious work, in the vein by which whatever happens in the meantime I shall ultimately make the most money. . . . It cannot be too clearly understood that though one may do lighter work for the sake of a contemporary splash etc. and for relief, it is the *Leonora* type which is and will be the solid foundation of the reputation. It is Leonora and Anna which will be talked of twenty years hence, when people will wonder why they attracted so little notice at the time.'[16]

As we know, he was right about *Anna*, which was reprinted in 1970 by Penguin: but not so right about *Leonora*, of which the last edition is dated 1931, the year of his death. Nevertheless, *Leonora* has its points. It is set in a slightly more elevated social sphere than *Anna*: Leonora is the forty-year-old wife of a wealthy earthenware manufacturer, John Stanway, who is no miser, though he has other failings. They have three children; they live comfortably, in a large house, and take part, like the Bennetts and their circle, in local affairs. Their lives are disrupted by the return of Arthur Twemlow, son of Stanway's old partner. There is a mystery about some financial dealings in the past, and John Stanway finally commits suicide, leaving Leonora to Twemlow, whom she accepts after some heart-searching as to whether or not she can leave her grown-up daughters to go to live in New York. As ever, the details of provincial life are well done; a review in the

Scotsman comments on 'the smug prosperity of the home, with its six o'clock meat-teas, and its subservient attitude to the blustering head of the house',[17] and it is this part of the novel which is the most successful. There is a fine description of a meal which John Stanway fails to attend. The girls squabble among themselves and with their mother, idly, amiably, and Bennett writes: 'The repast, which had commenced with due ceremony, degenerated into a feminine mess, hasty, informal, counterfeit. That elaborate and irksome pretence that a man is present, with which women when they are alone always begin to eat, was gradually dropped, and the meal ended abruptly, inconclusively, like a bad play.'[18] One might well ask oneself, how did he know about such things? Jane Austen never left two men alone together in her novels; Bennett deals quite confidently with a whole table full of women. And again, why a woman for the main character? Leonora is far more real than any of the other characters in the book. Her emotions as she watches her daughter Millie succeed on the stage, her jealousy when telegrams arrive for Millie and not for her, her confusion when she finds Rose competently working in a lying-in hospital, her mixture of competence and panic, her yearnings for wicked luxury – all these aspects of her character are handled with expert control. At times she gets a little out of hand: her passion for Arthur Twemlow is described at moments in phrases which are not too happy ('Then, in a delicious surrender, she felt towards him as though they were on the brink of a rushing river, and he was about to pick her up in his arms like a trifle, and carry her safely through the flood. . . . "Oh, you innocent angel," he cried . . .'[19]), but on the whole the fine tension between Leonora's fantasies and her reality is very well maintained. The ending, with the convenience of the union between the two middle-aged lovers, might seem contrived and improbable; but one must set against it the really quite ruthless account of her reflections on her husband's deathbed. There is nothing sentimental or palliative about these. He kills himself as a result of a financial crisis, brought to a head partly by her refusal to sell the house, which is her own. As he dies of prussic acid poisoning, she sits over him. 'I would not sell my home,' she reflects, 'and here is the consequence of refusal.' She wishes she had yielded – and she can perceive how unimportant, comparatively, bricks and mortar might be – but she does not blame herself for not having yielded. She merely regrets her sensitive obstinacy as a misfortune for both of them.

'Impelled by a physical curiosity, she lifted the sheet and scrutinized John's breast, so pallid against the dark red of his neck, and bent down to catch the last tired efforts of the heart within. And the idea of her extra-ordinary intimacy with this man, of the incessant familiarity of more than twenty years, struck her and overwhelmed her. . . . It was a trifle that they had not loved. They had lived. Ah! She knew him so profoundly that words could not describe her knowledge. He kept his own secrets, hundreds of them; and he had, in a way, astounded and shocked her by his suicide. Yet, in another way, this miserable termination did not at all surprise her; and his secrets were petty, factual things of no essential import, which left her mystic omniscience of him unimpaired.'[20]

Marcel Schwob said to Bennett that in Leonora he had 'got hold of the greatest of all themes, the agony of the older generation in watching the rise of the younger'.[21] Schwob was speaking personally: he had only two years to live, and ill health was making him incapable of work. But the theme is there, although it is not so central as Schwob suggests; and it was to recur again in Bennett's work, more and more powerfully. The mixture of coldness and illumination which holds Leonora at her husband's deathbed, as she thinks of the past, is a foreshadowing of the classic scene where Sophia, in *The Old Wives' Tale*, gazes at the aged corpse of Gerald Scales.

Bennett's next full-length book was in a completely different vein. He began it on 7 December 1903, having been working throughout the autumn on a daunting number of short stories and articles, as well as an idea for a play with Eden Phillpotts. He describes *A Great Man* as 'a humourous novel', and when published it was subtitled '*A Frolic*'. When it was published he was eager to urge Chatto and Windus to advertise it as 'humourous', and quite rightly, for it is a very funny book. It combines, in a very happy, confident fashion, the elements of his earlier works: there is the romance and gloss of high life from the serials – grand restaurants, scenes at Monte Carlo, scenes in the theatre in Paris – but there is also the lower middle-class, solid, Wesleyan background of the hero, who is transported to a new world of fame and fashion. The hero, Henry Shakspere Knight, is in many ways a parody of Bennett himself: he is (like so many Bennett characters) the son of a draper, though a London draper this time, and he starts life as a short-hand clerk – for 'shorthand, at that date, was a key to open all doors, a cure for every ill, and the finest thing in the world'.[22] A bout of measles obliges Henry to take a little time off work, and during this rest he discovers a talent for writing: he writes a story called *Love in Babylon*, which he has at first great difficulty in marketing. However, finally, through the intervention of an agent and his lovely secretary Geraldine, he gets his book published, and it is an instant success. The novel charts Henry's meteoric ascent, marred only by spasms of dyspepsia, the final accolade being success in the theatre, and the birth to Geraldine, now his wife, of twins, who have a nurse and a perambulator each, but who, 'when they are good, are permitted to crowd themselves into one perambulator, as a special treat'.[23]

The book, rather like *The Truth about an Author*, is a satirical yet affectionate description of the professional literary world, and the types that compose it. The charm of the hero is that, unlike Bennett, he is a complete innocent, not financially (for he is shrewd, quite the card in his dealings) but artistically, and has no notion that his clearly dreadful novels are not the height of literary talent. When, occasionally, a faint whisper reaches him, that Stendahl (unlike himself, he wonders?) is a *really* great writer, he is puzzled and uneasy, but not quite sure what is meant. His mixture of sharpness and gullibility is fanciful but convincing and entertaining; he is a successful fool, rather in the Wodehouse style. Much of the material is very clearly drawn from Bennett's own experiences: the encounters with agents and theatrical directors, the attraction of the chic of being 'at home in two capitals', the lionization, the double attitude from the establishment of patronage and envy – all these are things he had been through himself. There is a charming little sketch of Henry meeting a *divette* called Cosette, at the theatre, where he takes a great interest in her un-English lipstick and the curious way she wears a hat with an evening dress. He has lunch with her the next day, in the informality of her tiny apartment – she is in a crimson peignoir when he arrives, asks him what he wants for lunch, changes, goes out, buys it, returns, cooks it deliciously, all in 'about three minutes', explaining the while, when Henry points out that she is about to go out without her hat, that she is no duchess: 'Never can I do the shops in a hat, I should blush.'[24] This is an echo of similar real-life scenes with the Chichi of his journal: Chichi too cannot shop in a hat.

There are scenes towards the end, in Monte Carlo, where Henry learns to gamble, and breaks the bank. Bennett himself, whilst in the middle of writing the novel, on 14 January 1904, travelled to the south of France with Phillpotts, to visit Monte Carlo and stay at Menton. He and Phillpotts were writing a play together, but Bennett was also working hard at the novel, writing sometimes several thousand words a day, and it is clear that the Monte Carlo scenes must have come to him, whole, while he was there. He was, as one would expect, thrilled by the whole excursion: by the train de luxe, by the Italianate scenery, by the yachts in the bay, but above all by the Casino. One sees, in the journal, exactly the moments of temptation to gamble that

Henry goes through in *A Great Man*: the initial, sound, common-sense suspicion, the desire just to have a little flutter, the pretence that it is the human interest only that is absorbing: 'There is no doubt that the human spectacle of the gaming saloons is tremendous: unequalled; the interest of it could not easily fail for an observer. To a stranger, of course, one of the most curious things is the sight of large sums of money in notes and gold constantly being flung about the tables. . . .'[25] Then, tempted like Henry, he begins to dwell on systems, and finally begins to play: like Henry, he wins at first – 'I began on my system at once, and made 45 francs in three quarters of an hour . . .'[26] and like Henry, after beginner's luck, he loses. The entry for 31 January is very touching:

'Sunday, January 31
'Having nothing to do yesterday afternoon, and Eden being at work, and two others being out, and the day being wet, I could not resist going over to Monte Carlo in the tram. I lost money at the tables, and came home depressed. . . .

'Today, bad weather again. I wrote an excellent T.P. article on Monte Carlo.

'But at present my interest in this journal is not what it was. Monte Carlo and other things have disturbed it.'

However disturbed he was, he made good use of the whole experience in the novel. When he returned to Paris in the middle of February he got back to work, finishing it a month later, at 11.30 in the morning on 13 March. He had written, on some days, as much as 3,400 words a day. And, with yet more proof of the extraordinary expedition of publishing in those days, he had received a hundred pages of proofs by 24 March, and was expecting the rest in the next couple of days. It was published by Chatto and Windus on 19 May, just over five months after he had begun to write it.

In some ways, its reception was disappointing. It had the qualities of a real best-seller, yet it was not taken up and published by American publishers until 1910, despite rumours of pirated editions. Both Marriott, to whom he dedicated it, and Wells said it was his best book: Phillpotts was 'enchanted with it'. It was well reviewed; and yet somehow it never took off. Perhaps the publishers were to blame, for poor promotion; and Bennett, being abroad, could not look after his own interests.

His interests were, however, at this stage, being well cared for by his agent Pinker. One of the characters in *A Great Man* is Mark Snyder, literary agent, who inhabits an office so plush and glorious that Henry, accustomed to the gloomy austerity of Lincolns Inn Fields, is quite astounded. Staring at the Chippendale chairs, the Turkey carpet, the chandeliers, he asks himself 'Is this a business office? Or is it a club?' Whether or not Bennett found Pinker similarly opulent he did not record, but the relations between the two were growing increasingly close. In December 1903 Bennett had returned to Burslem for Christmas; on the way he called on Pinker, twice, on 22 December and, 'after some hesitation on his part, he arranged that he should pay me £50 a month certain during 1904'.[27] This was an unusual arrangement for the time; and indeed, would still be so. There are occasions when agents or publishers are prepared to back an author to the extent of guaranteeing him an income against profits, but such agreements are unusual. However, Pinker was an unusual and enterprising agent, and it was to this that he owed his success. He had established himself as an agent in January 1896, after working for *Black and White* and editing, briefly, Pearson's magazine; he quickly gained a national and an international reputation. It was Wells, one of his first clients, who recommended him to Bennett; he also handled the affairs of the well-established Henry James. His care of Conrad, who was a difficult and temperamental producer of words, was characteristic: he constantly loaned him money, nursed his talent and encouraged him; and the two became very close friends, despite the fact that at times Conrad owed him thousands of pounds. Bennett was a more reliable author than Conrad – both more versatile and more business-like. It might seem strange that Bennett was asking him for loans of what were in fact fairly small sums, when Bennett was already earning so well: his income for 1900 had been £620, so £50 a month for 1904 did not involve much of a risk. But Bennett needed the money; he had heavy family commitments.[28] The request may reflect, as well, Bennett's continuing sense of insecurity; he still had a long way to go before he was earning the £50 a day that he got towards the end of his career. And it also certainly reflects the irregularity with which even assured income comes to writers, a fact of life with which all writers are too well acquainted. One can have a best-selling book on every bookstall and still not have a penny in the bank, because the book has taken months if not years to produce, and the income of it does not begin to arrive until long after publication, owing to the curious system of half-yearly royalty statements, always several months out of date, so beloved by publishers, then as now.

In backing Bennett, in any case, Pinker was backing a winner, as both of them knew. Both behaved in a business-like fashion. When the debt was high, as for times it was, Pinker charged Bennett 5 per cent interest. And

Bennett, for his part, played fair: when he sold, himself, a French translation of *Anna of the Five Towns* to a French paper, a transaction he might well have concealed, he writes to Pinker, 'The price is *nothing*, but I will account for it to you in due course.'[29] Bennett, in fact, used to write to Pinker constantly, about every small negotiation, keeping him well informed of all his plans and progress, issuing instructions and asking for advice. His letters, collected together in Volume I of James Hepburn's edition, are only a small proportion of the number he actually wrote. How he found time to write them is a puzzle. But then, living in Paris as he did at this point, there was no temptation to use the telephone; and in any case, Bennett disliked the telephone, very sensibly, because of his stammer.

Despite their close business relationship, Pinker and Bennett never became intimate friends, and one receives a very vague picture of Pinker as a man from their correspondence. Conrad, whose affairs were more vexed, felt more warmth for him, and describes him as the 'Pinker of agents', and he seems to have been on closer terms with Wells, who was a neighbour of his at one time in the leafy suburb of Worcester Park. It's surprising that he and Bennett never became more intimate, as he, like Bennett, was a self-made man, the son of poor parents. He started life as a clerk at Tilbury Docks, and made his way up through journalism, assistant-editing, and working as a reader for a publishing house – they must have had many experiences in common, and Bennett tended to prefer friends from his own kind of background. Photographs show Pinker looking fairly Bennett-like: dapper, bow-tied, pleased with himself. Swinnerton, another client, describes him as being 'short, compact, a rosy, round-faced clean-shaven grey-haired sphinx with a protrusive under-lip, who drove a four-in-hand, spoke distinctly in a hoarse voice that was almost a whisper, shook hands shoulder-high, laughed without moving. . . .'[30] Whatever the reasons, he and Bennett maintained a fairly formal but mutually profitable relationship: Pinker was reliable, energetic, deeply respected if not feared by publishers, and imaginative about the role of agent, and it was these qualities that Bennett admired. One must add that Bennett himself was always equally business-like in return.

After *A Great Man*, Bennett did not waste much time in getting back to work. Some of his journalism had packed up: *T.P.'s Weekly*, for which he had been writing regularly, decided to dispense with his services in order to economize, a decision which would cost him £165 a year. So, as he notes in his journal, he would have to make it up by fiction.[31] (He started a new series for them, the Savoir Vivre Papers, on 1 December 1905 – T.P. found that dispensing with Bennett was a false economy.) For the time being he was without regular journalism: and on 20 April, little more than a month after finishing *A Great Man*, he began 'with great fervour' a new serial: *Hugo, A Fantasia on Modern Themes*. Unlike the *Grand Babylon Hotel*, which it resembles in tone, *Hugo* hasn't survived, and hasn't been reprinted since 1906, but nevertheless it is quite an amusing work. Hugo is the proprietor of an enormous department store of magnificent luxury and unparalleled efficiency: the kind of place, Bennett says, where one can wander idly all day amidst onyx pillars on thick carpets, and end up buying a threepenny packet of pen nibs, which are immediately delivered to one's home in a two-horse carriage. Hugo's supplies funerals, dinners, handcuffs, hats, elephants, chloroform – in fact any ingredient of the detective mystery is there on the spot, and the plot hinges on the amazing modern security of Hugo's safes, the impregnability of which are almost responsible for Hugo's death. Other ingredients are the middle-aged bachelor (Hugo himself); half-brothers, as in *A Great Man* (Hugo and the villain, Ravengar); the mysterious beautiful milliner who dies prophetically of typhoid in Paris, and then reappears alive later in the plot; references to Bruges, Paris and Mustapha Supérieure, the healthiest suburb in Algiers, reflecting Bennett's growing familiarity with foreign parts; and ghostly scenes in Brompton Cemetery. The story is indeed fantastic and absurd, but quite entertaining, and there are, as usual even in Bennett's lightest work, moments of carefully researched realism, such as the description of the taking of the plaster mask of the heroine's face, and the way she had to breathe through two straws while it was being made. But what really fascinates Bennett in the book is the store itself, and all its modern and extravagant ingenuities. It is a super-Harrods, supplying all whims, foreshadowing his later enthusiasms in, for instance, *Imperial Palace* and showing also his kinship to Zola, whose novel *Au bonheur des Dames* he much admired for obvious reasons. In fact Hugo is a mixture of Zola and Gaboriau; he was reading Gaboriau's detective fiction enthusiastically at this time, and makes several polite acknowledgements to him in the text itself, as well as in his journal.

It's easy to laugh at Bennett's enthusiasm for the modern and the grand, and to speculate about which parts of modern living he would have now found most amusing; how he would have approved of Dial-a-Meal and of Dial-a-Poem. Technology fascinated him; computers and telex machines would have been a delight. But there is something very infectious and very sound in his admiration. He came from a world where badly paid skivvies spent entire lifetimes on their hands and knees scrubbing floors and steps, and living in cold damp basements. Why not hail the vacuum cleaner, central heating, washing machines? They have liberated a whole social class. Who would not rather work on a conveyor belt packing biscuits than scrubbing, with one Sunday a month off, and no followers allowed? It is only those who can remember what it was like who can afford to welcome change. J.B. Priestley, not long ago in the pages of the *New Statesman,* had the courage to say that the television was a great blessing, and would have cheered the last days of his father's life. Bennett, one feels sure, would have welcomed television, as he welcomed the possibilities of anything new. His excitement in Hugo's emporium doesn't negate the intensity of his memories of his grandfather's draper's shop; but both he and Wells had seen too much of poverty and subservience to believe in the golden age of the little shop. It would be interesting to hear what Bennett and Wells would say about the supermarket. Priestley, it is true, I have heard expound the virtues of domestic service as compared with the slavery of a dull factory or office job; but then Priestley as an employer must rate very much higher than the average, as he must surely realize; and must also realize why it was that domestic service got such a bad name. (In many ways it still deserves it.) How much pleasanter, thought Arnold Bennett, to be a shorthand typist, or a girl in a millinery department, than a slave in a cellar. And he was right.

He does, however, one must admit, at this stage begin to utter some curious views about the female sex, which would be highly suspect these days. At one point, one of the characters says of Camilla, the heroine, 'She's so sensible, Camilla is. She's like a man in some things; all really great women are.'[32] The choice of name, too, is revealing. Bennett liked to call his women characters names like Carlotta and Camilla and Leonora; he liked them to be strange, to be different. Despite his solid creation of characters like Anna Tellwright, or even of Leonora, who is certainly real enough, there is, and particularly in his lighter fiction, an implication that women are utterly mysterious, unreasonable, strange creatures, interesting largely because they are so remote and unfamiliar. Perhaps it was this attitude of distance, so at odds with his understanding of women in his great novels, that led to some of the disastrous and unfortunate sexual misunderstandings that were shortly to preoccupy him, and to alter his whole life.

Bennett wrote *Hugo* in three months. He was not as light-hearted during the composition of it as might be supposed; there are one or two references in his journal to living too far from his friends, to being left 'stranded' one evening by Lewis Hind (his solution was to rush straight into the opera), to agreeing with a Mrs X that his life was miserable.[33] On Saturday, 14 May, he 'contemplated his future'.[34] On Friday, 27 May, there is a most interesting entry which reads:

'Today I am 37. I have lived longer than I shall live. My new series begins to appear today in the Windsor. My name is not on the cover. Anthony Hope's stands there alone. And I am 37. Comment is needless.

'I have now warned both Mater and Tertia that I shall get married before I am 40.'[35]

He was to fail of this intention by thirty-eight days only. He married, on 4 July 1907, at the age of forty. But, as will be seen, his determination to live according to plan did not work out as happily on this front as it did on others.

The truth is that one cannot help receiving, from Bennett himself, the impression that this period of his life was rather empty and emotionally unsatisfying. In Paris he was not in the thick of things, as he liked to be. He mixed mostly with Americans and other expatriates, and his French friends were not serious creative writers like himself, but scholars and critics like Davray. He spent a great many evenings at the opera or theatre or music hall, filling in time. He ate alone in restaurants. This may have been good for work, but it was not cheering to the spirits. His letters home – to the Wells, to the Phillpotts – express a more than polite desire to be visited. The Paris he had found was interesting enough, diverse enough, but it certainly lacked the glamour and intimacy and brilliance of the circle of the Goncourts, which must have been one of the models in his mind. One has only to think of Proust's circle to realize how very peripheral was Bennett's contact with literary life. This was the very period when Proust was gathering material for *A La Recherche*, busily observing Montesquieu, Madame de Noailles, the Bibescos, de Régnier, the Daudets; playing tennis as Bennett did, sitting on yachts as Bennett did, but in how different, how utterly removed, how eclectic and élitist a world. Proust and Bennett went to the same exhibitions, they listened to the same music by Saint-Saens, they went to the same theatres; but Proust was on the inside, in his total obscurity, while Bennett, a moderately successful writer with several books behind him, was on the outside. Not that Bennett would have liked the Guermantes way: one of the popular misconceptions of him, now, is that he was a snob, which he certainly was not. He would have much preferred the literary dinners and gossip of the Goncourts, with their bohemian egalitarian gaiety and (as he would have put it) their *sans-gêne*. But he hadn't yet really found it; except, perhaps, at the Schwobs'.

He expresses his mixed feelings about life in Paris, allusively, in a letter to George Sturt, dated 22 June 1904. Sturt had written to congratulate him on *A Great Man*, after a long lapse of correspondence, and had clearly said something in his letter about his own low productivity, which did not prevent him from being 'pretty happy'. Bennett writes back that although he knows he is doing well, he is no happier than he ever was. He says: 'I do nothing but fiction now, and have arrived at the stage where I can make £20 a week at it, minimum. Five years ago I would have looked on this as the *ne plus ultra* of paradisical bliss, but I am no more content than ever I was.... My belief is that some people are born happy and some aren't. I enjoy Paris tremendously. Indeed, I can't imagine myself living in any other city. It has spoilt me for London....' And then, after a few compliments to Sturt on Sturt's own work or lack of it, he says: 'A man who *can* write, and who at 41 has the effrontery to say that he is "pretty happy", cannot fairly ask for anything more. I am in a position to state that constant honest artistic production does not produce in the producer any particularly ecstatic sort of bliss. At best it is an anodyne.'[36] One can read, in these confidences, and in their arrangement in the letter, a distinct note of gloom.

It was this summer that he made another attempt to cure his stammer, Whether it had been getting worse, as cause or effect of gloom, we do not know. Certainly it was no help in the search to find a wife before forty. Plenty of girls were introduced to him; his hostess friends, like Mrs Devereux and her sister, seem to have made efforts to set him up. A stammer is no help in society. On 27 June he went to visit a M. Berquand, who claimed to have cured his own stammer, and to have orders from 'most European sovereigns'; he arranged to visit him for treatment in Aberdeen in August. Bennett says: 'He asked me a lot of questions, and said he was quite certain of success in a month or five weeks. In spite of the interview with him I felt rather depressed than otherwise.'[37] His depression was well judged. He went to Scotland in August (visiting the Wells on the way, and hearing the tragic story of Gissing's recent death), and stayed there for several weeks, returning to Paris on 23 September. The treatment was not a success. The following January, looking back over the triumphs and failures of the preceding year, as was his habit, he notes as one of his 'grave disappointments', 'the result of my visit to Scotland'.[38] (Another disappointment that he notes, incidentally, is the commercial failure of *A Great Man*.) The stammer was not to be cured; he had to learn to live with it.

When he returned to Paris from his visit to Scotland, he was delighted to find he had been missed, and that his return was greeted with 'the warmest cordiality'. He was settling in, after all, and to prove it he had his flat re-decorated and brought more of his books and pictures over with him from England. And, repeating exactly the pattern of his victory over London, as soon as he decided he felt at home, he acquired a little retreat in the country, this time in the form of lodgings at Les Sablons, a little village near Fontainebleau. He stayed there with an old couple, the Leberts, who looked after him, and who were to regale him over the next year or two with stories about life under the Commune, thereby making their mark permanently in *The Old Wives' Tale*. His life continued much as before: reading and writing at Les Sablons, social visits to the Schwobs, the Devereux and the Ullmans in Paris. He had a new French friend: Émile Martin, who introduced him to club life in Paris. Schwob (by this time) was a very ill man, though well enough to accompany Bennett one evening to the music hall in his wife's De Dion carriage – she was away on tour at the time. He was also well enough to crack jokes: when Mrs Devereux told the story of a man who had tried to cut his mistress's throat and had succeeded in severing only the skin, Schwob delighted himself by saying, at once, 'A close shave!'[39] He was doubtless pleased by the rare opportunity for making a pun in a foreign language. But on 26 February he died. Moréno, again, was away on tour at the time of his death. Bennett records that he dined with him a week before his death and found him 'vivacious enough';[40] also that Davray wept on hearing the news. As recently as 11 February, Bennett and he had been discussing antiquarian book-dealing, a conversation that was to be used many years later in *Riceyman Steps*. Bennett demonstrated his loyalty to his dead friend in immediate practical terms, by writing directly he heard of his death to Edmund Gosse, asking him to write a notice for the *Athenaeum*. Gosse, who had known Schwob for years, was happy to oblige, and the notice appeared on 4 March. He writes: 'He has been described as perhaps the most learned man of his generation. The learned man is often very dull outside his study, but Schwob was brilliant, whether as a conteur, as a critic, as a dramatist, and in more than one other direction of literary activity . . . he had a morbid horror of "popularity", and it was for this reason that he ceased some time ago to write for the daily papers . . . he had few intimate friends, whom he received once a week at his house far from the noise and strife of Paris life . . . his untimely and unexpected death is a serious loss to French literature.'[41] It was also a loss to his friends. Bennett had felt accepted and at home in the informality of the gatherings at Schwob's bedside; he liked the meals pre-sided over by the Chinese manservant Ting, the intellectual and theatrical conversations. Schwob was an exceptionally kind and unselfish man –

Colette records that when she was ill he would go and read to her for hours – and he must surely have taken up with Bennett partly through kindness. He saw that Bennett was lonely, awkward and shy, so he took him into his circle and looked after him. Not many Frenchmen would have done the same for a not immediately attractive foreigner, and one hopes that he saw enough rewards in his protégé's progress. He certainly liked *Leonora* and *Anna*; but what would he have made of Bennett's next novel? And what indeed has anyone ever made of it?

It was to be called, finally, *Sacred and Profane Love*, and he had begun it in November 1904. He describes it to Sturt as 'a bawdy novel',[42] but then one must remember the standards of the day, which had obliged Bennett to insert a housekeeper into a scene in *Hugo* because T.P. had objected that it was indecent for a fiancé and a heroine to meet alone in a flat, even in a completely frivolous fantasy and with no villainous intentions on either part. He planned it even before he wrote *Hugo*, which is why there is a certain overlap of names; originally the heroine was to be called Camilla, but Camilla got into *Hugo* first, and therefore Camilla became Carlotta – another splendid romantic name. Bennett refers to the novel under the title of 'Carlotta' during a great part of its composition; the final title seems to have crept in round about June, and he finished the novel in July. He calls it a serious novel, but it reveals his weaknesses more clearly, perhaps, than any of his serious work had done so far: it strays far too frequently into the absurd, the lavish, the unreal. Its plot is, indeed, quite daring, if not exactly bawdy: the heroine, Carlotta Peel, is a sheltered young girl from the Five Towns who has an affair with a pianist, another affair with a married man, writes novels, gets herself involved with drunkards and prostitutes, and dies in Paris somewhat bathetically of appendicitis brought on by swallowing strawberry pips. The Five Towns background, and the pressures from which she was escaping, are unfortunately very briefly sketched in, though there is a good description of the way in which she sees the light through reading Herbert Spencer in a secret binding. Bennett is trying to depict in her the kind of forceful, physical, impetuous woman who did not exist in English fiction: significantly, another book admired by Carlotta is *Mlle de Maupin*, and she finds liberation by travelling rather closely, in Bennett's wake, on trains de luxe, first from Stoke to London, then from London to Torquay, from Torquay to Menton, from Menton to Monte Carlo, and from Monte Carlo back again to Paris. It is a brave attempt, particularly as Bennett writes in the first person, but it cannot be called a success. The alacrity with which Carlotta leaps into bed with the pianist Diaz, in the Five Towns Hotel, after her first meeting, mesmerized by absinthe and Chopin, is admirable but implausible. But even here Bennett is such a good writer that he cannot wholly miss the mark – there is a touching scene the morning after, when Carlotta creeps out of the hotel and buys a straw hat from the maid, because she dare not be seen, though disgraced, without her hat.

Carlotta is at times almost a fine comic creation. It is hard to tell what Bennett himself thinks of her – are we meant to take her passions seriously? The novel is full of bathos, as in this scene between the heroine and her newly declared lover, who is also her publisher (can Bennett have been thinking, even remotely, of George Eliot and the Chapmans?); there are pages of passion and sorrow and remorse about the poor wife, then Carlotta suggests they go abroad. Her lover, Ispenlove, demurs.

> ' "My dear," I said submissively, "I shall leave everything to you. The idea of travelling occurred to me, that was all. I have never travelled further than Cannes. Still, we have all our lives before us."
>
> ' "We will travel," he said unselfishly. "We'll go round the world – slowly. I'll get the tickets at Cook's tomorrow." '[43]

Bennett clearly admires his heroine's enterprise, and her lack of false modesty and scruples, but he fails to embody them, as he was to fail in his original conception of Sophia. Some of the bathos must be intended. The last page of the book, after Carlotta foresees her own death from the strawberry pips, is taken up with an obituary from *Le Temps*, in which her name is misspelt. The idea for this, according to Bennett himself in his 1910 preface to the American edition, came from the 'terribly brief account' in the *Journal des Débats* of the death of Sybil Sanderson, the once famous opera singer for whom Massenet had composed *Thaïs*. Sybil Sanderson had other similarities with Carlotta, for just as Carlotta turns her career to help the alcoholic Diaz, so the opera singer had left the opera at the height of her fame to marry a Cuban planter. The obituary is cursory and dismissive: Carlotta is put firmly in her place by time. But Bennett himself doesn't manage to place her. It's not that he doesn't know the world he describes. The book is full of portraits of people he knew well. Moréno appears, as an actress called Morenita. The theatrical chat is hit off well. Some of Diaz is drawn from Viñes, his pianist friend. And he knew enough lady novelists, some of them, like Violet Hunt, disreputable and adventurous enough in their own right. But he doesn't manage to make her real. He was handicapped by writing in the first person. Carlotta's style, as he points out in a letter to Wells, was not his own, and it 'cost me a Hades of a lot of trouble'.[44] Although he seems to have been tolerably pleased with the book while he was writing it, he lost faith in it quite quickly, and had moments of doubt even before he finished it. In 1908 we find him writing to Edward Garnett describing it as nothing more than a *tour-de-force*: in 1910 he reread it himself and found it 'very young'.[45]

It is hard to imagine quite why he wrote it. He never aspired to be a shocking writer. On the contrary, he prided himself on being able to do without the effects of shock. And why write about passionate love, when, as he admitted to Wells, he had never experienced love himself? ('I have never been in love. Sometimes the tears start to my eyes, but they never fall.'[46]) Was it a desire for technical virtuosity, the desire that makes a woman writer suddenly write in the first person as a man? Such experiments can be genuinely mind-expanding, and maybe Bennett got more from the release of writing sloppily and passionately, as Carlotta, than the critical reader could receive. Perhaps, also, he had begun to despair of feeling love, and felt he ought to try to imagine it before it was too late.

Sacred and Profane Love was published by Chatto and Windus in September 1905. It was also serialized (one of his few serious novels to be serialized before publication). Bennett by this time was far from satisfied with his publishers. (Nor were they entirely satisfied with him: according to Frank Swinnerton, old Mr Chatto couldn't take the book seriously and didn't like it.[47]) Bennett's letters to Pinker are full of criticisms of the way they were advertising and handling his work, and he writes on 5 April 1905: 'What I want is to be published by Methuen. How soon can I get there? Chatto's list gives me appendicitis. I wish we could have *Hugo* published by Methuen.'[48] Appendicitis was clearly much on his mind at the time. He was to go to Methuen's, but not for a few books yet. In fact, the next book he wrote was not for Chatto's either, but for a small publisher called Alfred Nutt, who suggested to Bennett that he should write for him a specific novel on a specific theme – the theme of divorce. Nutt had had a considerable success with a French novel on the same subject by Paul Bourget which was published in 1904, and was called, simply, *Divorce*. It paints a horrific picture of a woman torn between her religion and her second husband, and ends up, firmly, on the side of the Catholic Church. The woman, Gabrielle, is described as 'a mere incident of a civil religious war', and it is the divorce laws themselves that are blamed for her ensuing sorrows. If she hadn't been allowed to divorce her appalling husband, Bourget implies, she would have been better off. The crux of the plot is, as in Bennett's novel, a legal technicality: because of her divorce, Gabrielle cannot forbid her own son's indiscreet marriage. She ends up in despair, 'cursing once more that impious law, to whose seductions her feminine weakness had succumbed. Destructive of family life, subversive of religion, the source of anarchy and revolution, this law had promised her freedom and happiness, and all she had found, like so many of her sisters was captivity and wretchedness.'[49]

Nutt evidently wished to follow up the success he had had with this dramatic work. Perhaps he also wished to offer a more reasoned, British, Nonconformist view of the matter. He had picked his man well: Bennett was attracted by the documentary and legal aspects of the commission, and after some haggling about terms he settled happily for an advance of £125 and a 20 per cent royalty. The subject was a very suitable one for Bennett's talents, and he brought to it everything that *Sacred and Profane Love* lacked – sobriety, local colour, domestic scenes, realism, the petty sorrows of ordinary and not particularly sympathetic characters drawn in a sympathetic light of understanding. Nutt's letters to Bennett have been lost, so we don't know how much detail he himself suggested. The plot is about a well-to-do Five Towns lawyer and his employee, both of whom quite plausibly get themselves sued for divorce. The embarrassments and the humiliations of the divorce system are brought out with skill and indignation; the daughter of the solicitor, who had witnessed her father's affair with the governess, breaks down under the ordeal of appearing in the witness box, and the solicitor's clerk loses his case on a technicality about his place of domicile. It is a well-written, interesting, moving piece of propaganda for a more humane law. But it is more than that: Nutt got more than his money's worth. It is also a fine description of life in the Five Towns, a fine provincial piece, with shades and details that are not to be found in *Anna* and *Leonora*: a reminder to Bennett of where his true talent lay, a pointer-forward to the achievements of *The Old Wives' Tale* and *Clayhanger*, now not so far ahead. He was himself pleased with the work, and rightly. Lawrence Ridware, the clerk, with his sexy dissatisfied wife, his artistic brother, his bicycle, his enthusiasm for old books, his admiration for his boss's daughter, his grey life, is admirably done; so too is the gay dog of a solicitor, and his understanding wife, who are forced into an intolerable position by their difficult, pure young daughter, who can't and won't pretend that she didn't see what she did see. There are many moments worthy of the greater novels, and none of the uneasy romanticism which mars even *Leonora*, and ruins *Sacred and Profane Love*. The theme did not lend itself to romance. But the circumstances in which he wrote it were another matter.

127

7
Marguerite

He began *Whom God hath Joined* on 9 November 1905, and finished it in July 1906. During this period he was to go through the first great emotional upheaval of his life. He was already in his late thirties, and perhaps not well equipped to deal with such disturbances. As we know, he was at this time looking for a wife. How earnestly he searched we cannot tell, but he certainly had his eyes open; he had resolved to marry before the age of forty and there wasn't much time left. Certain names recur hopefully in his journal, as the name of George Paston had featured in earlier days – principally, perhaps, that of the American painter Miss Thomasson, who dined with him frequently, invited him to little parties in her studio, introduced him to interesting people like 'Hubert Bland and his Liberty-clad daughter Rosamund'.[1] (Bland was a Fabian friend of Wells, the husband of Edith Nesbit, and a well-known philanderer.) Miss Thomasson always seemed to encourage his mind to dwell on 'the relations between the sexes'; she was an independent girl, who lived a life of her own, and did and discussed what she chose. They saw a good deal of each other in the spring and summer of 1905, but then she disappears from the scene, to reappear a decade later, with her studio and her mayonnaise-making, in *The Lion's Share*. She was not replaced until the following year, when Bennett took up with another American girl, Eleanor Green. The story of his relationship with her is complex, miserable and uncertain; the damage she did him, however unwittingly, was immense.

Various people have tried to account for the misunderstandings of this affair, but none of the reporters seem wholly convinced by their descriptions. The facts, as far as can be told, are as follows. Bennett met the Greens through his friendship with other American families living in Paris – particularly through the Farleys, Willie and Agnes Farley. They were typical of the kind of family which Bennett had got to know: like Mrs Devereux and her sister Mrs Laye, the Farleys were easy-going, outspoken, informal people, interested in the arts, amusing, sociable. Bennett became friendly with the Greens' eldest daughter, Eleanor, a red-haired penniless beauty, with ambitions to become a singer, who had been educated partly in America and partly in Paris. She was about twenty-four at the time. He became engaged to her. Eleanor behaved in a strange manner during their engagement, and finally broke it off at the last moment, when everything was arranged. Bennett had taken a flat for them, the wedding presents had arrived, Bennett had written to all his friends in England, and congratulations were pouring in. The breaking-off was a great shock to him, understandably. Eleanor married an American, Kenneth Joll, shortly afterwards; he was a nephew of Agnes Farley and Eleanor had known him for some time.

How could such a situation have occurred? One can only speculate, from what one knows of the characters of both of them. First of all, evidently, the age-gap was very large. Bennett was many years older than his fiancée, and having once accepted him, she may have felt some alarm and fear at the prospect of breaking off. Communication between the two of them cannot possibly have been intimate; Bennett was courteous, diffident, shy, possibly rather in awe of a young girl whom he took to be innocent, virtuous and ignorant, so he may not have been a very pressing lover. He records in his journal that he took her to the theatre to see a play, which proved to be improper. He says: 'I felt myself shocked. . . . I can't at the moment remember ever having been shocked before. The experience gave me an idea of how pious philistines must often feel, and was therefore useful. My being shocked was absurd.'[2] Was he shocked only because he was seeing the play in the company of a young girl whose innocence alarmed and disturbed him? It is easy to see what attracted him to her: she was young, she was vivacious, she was beautiful. It is less easy to see why she ever responded to him at all.

The most cruel explanation would be that she found him financially eligible. The Greens were a large family, and far from wealthy; a respectable marriage, with the prospects of status, luxury and reliability, had its attractions. She seems to have been at once spoiled and opportunist, and perhaps she did flirt with the idea of a good marriage, and then lose her nerve as the day got closer. It is impossible to suppose that she had any real feeling for him, or she could not have used him so badly. It is more likely that some parental pressure was brought upon her. The Greens, who were struggling to support seven dependent children, would have been glad to get a daughter off their hands, and may have put it to her that she would be silly to refuse such an offer – though it is only fair to say that this is pure speculation backed by no evidence at all. What one cannot believe is that Bennett himself brought any real pressure to bear upon her. One of the accounts, by her sister Anne, suggests that when he proposed to her in the forest of Fontainebleau, he wept, threatened, said he would kill himself if she would not accept – but such a scene from a man like Bennett is most implausible. It is possible that she did not take his proposal seriously, and accepted, or was thought to accept, in a joking spirit, and then found herself trapped in a situation beyond her control. But she must have realized, during the six weeks of their engagement (15 June–3 August) that he was perfectly serious, and was making plans for the future. During this period she did not open his letters, she flirted with other men, and generally behaved in a most unengaged way, to the professed bewilderment of her family, who had to cope with the consequences.

Some of the explanation lies in the Green family itself. They were a strange, temperamental, vain, self-admiring family, as can be seen from Anne Green's book about them, *With Much Love*.[3] The parents had been born in the South, in Savannah and Virginia, and had come to Paris in 1893, after various financial disasters at home. The father, Edward Green, was the manager of a cotton agency, and the mother was a red-haired Southern belle, alternately child-adoring and child-hating, irresponsible, talkative, and evidently immensely self-admiring. She was self-consciously dramatic and crazy, and the family had to admire her caprices. They were talented – the baby of the family, Julian, was to achieve distinction as a writer, and he too, like Bennett, became a good friend of Gide's. But the talent in the parents was somehow dissipated: Mrs Green, although her daughter Anne purports to write with admiration, comes across as a dissatisfied and destructive woman. And she clearly did not look after her children as well as she might have done. They were always having accidents, which seemed to amuse her enormously. Henry James, one feels, might well have portrayed Eleanor as a kind of unprotected Daisy Miller, let loose in Europe amongst the wolves, unsupported by her amoral family, innocently or ignorantly unaware of the dangers of engaging herself to middle-aged men of letters. Certainly, like Daisy, Eleanor wanted to cut a dash, and did not much care how she did it; she enjoyed clothes and admirers and excursions, she had ambitions to be an opera singer, she had not been brought up to think of the proprieties. Perhaps Bennett's style of wooing seemed to her to come from another age, and therefore to mean nothing. She pretended to be older than she was, a conspiracy in which her parents, one feels, must at least have connived. Anne Green's description of the way she conned her mother into writing love letters to Bennett for her when she didn't feel like doing it herself is extremely unattractive, even allowing for sisterly malice; nor is Anne's support of her mother's innocence in the matter particularly convincing. One must indict Mrs Green either of extreme negligence or of complicity. There is a peculiarly unattractive account of Eleanor's behaviour after the disaster: 'Eleanor behaved very badly over the wedding presents. The checks and sundry valuables given her for her engagement to Bennett were relinquished after undignified scenes with Mamma. For her second betrothal she received little and mourned her mother's honesty in sending back the first lot. . . .'[4] It is interesting that although Anne Green condemns her sister's behaviour we are in no way intended to think her anything other than amusingly 'naughty' or daringly 'wicked'. And what can one think of the responsibility of a mother who is obliged to have a scene with her daughter in order to persuade her that wedding presents for a cancelled wedding must be returned? Even allowing for the fact that Anne does not pretend to be a very accurate witness, and reconstitutes whole pages of dialogue that she cannot have heard or remembered, one must conclude that Bennett was in some ways mercifully delivered from the Greens.

He could not have seen it that way at the time, however. There is no doubt that he was deeply attached to the idea of her, if not to the girl herself, and much taken with the idea of marriage. He wrote to his friends – the Phillpotts, George Sturt, the Wells, Violet Hunt, Pinker – and received from them letters of congratulation, which he claimed pleased her as much as they pleased him. In correspondence, he usually refers to her as Eleonora, betraying again his weakness for the romantic name. He does not betray much beyond the conventional in the way of passion: he writes to Phillpotts: 'I may tell you that this courtship has been rather violent. Eleonora is recovering with her mother in the country, and I have been near collapse. One doesn't know what one has been through till afterwards',[5] and to Violet Hunt: 'Since tasting the extremely mixed sensations of love, honestly for the first time in my life, I have re-read all that I had written on the subject. And I am astounded at the sheer insight I had. It has given me quite a new belief in myself (not that that was needed, by the way, as you must always have seen).'[6] But after the event, he seems deeply affected: his letters of cancellation to his friends are terse and pained, as is his abrupt entry in his journal:

'August 3rd
'At 11 a.m. on this day, at Caniel, my engagement to Eleonora was broken off.

'In the meantime I had, with the utmost difficulty, finished my novel: *Whom God hath Joined.*'[7]

He tries a little gallantry when writing to Violet Hunt, but that is as far as he rises. He says to her: 'I may tell you that in spite of everything I wouldn't blot out the last six months even if I could. I knew a devil of a lot about women before. I know more now, and I have never yet bought knowledge too dearly. Besides that, I know more about myself, and can write infinitely better books. And I am a writer first; all the rest comes afterwards.'[8]

The movement of wounded pride, in assuring himself that he cares more about his work than his loss, makes him appear more than usually vulnerable.

What the scene of their parting was like, again, we can only conjecture, but the probabilities are that it was unpleasant and ill-managed. Anne Green describes a scene on a railway station when the two of them are on holiday, though Eleanor has already decided she must tell him she cannot go through with it; she finds him going through her bag and finding compromising letters, and breaks off the engagement in a rage. Eleanor Green herself told Reginald Pound that she 'had clear recollections of the final scene, but thinks it unfair to Arnold Bennett's memory to recall them publicly in detail. It is sufficient to say that his speech difficulty appeared at its worst, that every aspirate deserted him in this extremity, and that he was reduced to uttering comically pathetic threats of social excommunication for Miss Green. "You'll lose the respect of the 'ole world, – and Mr and Mrs Farley too." '[9] The extraordinary vulgarity of this account does as much as anything to illuminate the character of the girl who had been his first love. Certainly the last things that can have distinguished the end of the affair were her tact and consideration.

The truth is that Bennett, all his life, had had a curiously and dangerously ambivalent attitude towards women, an attitude that prevented him from seeing them straight, unless they were fictitious or ineligible. It is not an unusual handicap. It is interesting to note that in his letter to Violet Hunt, he writes the affair down as experience about 'women' – not about a woman in particular, but women as a species. In much of his less serious writing one sees a kind of nervous mockery that is partly bred of fear: the tone of *Journalism for Women*, for instance, betrays a desire to keep women in their place, to make them acknowledge their unprofessional weaknesses. Half of him wanted to see women as delicate, innocent, luxury-loving, foolish creatures; the other half was attracted to women as they really were, tough, adventurous, spirited, independent. The division is partly the division of the age he lived in, an age of transition: the heroines of George Paston are half

Frank Swinnerton

George Sturt

in the direction of St. Luke's Church. The music ^appeared^ ~~seemed~~ to linger
a long time in the distance, and then it approached, growing
louder, and the Bursley Silver Prize Band passed under the
window, at the ^solemn^ ~~funereal~~ pace of ~~the~~ Handel's "Dead March".
The effect of that ^requiem,^ ~~dirge,~~ heavy with its own ^inherent^ beauty and with
the vast weight of ~~tragic~~ harrowing tradition, was to wring the
tears from Constance's eyes; they fell on her aproned bosom,
and she sank into a chair. And though the cheeks of the
trumpeters were puffed out, and though the drummer had
to protrude his stomach and arch his spine, ^backwards^ lest he should ~~fall~~
~~over~~ tumble over his drum, there was majesty in the passage
of the band. The boom of the drum, desolating the ~~pauses in~~
the interruptions of the melody, made sick the heart, but with
a lofty grief; and the dirge seemed ~~to weave~~ ^be weaving^ a purple pall
that covered every meanness.

The bandsmen were not all in black, but they all wore
^on their^ crape ~~been~~ sleeve ~~bands,~~ and their instruments were knotted
with crape. They ~~wore~~ ^carried^ in their hats a black-edged card. Cyril
held one ~~of these cards~~ in his hand. It ran thus:

Sacred to the Memory
of
Daniel Povey
a Town Councillor of this town
judicially murdered at 8 o'clock in the
morning of ~~18~~8th February 1888
"He was more sinned ~~against~~ than sinning."

In the wake of the band came the aged rector, bareheaded,
and wearing ^a^ ~~his~~ surplice over his overcoat; his thin white air
was disarrayed by the ~~chill~~ ^chilly^ breeze that played in the sunshine;
his hands were folded ^on^ ~~over~~ a gilt-edged book ^A curate,^ ^churchwardens^
and sidesmen followed. And after these, ^tramping through the dark mud^ in a procession that
had apparently no end, ~~came~~ the unofficial ^male multitude^ ~~, nearly all in~~
~~black~~ mourning, and all, save the more aristocratic, ^carrying^

A page from Arnold Bennett's manuscript for THE OLD WIVES' TALE.
A complete fascimile of the manuscript was published in 1923.

A page from Bennett's manuscript of *The Old Wives' Tale*

J. B. Pinker

The Baines's shop from *The Old Wives' Tale*

left Bennett in early middle age
below Eden Phillpotts

H. G. Wells

one thing, half the other, and Wells's Ann Veronica, one of the first wholly successful new women, was not to be created for another few years. Bennett's friend Mrs Devereux had published, in 1896 with John Lane, a curious little book called *The Ascent of Woman*, of which the first half deals quite boldly and openly with women's education, the need for easier divorce, the reasons why 'Trade Unionism among women is still a farce'; the second half deals with fashion, tea gowns, corsets, and the reason why Paris fashions are so superior to London fashions. There is hardly any link between the two, or any attempt to forge one. Yet Mrs Devereux, herself an independent woman, wrote novels in which daring lady playwrights wrote daring plays about syphilis, and went to live on their own in Paris and Algiers. So Bennett must have lived in an atmosphere in which the double attitude to women was strangely pronounced. The women whom he knew well, like Mrs Devereux and Marguerite Moréno, were artists and intellectuals; but when he fell in love, he fell in love with a girl whom he took to be innocent, whose hats and gowns he admired, and whom he did not understand at all. And again, disastrously, the very next woman with whom he was to become involved, and whom he in fact married, had qualities that were exactly the reverse of those which he in cold blood and with his more sober judgement admired. One cannot help feeling that the women he met were not quite worthy of the women he created; that he had too firmly and finally rejected the virtues of the women of the Five Towns, of Anna and Leonora and of his own family. It was reasonable enough, perhaps, to look for sex in Paris, but had he strayed too far from home for his judgement to operate?

There are some aspects of the Eleonora affair which will never be cleared up. Her attitudes, his behaviour, are lost for ever. Even her age remains clouded in mystery. Bennett thought she was about twenty-four, which would be a reasonable assumption. Her parents had married in 1880, and as she was the oldest of a prolific family it seems fair to assume that she was born soon after the marriage. However, Reginald Pound states that she was only eighteen at the time, and just out of the schoolroom. As he had the information from her, one might imagine she was exaggerating out of self-defence, or out of characteristic feminine vanity. Certainly, her conduct would appear less reprehensible, if not less mysterious, had she been eighteen rather than twenty-four or twenty-five.

The loss of face which Bennett suffered must have been the worst to endure. The girl he was well rid of, but it is no easy thing to write to friends announcing cancelled engagements. He had introduced her to Tertia and persuaded his family that they would like her; and he had also committed himself in practical terms – 'taken a flat, bought a lot of furniture, given up the old flat',[10] and taken out a new insurance policy. Prudently, he kept the insurance policy. It would have been natural for him to throw himself into work as a solace, but in fact he was not to start another serious novel for some time. Perhaps more wisely, he went to England to stay with the Phillpotts, where he planned a new serial, and worked with Phillpotts on more of their innumerable dramatic and serial projects. They had already collaborated successfully on a novel called *The Sinews of War*, which appeared in *T.P.'s Weekly* as a serial from March 1906 onwards, and in book form in November 1906, and they were planning a new one to be called *The Statue*. He was also kept busy with the publications of various finished works, pointing out to Nutt that he might as well cry for the moon as expect a serious work like *Whom God hath Joined* to get the rapturous reception of a sensational serial, criticizing Chatto for not selling enough of his old work, *The Ghost*, and so on. After leaving the Phillpotts, he went yachting with a couple of friends (one of them Ochs, a newspaper proprietor) and returned to Paris after a a short visit to Brussels. At the end of November, he moved to a new flat in the rue d'Aumale, in Montmartre – it was a street he had always admired, for it was 'austere, silent, distinguished, icy and beautiful'[11] and he was later proud to describe it in one of his novels as a good address, well known to taxi drivers. As he had already relinquished his old flat, he had to move anyway; but he was not at the best of times a man who enjoyed rearranging plans. He was a rigid thinker: if he had arranged to move, he would move.

It would have been quite possible for the shock of the Eleanor affair to ruin his hopes of marriage for ever; he might well have retired into bachelor-hood, like his friend Émile Martin, who, however, prophesied that 'there was a good chance of my being married within a couple of years. Why? I asked. *Vous deviendrez trop riche*,' he said. '*Vous serez visé, et sans vous en apercevoir*, measures will be taken to catch you . . .'[12] And it's noticeable that at this period his journal becomes much freer in its references to sexual matters. Before this, he had indeed kept two journals, one as it were for publication, and one containing 'matters relating to the sexes' – another example of the division he suffered on the subject of women. But in September 1906, after his engagement fiasco, instead of deciding to blot out the thought of women for ever more, he decided very wisely to let them have a better place. He writes: 'I got tired of doing my journal in the old journal, and this is the result. Practically I have kept no journal for quite three months. But up to
· that time, for a year or so past, I had kept two journals – one for general matters, and the other for matters specially relating to the sexes. I did this,

at first, because there were things in the second that were not fit for every eye. Then I gradually perceived the absurdity of any such timid scruples in the composition of a private journal. . . .'[13] And after this point, his journal does change slightly in character – not a very marked change, but a change. He mentions more freely his friends' anecdotes about brothels and sexual irregularities and eccentricities. But there are still no confessions of his own, nor many signs that he is being 'visé', although he records, in his usual end-of-the-year stock-taking, that for the first time, in 1906, he had made 'over £1,000 clear'.[14] His constant female companions were still married women, like Roy Devereux, Violet Hunt and Mrs Farley, who flirted with him safely, dined with him, told him stories and left him alone. Perhaps Mrs Farley had lost her nerve as a matchmaker; in her novel *Ashdod*, which was published by Chapman and Hall in 1907, there is a disastrous relationship between a young girl and an older man, at the end of which one of the characters says: 'What do you think a girl of 23 can be to a man of 45? a nervous, fussy man, at that?'[15] Bennett was not yet forty-five, but he might well have been described as a nervous fussy man. He was not, however, to remain unclaimed for long.

His wife-to-be, Marguerite Soulié (or Solié, as she sometimes spelt it) was introduced to him by his friend Calvocoressi, who had heard that Bennett was looking for secretarial help. The first mention of her appears in the journal for 16 January 1907, when she visited him in his flat in the rue de Calais. This first meeting is described by her in her *Memoirs*, but as she was an unreliable witness, much given to rethinking and rewriting her own memories, one cannot tell how accurate the account is: she says that she found him attractive, rather like Edward the Seventh, she was impressed by his furnishings and his manner, and had reservations only about his voice. In three days she was telling him about her career and aspirations; within a week, they were dining together in the Place Blanche where, he says, 'We recounted to each other our chagrins. Hers appeared to be much worse than mine.'[16]

She had indeed had a hard life. She was thirty-three when she met Bennett, and an experienced woman. She was on her own, and had been for some time. Her family came from the south-west of France, from Négrepelisse, a small town just north of Montauban in Tarn-et-Garonne. Her father was a baker and an alcoholic. Marguerite was a spirited child, determined not to spend the rest of her life in a village; thanks to her grandmother she received an education in Toulouse, then became apprenticed in a dressmaking firm. She was an expert dressmaker throughout her life. Her first job, however, was not in couture, but as a companion to a lady in Paris, whom she left because she ran into trouble with her employer's husband, like the French governess Renée in *Whom God hath Joined*. Thereafter she drifted in and out of jobs, she visited England as a governess, she worked as model and *vendeuse* in dress shops, and at one point set up business in a dress shop with her young aunt, Hélène Bion, a venture which failed. But her real ambitions were theatrical: she wanted to be an actress, and one of her first discussions with Bennett was about the miserable salary which the manager of the Comédie Mondaine had offered her for a job in his company. Some years before her meeting with Bennett she had become the mistress of a notary, an affair which she discusses with him openly: Bennett refers to this man as 'her protector'. He died, conveniently, leaving her a small legacy. She claims that his death was a great shock, but his legacy enabled her to train for the stage. Bennett must have appreciated the Balzacian flavour of her career. One wonders whether he would have regarded her past differently if she had been an English girl. When they met, she was on the fringe of the theatre. She wanted to be an actress, but her yearnings were highbrow; she liked to recite, dramatically, the poems of Verlaine and Baudelaire, and used to do this, both before and after her marriage to Bennett, at evening parties. This was the age of Isadora Duncan and Colette, both of whom used to make similar exhibitions of themselves in drawing rooms. And an evening with dramatic recitations of Verlaine was not so far removed from the musical evenings in Fulham with the Marriotts, or even the Christmases at Burslem. These recitations were to become something of an embarrassment to Bennett back home in England, but in Paris in 1907 they were quite the thing. Moreover, Marguerite had the looks to carry such performances off. She was dark, dramatic, striking; later photographs of her in the 1920s, when Bennett was a wealthy man, show her elegant, stylishly dressed, doing credit to the luxury he had brought her. Bennett must at once have seen in her possibilities for the future: here was a sensible, practical woman, attractive and experienced, without a mother or father around to fuss and create misunderstandings, not the kind of person who would expect a lavish courtship – he couldn't have faced that again, so soon after the disaster of his first. She would be content with little, would Marguerite, perhaps he thought to himself; she would be grateful to him for rescuing her from a hand-to-mouth existence and taking her into the world of literature which she so enthusiastically revered. He would receive from her flattery and admiration; not mockery, as he had received from Eleanor. He can hardly have foreseen that Lytton Strachey, thirteen years later, would be writing:

'Last night the Sitwell dinner was dreadfully dull, and they took me off afterwards to an incredibly fearful function in Arnold Bennett's establishment. *He* was not there, but *she* was – oh my eye, what a woman! It was apparently some sort of Poetry Society. There was an address (very poor) on Rimbaud, etc. by an imbecile Frog; then Edith Sitwell appeared, her nose longer than an ant-eater's, and read some of her absurd stuff; then Eliot – very sad and seedy, it made one weep; finally Mrs Arnold Bennett recited, with waving arms and chanting voice, Baudelaire and Verlaine till everybody was ready to vomit. As a study in half-witted horror the whole thing was most interesting. The rooms were peculiarly disgusting, and the company very miscellaneous. . . .'[17]

Setting aside Strachey's characteristically offensive tone, one cannot help receiving a strong impression of Marguerite Bennett and her milieu. Nor, remembering Bennett's strictures on the Stage Society, on vegetarians, on poets, can one wonder that he was not himself there.

However, when Bennett first met Marguerite, such events were far in the future. Their relationship was at first comradely; she told him about her past struggles, he doubtless told her of his. She impressed him immensely by meeting him off his train from San Remo, at some unearthly hour in the morning, having said in a moment of bravado, before he left, that she would do so. It was the kind of gesture that appealed to him. This was on 3 April; a fortnight later he took Marguerite to Les Sablons with him for a week. Whether or not she became his mistress during this week or a little later is not clear; certainly the Leberts offered encouragement rather than disapproval. While he is at Les Sablons, during this week, he makes a most curious and unusual entry in his journal. On Friday, 19 April 1907, he writes:

'I acceded to the desire of May Elliot last Friday afternoon. En voilà ma préoccupation. There was an accident, and for aught I know consequences may follow in the shape of the younger generation. The affair gave me no satisfaction. I sent for her on Monday night to come and see me and in $3\frac{1}{2}$ hours of talk made it fairly plain to her what I thought. I was as careful as I could be, but she wept again and again.'

There is then a space in the manuscript. He then goes on: 'I came down here with Marguerite S. on Tuesday, and I stay till next Monday. Voilà une affaire qui me plaît infiniment.'[18]

This entry is unusual, in that it is more or less the only direct record of sexual activity on Bennett's part. Perhaps he put it in in order to be true to his resolve to tell all, in his journal, at last. His embarrassment over the episode is clear: he does not achieve the tone of the man of the world, and his nervous descents into French are clear indications of a man uneasy, even to himself, about his own emotions. We do not know who May Elliot was, nor how many such episodes there had been. Why does Bennett say that he 'acceded to her desire', rather than the other way round? Was it really so? Did he not like to admit to himself his own desires, or was May Elliot out to trap him, as Émile Martin predicted that girls would? His stilted phrases about 'the younger generation' betray a high degree of anxiety, if not exactly of guilt; they are not like Bennett at all, and perhaps he felt himself to have acted out of character. If many more of such episodes had occurred, why did he never record them? Perhaps, just as he never much cared to write of sex in his novels, and prided himself on his ability to do without it as subject matter, he found himself unable to find a style in which to discuss these things, even with himself.

He and Marguerite, in any case, were happy together. She certainly knew better how to manage him than the unknown May Elliot. At the beginning of May, Bennett developed an acute gastric illness (diarrhoea with blood, he says in his journal) for which he blamed a dinner at the Ullmans'. Marguerite nursed him with care, and he says: 'not once has that creature (who is clearly a born nurse) made a gesture or used a tone that grated on my nerves. This is one of the most wonderful things that ever happened to me.'[19] She was with him in his flat for three weeks; when she left, he wrote that he 'felt like a widower'. For the first time, he had experienced the pleasure of living with a woman, and being cared for by her, and he had enjoyed it. She must have been very clever and careful to have managed not to annoy him, for he was a difficult, hypochondriac patient, his domestic habits were even more rigid than they had been in London, and he was settled into solitary bachelor indulgences. But she had managed it, and over a three-week period. He was pleased with her, and at the end of the three weeks we find him showing her off to his friends, at a reception, his first 'miscellaneous hospitality' for four years. Marguerite acquitted herself well, despite nerves beforehand. It was a musical evening. Bennett's friend Ricardo Viñes, the pianist, played, Mrs Boddington sang Strauss, Marguerite recited, and Bennett, carried away, sang 'Sucking Cider through a Straw', just as he would have done back home. He was pleased with the evening, for Marguerite passed the test of inspection: Mrs Devereux pronounced her a success, and said she was like a drawing by Helleu. He took her off to Les Sablons again; on 11 May he refers to her as 'the ideal mistress'.[20] They spent much time there during that summer: working, walking, eating out, eating in. She was making herself indispensable to him. They were drifting towards marriage. She said to him, with some courage, that she belonged to him completely, that she was full of happiness and security, but felt a certain regret at having come to the end of adventure. They spent his fortieth birthday together. He says, 'I think perhaps the most satisfactory birthday I have spent for a long time. But now of course my circumstances are very different. Still, to enjoy a liaison with a woman who thinks of nothing but you, you have to give up a fairish lot of things. You are no longer a bachelor. You regret it, of course. But you can't have everything.'[21] What had he given up, apart from privacy? Four days after his birthday he decides to marry her, and records the decision in his journal. He does not decide to ask her to marry him, but to marry her; presumably there was no doubt of her reply.

From his journal over this period we get a fairly clear picture of his emotions as he drifted into marriage – on the whole optimistic, but by no means passionately committed. There are plenty of doubts, expressed and between the lines. It's perhaps for this reason that this volume of the journals disappeared for some time, presumably removed from Bennett's house years later by Marguerite, who may not have liked to see so frank an account of her relationship with him, and so frank a description of his other sexual interests; it ended up apart from the other papers, and extracts from it were published for the first time in the Penguin edition of the *Journals* in 1972. At first it had been assumed that this year's journal didn't exist, and that the shock of the Eleanor Green affair had put him off writing it, as did the trials of his father's death, but it was there all the time. Marguerite need not have protected it so carefully, as its revelations are not very surprising, but they do help to contribute to an overall picture which later events certainly confirmed. One might fairly conclude, at the least, that she intended to marry him before he intended to marry her, and that she had more to gain from the formality. He, being an honourable man who disliked casual affairs, agreed to marry her when he saw what her expectations were. It seemed suitable, his friends seemed to approve, and she seemed to expect it. Why not? He had misgivings, but it was too late.

He visited England in June, leaving her in the care of an English lawyer called Bodington who was to arrange the practicalities of the marriage. He wrote to her constantly of his affairs, vowing earnestly that he was very bored without her, and missing her constant 'interruptions'. He had family business to attend to: he saw his sister Tertia in London, who had just had a new baby, Mary, then he went up to Burslem to see his mother, and to do some research for *The Old Wives' Tale*. While he is there, although he insists that all his family send loving messages and long to see her, he also warns her: 'When you come here you will have some rather tiresome experiences, in this filthy factory region.'[22] He writes that he and his family are buying wedding presents – old silver, servants' aprons – but a querulous note creeps into the otherwise amiable correspondence: some inefficiency about the publishing of the banns and the drawing-up of Marguerite's mother's certificate had occurred, and he sounds far from pleased about it. However, all the difficult technicalities of getting married in France were finally sorted out, and on 1 July Arnold returned with his wedding presents and a white hat which was 'the dernier cri of chic'. On 5 July, six months after their first meeting, and less than two months after his fortieth birthday, he and Marguerite were married, at the Mairie of the 9th Arrondissement. He had talked much less about this marriage than about the previous one that did not come off; to Wells, in a joking note, he refers to it as 'the accursed union',[23] to Pinker he says, 'this time I really *am* going to be married, to a French lady, and soon . . . the fact is that money spent in anticipation of one marriage will not obviate the necessity of spending money on another. . . .'[24] He had regained his detached, ironic tone; he had played up one great romance, and this time he was going to take his marriage calmly. He took it so calmly, in fact, that he and Marguerite were joined almost immediately after the wedding by the Marriotts, who had been intending to visit France that summer before Bennett's marriage was proposed. When they heard of it, they wrote to cancel arrangements, but Bennett wrote back on a postcard that he would need them all the more. This has been seen as a hint that he was already feeling the inconveniences and drawbacks of marriage, as he was indeed very soon to do; but perhaps it was no more than his usual courtesy to old friends, and a desire not to make too much of a fuss this time. In fact, the Marriotts didn't arrive till 26 July, nearly three weeks after the wedding, so the Bennetts had time to settle in at Les Sablons on their own. Bennett seems to have been very happy that summer; he was working as hard as usual – he refers to 'the industrious calm of my honeymoon' – and yet at the same time he was enjoying strolls with Marguerite, bicycle rides with the Marriotts, excursions to Nemours and Fontainebleau, discussions about Marcus Aurelius late at night in the garden under the Chinese lanterns.

He was writing poetry, not very successfully. He got some of it into print,

in the *New Age*, but cannot have received much encouragement from discriminating friends and editors, as it is very bad. He was experimenting with
calligraphy, more successfully; he had decided he needed a hobby, amazingly
but characteristically enough, and had decided on something that combined
'utility with beauty' – the whole of the manuscript of *The Old Wives' Tale*
is written in his new and beautifully developed hand. Perhaps he needed a
hobby because he wanted to compete with Marguerite – she had a great
gift of sitting around elegantly of an evening sewing beautiful garments, a
vision which also combined beauty and utility. (Ottoline Morrell was to
remark coarsely that Marguerite Bennett was the only woman in society who
could make her own corsets, but she was in fact a very capable dressmaker,
and enjoyed making things for herself.) In such domestic pursuits, the
summer passed. The Marriotts stayed for a month; after their departure in
early September, Bennett and Marguerite went off for a short cycling tour
on their own, through Charny, Vézelay, and St Julien – Marguerite got
rheumatism in her knees, but her husband thought cycling was good for it.
For one so careful about his own complaints, he was always less than wholly
attentive to those of others. He was pleased by the economy of the holiday:
she, no doubt, less so.

And so they settled down together, in the French countryside. They were
content: they agreed that they preferred the country to the town. Bennett
had no need to worry about women any more, for he had got one, and she
was eager to show herself in her most favourable light. And Bennett was
happy. He was working on his first great masterpiece, *The Old Wives' Tale*,
and he knew that it was good.

The Old Wives' Tale is one of the most English of masterpieces. Yet it was
written in France, and much of its action takes place in Paris. Through it,
one can see clearly what Bennett gained from his years in France. He gained
definition, and distance, and understanding. The resentments were over. He
was free, he had escaped, he could say what he chose.

Such freedom had not come easily, nor had he found it easy to express his
feelings about the Five Towns. Even in France, moreover, he was not free
from demands and irritations from the family at home. He worried about his
mother's health; he wrote to her daily, and visited when he could, usually
twice a year. His brother Frank and his sister Tertia visited him in Paris;
these were presumably happy visits. Less happy was some financial worry
to which he alludes in a letter to Pinker in November 1904. He writes,
acknowledging that his debt to Pinker stands at £400, 'I have lived like a

trappist monk this year, but the family matters which I mentioned to you have been such a drain on me that I am no better off than I was before. And I shall really be very much obliged if you will continue the arrangement for another year.'[25] Which of the family was claiming his financial support? Was it his brother Frank, who had gone into his father's business as a solicitor, somewhat reluctantly, and had never managed to get on? Was it the expense of his sister Emily's divorce?; she and her husband Spencer Edge were planning divorce in 1907, and on 14 May 1907 Bennett is writing in his journal that he really doesn't want to get mixed up in it, being 'horribly *embêté* to find myself right in the middle of a matrimonial row that did not concern me'.[26] But despite these claims upon him, he was at a safe distance. And from that distance his thoughts returned increasingly to the world he had left.

He had, as we have seen, used the Five Towns as a background quite often, after that first descriptive article in *Black and White* on 12 March 1898. Anna of the Five Towns and Leonora were local heroines; so, too, more oddly, was the glamorous Carlotta in *Sacred and Profane Love. Whom God hath Joined* was set firmly in the Potteries. And in his short stories Bennett became more and more interested in the provincial ways and provincial memories. He was an extraordinarily prolific writer of short stories, most of them ephemeral; the good ones, those that were worth collecting, are nearly all in the two volumes, *Tales of the Five Towns* and *The Grim Smile of the Five Towns*. The first of these volumes, dedicated to Marcel Schwob, was published by Chatto in January 1905: it contains stories, most of them published previously in magazines such as *Grand Magazine* and *The Windsor*, and though not all of them are strictly tales of the Five Towns – there's one about a luxury hotel, one about a trapeze artist – the best ones, such as Bennett's own favourite, 'His Worship the Goosedriver', are based on some anecdote or incident from local history or gossip. The second volume, *The Grim Smile*, was published in June 1907, just after Bennett's pre-marriage visit to Burslem; it was published, after lengthy negotiations, by Chapman and Hall, who were willing to pay the starting royalty of 20 per cent that Chatto and Windus refused. (Bennett didn't stay with Chapman and Hall long: he quarrelled with them too, and moved to Methuens, and the two volumes of stories were subsequently republished in one volume by Chatto, and are still in print.)

This second volume contains one of the best short stories, if not *the* best, that Bennett ever wrote: it is a long story, so assured and well sustained that it must have encouraged Bennett considerably in his conception of *The Old*

Wives' Tale. It is called 'The Death of Simon Fuge', and Bennett wrote it in March and April 1907, in Sam Remo and at Les Sablons. He liked it himself, commenting while writing it that it was a pleasure to be writing a story '*not* destined for any magazine',[27] and that 'not to have the fear of the unperceptive stupidity of the magazine public before your eyes is certainly a wonderful release'. He notes when he finishes it: 'It seemed to me very excellent and very original.'[28] Excellent it is, but in a sense not so original, for it bears a very close resemblance to a story by de Maupassant, 'Le Rosier de Mme Husson', which Bennett certainly must have read. It is hard to tell whether he was aware of his debt while he was writing or not; he had read so much of de Maupassant, and had admired him for so many years, that probably his manner and his conceptions had sunk into his subconscious. As he said himself, on rereading 'Bel-Ami' after ten years, in 1903 – 'People might easily say that in *A Man from the North* I had plagiarized from it: the scene at the Folies-Bergeres, the handing of her purse to Duroy by Clotilde de Marelli at the dinner, etc., etc. But I am not conscious, now, of having imitated.'[29] A couple of days later he is accusing de Maupassant of a 'feeble imitation' of Balzac, in the same book. And this is the point about 'Simon Fuge': it is not a feeble imitation, it is a new work, which draws strength from its model, but also adds to it. Bennett himself, in fact, was later to find Chekov in 'Simon Fuge', and with cause: but he hadn't read any Chekov when he wrote it.

Both stories are about the contrasts between provincial culture and metropolitan culture, a theme which preoccupied Bennett profitably throughout his life, and one which he was particularly happily placed to contemplate from a second metropolis. In de Maupassant's story, a Parisian is stranded unexpectedly in a small provincial town, and looks up an old schoolfellow, now the local doctor. He finds him at first sight fat, deadened, coarsened, aged by provincial life, yet full of unexpected interests, a keen defender of his local culture. In Bennett's story, a Londoner is travelling to the Potteries for the first time in his life; he is an expert on pots from the British Museum, and he is going to consult with the chairman of the committee of management of the Wedgwood Institute about loan exhibits. On the train, in his cultural paper, *The Gazette*, he reads of the death of Simon Fuge, a painter from the Potteries, who had enjoyed a distinguished, rarefied reputation. The story deals with the narrator's responses to the Potteries, with the differing attitudes to Fuge's reputation, with the difference in cultural climate between Knype and London. The distinctions drawn are subtle and finely observed: there isn't a word out of place. The creation of the narrator's character –

sophisticated, dilettante, yet willing to learn, impressed despite himself by the vigour of his hosts – is superbly done. The Five Towns is seen by Bennett for the first time from outside, through the eyes of an outsider. He sees how it strikes the Londoner, and his observations have the mixture of love and recoil that so many exiles feel for their native land; Lawrence himself could not have seen more. Here is Loring, the British Museum expert, on his arrival:

> 'Well, my impressions of the platform of Knype station were unfavourable. There was dirt in the air; I could feel it at once on my skin. And the scene was shabby, undignified, and rude. I use the word "rude" in all senses. . . . In truth, I felt myself to be a very brittle, delicate bit of intellectual machinery in the midst of all these physical manifestations. Yet I am a tallish man, and these potters appeared to me to be undersized, and somewhat thin too! But what elbows! What glaring egoistic eyes! What terrible decisiveness in action!'

As he stands there, watching, a porter says to him, 'Now then, get in if ye're going.' He replies that he's not going, he's just arrived, thereupon the porter replies, 'Well then, why dunna ye stand out o' th' wee and let them get in as wants to?'[30]

The shock of arriving in the North has rarely been better done.

The story is full of ironies – the most delicate of them is that Fuge, the local painter, did not paint his locality at all; he was amorous, elegant, exquisite. Which was real, which was enduring, the industrial scene, or Fuge the artist? Which would live for ever? Loring says, after attempting to record his impressions of 'squalid ugliness on a scale so vast and overpowering that it became sublime', that: 'I do not think the Five Towns will ever be described: Dante lived too soon.'[31] Fuge was totally inadequate, before such a scene. On the departure platform, after an emotionally exhausting visit, Loring reads two headlines in the local paper, which say

HANBRIDGE RATES LIVELY MEETING
KNYPE F.C. NEW CENTRE FORWARD

There is no mention of the famous Simon Fuge's death. Loring reminds his host of Fuge; but his host grew 'if not acrid, a little impatient'. 'After all,' he said, 'rates are rates, especially in Hanbridge. And let me tell you that last season Knype Football Club jolly nearly got thrown out of the First League. . . . You don't understand these things. Who the devil was Simon Fuge?'[32]

But Loring knows that his host, Brindley, is no philistine. He is a well-informed, deeply cultured man, who has impressed Loring by the variety of his interests, by his opinions. And Loring, quite lost, says, 'They joke with such extraordinary seriousness in the Five Towns that one is somehow bound to pretend that they are not joking.' The complexity of feeling, the distinctions drawn in this story are truly remarkable; and above all, the whole thing is achieved with a remarkable objectivity, with a real command of the material. It was to do this that Bennett moved away. It cannot be done from within: the contrasts and the fine shades can be perceived only by a man who has lived elsewhere. Bennett himself was neither the expert from London nor the proud provincial; but he knew both. He had arrived at a position ideal for the novelist: he knew the material was there, and he was no longer afraid of it, he was no longer afraid of being sucked back into the smoke. He was not afraid of causing offence. He was no longer needing to amuse or to please. He knew, precisely, where provincial life differed from life elsewhere, and how it had evolved; he could see the Wesleyan Chapel without shuddering, he could give credit where it was due without fearing to be deprived for ever of the joys of London and Paris thereby. There is a marvellous description of the Potteries made on a return visit in December 1907. He says in his journal:

'December 22
'We came down to the Potteries yesterday afternoon. Seemed to have better ideas as to the scientific causes of provincialism.

'I went for a walk this morning up Sneyd Green. Untidiness; things left at a loose end. Broken walls, deserted entrances to what had been spacious gardens. Everything very misty.... Men in bright neck ties sallying forth, rather suspicious, meanly-shrewd look. Mean stunted boy crouching along smoking a pipe which he hid in his hand while holding it in his mouth. Complete waste of Sunday: deserted goal posts in gloomy mist. Mild wind. Cold, chilling, clammy.'[33]

And that is how it is now, unchanged. And in Bennett, these things had found their poet and their chronicler. Others have described the ruin of the countryside and the miseries of the coal mine, but Bennett alone described the living world of high teas and gloomy goal posts and savage jokes and damp basements and *Manchester Guardian* readers and mean rich men; a world that is more there, now, ignored then as now by the Clive Bells of Britain, than many of us know, or like to think.

Bennett had not merely come to terms with his material: he had also, at this point of his life, developed the stamina and the technique for the real climb. He began to write *The Old Wives' Tale* on 8 October 1907, but he had been planning it for years. The first notion of it, which he had taken as an idea for a long short story, had come to him as he was eating in the Duval on 18 November 1903; and between then and his first chapter he refers often, in correspondence and in his journal, to the novel that is growing in his mind. There was too much there, he saw almost at once, to waste in a short story: he refers constantly to the fact that this novel will be 'long' and 'serious' and 'noble'. Despite the predictions of some of his friends, who had long bewailed his ability to turn out stories and novels to order, he had not lost the ambition nor the ability to do the real thing. On the contrary, he had been training himself to do it. Journalists often complain that they have ruined their ability to write a sustained work by working to deadlines and within limits of so many hundred or thousand words; but Bennett had never ceased to set before himself the image of a big work, he had never allowed himself to relax and think only in terms of little novels of forty thousand words (like *A Great Man*) or pleasant little serials, like *Helen of the High Hand*, which he managed to dash off in the middle of the composition of *The Old Wives' Tale*. And so, quietly, for years, he had been collecting material.

Some of the material came directly from life. The woman in the Duval, 'a mysterious pretty Englishwoman from Liverpool who gave lessons in English to a constant stream of messieurs chics, and expired alone at 7 rue Breda after being robbed by a Spanish male friend',[34] reminiscences brought from home by Frank and the Marriotts, conversations about the siege of Paris with the Leberts – all these things were joining together in his mind. He also, himself, mentions fictional models, principally de Maupassant's *Une Vie*, which tells the sad life story, from youth to old age, of a provincial girl Jeanne, who marries, is deceived, produces an adored child, is neglected by the child, and ends up alone with an old servant. The resemblances are certainly there: de Maupassant, like Bennett, writes movingly of time and age, like Bennett he evokes the feeling of a house much lived in, changeless and finally changing, of furniture loved as though it were alive, of maternal anxiety, delight, sorrow and loss. Like Constance Povey, his Jeanne is a simple, loyal, enduring victim. In his preface, Bennett writes:

'In the nineties, we used to regard Une Vie with mute awe, as being the summit of achievement in fiction.... Une Vie relates the entire life history of a woman. I settled in the privacy of my own head that my book must

146

be about the development of a young girl into a stout old lady, must be the English Une Vie. I have been accused of every fault except lack of self confidence, and in a few weeks I settled a further point, namely that my book must "go one better" than Une Vie, and that to this end it must be the life history of two women instead of one. . . .'[35]

Of course, his decision to have two heroines instead of one did not arise simply from a desire to outdo his model, and dates from early in the conception of the book (at least as early as November 1903, when he described it in a letter to Pinker as *The History of Two Old Women*). He wanted to cover, he saw he had a unique opportunity for covering, the two most powerful influences currently working upon him: the past, to which he was still bound by family ties as well as by memory and inheritance, and the present, which was Paris, and all that it stood for. The contrasts between the two, and their final dour reconciliation, gave him his structure and his theme. Most critics have thought the Parisian scenes of the novel less achieved than the Potteries scenes, but perhaps they give too little credit for the overall effect of contrast and reinforcement: just as, in 'The Death of Simon Fuge', the Potteries are seen in all their immutable self-ness by a lightweight outside, so Constance's unmoving life could only have been seen in terms of the possibility of adventure and escape. It is seen, not defended.

Bennett had read de Maupassant so early and so deeply that it had become part of him. When he reread *Une Vie*, in March 1908, he could find faults, but they were irrelevant to the work that had been done to him. A more recent influence was Huysman's *Les Soeurs Vatards*, a novel about artisan life in a lace-maker's *atelier* in Paris, which he read with great admiration in March 1907, and which he admired for its uncompromising realism, for its shocking of the bourgeoisie, for being 'so superbly crude and magnificently disgusting in its minor detail'. Another book to which he may have referred is Balzac's *La Maison du Chat qui Pelote*, a novel which also contains two draper's daughters, one domestic, one adventurous. One could doubtless find other sources: but it is worth remarking that it's no coincidence that most of them are French. When one thinks of other writers working in English at the time, Bennett's confidence and distinction appear the more remarkable. He had studied, and he had used what he had learned. Perhaps the only other writer to learn so much was George Moore, whom Bennett also deeply admired; but Bennett, in human feeling, was immensely to surpass him.

The English sources for the book, then, are not novels, but life. Louis Tillier, in his study of the sources of Bennett's novels, has traced many of the local incidents, reported in local papers or remembered from childhood, that have gone into the novel: there was the affair of the elephant belonging to Wombwell's menagerie, which in the novel dies but which in life had crushed a boy to death at Hanley in 1872, there was the affair of Horry the murderer, who was executed in 1872, and whose fate suggested the story of Daniel Povey. There was the whole row over federation, which kills Constance as the murder case killed her husband. There is the balloon ascent of Dick Povey, which is clearly a description of the balloon ascent of an old school friend of Bennett's, H.K.Hales, who was, like Dick, a bicycle and motorcar dealer and enthusiast, and who was, in later years, with perhaps less reason, to claim that he was the origin, not of Dick Povey, but of the Card. And there are countless other recollections and reminiscences, showing that Bennett, like most writers, had remembered his childhood with startling clarity. The Longsons' shop, which he had already briefly described in *A Man from the North*, is here in every detail: after Balzac and Zola, he allows the details their space. But for this novel, he did less actual research into local history than he was to do for the *Clayhanger* books. He stated that he disliked research; and most of the research that he did for this novel was into French, not English history.

By his own account, the notion of using certain parts of the French material came to him only when the conception (and indeed the writing) of the book were well under way. For instance, it wasn't until August 1907 that he had the idea of using the execution scene, and it came to him quite by chance, from a series of six articles in *Le Matin*, which appeared between 22 and 27 August. The parallels between the newspaper articles and Bennett's descriptions are very close: the section would not have existed without them. His information about life in Paris during the siege he got from the Leberts, but he supplemented it with Sarcey's diary of the siege,[36] and Jules Claretie's *L'Histoire de la Révolution de 1870-1871*. He says that he 'looked at the pictures' in Claretie (though there is little doubt that he read it too), and one of the pictures that particularly caught his attention was that of the slaughter of the elephants.[37] He used, too, the story of the balloons which left Paris, and were never seen again; Sophia's admirer, Chirac, disappears in one of them. And thus, neatly, all his material is drawn together: an elephant dies in Hanley at the beginning of the novel, elephants are eaten in Paris in the siege, balloons leave Paris, balloons fly over the Five Towns. Balloons, elephants, and fat old ladies: he had found some strange large images for his large book.

He knew he was working at full stretch, with satisfaction. He knew that what he was doing was good, and on a grand scale. But he didn't so completely immerse himself in *The Old Wives' Tale* that he left himself no time for other work: he was incapable of doing only one project at a time, no matter how serious the project. He began the writing of *The Old Wives' Tale* on 8 October 1907, three months after his marriage, and he finished it on 30 August 1908, less than a year later. For a work of 200,000 words, of considerable constructional complexity, this was an achievement. But he also, during that period, wrote two complete short novels, *Helen of the High Hand* and *Buried Alive*, many articles, short stories, a scenario of *Antony and Cleopatra* for his friend Calvocoressi, toyed with the idea of publishing a book of poems, finished a play with Phillpotts, wrote one or two books of popular philosophy, and saw his play, *Cupid and Commonsense*, on to the London stage. He also, during this period, managed to spend three months in England, from December 1907 to March 1908, and to move house. The explanation, which he himself recognized, was that he had become addicted to work. On Sunday, 5 April 1908, he writes in his diary, as he sees the end of *The Old Wives' Tale* in sight: 'Habit of work is growing on me. I could get into the way of going to my desk as a man goes to whisky, or rather to chloral. Now that I have finished all my odd jobs, and have nothing to do but 10,000 words of novel a week and two articles a week, I feel quite lost, and at once begin to think, without effort, of ideas for a new novel. My instinct is to multiply books and articles and plays. I constantly gloat over the number of words I have written in a given period.'[38]

And of course, reading this, and remembering that Bennett at this period was a newly married man, one cannot help wondering what he can have been like to live with, and how much spare time was left over for society. His marriage began to show signs of strain before long; in some ways it is hardly surprising. Though at the same time, one of the explanations that Bennett gives for his productivity is his ability to settle better now that he is married. He feels released from some of his domestic anxieties, for his wife was competent in the house, and he was also released from the strain of looking for sex or a wife. From his point of view, this probably worked out well. He writes to his friend Sturt in November 1907: 'I have practically lost all my ambitions except the ambition to be allowed to work quietly. This remarkable phenomenon coincides with my marriage, but I do not honestly think the two things are connected, as it has been "coming on" for a year.... Now that I am no longer alone, you won't catch me living any more in Paris.'[39] One does not hear Marguerite's side of this story. Was she as happy as Arnold to give up the flat in the rue d'Aumale, which they did in the spring of 1908, and move permanently into the quietness of the Villa des Néfliers? Had she hoped for a more dazzling social life? There were certainly clashes between them from the beginning; as early as October 1907, two months after their marriage, Bennett had written to his sister Tertia, saying, 'The only worm gnawing at the root of my mind is that this business of being married cannot possibly last as it is. It can last perfectly well on my footing; but it can't last on *her* footing.'[40]

One of the later problems was to be her extravagance, but at this stage she seems to have been sensible about money: on the visit to London she tries to persuade him to take a cheaper hotel. They were both careful: they had hoped to negotiate a long lease with the Leberts for Les Sablons, but it broke down because both sides wanted to strike a hard bargain. The Villa Néfliers was a charming house with a walled garden, a 'toy house', and they both took pleasure in their new carpets, their garden, their walks across the park, their purchase of little objects like 'a most charming brocanteur, with lovely Empire gueridons'.[41] Bennett says that he resents visiting Paris, and is glad to get back to the country; but now as ever, he is a countryman as much in the imagination as in reality. At one point we find him complaining, in his journal, that he lacks 'masculine company', and he clearly enjoyed his visits to Paris. He was particularly delighted with a new friendship which he struck up at this period. On 28 May 1908 his friend Calvocoressi took him to meet a Polish family, who were to become close friends for life, and through many vicissitudes. These were the Godebskis, Cipa and Ida, who, after Marcel Schwob, introduced Bennett to the real as opposed to the expatriate cultural life of Paris. They were a very artistic couple – he painted, and had edited a review. Bennett found them 'among the most charming people I have ever met'.[42] The Godebskis – familiarly known as the Gods – knew everybody: their flat in the rue d'Athènes was visited by Cocteau, Gide, Valéry, Valery Larbaud, Fargue, Satie, the pianist Viñes, the composers Roussel and Ravel, and many others. Ravel was particularly close to them: he saw them constantly, played with their two children, Mimi and Jean, dedicated a sonatine to Ida, and wrote *Ma Mère l'Oye* for Mimi and Jean in this year, 1908. It was presumably through the Godebskis that Bennett also came to know Ravel, whose work he much admired. Cipa Godebski's half-sister, Misia Godebski, may also have influenced Bennett's artistic tastes. She herself was a woman of great character, a well-known patron of the arts, a friend of Picasso and Diaghilev, and the favourite model of Vuillard. Bennett, from Paris, was to encourage the apathetic British public to take an interest in Russian ballet, and he was one of the earliest purchasers of Vuillard's paintings. Bennett found the Godebski home and atmosphere very welcoming and congenial. It was natural that he should. But there's something slightly ominous about his delight in meeting them on this first occasion in May. Was he getting a little bored, out there in the country with his wife? At the end of this entry in his journal, having said how delighted he was to meet such delightful new people, having commented that he lacks male society, he complains of monotony, complains of the gardener, and says: 'Tonight I felt as if I wanted a change rather acutely.'[43] Considering how large a part disputes over gardeners were to play in his married life, this collection of grievances augured ill: disputes over servants finally helped to separate himself and Marguerite.

There are also signs of restlessness and unease about his feelings about sex. In a moment of unusual frankness he says he likes to feel independent, and 'could not ask for a caress, except as a matter of form, and to save the amour-propre of her who I knew was anxious to confer it'.[44] He had lived too long alone. He always, to the end of his life, liked to sleep alone, could not let himself go, could not share his bed. And unquiet speculations about the female sex are creeping into his mind, at the same period. He invited his sister Emily, whose marriage had broken up, to stay, and there are hints that she and Marguerite did not get on, for, he writes: 'It occurred to me, for the first time I do believe, that women, when very intimate, have coolnesses and difficulties just as men do and perhaps more.'[45] Emily was an eccentric girl; later photographs of her show her with a parrot on her shoulder, a handsome, slim, upright old lady, sitting in a deck chair with her parrot. She was a health-food believer, and did exercises, fads that should have been after Bennett's own heart and certainly came from the same origins. But that did not mean that they would get on. There were more problems in women than he had bargained for.

What he really wanted, one sometimes feels, was a completely docile, subservient, self-effacing housekeeper of a wife, such a one as he might well have found in the Five Towns. But he also wanted an approving, un-censorious, glamorous and intelligent wife, and he couldn't get both at once. In *Buried Alive* he paints a fantasy picture of the ideal wife: Alice, the widow of a small builder from Putney, marries the shy artist hero, Priam Farrl, and continues to look after him in her solid, motherly, comfortable way, providing him with money and muffins, even when she thinks he has married her bigamously. (Bigamy, like half-brotherhood, was a theme that haunted Bennett, for no very evident reason.) Alice, as a wife, is perfect, except for one thing: when she talks about paintings, Farrl feels that she sticks a knife into his soul, for her remarks are of 'exceeding puerility'. Despite himself, despite Alice's excellence with the pastry, her ability to lay a cosy tea table, her shrewdness in the witness box, her tolerance of his foibles, he finds himself yearning for conversation, for the 'voice of informed common sense', even when it issues from a dealer who is trying to double-cross him, or a plain, clever, middle-aged lady whom he had jilted. Bennett's idea of informed common sense about painting, incidentally, include discussion of 'Segantini, then J.W.Morrice, then Bonnard' – and it was doubtless from Morrice and O'Conor that he picked up many of the hints for this admittedly frivolous work, the plot of which hinges upon the inability of the ladies of Putney to recognize a great masterpiece unless it is hanging in the National Gallery. Alice is one such lady – when her husband starts to paint masterpieces worth thousands, she asks him, sniffing the paint, if he is 'aspinalling the bathroom chair'. When she sees the work, a view of Putney Bridge, she says he should write some letters like 'Vanguard' or 'Union Jack' on the omnibus so that people will know it is an omnibus, and then tries to cheer him up for this criticism by telling him that he was clever to 'get in' the Elk Public House in the corner. And yet, this is the woman who serves him his breakfast 'in her white apron', hands him the *Telegraph*, toasts his muffins to perfection – she never reads the paper herself, she ignores politics and the machinery of living. 'She lived. She did nothing but live. She lived every hour. Priam truly felt that he had at last got down to the bed rock of life.'[46] As I said, she is a fantasy figure, as the novel is a fantastic juggling of current stock notions. Bennett knew well enough that suburban wives were in reality querulous and humourless, like his mother and Constance Povey, or ferocious and hypocritical, like Auntie Hamps, or endlessly moaning about money and their offspring, like Edwin's younger sister Clara. But, nevertheless, the image of a quiet little wife in a white apron, like a servant, whose only aim is to please her husband and make his life quiet, was the image he had been reared on. And what was he to do about it, when he had spent so long mixing with actresses and women journalists, with lady novelists and poets, with artists and singers? Violet Hunt and Roy Devereux would hardly have recognized even the image – they came from a different world.

Marguerite was doubtless the one that suffered from this clash of expectations. It was in a way lucky that she had first met Bennett in the position of an employee: she must have been presented at once with his notions of order and his habits of work. In her not particularly reliable *Memoirs* (suspect, amongst other reasons, because she wrote them after leaving him) she paints a convincing portrait of his need for service and attention, and her diffidence in the face of his already well-formed tastes. She was willing to be guided by him; the furniture that Clive Bell and Somerset Maugham found so hilariously tasteless she found rich, distinctive, harmonious, and she was overawed by his sheer knowledge about running a house – much of it acquired, as she reminds us, when he was editor of *Woman*. It must have been an alarming task, rather like inviting a well-known cookery expert to dinner. She says:

'To share a home with such a well-informed and practical husband was a privilege, but a somewhat terrifying prospect, although the surroundings appealed so much to my natural instincts and taste. I felt that there was no possible way for me to learn through my own experience the best place in a room for a picture or a piece of furniture. Like a naughty child, I would rebel at times, and would change the position of the furniture, secretly thinking it might even improve the room. But alas! every time I tried such a daring experiment I had to admit to myself that the place first chosen by Arnold Bennett was the only possible place. . . .'[47]

One remembers the more overt resistance of Hilda Lessways over the arrangement of the chairs and piano at the musical evening; and one wonders how real, and how long-lasting, was Mrs Bennett's claimed humility. Not many women would put up quietly with the treatment she got, and she had a strong personality, like Hilda. She says that for the first few years of marriage her personality was completely effaced and subdued by his, and she may well have felt it to be so, or to be so threatened, without necessarily having conceded every point to him, as she tries to imply. She certainly did try hard, to please him and his friends, to do what was expected of her. She was, as he had found out early enough, a good nurse: she enjoyed nursing him, and respected the delicacy of his health rather more than he at times respected hers. She did not mind being asked to sew in the room where he was working to see if it would help to settle him, only to be banished when she dropped a thimble. (She kept up her dressmaking; what had been a profession had become a hobby, and she did a great deal of sewing.) But at times, she broke out. We have a record of this from Pauline Smith, the novelist, who was one of Bennett's protégés: she went to stay with the Bennetts at the Villa des Néfliers in the summer of 1909, having met them the Christmas before in a hotel at Vevey; and although on the whole she describes an atmosphere of tranquillity and industry, with Bennett working, Marguerite sewing, and evening discussions of literature, she admits that at times there were 'big and little Anglo-French difficulties and differences of opinion' from time to time between husband and wife, and that she herself was some-what startled by Marguerite's 'sudden Latin tempests', which seemed to her to be heading straight for disaster. Pauline Smith herself was a shy and quiet girl, likely to be easily upset by public rows, and she says that the storms quickly died down, leaving her a faith in 'their romance in domesticity'.[48] But rows there were. Perhaps, at this time, they were of the essentially loving nature that Bennett catches so well in *These Twain*: the rows which are, as he indicated to Wells, part of the intimacy of marriage. It is difficult to re-capture the quality of dissension, or mark the point at which it goes beyond repair. At this stage, all one can say is that there was sometimes trouble, and that Marguerite had a far from easy job. Whether, and how much, Bennett regretted his marriage, he keeps to himself. But it certainly gave him some-thing to think about. On 11 June 1910, when he was working on *Clayhanger*, he writes: 'I didn't seem to be getting near to the personality of Hilda in my novel. You scarcely ever do get near a personality. There is a tremendous lot to do in fiction that no one has yet done. When M. comes downstairs from the attic, in the midst of some house arrangement, and asks me if such and such a thing will do and runs up again excited – why?'[49] Marguerite had done more for him than make a good breakfast, keep out of the way at the right times, and sew decoratively in the evenings. The long experience of mystery was to be in itself of immense value, although it was probably not the experience he would have chosen.

8

Success

The Old Wives' Tale established Bennett. He had intended it to do so, and it did. The year in which he wrote it also saw the maturing of various other ambitions. He got his first stage play on to the stage, after many abortive efforts; and he began one of the most influential stages of his career as a reviewer, with a series which he undertook for *The New Age* under the pseudonym of Jacob Tonson. But it was *The Old Wives' Tale*, his most serious work, as he had always predicted in his earliest letters to Sturt, that really tipped the balance in his favour. It was admired by his friends, it brought him important new friends; it was well and widely reviewed; it went into several editions; and it found for him for the first time an influential American publisher, George Doran.

He finished the book on 30 August 1908, and it was published in October of the same year, by Chapman and Hall, who had already published *The Grim Smile of the Five Towns*, and who were to get *Buried Alive* and *The Glimpse* before Bennett moved off yet once more, to Methuen. The book began slowly: Chapman and Hall didn't seem to realize quite what they had got hold of. In his correspondence with Pinker, Bennett describes Arthur Waugh (his editor at Chapman and Hall and Evelyn Waugh's father) as a 'grumbler', and was less than enthusiastic about his offers for the book. He finally accepted £150 advance – which had to be 'got out' of Waugh. (*The Grim Smile of the Five Towns* wasn't selling too well, owing, according to Bennett, to inadequate advertising, which may explain some of Waugh's reluctance.) The first edition of *The Old Wives' Tale* was small and its rise to success, through the original publication and through American and Tauchnitz (and many subsequent other) editions, was slow, though Bennett had confidently predicted that it would happen. He knew what the book was worth, and did not hesitate to say so. Nevertheless, he was perhaps disappointed by the slow financial response, for he makes several references to the fact that it was hardly worth his while to expend eight months of his time for £50, and if he can take such a risk why can't his publishers? And he writes on 29 November 1908 to Pinker: 'I am not coming to England for Christmas. It always costs me such a deuce of a lot. We are going to shut up house for a couple of months, and live in a hotel in Switzerland at 13 fr. a day, for the two, and I have got three railway tickets thither. This is the French woman's answer to the lack of spontaneity shown by the British public towards the O.W.'s Tale!'[1] On the other hand, though the British public hadn't responded instantly by buying thousands of copies, the reviews and his friends had done him proud, and in his heart he knew that this was more important – and even, so delightfully arranged is life for the successful, more profitable.

H.G.Wells had been particularly enthusiastic. He had been strongly critical of some of Bennett's early work, though always encouraging: but now he writes: 'Ripping. Enormous, various Balzac. Arnold has surpassed himself. No further question of First Rank. A great book and a big book.... Nobody else could come anywhere near it. We are satisfied with our Bennett ...',[2] and, in a second letter written a month later, he says: 'it at least doubles your size in my estimation. ... I am certain it will secure you the respect of all the distinguished critics who are now consuming gripe-water and such-like, if you never never write another line.'[3] Bennett was delighted; he respected Wells's opinion greatly, with cause, and their friend-ship, which had begun on a professional and literary level, had flourished through correspondence. He writes back: 'What can I say in reply to your remarks? Considerable emotion caused in this breast thereby! ... We must strive to live up to this. That is all.'[4] He was also delighted with the atten-tions of Frank Harris, who had written to him asking him to review his novel *The Bomb* for the *New Age*; they entered into mutually admiring correspon-dence, Bennett gave *The Bomb* a good review, and Harris wrote a long letter praising *The Old Wives' Tale* in the highest terms: 'The workmanship is astounding ... the style is always beyond reproach.... The architecture too, as Goethe calls the skeleton, superbly designed – no faults anywhere in design – no flaw. The storyteller's unique faculties everywhere apparent – then a masterpiece?'[5] As stated earlier, Harris withheld his final approval because he deplored Bennett's failure to make Sophia a magnificent cour-tesan. 'You give her a muck-rake instead of a soul. It is all right but it depresses me, it disappoints me.' He goes on to make certain references to those who 'live the usual Pentonville life and like-minded die the usual

Pentonville death. . . .'[6] Bennett must have been more than satisfied with this letter, for it takes him entirely seriously, it criticizes at the highest level. He writes back, also at length, defending his position, but again on a high, not hostile level. Yes, he admits, he did falter in his original conception of Sophia, but, he says firmly, 'what she did in fact become was just as interesting and good as anything else. What *you* want in life and in art is the *expensive* – I mean the spiritually expensive. I want it too. But not much of it (I did it in Sacred and Profane Love). At bottom I regard your attitude as flavoured with a youthful sentimentality. At bottom I am proudly content with the Pentonville omnibus. If I cannot take a Pentonville omnibus and show it to be fine, then I am not a fully equipped artist. (And I *am*.)'[7]

The Old Wives' Tale also brought Bennett the attention of important reviewers like Edward Garnett, who said in *The Nation* that: 'Most novelists are rarely quite one with their subject; a little above or below it. But Mr Bennett really is his subject, the breadth of it, intellectually, in a remarkable way.'[8] Bennett wrote to him, taking him up on an earlier review of *The Grim Smile* in which Garnett had accused him of being incompetent when dealing with any other than provincial subjects. Again, a flattering correspondence ensued. Ford Madox Ford, who was launching his new periodical, the *English Review*, which was to be, with the *New Age*, one of the most respected literary journals of its time, wrote asking for short stories: Bennett gave him 'The Matador of the Five Towns', which appeared in the issue of April 1909, following issues with Hardy, Conrad, Wells, Galsworthy and Henry James. Intellectually, he had reached the top.

Another tribute which pleased him, but which must have given him mixed emotions, came from his old friend Eden Phillpotts, with whom he had now quarrelled. He writes to Pinker: 'Phillpotts has broken a long silence in order to say that, though he regards our friendship as definitely broken, he must tell me that The Old Wives' Tale stands on a higher plane than any novel of modern times. This may amuse you, but it pleases me.'[9] It was generous of Phillpotts to offer this tribute, for he and Bennett had quarrelled, characteristically and perhaps inevitably enough, about money and contracts. They had, in the years of their collaboration, produced a good deal of work together: four plays, all of them unproduced, and two serials, *The Sinews of War*, which was published in November 1906, and *The Statue*, which was published in March 1908. It was *The Statue* which had been the cause of the trouble: the writing of it had gone pleasantly enough, most of it during Bennett's visit to San Remo in the spring of 1907, where he and Phillpotts would plot chapters together, and then go away and write five thousand words a day each. But there was already, perhaps, a little friction: Bennett comments on 'the extreme singularity' of Eden and his wife in his journal, and had quarrels with Emily. It was over the contract for *The Statue* that dissension finally broke out. Phillpotts had offered it to Moberley Bell without telling Bennett; there were long and irritable letters flying backward and forward between the two authors and their two agents, Pinker and Curtis Brown. The book was sold, finally, to Cassell's in August for £600, but it proved the end of their collaboration. Bennett's letters to Pinker remain full of comments on Phillpotts's bad manners and 'unbusinesslike childishness'. They were not to meet again for many years, but managed to get over their ill will, and they kept a watchful and friendly eye on one another's successes, as Phillpotts's appreciative letter about *The Old Wives' Tale* proves.

Having reached such a dignified and eminent literary position with *The Old Wives' Tale*, writers other than Bennett might have thought twice about the wisdom of continuing to produce light fiction. But for Bennett, the choice was hardly open. He could not support himself and his wife on £150 for eight months' writing and several years' thinking: he would have to keep on with the usual routine. *Helen with the High Hand* and *Buried Alive* he wrote actually in the middle of *The Old Wives' Tale*, and shortly after he wrote two other novels – *The Card*, which he wrote in the first two months of 1909, and *The Glimpse*, which nobody has ever taken as seriously as Bennett did. Of these novels, two were set in the Five Towns: *Helen with the High Hand* is almost a comic treatment of the theme of *Anna*, for it is about a rich old miser who is wheedled and coaxed into marriage, expenditure, the purchase of a large house and other such extravagances by his forceful schoolteacher niece, Helen. It is slight, impossible, but funny, another example of his ability to handle stock characters and concepts with an ironic and stylish touch. *The Card*, equally frivolous, he if anything underrated: he wrote in his journal as he finished it: 'I finished *Denry* or *The Card* yesterday at 11 a.m. Began it on Jan 1, I think. 64,000 words. Stodgy, no real distinction of any sort, but well invented and done up to the knocker, technically, right through.'[10] He was surprised by its good reviews, though he need not have been, for the book is very entertaining, and has remained popular since it was first published: Methuen published forty editions (the last one in 1964), it was filmed with Alec Guinness as the hero, and produced as a straight play in August 1973 at the Victoria Theatre, Stoke-on-Trent. It has been translated into many languages, including Arabic, and a musical version recently reached the West End from Bristol.

Denry is a classic Bennett character: card, joker, opportunist, money-maker, heart of gold. To create him Bennett drew on his childhood memories and made good use of chapters of his own life, from his days as a rent col-lector for his father, to the triumphal climax in a hotel in Switzerland, where Denry takes his wife Nelly for her honeymoon – Bennett wrote the entire book in the hotel at Vevey, and must have enjoyed bringing his hero thus up to date with himself. Several of the incidents are related to real incidents in his own past – the great newspaper war between *The Signal* and *The Five Towns Daily* echoes the struggle between his father's paper and the old-established *Sentinel*, the episode at Llandudno recalls Bennett's first piece of journalism, which he began so cardishly, so defiantly, so confidently, with the forbidden word 'And'. Some of the characters are local characters: the Countess of Chell, known as Interfering Iris, is quite clearly inspired by, if not closely based on, the local duchess, the Duchess of Sutherland, who took a great interest in public affairs; she opened bazaars for cripples, lectured on infant mortality and Benjamin Constant, wrote several books, wrote a paper on lead poisoning in the pottery trade, worried about the high incidence of phthisis in the district, and spoke about the teaching of Gaelic. No wonder she was known as Meddlesome Millie. The Card himself is clearly a fictitious character, a kind of dream hero, who says all the things one would like to have said oneself, a master of *l'esprit de l'escalier*. His quickness with a ready retort, his shrewdness with money, his love of display, his courtesy to his mother, are all qualities which Bennett possessed or would have liked to possess. So would many others, and his identity was claimed by a school friend of Bennett's, H.K.Hales, who published an autobiography which he entitled *The Autobiography of 'The Card'*. Hales did indeed have a successful career, and no doubt furnished many of the ideas for Dick Povey, for instance, the cyclist and the balloonist in *The Old Wives' Tale*, but it's doubtful whether Bennett was thinking much of him when he invented Denry. The two men were to meet again, in 1923, when Hales challenged Bennett with having used him, and demanded royalties, in Denry style. But Bennett, with equal style, replied that Hales should pay him for all the free publicity. Hales admits that, though Bennett was friendly and courteous, he was also cautious and withdrawn; perhaps he had had enough, by that stage, of ghosts rising from the past and demanding intimacy, friendship and advice. Hales wanted advice about his writing: that in itself must have been enough to make Bennett's heart sink, but he gave Hales 'a letter to his publishers with the air of an ambassador granting a safe conduct'.[11] Whatever his origins, the Card was such a popular hero that he had to be brought back again in a sequel, a tribute which Bennett never paid to any other of his comic characters.

The other two novels owe far more to Bennett's Paris years; they deal, not with misers and rent collectors, but with artists and music critics. *Buried Alive* is a highly successful joke about art and the artist. It deploys the stock notions of what artists ought to be like and what they are really like with a good deal of skill. The plot is simple, preposterous, and well worked: Priam Farrl, famous painter, is chronically shy, and when his valet Henry Leek dies, Priam seizes the opportunity to disappear. Leek is buried in Westminster Abbey; Farrl disappears into the wastes of Putney, and marries a woman whom Leek had been pursuing through a matrimonial agency. He is happy, but he is undone by his urge to start painting again. He paints; his wife sneers; but ceases to sneer when she finds she can sell his paintings for a fiver at the tobacconist's on the corner. But, of course, Farrl is discovered by the dealers, and forced to admit to his identity in a very good court scene, reminiscent of the Whistler trial, where identification rests not upon his unmistakably distinctive paintings, but upon whether or not he has two moles on his neck. Current attitudes to art – philistine, fashionable, and thoroughly informed – are played off against one another in a very nice pattern. Bennett had been close enough to the real artists of Paris, he had visited enough studios, he had talked long enough to Ullmann and O'Conor and Morrice (whom he credits in the text) to know what he was doing. The dealer, for instance, is a thoroughly credible character sketch. He was not offering aesthetic art criticism of the sort that would have pleased a Clive Bell or a Roger Fry; he was doing something more rare and just as difficult. He was sketching in, to his ordinary readers, with a real sureness of communication, the areas of which they knew nothing, and in such a manner that they could read with sympathy. Bennett's achievement as a communicator, as a popularizer, as a breaker-down of prejudice, has not been much recognized, but it is very real. The book may be preposterous and far-fetched: he would never have said that it wasn't. But it is dealing in realities of attitude, which Bennett felt for, and Clive Bell could never have comprehended. He knows why Priam's wife Alice is amazed when he says, rashly and desperately, that his works are worth £800 – 'The tears rose to Alice's eyes. She saw that he was infinitely more mad than she imagined – with his £800 and his £1,500 for daubs of pictures that conveyed no meaning whatever to the eye! Why, you could purchase real, professional pictures, of lakes and mountains, exquisitely finished, at the frame-makers in High Street, for three pounds apiece. And here he was, rambling on of hundreds and thousands. . . . Who could have guessed that the seeds of lunacy were in such a man?'[12] And although Priam Farrl is not intended as a serious sketch of the artistic temperament, there are nevertheless touches that are entirely persuasive, in a very disarming way – as when, confronting the first canvas he has painted in months, he steps back to admire it.

' "By Jove," he exclaimed, surveying the picture, "I can paint!" Artists do occasionally soliloquize in this way.'[13]

Yes, indeed they do; and one can well imagine Bennett himself laying down his pen, after a morning's work, and saying 'By Jove, I can write!' with the same mixture of pride, innocence, astonishment and certainty. *Buried Alive* may be written for a popular audience, but it rings true at the most surprising points, and foreshadows the role Bennett was to play in educating the taste of the English public, in castigating it, in the most amiable and persuasive fashion, for its philistinism. There is something in itself fantastic and delightful in the spectacle of Bennett, who had been born in the most provincial of the provinces, and who had become cosmopolitan through immense efforts of the will, chastising the smart gallery-going London public for its insularity of taste.

Bennett's other aesthetic novel of this period is less successful, and is one of the few occasions on which his own judgement seems to have been at fault, for he seems consistently to have overrated it, with as much persistence as he underrated *The Card*. The novel is called *The Glimpse*, and it began as a short story, which the *New Age* published on 4 November 1909, and which appeared in the volume of *The Matador of the Five Towns*. Bennett was clearly very taken with his theme, for he expanded it into a short though full-length novel, which he obstinately continued to believe to be as good as the best he could do. The theme is a curious one for a man of Bennett's materialist and humanist temperament: it concerns the moment of death experienced by the hero, aesthete and music critic, Morrice Loring. In this moment, he glimpses the other world, and it is a world of radiant shapes, thought forms, prismatic quivering seas of floating shapes, transparent envelopes, etc. Bennett had been reading Annie Besant's book on spiritualism and the transmigration of souls, and was toying with the idea of believing it. Wells and his own innate sense dissuaded him, in the end, but not before he had written a whole book as a memorial to this phase of belief. Several chapters are devoted to the condition of being dead, and the various stages of the soul in this state: most of them are rather dull, but there are some revealing similarities to the classic opium dreams analysed by Alethea Hayter in her work on *Opium and the Romantic Imagination*. For instance, in this state of death he sees 'immense gardens, strictly formalised: avenues, alleys, borders, fountains, trained trees, geometric spaces, canals, fountains, patterns of flowers, statuary, pergolas. . . .'[14] Had Bennett been sampling opium, under the guidance of his artist friends? It would not have been surprising, as nearly everybody else in Paris at that period did. Or were such descriptions simply the result of the equally intoxicating effect of the classic French gardens of Fontainebleau on one reared with the sooty herbaceous park of Burslem as the ideal in landscape gardening? Further on, Loring, who is after all an art critic, says, 'I saw that the supreme experience of music had been reserved for me. I understood the logical order of the phrases.'[15] Again, a whiff of opium, curious in so sober a writer.

But, of course, the narrator of this strange story is not Arnold Bennett, but Morrice Loring: as in *Sacred and Profane Love*, Bennett has risked having his own prose style confused with that of his narrator. And Loring is certainly a little flowery and delicate in his phrasing. He adores Ravel, he quotes Swinburne, he collects fine books, expensive vases, he writes of the 'surging of pale gauzes over cushions . . . flowering of monstrous hats and chromatic expansion of parasols . . .', he says that the colour of his eiderdown in his bedroom 'showed richly, amid the general severity of tone, like a piece of rhetoric'.[16] All this is a deliberate imitation of a certain style, a style with which Bennett identified in some ways but certainly not in all. The admirer of fine things is Bennett; the writer of colourful prose is not. One can imagine what Loring's music reviews were like – here are Ravel's 'Mournful Birds': 'the tragic grief of the birds, the febrile and yet majestic sorrowing of that singular bark, the evasive sweetness of bells in a most sinister valley. . . .'[17] This is not much like Bennett's style of book-reviewing: it is deliberate pastiche. Bennett knew Ravel personally, through the Godebskis, and liked him; they were friends for life. But he didn't write about him in this manner. He did at one point claim that he was more like Loring than any of his other protagonists, and other friends and critics, such as Walpole, spotted the resemblance; but it was an affinity of tastes, expensive bachelor tastes, not of character or style.

The story underlying this aesthetic prose is perhaps more revealing than Bennett's temporary interest in spiritualism. Loring has a wife, Inez, who is bored with him. She is a good nurse (odd how the theme of nursing, clearly connected with Marguerite, recurs), she is an attractive, mysteriously feminine woman, but she is bored with him and he with her. He discovers that she is plotting to run away with his best friend, dashing cosmopolitan artist Captain John Hulse. Loring has a heart attack, and is assumed dead. Inez, in a fit of guilt and fury, drinks a bottle of oxalic acid. Loring recovers;

Inez dies. Loring and his sister Mary go off on holiday to Fontainebleau, are pursued by Captain Hulse, who proves to be really in love with sister Mary. She refuses at first to marry him, because of the recent death of Inez, but he drives her masterfully and passionately around the forests of Fontainebleau in his automobile until she succumbs. Mary and Johnny go off and get married, leaving Loring, the spiritual bachelor, in solitude, to contemplate his glimpse of God. Various parallels with Bennett's life immediately suggest themselves. The drive round the forest clearly echoes Bennett's hard day with Eleanor Green, and indeed there is a little portrait of a talentless opera singer at the very opening of the book which may also be a reference at her expense. Loring and Hulse would not have existed had it not been for Bennett's friendships with Calvocoressi, Morrice and O'Conor, though none of them are direct portraits. But, most interestingly, why did Bennett choose, at this point in time, when he had been married only a year, to write a novel about an unhappy marriage? Inez, glamorous, difficult, unsatisfied with her preoccupied husband, has far more in common with Marguerite than have the down-to-earth good wives of his novels of this period: Nelly in *The Card*, Helen, Alice in *Buried Alive* are all sensible, domestic, managing women. Was Bennett, perhaps, like Loring, wondering whether or not he was at heart a bachelor, more satisfied and amused by his first edition catalogues and his music than by the tussle and claims of domestic conflict? Inez is a good nurse, but otherwise too much trouble as a wife; and in his limbo-like visions the spiritual disembodied Loring associates with another disembodied woman, 'more feminine than any being of her sex that I have ever seen. She was yielding; she was acquiescent; she was the embodiment of surrender. . . . Her receptivity exalted me, but did not lower herself. . . .' One of the spiritual Loring's pleasures is to browse in a heavenly library (another touch of opium and Borges) and 'the woman was happy in my absorption, and she was happy when I drew out of it and lost myself in her. Part of her destiny was to be solitary when I had no need of her . . . it was inconceivable that her glance should reproach me, or that I could be guilty towards her.'[18] Very convenient indeed: much better than Inez, who cries, very convincingly, as an explanation for her infidelity: 'I've stood it too long . . . getting up in the morning with the feeling that no man in the world was thinking about me – was neither happy nor unhappy because of me. . . . How many years have I stood that? . . . Do you suppose I got used to it? Never!'[19]

Bennett, clearly, was going through an acute and difficult reassessment of his views on women. Proximity to a wife with a ready developed and powerful character had forced it upon him. He was not, one must admit, alone in this struggle: his whole age had divided views, views that resulted in the dichotomy between the women who inhabit, graciously, the novels of Virginia Woolf, and those whom she politically defended. A similar dichotomy, though rooted in very different experience, can be found in Bennett. He, too, defended the rights of women, believed in their education, their right to work, corrected the prejudices of those who thought women shouldn't work by reminding them of the housemaids and laundresses; and yet, just as Virginia Woolf is irrationally haunted by the image of a gracious hostess whose justification is simply, or rather in much complexity, to be, so he is haunted by the idea of a wife at once docile and beautiful, well-dressed and gracious, intelligent yet servile, a kind of secretary–mannequin–housekeeper–companion all rolled into one. He even says so, in *The Glimpse*. He says he wants 'all women rolled into one woman for the companionship of a man'. And, of course, he probably suffered more anguish on this point than many, because of the distance he had travelled from his social origins. Nobody expected Violet Hunt to be a cook or a secretary; there were servants to do that kind of thing. Although Mrs Ramsay knits stockings and Mrs Dalloway does a little sewing, neither they nor Virginia Woolf herself possessed the domestic virtues of Alice Farrl or Constance Povey. Most men, perhaps, at this period expected the impossible from their wives: but Bennett expected it more than most. No wonder he was disappointed, and his wife dissatisfied.

The early years of their marriage, however, were by no means permanently overcast with gloom or quarrels. It was a great period for Bennett as a writer, and success seemed to attend all his efforts. After his long writing holiday at Vevey, he and Marguerite went to England, in March of 1909. They visited, naturally, his family, and he makes notes in his journal of a snowy funeral in Tunstall – he was already collecting ideas for *Clayhanger*. Then they went to London, and Bennett enjoyed his new prestige, seeing old friends like Wells and Whitten, dining with Frank Harris and Ford Madox Ford, and meeting for the first time, with some apprehension, Galsworthy. The apprehension was caused by the fact that Bennett had been less than polite about Galsworthy in two recent articles in the *New Age* – in February he had written of his 'fierce animosity' to the great stolid comfortable novel-reading public, which in his view 'vitiates his right to be considered as a major artist. . . . Major artists are never so cruelly hostile to anything whatever as Galsworthy is to this class.'[20] He had followed this up with a signed piece (rather than a Jacob Tonson piece) on Galsworthy's new

above Arnold Bennett and Marguerite
by the tennis court at Comarques
below Caricature of Bennett by Rickards

previous page Comarques at Thorpe-le-
Soken
previous page The drawing-room at
Comarques

above The yacht *Velsa*
below Marjorie Gordon

Beaverbrook

Hugh Walpole

play, *Strife*: it was very cool, allowing Galsworthy honesty and ideas, but not much else.[21] However, he found that he and Galsworthy got on well together, personally if not professionally (Bennett was never much to admire his work) – and they became good friends, over the years.

Such moments of strain are inevitable for a reviewer who mixes in society and has some influence. And Bennett had now become a man of influence, largely through his *New Age* pieces. These articles, which he had begun in 1908, were widely read and widely admired: he had found in this periodical an ideal place for expressing his particular views and interests. He was now regarded as one of England's few contacts with Continental taste. He taught the English to admire the Russian ballet (as Compton Mackenzie records), and the Russian novel – particularly Chekov and Dostoevski, who were more or less unknown in England. He introduced his own favourite French writers, such as Romain Rolland, Gide, Valéry and Claudel. As a result of Bennett's enthusiasm for Chekov, the *New Age* began to publish his short stories; his praise of Dostoevski encouraged Constance Garnett and Heinemann to produce a translation. (He read the novels in French.) And yet, while conveying all this new and exciting information, he manages to avoid sounding either patronizing – he is rude at times, but not patronizing – or élitist. He has a remarkable capacity for imparting information with feeling: one wants to read the books he recommends. And the *New Age* suited him, politically: it was radical and highbrow, but at the same time it aimed at a wide cross-section of the public, the 'intelligentsia' (a new word of the day) – those who had had a little education but not enough, the readership provided by the Education Acts. Bennett was their natural spokesman: he was one of them. He had written with flair for lower-brow weeklies, such as *T.P.*'s, but he could really offer more powerful stuff than T.P. (rather a prudish editor, morally and intellectually) would take. Ford Madox Ford, writing in 1918, described the readers of the *New Age* as 'very numerous and from widely different classes ... army officers ... colonial governors ... higher Civil Service officials, solicitors and members of the Bar. On the other hand, I have known it read regularly by board-school teachers, shop assistants, servants, artisans, and members of the poor generally. . . .'[22] Bennett was exactly the right person to reach this variety of people: he offends none of them. Genuinely *avant-garde* and well informed in his views, he is never precious or pedantic in his expression. His pronouncements were widely respected even by the most literary and literate: Frank Swinnerton records how Katherine Mansfield and Middleton Murry agreed with his assessments, and says that his pieces 'familiarised us with the language and views of

Parisian critics. It was quite different from the literary letters of C.K.S. [Clement Shorter] and Claudius Clear [W.Robertson Nicoll] and the sedate gossip of other bookmen; and it opened our eyes.'[23] His move to France, if it had been a calculated effort to gain himself a new literary corner, had been highly successful. He was now listened to with respect, as a leader of opinion, and when he visited England he could really play the role of the well-informed man at home in two capitals, successful as a novelist and powerful as a critic.

The real purpose of this visit to England in 1909 was to see his play, *What the Public Wants*, on to the West End stage. After years of discipline, hopes and expiring options, he was at last to see a play of his given a sizable production. It did not happen very smoothly, however. The play had been originally accepted by Sir Charles Hawtrey on behalf of his syndicate, but the syndicate refused to back him up, so the first production was given by the Stage Society at the Aldwych Theatre; the Stage Society had already put on *Cupid and Commonsense*, an adaptation of *Anna of the Five Towns*, at the Shaftesbury for a couple of nights in January, but they had not done it very well. Bennett had mixed feelings about them anyway. He was inclined to regard them as an arty lot, and made fun of their more *avant-garde* and poetic productions in the Regent. He was not much interested in the revolutionary staging techniques of Granville Barker: he would have been more at home with a commercial organization. Still, it was something, and he became very excited by and involved in rehearsals. The first performance was on 2 May; the play seemed to be well received, but Bennett had to go through the inevitable cold dawn of finding that critics who had been rapturously enthusiastic in person in the theatre had gone home and written 'Cold carping' notices. The experience is faithfully recorded in *The Regent*: Denry the Card, now Edward Henry the theatre-owner, reads the press of the first night in his new theatre, expecting to find accounts of the sensational success and rapturous applause he had heard the night before, but instead he finds harsh criticisms of play and actors, remarks varying from 'The reception was quite favourable' to 'a reception tumultuously enthusiastic', and concludes that there is a vast difference between the world of gossip and the world of reviewing. He reflects: 'In those columns of theatrical gossip there was no flaw in the theatrical world. In those columns of dramatic gossip no piece ever failed, though sometimes a piece was withdrawn, regretfully and against the wishes of the public, to make room for another piece. In those columns of dramatic gossip theatrical managers, actors, and especially actresses, and even authors, were benefactors of society, and therefore they were treated with the deference, the gentleness, the heartfelt sympathy which benefactors of society merit and ought to receive. The tone of the criticism of the first night was different – it was subtly, not crudely, different. But different it was.'[24]

Bennett, himself an ex-theatre-reviewer and a man of sense, must have known all this. But it is a different thing to experience it. Compared with some authors, such as the ill-fated Henry James who was booed from the gallery, he got off very well: though, like James, his works have since proved successful in adaptation, as television serials, and notably in dramatic versions in the Victoria Theatre, Stoke, whereas his own dramatic efforts are rarely revived. They are, however, not uninteresting. *What the Public Wants*, *Cupid and Commonsense* (which was produced in Glasgow by Frank Vernon, also in May 1909) and his next play, *The Honeymoon*, all have their points. *What the Public Wants*, which Bennett wrote in November 1908 at Vevey, and which was originally conceived as a short novel (and indeed, to Bennett's surprise and amusement, sold as a serial in America), is about the popular press. Its hero is a newspaper magnate, Sir Charles Worgan, a self-made man from the Five Towns, who believes in making money out of the press but who is yet nevertheless always sentimentally ready to see 'anyone from the Five Towns, especially from Bursley';[25] the millionaire with the heart of gold, in fact, though his heart is not quite as golden as the plot at first indicates.

The play is a not uninteresting discussion of newspaper ethics and cosmopolitan and provincial culture: Bennett, who had written for the popular press for years, and knew its morals exactly, was interested in the phenomenon – fairly recent – of a powerful pressman who could print, for the consumption of millions, horror stories and scandals which would previously only have reached the local papers. At this stage he didn't yet know Rothermere, Northcliffe and Beaverbrook personally, as he was to do – the character of Worgan is drawn from speculation. But it does have some of the feel of reality, and the life of the newspaper office is not badly portrayed: Bennett was good at making a little knowledge go a long way.

The play was successful enough in its original Stage Society run for Hawtrey to regain the confidence of his reluctant syndicate and he appeared in it in the role of Sir Charles at the Royalty on 27 May; the play was put on, however, after only two weeks of rehearsals, and Bennett was not at all happy with the production. Indeed, some years later, writing to the actress Doris Keane about difficulties over another play, he says, looking back on this experience: 'I have never got a play produced except after extreme difficulty and amid prophecies of disaster. With one exception, in which the circumstances were in my judgement so impossible that I left the country before rehearsals began, I have not yet had a failure.'[26] But the play was by no means a total failure; it got some very good notices, and ran, respectably, for a month. Beerbohm, perhaps surprisingly in view of his own sophisticated literary tastes, praised the play in the *Saturday Review*: after paying some fine tributes to *The Old Wives' Tale*, he devoted a long piece to the play, describing it as 'one of the best comedies of our time'[27] and not at all, as he had feared, written down to the public.

The *New Age*, perhaps in a slightly partisan spirit, had a long article by J.E.Barton, praising it very highly, and also giving enthusiastic support for Bennett's novels on the side – *A Great Man* is described as 'one of the most amusing books for the cynical and bookish reader ever written'.[28] Nor was the play's life over when the run ended – it has had many repertory productions, was published in *McClure's Magazine* in the United States, in the *English Review* in this country, and in hard-back edition by Frank Palmer in 1910. Bennett had probably done better out of this so-called failure than out of any other of his plays to date.

He was clearly very much taken with the theatre world, for on his return to France in May, far from brooding over his disappointment with Hawtrey, he immediately dashed off a scenario of a play about Don Juan for Beerbohm Tree, whom he had met in London. Tree had seen nothing in *What the Public Wants*, but had presumably seen something in Bennett. He was also on intimate terms with his theatrical agent, William Lee Mathews, whom he invited to stay with him in Fontainebleau, and whom he addressed in correspondence as 'Dearest William', a form of salutation that Pinker never achieved. The next play he wrote was *The Honeymoon*, which was commissioned by Herbert Trench. He began it in September, after a fairly idle summer full of guests. He says the idea came to him 'during influenza', and he intended it to be a light comic piece – adding defensively, in a letter to Mathews, that *What the Public Wants* had not aimed to make people laugh, so it was no use complaining if they didn't.[29]

The plot of *The Honeymoon* is certainly slight enough – a young couple just married embark on their first post-marital row. He wants to fly over Snowdon in competition against a German aviator, for he is a celebrated aviator, whereas she wants to have a month's honeymoon. When he points out that he must make his flight now, whereas the honeymoon can take place any time, she embarks on an interesting defence of herself as a highly trained woman. She has, she says, made the most elaborate and expensive preparations for her honeymoon, and could not postpone or cancel the 'sensational exhibition flight' she had arranged for him. He concedes her point, as he has to, but she, realistically enough, is not best pleased by his concession. Then, unrealistically, the news arrives that the couple are not really married at all: the ceremony had been performed by a 'false curate', a good comic character who arrives on stage to give his explanations for his conduct. Deadlock. Should the couple, who have discovered themselves to be so ill-suited after only a few hours of supposed marriage, get married again the next morning, or should they take advantage of this second chance and call the whole thing off? The situation recalls that in J.B.Priestley's old favourite, *When We Are Married*, and yields a good deal of amusement. It is slight, but accomplished, and Bennett could reasonably have hoped for its success. But, inevitably, there were difficulties. Trench wanted him to alter the last act: Bennett agreed, then disagreed. On 8 March 1910, four months after he had finished it, he got a letter from Trench accepting it for the Haymarket, and 'had a great fit of triumph',[30] but his rejoicing was premature, for Trench finally turned the play down. Bennett pocketed the option money, and waited. It was sold in 1911 to Marie Tempest, who appeared in the leading role opposite Dion Boucicault, a distinguished enough pair. It opened on 6 October 1911 at the Royalty Theatre, which Marie Tempest was then managing, and it ran for just under four months, to reviews acclaiming Bennett's witty dialogue, but showing even more enthusiasm for Marie Tempest's performance, which elicited the 'most melodiously spontaneous laughter' and 'plenty of mirthful appreciation'.[31]

Miss Tempest certainly took all applause as a personal tribute and there is an account of her first meeting with Bennett which sums up so many people's attitude to him that it is worth recounting. She had admired his work, his sophistication, regarding him perhaps rather oddly as representative of the 'new drama', and had expected to meet a well-dressed, suave playwright. Instead, he arrived at her house 'in a grey bowler hat, and a red tie fixed to his shirt by an enormous ruby pin',[32] and suffering from a large carbuncle inadequately covered with elastoplast. The typical snobbery of this account, which is perhaps as much the biographer's as the actress's, is softened by the fact that she became extremely attached to him as she got to know him. The same biographer reports that 'one of the few dead people I have ever heard her speak of sadly is Arnold Bennett. "I miss him," she once said to me. "He is one of the two or three dead friends I miss." '[33] His personality had clearly triumphed over his ruby tiepin – though one cannot help wondering whether he really did dress as oddly as this account suggests. He was proud of his taste, went to good tailors and dressed expensively. It seems at least possible that a woman like Marie Tempest, hearing a broad

Five Towns accent, immediately assumed that his dress must be as vulgar as his voice. I met an elderly aristocratic friend of his recently – and a close friend, who really liked him – who referred to his 'cockney' accent, which is one defect from which he surely never suffered. It is curious how undiscriminating the discriminating can be.

The autumn during which Bennett composed *The Honeymoon* was, domestically, a happy one. He was planning *Clayhanger*, which he intended methodically, to begin on 1 January 1910. (In fact he began it on the 5th, a slight margin of miscalculation.) He did a good deal of research, reading up the *Victoria History of the Potteries* and various other documentary sources. He read other things at random. He attended exhibitions of painting and of aviation. He continued to do his own watercolours. He wrote a poem, he wrote articles. He thought he might write an anthology of the literary ideas of W.S. Landor. And during this period his lifelong friendship with Pauline Smith, whom he had met the winter before at Vevey, prospered. She came to stay at the Villa des Néfliers in October, and she, in her memoir '*A.B.*',[34] recalls his mornings of hard work, his daily solitary walk in the forest, his friendliness in the 'lovely golden afternoons' when he would accompany Pauline and Marguerite on walks along the river bank, or in search of poisonous-looking mushrooms. He would read acts of *The Honeymoon* aloud to the two women, conscious that he did not read well, but considering it a good test, to see if his lines could withstand a bad rendering. He fussed about the geyser, and talked in the evenings to the local chemist, Devic, who used to impart interesting information, such as the fact that, if a man dies in the French Alps in winter, his corpse is stored in the attic until the spring, preserved in nature's own refrigeration. And every now and then he would divert his attention from these things to concentrate, rather alarmingly, on Pauline.

Pauline Smith was a timid girl, socially self-conscious, not very strong, with aspirations and indeed a real talent as a writer, but very little self-assertion or confidence. Bennett was an ideal mentor. He had noticed her and her mother at the hotel, had talked to them, had brusquely defended Pauline's social vagueness, and had criticized her writing: he liked her children's stories, but not her projected novel. Now, in his house, she was going to be compelled to write a novel, and to make conversation. He also widened her taste in literature greatly; until then she had led a narrow and sheltered life, and he revealed to her 'the world of modern literature, in France and Russia as well as in England'.[35] Bennett, never one himself to despise guidance or reject the revelations of others, was always keen to impart his own enthusiasms, and Pauline was an eager pupil. She says of him: 'To the end the discovery of beauty in any form was adventure to him – and adventure to be eagerly shared. In later years I never went with him to any play or art collection without being in this same way enriched....'[36] As a protégé, as well as an admirer, she was a success: her short stories, *The Little Karoo*, all set in the South Africa of her childhood, were widely admired and are still remembered. Bennett must have felt a justified pride in writing an introduction for the collection, in 1925, describing himself as 'the earliest wondering admirer of her strange, austere, tender and ruthless talent'.[37]

Pauline stayed throughout the autumn with them in Fontainebleau, and returned with them to Paris in falling snow, on 27 November. She was going to travel with them to London after a week in Paris, but left precipitately to join a sick sister. They were to meet up again on a trip to Italy in the spring of the next year. The Bennetts spent the week in Paris. Arnold was tired and suffering from lumbago and the intense cold. Perhaps, also, he was not much looking forward to his statutory trip to Burslem, where he arrived on 1 December, with the weather still appalling. He had looked round on his visit a couple of years earlier, in 1907, for details for *The Old Wives' Tale*; now he was looking for background for *Clayhanger*, particularly from his friend Joseph Dawson, the printer and bookseller. Those who think Bennett was a purely methodical, dull, workmanlike writer should look at the pages of his journal covering this visit, for it is clear from them that he was in a state of intense creative excitement, possibly expressing itself in ill-health (he was on a Sanatogen cure), and certainly, as he records, expressing itself in an inability to settle down and read. He says: 'I cannot read in Burslem. All I can do is to go about and take notes. My mind is in a whirl all the time. I have only been here 5 days, and yet all Paris and Avon seems years off....'[38] Revisiting the scenes of his childhood, thinking back over his childhood, as he did more intensely in *Clayhanger* than in *The Old Wives' Tale*, had a highly disturbing effect on him – he saw things he had hardly noticed before, such as the clog-dancing, which was to be used so splendidly in the novel. He says, after watching the clog-dancing: 'I had got into an extraordinary vein of "second sight". I perceived whole chapters.'[39]

After nearly three weeks of Burslem, which must have been fairly trying for Marguerite, they went off to London for Christmas, where they saw old friends – Wells, Rickards, Frank Palmer. At a dinner at Wells's he met the William Rothensteins: he liked Rothenstein, who was 'a good talker' (21 December 1909) and the friendship prospered, for both William and his son John were to turn to Bennett in later years for help and literary advice.

He saw a good deal of Wells during this patch, for Wells had a lot to talk about; while Bennett had been in Paris, he had been through the affair described in *Ann Veronica* and was clearly willing not only to write about it but also to talk about it. Bennett had read *Ann Veronica*, which Wells had sent him that October with an inscription 'The Young Mistress's Tale, to Arnold B. with love from his nephew H.G.': he hadn't been over-impressed with it, surprisingly, perhaps. Or perhaps his view of it was clouded, inevitably, by his personal friendship with Wells and his wife, and he preferred to hear the story direct from Wells himself. Like most exiles, Bennett had a good deal of gossip to catch up on. He also had the gratification of finding that his reputation was growing steadily: he received compliments on *The Old Wives' Tale* wherever he turned. After three weeks' hard work on Burslem, he gave Marguerite her turn: he took her to Bournemouth, which he detested, to the theatre, which made him reflect yet again upon the impossibility of getting a play put on properly, and, on the last night of their stay in London, to the Tivoli where they saw Marie Lloyd (very young and spry for a grandmother) and George Formby, whom he liked better than Marie Lloyd. From London they went to Brighton, where Bennett, for the first time, was recognized by a hotel manager: when Bennett gave him his card, the manager said, 'My God! Is it you?' He had achieved fame indeed. And perhaps it was this new thrill that made him write, on the same day, in his journal: 'Our first stroll along the front impressed me very favourably, yesterday afternoon. But I am obsessed by the thought that all this comfort, luxury, ostentation, snobbishness and correctness, is founded on a vast injustice to the artisan class. I can never get away from this. The furs, autos, fine food, attendance and diamond rings of this hotel only impress it on me more.'[40] In similar mood, he had written in the hotel at Vevey: 'In the basement of this hotel, very dark with windows that look on a wall that supports the earth, is the laundry, where human beings work all day washing linen. We live on top of all that, admiring fine literature, and the marvellous scenery!'[41] It was not only the comfort of the big hotel that appealed to him, pioneer advocate though he was of the private bath: he also enjoyed the sense of disparity. He took no pleasure in the injustices of the artisan; he saw them for what they were. But the contrasts of life fascinated him. He tried to catch them, seriously, in *Imperial Palace*, and failed only marginally, through a loss of energy, maybe: but already, years earlier, the scheme was planning itself in him.

The Bennetts stayed in Brighton until 18 March, and it was there that Bennett wrote a fair amount of *Clayhanger* – the whole of the first part, and a good deal of the second. He finished it at home in France on 23 June; an amazing achievement for so long and carefully worked a novel. But, as we have seen, he had been working on it for months, and had made copious notes. It must have been a curious experience, writing of his childhood in a luxury hotel on the south coast, surrounded by the blandishments of smart writers and theatre folk – Mrs Granville Barker, the actress Lillah McCarthy, was there; she begged him constantly to write a monologue for her – as well as being distracted by the turmoil of the 1910 general election. He watched its progress with hope and disgust. He discussed politics with fellow hotel guests, and was surprised to note in himself 'the faults shown by the Tory mentality', by which he may have meant a kind of bigoted partisanship. He reflected that no political changes could make much difference to 'the situation of middling comfortable persons like me',[42] but he couldn't prevent himself from becoming involved and agitated. He expressed his feelings in a piece for the *English Review*, published in February 1910, called 'The Elections and the Democratic Idea'. It's one of his better political pieces: in it he describes the voters, the conquerors and the conquered of Britain. Brighton, for him, represents perfectly the ideal of the governing classes, with its leisured life, grand hotels, luxury, obliging servants and policemen; its residents are 'comfortable . . . replete . . . honest, respectable, kindly, educated, experienced . . .' – that is, until they get on to the subject of politics: then they start abusing Lloyd George and Winston Churchill, and 'almost shout that if the Radicals are returned England is eternally ruined'. Intellect, which was once one of their possessions, has now gone over from the Tories to 'this newly-invented democracy'. Having described Brighton, he then goes on to describe its antithesis, the industrial Midlands, where houses have no wine cellars or tradesmen's entrances, nor even any vacuum cleaners. He pictures a street full of colliers boarding a tram and says: 'Set yourself to wonder why they don't use their brute force to wreck the tram car. But they don't. They vote, many of them, Tory. Why?' He discusses the fatalism of some, the hopelessness of many, the lack of information, the lack of anger, even, of those who have never seen a place like Brighton; and concludes that democracy, 'the uncompromising democratic idea', 'the passion for justice', which he says has the force of a religion, is felt only by a few thousand men, who are the true leaders and the lifeblood of the Radical Party. Their problem is that they are so far removed from those they would help, though 'the abyss must narrow every year'.[43] It is a good piece, written with some faith and some feeling; as a writer with a foot in both worlds, he was well placed to write it.

Politics didn't distract him, however, from his work on *Clayhanger* – which is, in some ways, a political novel, embodying a democratic ideal. He wrote 33,000 words of it in January alone. It was also an intensely personal book. The extremely heightened state in which he planned and composed it must have been induced by looking back over matters which he had long forgotten, or tried to forget. The death of his father in particular must have risen up like a ghost. Clayhanger is the boy that Bennett might have been, had he not escaped the family net; the speculation about one's other self, about the self one might have been had a degree of determination or talent or luck not intervened, is a painful process. Yet the novel is by no means a straight autobiography of an *alter ego*. Darius Clayhanger, as we have seen, can by no means be equated simply with Enoch Bennett; he owes a great deal of his character to Arnold Bennett's conversations with Dawson, but most of all to his reading of that remarkable book, *When I was a Child, Recollections of an Old Potter*. This book had been published by Methuen in 1903, with an introduction by Robert Spence Watson. The Old Potter was a man named William Shaw, who worked at the Hill Pottery in Burslem and became a Methodist minister in the New Connexion. He relates both his own life story and the story of the struggles of the potters to gain fair working conditions and wages: struggles so unsuccessful and fraught that, as the *Manchester Guardian* said when reviewing Harold Owen's *The Staffordshire Potter*, published in 1901, 'The wonder is that a body of workers of singular skill, holding a virtual monopoly of a great trade, in what is virtually a single town, should have failed so singularly to do for themselves what artisans under most exacting conditions have generally managed to achieve. The stamp of futility is set on everything these unfortunate potters touch.'[44] The helplessness of the working man in face of the march of industry is brought out with passion; so too is the despoliation of the countryside, in Shaw's childhood so recent and therefore so much more shocking.

William Shaw was one of those early Methodists who preserved a deep affection and loyalty for the Sunday School education. Bennett, to whom Sunday School was a symbol of hypocrisy, doubtless reinforced family memories of his own grandfather and other simple and sincere characters from the past with the admiration of Shaw for his school, which was 'an oasis in the desert'. Through Shaw's recollections, he was able to re-create the early days of Methodism, its genuinely democratic nature, its true generosity; he embodies these in the character of old Shushions, whom we see literally falling by the wayside and dying, as the grand new age bears onward. Shaw's own teacher, to whom he owed so much, was one Ralph

174

Lawton, 'A butty collier' – a far cry from the middle-class Methodism of Swan Bank and Auntie Hamps and Minister Crabtree. Shaw, like Darius Clayhanger, started life as a boy-worker in the Potteries; he was a mould-runner, at the wage of a shilling a week. His descriptions of the long hours of labour, of the appalling conditions, of the joy of eating a cheese roll with some beer in the public house on pay day, are transcribed almost word for word by Bennett. And, like Darius, Shaw was sent with his family to the work-house – Chell workhouse, known as the Bastille. The Clayhanger family was released after one night by the kindness of Shushions, but the Shaws, who had a black mark against them for some political activism of the father, were there for weeks – this is one of the few occasions on which Bennett makes his character's experiences less appalling than those of his source.

The details of Darius's childhood are thus taken almost directly from Shaw, and it seems pointless to inquire why Bennett included so much of them. It was certainly not through a lapse in artistry, as Louis Tillier implies, for they are so far from being an irrelevance (although they appear as a lengthy flashback) that they are one of the most central, moving and powerful parts of the book. In them, Bennett's passion for justice and accuracy unite with a feeling of personal deprivation. For although he was not the son of this savage and savagely exploited infant, he was the son of an environment as harsh, of doctrines of self-help as severe and ineffectual, of a father as ruined by labour. Darius Clayhanger is the suffering of industrial England, with all its fortitude and grit and gracelessness, and through Shaw's tones Bennett takes on himself a note of biblical denunciation, less neutral than usual, as certain and as partisan as Dickens. Here is Shaw, describing the changed scenery: 'This lovely, peaceful and fruitful valley is now clotted with smoke and disfigured by mining and smelting refuse ... huge mounds of slag and dirt are seen now, filling the valley, burning for years with slow, smoky fires within them. Poor Chatterly Farm stands like a blasted wraith of its once rural buxomness. ...' And the new industry, which came 'like an ogre, devouring the domesticity and child life of England ... to its everlast-ing disgrace the aristocratic statesmanship of England lent itself to the dread carnival of greed and cruelty.'[45] We are in Bunyan's territory here, and the passion stirred Bennett's inescapably Nonconformist spirit. It is a land-scape, though, peopled with human figures. Here is Shaw's description of the long stagger home from work, so different from the privileged Edwin and Arnold's walk from school: 'Many a time, after fourteen and fifteen hours' work, I had to walk a mile and a half home with another weary little wretch, and we have nodded and budged against each other on the road, surprised to find our whereabouts. No wonder ghosts were seen in the dark gasless "Hollow".... Boys don't see ghosts, now, because the Factory Act sends them home at 6 o'clock, and because the road is lit with gas lamps.'[46] Here the echoes from Bunyan and Blake mingle strangely with Shaw's faith in the Factory Acts and political reform and scientific progress – a faith shared by Bennett, and who can say it was misplaced? Certainly one who had known the horrors of working in a pot bank as a small boy could reasonably thank progress that such things were no more allowed. The section of *Clayhanger* which describes Darius's first day at work, close though it is to a fine original, is at the same time one of Bennett's finest pieces of writing, where the irony of the style ('The man Darius' – 'As no man of seven could reach the upper shelves, a pair of steps was provided' – 'At a later period it was discovered that hydraulic machinery could perform this operation more easily and more effectually than the brawny arms of a man of seven') merely reinforces the feeling of the author, and leads into the concluding paragraph, which has a more convincing pathos than Dickens: 'Darius reached home at a quarter to nine, having eaten nothing but bread all day. Somehow he had lapsed into a child again. His mother took him on her knee, and wrapped her sacking apron round his ragged clothes, and cried over him and cried into his supper of porridge, and undressed him and put him to bed. But he could not sleep easily because he was afraid of being late the next morning.'[47]

In *Clayhanger*, Bennett pays his debt to the world which he escaped so narrowly. Born himself into a relentlessly aspiring family, he himself aspired: there was nothing else he could do. He removed himself, in spirit and in body, as far as he could from his origins. But writing in Fontainebleau, or in the luxury hotel in Brighton, he still feels his kinship with those left behind, in time and in place. He continued to feel this kinship, and perhaps the accompanying sense of exile felt by those who move too far from their social origins; but rarely does he find an opportunity to express it with such power. Here are the people from whom he had his being – 'a crowd of shivering, moaning and weeping wretched men, women and children – the basis of the population of Turnhill. Although they were all endeavouring to make a noise, they made scarcely any noise, from mere lack of strength. Nothing could be heard, under the implacable bright sky, but faint ghosts of sound, as though people were sighing and crying from within the vacuum of a huge glass bell.'[48] These are the ancestral ghosts of the well-fed Clayhangers, with their roast goose and jam, their Conservative Clubs and safe deposits, and they are Bennett's too. He describes them with a poetry as fine as Zola's.

Clayhanger, begun in Brighton in January in 1910, was finished in Paris in June, 'one week in advance of time. 160,800 words'.[49] Once again, one can only marvel at his productivity. It was not even as though he devoted himself exclusively to the task of writing the novel. During this period he dined out, met new friends (among them Hugh Walpole), read other people's books, worried about the election, wrote other articles, and, most amazingly, travelled extensively. After a long stretch in Brighton, he and Marguerite left on 18 March, spent three nights in Paris where he visited the *Exposition des Indépendants* and met old friends such as O'Conor, the Godebskis, Ravel, Calvocoressi, and then travelled on, after a week in Switzerland, to Italy. (In Switzerland he managed to fit in three articles and 11,000 words of novel in what he describes as 'seven clear days'.) They stopped in Milan on the way to Florence, where Bennett met his Italian translator, Auguste Foa, and Marguerite was 'enchanted with everything'; then they went to Florence for a long visit, where they were joined by Pauline Smith.

The Bennetts stayed in a very English *pensione*, which, in his descriptions and Pauline's, evokes the atmosphere of the *pensione* in E.M.Forster's *A Room with a View*, a novel published in 1908. Bennett pretends to enjoy its eccentricities, its 'drawing room at night, full of melancholy and polite women, and the sound of violins',[50] as well as the women who accost him on the stairs, saying they admire *The Old Wives' Tale* and is it his first book?, a question which receives the fine reply, 'No, it's my thirtieth.' Finally, after a day out with artists, he admits to 'the dreadful dull social atmosphere of this excellent but damned pensione'.[51] Pauline Smith had noted the difficulties, too, and says, in her delicate manner, that 'We all suffered, I think, from the treacherous winds of the treacherous Florentine spring, and in our too English *pensione* M. had no natural outlet for her energies!'[52] Marguerite, at this stage, had embarked on writing short stories as an outlet. The fact that none of them ever reached publication indicates that it was not a satisfactory one, and doubtless added to the friction. Nevertheless, between the rigours of the *pensione*, the rigours of sight-seeing, the miseries of ill-health, the failing energy of Pauline and the bounding energy of his wife, Bennett managed to press on with *Clayhanger*, searching for ideas in cathedrals and back streets. He was ill at times; though he finished the novel, contrary to his usual practice, in 'magnificent health', he was not well at this period, for Pauline remembers him kept in bed for days by exhaustion, and he confides to his journal, 'Must have caught a chill while sketching last even between showers. A wreck this morning. I told the Mocks and M. that if only the code of literary manners permitted me to describe such a night in terms of literature, I could make it wonderful. But perhaps I couldn't.'[53] What a pity it is, in some ways, that Bennett spared us the workings of his bowels and his guts: like Joyce, he could certainly have embarked on a piece of fine realism. But he was right about literary manners; perhaps one of the first descriptions of a lavatory in a middle-class novel occurs in Proust in 1913. Bennett would have been before his time. Which leads one to another piece of speculation: was, perhaps, part of his enthusiasm for private bathrooms in hotels based very firmly and reasonably on the irregularity of his own digestion?

The beauties of Florence did not leave Bennett unmoved. He studied them and sketched them, and noted also the muck carts and the price of bread. He went to frightful operas and magnificent concerts. At the end of April Rickards called, and nearly infected him with a desire to see Venice at once. The Englishness of the *pensione* began to pall, and Bennett's opinion of the Anglo-Saxon race was deteriorating rapidly; he comments on 'their extraordinary unattractiveness'. There were other problems: Pauline fell seriously ill, had to be looked after by a doctor, was threatened with an operation on the throat, and was carried off to the nursing home of the Blue Nuns, a sinister-sounding resting place. Most of the inhabitants of the *pensione* were ill by this time, with various end-of-season afflictions. One ceases to feel scornful of their afflictions when one remembers how many English tourists did in fact die of travel, as did Virginia Woolf's brother Thoby in 1905, and as Bennett himself was perhaps to do. This time, in any case, Bennett escaped. They left on the 19th, and went straight to Paris, again via Milan. After three days of Paris, visiting friends and theatrical costumiers and exhibitions and buying hats, they returned home to Fontainebleau, where, on 25 May, after six months away, they found the garden like a jungle. And there he finished *Clayhanger*.

9
Fruits of Success

When he had finished *Clayhanger*, Bennett decided to 'finish up odd articles' and then to go and have a holiday, and he actually did it. Florence had been no holiday; it had been a schedule. But in Brittany, where he now went, he managed to do no work at all, and was rather proud of himself. By 'no work', he means that he merely wrote three articles for the *New Age*, answered his correspondence (which included among other items a request from Lillah McCarthy for a one-act play for herself in which she could appear in the next month) and for fun wrote an illustrated journal and did many sketches. He was joined on his holiday by various friends from the past – Fred Alcock, of the days of James Brown and musical evenings, and his sister Tertia. Perhaps he was feeling particularly relaxed because he knew he had *Clayhanger* behind him, knew that it was good, and could see the way clear ahead for his next book. On his return to Fontainebleau in the middle of August, he found the proofs waiting for him and 'was very pleased with it indeed. In fact it so held me that it distressed me. . . .'[1] He started to work on bits and pieces – a foreword for a book by Agnes Farley, a short story, a dramatic adaptation of *Buried Alive* – but really he was waiting for *Clayhanger*'s reception, which he records in detail. On the whole, it was excellent, despite minor disappointments – the *Manchester Guardian* gave his book to the wrong man, the *Evening Standard* wrote a 'damn silly review (10 inches)'.[2] His stature could no longer be questioned, he was taken seriously by all, the book went into a second edition in a month, and went down well in America, where *The Old Wives' Tale* was still selling excellently. All in all, he must have been delighted with his progress – which does not prevent a characteristic note of gloom from creeping in amidst the rejoicing, every now and then, as on 22 September, when he records that *Cupid and Commonsense* made only £75 13s. 10d. in Hanley, and that he has made a mess of another watercolour – 'Hence depression, though my affairs are prospering as they never prospered before. Which shows how little content has to do with prosperity.'[3] Was this a warning to himself, or a cry from the heart?

He finished his stage adaptation of *Buried Alive* in November, an exercise which he had on the whole enjoyed. It was to be one of his most successful plays, under the title of *The Great Adventure*, but was not produced until March 1913. It must have been a satisfactory coincidence to him that the first exhibition of post-impressionism, organized by Roger Fry, Desmond Macarthy and Clive Bell, had just opened at the Grafton Gallery in London, on 5 November 1910; the cries of outrage which greeted this exhibition more than justified the jokes which Bennett had made about the English art world. As Ian Dunlop in his book *The Shock of the New*[4] describes, respectable art critics responded with anger or bewilderment: Wilfred Blunt said that 'The drawing is on the level of that of an untaught child of seven or eight years old, the sense of colour that of a tea-tray painter, the method that of a schoolboy who wipes his fingers on a slate after spitting on them.'[5] Robert Morley wrote to the *Nation* saying that the paintings reflected the debased lives of painters living in the Gay City, and declaring that it was impossible to take them seriously. Bennett, in reply, in a letter to the *Nation* on 10 December, says: 'Numbers of plain profane men take these pictures seriously. I do, for instance. Mr Michael Sadler demands: "Did Van Gogh burn with the same passion when he painted his Boulevard as Cimabue when he painted his Madonna?" The answer is most emphatically, Yes! Let Mr Sadler enquire into the details of Van Gogh's career.' With what pleasure he must have written: 'The attitude of the culture of London towards [the exhibition] is of course humiliating to any Englishman who has made any effort to cure himself of insularity. . . . London may well be unaware that the value of the best work of this new school is permanently and definitely estab-lished – outside London. So much the worse for London. For the movement has not only got past the guffawing stage; it has got past the arguing stage. Its authenticity is admitted by all those who have kept themselves fully awake. And in twenty years London will be signing an apology for its guffaw.'[6]

After *The Great Adventure*, Bennett was free to turn his attention to *Hilda Lessways*, which had gradually been putting itself together in his mind. In November he and Marguerite took a furnished flat at 59 rue Grenelle, so some of the planning was done in Paris. Instead of walking round the forests of Fontainebleau, he would sit in the café at the Gare d'Orsay, to escape the seasonal rain. He began writing on 6 January 1911 and finished on 14 June – exactly, he says, 100,000 words. This book has generally been considered inferior to *Clayhanger*, and has suffered by comparison, but perhaps unjustly. In it, he traces the background and adventures of Hilda, Edwin Clayhanger's future wife, and at the same time, clearly, explores the character of his own wife, and begins to tackle the relation of his own marriage. It's not possible to identify Hilda with Marguerite, for Hilda is a girl of the Potteries; but equally one cannot help but see Marguerite in her inconsequential, rash, solitary behaviour. This book is a book about women – Marguerite, not surprisingly, had found *Clayhanger* extremely difficult to read, with its hunks of sociology and documentation drawn from a world more or less foreign to her, and *Hilda Lessways* shows the woman's side of the picture. In one of his first flashes, Bennett had conceived it 'as portraying the droves of the whole sex, instead of whole masculine droves . . . the multitudinous activities of the whole sex, against a mere background of masculinity'.[7] And this is what he achieves. The book, as it opens, is curiously deprived of men. Hilda and her mother move against a background of domestics and landladies and old spinsters. But Hilda is a modern girl: she despises domesticity, she wants to work. She is attracted by the masculine, as embodied in Mr Cannon the newspaper man, but somehow vaguely repelled by the falseness of his role: here is Hilda watching her own little servant Florrie, newly 'rescued' from a dire fate at the pot bank or the pub, and now covering the Lessways floor 'with liquid mud':

> 'Florrie, moving backwards and forwards, had now nearly got to the scullery door with her wringing and splashing and wiping; she had dirtied even her face. As Hilda absently looked at her, she thought somehow of Mr Cannon's white wrist bands. She saw the washing and the ironing of those wrist bands, and a slatternly woman or two sighing and grumbling amid wreaths of steam, and a background of cinders and suds and slop-piness. . . . All that, so that the grand creature might have a rim of pure white to his coat sleeves for a day! But the grand creature must never know. . . . And this was woman's loyalty! Her ideas concerning the business of domesticity were now mixed and opposing and irreconcilable. . . .'[8]

Mixed Hilda remains, but at least she has ideas. Perhaps she strikes the reader today as peculiarly modern because of her peculiar social status. She is the same age – early twenties – and living in the same age, as Wells's Ann Veronica, but the two girls come from different worlds. Ann Veronica is sickened by the society she lives in, by not being allowed to go to dances when she wants, by not being allowed to study what she wants, by the conventions that prevent her from borrowing money from a man without entering into a sexual contract – but her problems are essentially dated. Few girls now find themselves locked in their bedrooms by tyrannical middle-class fathers, locked in prison for suffragette activities, or trembling with fear and ignorance and courage while looking for a bedsitter in London. The world of over-protected middle-class girls has largely vanished; a father like Ann Veronica's today would at least expect his daughter to fill in her time before marriage by taking a course or a job. Ann Veronica is a child of the idle Victorian middle-class myth that women do not work. But Hilda is completely different. Although not a servant, for she and her mother keep servants, she is not a Putney lady of leisure either. Her mother, a widow, owns property, and Hilda knows herself to be above and below any career but that of teaching, which she 'abhorred'; but she is not idle in the empty Southern suburban way of Ann Veronica and daughters of the Fabian Party. Her energy, the springs of her energy, are true and timeless, and she comes from a place where character is not swamped utterly in habit. The very second sentence of the book could have come straight from a modern woman novelist's pen. It speaks. 'Hilda,' says Bennett, 'hated domestic work, and because she hated it she often did it passionately and thoroughly.'[9] Yes, indeed. One would not catch Ann Veronica, admirable though she is, facing such a situation. And here is Hilda as a child, at least as persuasive as that other rebel, Maggie Tulliver, and a great deal more confident. When she was thirteen, she was fussy about her food, and:

> '. . . at last, one noon, when the child had refused the whole of a plenteous dinner, Mrs Lessways had burst into tears and, slapping four pennies down on the table, had cried, "Here! I fairly give you up! Go out and buy your own dinner! Then perhaps you'll get what you want!" And the child, without an instant's hesitation, had seized the coins and gone out, hatless, and bought food at a little tripe shop that was also an eating-house, and consumed it there; and then in grim silence returned home. Both mother and daughter had been stupefied and frightened by the boldness of her daughter's initiative, by her amazing flaunting disregard of filial decency. . . .'[10]

This is the truth, reported here, unclouded by any preconceptions of behaviour – feminine, middle-class, Northern, whatever: it is a moment of pure character. The novel is full of them. Hilda is indestructible, she thrives on disaster. When she learns she is bigamously married, she thinks, there, at the very time, at the moment of confession, 'dizzied by the conception of the capacity of her own body and soul for experience', she thinks, 'my life is marvellous'.[11] Though perhaps this is not so far from Ann Veronica, embraced by Mr Ramage, aware that she should be dying of shock and outrage, but in fact, alas, enjoying herself. Hilda seems to me a more complex and first-hand creature than Ann Veronica: but perhaps I am merely falling into the trap of finding the North more 'real' than the South. Either way, we owe our thanks to Bennett and Wells, who saw and dared to say things that women hadn't got round to saying for themselves; and we must also marvel at the curious way in which the adventuress from Négrepelisse has inspired and coloured the widow's daughter from Turnhill. A strange cross-breeding, in which the similar traits – domestic toughness and competence, emotional enthusiasm, intellectual curiosity, a sense of adventure – in no way destroy the precision of the local portrait. There is not too much of the French woman about Hilda, despite her 'olive skin and black eyes and hair'; she is 'dramatic, dangerous, threatening', but she is deeply rooted in Bennett's own world of Sunday Schools and rent-collecting and small local newspapers and tripe shops.

In the middle of the composition of *Hilda Lessways*, true to his restless form, Bennett visited England. He went at the beginning of April, visited Burslem, and then spent some time at Whitehall Court in London. His thoughts were already turning permanently towards England. In January he had read Wells's *The New Machieavelli*, which made him wonder whether he had not arrived at a parting-of-the-ways in his own career – a parting which formulated itself in the question 'London or Paris?' Wells's novel had drawn him into English life in more practical ways: it had raised a storm of controversy and had been blacked by librarians and book-sellers. Bennett defended it vigorously, in the *New Age*, for he was strongly anti-censorship, and he wrote from Burslem to the *Manchester Guardian* attacking the views of a Dr Moulton, a professor at Manchester University, who had applauded the city council's actions in censoring the novel. The novel is, says Bennett, neither 'dirty nor nasty . . . but an absolutely sincere and righteous work, the product of a brain which . . . is one of the greatest forces for real progress in the world today'.[12] It is almost as though the backwardness of his own country, compared with the tolerance of Paris, is drawing him back to it: and understandably so, for he had now become a person of weight, whose views on post-impressionism and censorship would be earnestly requested, well paid for, and possibly heeded. He had progressed during his life in France, but perhaps he saw too an end to possible or desirable progress there. His friends in France, it is true, had become more and more distinguished and numerous, but was there not always some final barrier, as there was between himself and Gide? He and Gide were good friends, they were intimate, they corresponded at some length and admired one another, but there was nevertheless a barrier to perfect understanding: Gide, for instance, like Marguerite, could not possibly have appreciated the Englishness of *Clayhanger*, '*ce long ruisseau au cours tres lent*'.[13]

In London, on the other hand, life was full of new possibilities. The theatre world beckoned: he became involved in negotiations to get *The Honeymoon* on, visited concerts and ballets and a play by Masefield, was flattered and opportuned once more by Lillah McCarthy, planned a new play with Edward Knoblock. Once again, in one of his journal entries, one sees the perverse attraction of the English philistinism. '21 April. Palace Theatre. Pavlova dancing the dying swan. Feather falls off her dress. Two silent Englishmen. One says, "Moulting." That is all they say.'[14] He also had the mixed pleasure of meeting the Duchess of Sutherland, whom he was accused of portraying as 'interfering Iris', the Countess of Chell, in *The Card*. As there was good reason for the identification, it was an embarrassing meeting, especially as it was sprung on Bennett by surprise at dinner. He seems to have carried it off well enough, and wrote her a gallant letter when he returned to France, claiming to be 'admiring, apologetic, and unrepentant'.[15] It wasn't the last time he was to find himself in such a situation – they are, after all, well-known hazards of the novelist's trade.

However attractive he found London, he could not return to it immediately: a trip to America was planned for October, and before that he had arranged to return to Fontainebleau, finish *Hilda Lessways*, and write a new play. The new play was to be written in collaboration with Edward Knoblock, who had been introduced to Bennett by Frank Vernon, the stage director at the Royalty Theatre, and an old friend of both. Knoblock was a seasoned man of the theatre and had just achieved, in April 1911, after writing more than twenty plays, his first substantial success, in the form of *Kismet*, which ran to packed houses for a year and was played in many different languages all over the world. He had read plays for theatrical managements, had had adaptations of his own performed, and knew a great deal about the practical business of getting a play on to the stage. He had a good deal in common with Bennett, for though he was an American citizen he had spent some time in Paris studying at the Conservatoire, and knew both London and Paris well. They first met in the Authors' Club on 'May 27 at 4.30 in the afternoon'. Knoblock says: 'Vernon felt . . . what Bennett lacked, the technique of playwriting, could be supplied by me.'[16] Knoblock had the good sense to find the prospect of association 'flattering . . . since he [Bennett] was an author with an ever-growing reputation',[17] and Bennett for his part doubtless found out very quickly that Knoblock had a first-rate idea. After Bennett had proposed his own idea, which was the theme of *Don Juan*, a non-starter he never managed to abandon, Knoblock modestly proposed his – the idea of a drama spanning the generations, dealing with family tensions, to be called, possibly, 'The Family'. Bennett at once saw the virtues of this scheme, wondered why he hadn't thought of it himself, in view of its closeness to the theme of *The Old Wives' Tale*, 'and in his usual orderly fashion he pulled out his engagement book and it was agreed that I should be at Fontainebleau on August 1st, and we would begin work on the 2nd'.[18]

And so, of course, on 1 August, there Knoblock was, accompanied by his friend the playwright Edward Sheldon; they took a neighbouring villa and settled down to work. In the mornings they would work separately, and in the afternoons together. Both were businesslike: after his experiences with Phillpotts, Bennett was a seasoned collaborator, and he writes to his theatrical agent that '98 per cent of the dialogue is mine, and I have kept documentary proof of this. (But don't go and say so to Knoblock's agent!)'[19] The play was finished, after a hot summer of hard work, on 24 August; they sat in an arbour to read it, with an audience of Marguerite, Sheldon and Knoblock's agent Miss Kauser, but as they both read badly they didn't give it a fair hearing. The title, *Milestones*, came to Bennett suddenly one evening as they were driving out to dinner at a restaurant in the forest at Montigny-Marlotte, and they stayed with it. There were, inevitably, disputes about which company should be offered first refusal, but they all resolved themselves amicably. The play was taken up by Dennis Eadie for the Royalty Theatre, and relations with Knoblock remained friendly, so friendly that he and Bennett discussed the possibility of sharing a cabin on their projected trip to America, a possibility which was renounced because of Knoblock's habit of snoring, for, said Bennett, 'if I have a fancy to hear your snoring, I can always creep round from my own cabin and listen, can't I?'[20]

The trip to the United States was planned for the beginning of October. Bennett's mind was full of projects: he had already planned in his mind the third and fourth parts of his *Clayhanger* sequence and a Five Towns serial for *Harper's*, which he expected to write in 1913, and for which he was paid an unprecedentedly high advance.* He expected to write the fourth part of *Clayhanger* in 1914. In fact, the war intervened, and he did not manage it until 1916. How he kept all these ideas in his mind at once is hard to imagine. He had reached the stage in his career when invitations and offers were

* £3,000 for serial rights, £1,000 advance on the book, and a 20 per cent royalty.

reaching him from all sides, in the midst of which he still found time to try (without success) to persuade Pinker to persuade Methuen to buy *Whom God hath Joined* from Nutt – he evidently preserved an affection for this novel, and rightly considered it neglected. Between finishing *Milestones* and boarding the Cunard liner, he travelled to London, where he stayed again at the Authors' Club, Whitehall Court; he fitted in a flying visit to Glasgow, where Boucicault was rehearsing *The Honeymoon*, and then, on 7 October, departed, leaving Marguerite in the care of the Marriotts, where she could divert herself by going to the theatre, buying a motorcar, and in other ways no doubt getting rid of her excessive energy without him.

For Bennett, as one can imagine, a voyage on an ocean liner was a real treat. It offered everything – human interest, gadgets, the thrill of the modern and the grand, mechanical marvels, and the dramatic contrasts of the cook making *petits four* for the first-class passengers on one deck, while beneath blazed furnaces tended every ten minutes with new meals of coal. Bennett explored thoroughly and found out all he could, about the way the ship was run, about professional gamblers, about his fellow passengers – he travelled with Knoblock and met up with Forbes Robertson. They landed on 13 October and he found America all that he had hoped, and overwhelming in its welcome. He was an enormous success. He writes to Fred Marriott, persuading him and Marguerite to choose an expensive car with plenty of gadgets, 'I could have paid for 3 Lanchester autos by showing my face to audiences. So I think I ought to be able to afford myself *one* good one.'[21] He had hit the American lecture-tour circuit, so healthy a source of income to many subsequent visiting writers, and he was amazed.

He was received in New York by his publisher, George Doran, whom he had met in France, and whose enthusiasm for Bennett's works was great and undiscriminating, suitably enough in one who was doing so well from him. (In February, Arnold Bennett had noted in his journal that Doran had sold 35,000 copies of his book in eight months.) Doran boarded the liner accompanied by two pressmen, and the tour, which at times seemed like one long press reception, had begun: Doran said that no other visitor from Europe had had such a welcome since Dickens. At first Bennett stayed at Doran's home, later at the Waldorf, where he upset the management by trying to leave the telephone off the hook. Doran accompanied him everywhere, making sure that he saw all the sights he wanted to see, and Bennett was suitably impressed by most things – by the free-luncheon counters, by the sky-signs showing 'a mastodon kitten playing with a ball of thread and an incredible heraldry of chewing gum',[22] by the skyscrapers and by the cornices, which he compares to those in Italy. His good impressions are all recorded in articles which were subsequently published under the title *Those United States*, but into the journal and at times into the articles creep notes of dissent – alarm at the baseball, the chewing gum, the litter, and a glum little description of a less-than-scenic tour: 'October 21st. Journeyed by Elevator (change at 155th) and N.Y. and Putnam R.R. to Yonkers. Talk about the sadness and raggedness of this. Occasional ship. Broken down wooden warehouses. Sloppy planks. One house had drifted out into the Hudson river and sunk. Mrs D. said that really terrible crimes were committed here.'[23] Being a man of restless curiosity, he could not stick to the beaten tracks, and wandered off on his own on several occasions to less known parts of town. He felt that a frightening shabbiness and squalor lay just behind the smart façade, but wisely did not stay in it long enough to encounter any ill adventures. He 'did' the East Side, Sharkey's and Chinatown from the safety of an automobile, protected by Doran, a newspaper man, and an 'amiable Jewish detective who had come out first among eighteen hundred competitors in a physical examination . . .';[24] and whose chief interest was murder.

Business went as well as sight-seeing in New York. He was lavishly entertained by various concerns, and sold a serial to *Harper's* (it was to be *The Price of Love*) for £2,000, eight essays at £150 each to *Metropolitan* (*The Author's Craft*) and the American rights of the fourth unwritten *Clayhanger* for £3,000. He met fellow writers such as Upton Sinclair, millionaires like Guggenheim, old friends such as Arthur Hooley and Knoblock, and made new friends, particularly among the ladies: the wife of Paul Herzog, Mrs Elsie Herzog, was to be a devoted correspondent until her death. Herzog was a director of the George H. Doran company and was its legal adviser. Bennett also won the admiration of Mrs Hellmann, wife of George Sidney Hellmann, writer and antiquarian book dealer; on his departure she sent him a fine engraved gift 'for desk use'.

He did not of course spend all his time in New York: he paid a flying visit to Washington, a longer visit to Boston and the ancient universities. In Boston he particularly admired the Puvis de Chavannes paintings in the library and the Yacht Club; he had learned to admire his work in Paris. He was enraged with a reporter who bullied him into saying that Boston was just like England, and even more enraged with a sub-editor who headed his reluctant views with the headline 'Boston as English as a Muffin'. All Bennett would commit himself to in retrospect, unbullied by newspapers, was that 'Boston is less strikingly un-English than sundry other cities'. In

Cambridge he had an interchange which would have delighted Updike: 'October 27. Long walk with stalwart Basil King. Ex-parson. He said major vices did not exist in this community of professors, writers, and professional men.

'A.B. No adultery?
'B.K. None.'[25]

He also travelled west: on 14 November he took the train for Chicago, an epic journey which he describes with mixed respect and mockery, for the magnificent train broke down and stranded its passengers for two hours, cold and without breakfast, at seven o'clock in the morning. Chicago was rude, cold and dirty – 'a grey dirty bituminous region. Can't keep hands or linen clean'[26] – and Bennett was greeted there with a mixture of passionate welcome, from autograph hunters, and extreme abuse: a man inexplicably telephoned Doran to say, 'Tell Mr Bennett he stinks.' Bennett adds to his journal, mildly, 'This would probably happen in no other city in the world.'[27]

From Chicago he went on to Indianapolis, then to Philadelphia, continuing the round of meeting local celebrities and dining out; no wonder if at times he suffered from insomnia and dyspepsia, and had to offend his hosts by turning down expensive delicacies. At the end of November he returned to New York, and was seen off on the *Lusitania* on 30 November by a large group of friends and admirers. On the boat he met up with acquaintances, in the form of the Compton Mackenzies and Edgar Selwyn and his wife Margeurite Mayo. Selwyn, the actor and playwright, was to become Bennett's dramatic agent; his wife was an actress and playwright also. They were to meet up again very shortly in Cannes. The crossing home was rough all the way. Bennett notes 'the whole surface of sea white with long marmoreal lines of foam'.[28] The boat arrived at Fishguard on 4 December, and at Liverpool at 8.15 a.m. on 5 December. Bennett went straight to Burslem for lunch with his mother, then on to Paris, via Pinker and London. By this time he was suffering from abscesses and a chill, and admits also to having been extremely seasick. It is not surprising; a man with a stronger constitution might well have been shaken by so much ceaseless travelling and so many expensive meals. He did not linger in Paris, but went straight on to Cannes, where he was to stay at the Hôtel Californie for several months with Marguerite. The whole trip had cost him £252 5s. 8d.; he had made it back many times in contracts, and had he been able to make public appearances he could have multiplied his profits yet again.

In Cannes, he was able to enjoy the fruits of success, as far as his health would permit him; and also his reunion with Marguerite. Marguerite was learning how to live up to his income, no doubt with his encouragement. He enjoyed in particular such expensive visions as the sight of his wife and Marguerite Mayo trying on dresses in their hotel rooms ... 'the frothy garments lying all about on chairs and in the box, Selwyn, Alcock and me lounging on chairs, and M. and Mrs S. playing the mannequin'[29] – a tableau presided over by the *vendeuse* and the *essayeuse*, with their liquid persuasive voices, obliged to wait passively while the customers chatted of other things. This was the power of money; and Marguerite deserved a little indulgence, after her husband's long absence.

At the end of January he had a bad attack of gastro-enteritis, which lasted for several days; in his last illness this attack was recalled, and it was thought that it may possibly have been a mild attack of typhoid. Probably, also, Bennett never quite recovered from the chills of the voyage. This attack was certainly with him for some time: he is still mentioning it ruefully in a letter to Jane Wells in the middle of February, and it delayed the beginning of his new light novel, *The Regent*. He began, in the end, on 16 February, and finished on 11 April.

The Regent is a sequel to *The Card*, and tells of Denry's adventures as an impresario in the London theatre – it also incorporates, naturally, a voyage to the United States. This time, by coincidence, he had the happy experience of writing the novel over the period when his first big theatrical success appeared upon the London stage, for *Milestones* opened at the Royalty on 5 March, and was to have a long and remunerative run. Bennett urged William Lee Mathews to go to the first night and then stroll down Charing Cross Road, to 'telegraph a truthful description of the first night'.[30] He did: his telegram read 'Unparalleled success'. Three other telegrams arrived, declaring the play a hit. Bennett had made it at last.

The play ran for more than a year, bringing in about £60 a week. He may have been sorry to miss the first night himself, especially as the audience shouted for authors, but he had had enough of theatrical uncertainty, and anyway would not have been well enough to travel. Knoblock went to it, but would not take the stage alone. It was left to Eadie, the producer, to make 'a pretty little speech' to the enthusiastic audience.[31]

The cast of *Milestones* was distinguished, and included Mary Jerrold, Gladys Cooper, Owen Nares and Haidée Wright. The play was directed by Frank Vernon, who must have been delighted with the results of his match-making the year before. The play's success was not surprising – it was clearly very well done, and its theme was large, simple and sentimental. Hugh Walpole, who went to see it with Henry James, says that James 'thought its simplicity incredible',[32] but that, in a sense, was its virtue as a stage piece. James's complexities had certainly not proved themselves to be very theatrical. The trick of requiring actors and actresses to age decades during the show brought forth some bravura performances. Gielgud, who enjoyed the play, recalls: 'Haidée Wright was the spinster aunt, thwarted in early life through some passionate romantic attachment which had gone wrong. Halfway through the play she had a dramatic outburst, dressed in a Victorian bonnet and a dress with a bustle, and carrying a tiny folded parasol in the crook of her arm. In the last act she entered leaning on a cane, and later played her final scene crouched in a low chair before the fire, dressed in a long grey satin gown, with a shawl over her shoulders and a lace cap on her white hair.'[33] This was the kind of thing that audiences loved: Bennett's favourite theme of the passage of time had been made truly dramatic, for once. Even Mrs Belloc Lowndes, who showed some hostility to Bennett at times, confided to her diary that it was the best play she'd ever been to – though confiding at the same time the no doubt current gossip that of course Knoblock had really written it all.

Knoblock was so thrilled with this new triumph that he could not resist travelling down to Cannes to discuss the success with Bennett, but on the way down he too was struck down with an illness which, he tells us in his autobiography, was diagnosed as colitis. He was ill for days. Is there something in the prevalence of gastric illnesses in the South of France at this period that confirms the typhoid diagnosis?

Not even a national coal strike could stop *Milestones*. Bennett's views on the strike, which lasted from 26 February to 6 April, are interesting, for one would surely not be surprised (though a little disappointed) to find him, when his own interests were so much at stake, joining the ranks of the right, and sympathizing with such ladies as Mrs Julia Frankau (the novelist Frank Danby) who declared to him, safely in Cannes: ' "I'd batten them down. I'd make them work. They *should* work. I'd force them down." '[34] But all he will concede, in a letter to Matthews, is that 'as an example of a revolt of the poor against the rich, this strike has been a dazzling proof of the ineffectiveness of such a thing even when well managed under discipline. The poor have *suffered* all over the country. The rich have merely been infinitesimally inconvenienced.'[35]

When he had finished *The Regent* and his *Harper's* articles on his trip to the United States, he came back to England, in April 1912, for good. He was finished with France, and never returned there to live, though his frequent trips to that country were interrupted only by the war. He had made many and permanent friends there, and kept up his contacts: Gide, who visited him that spring in Cannes, was to stay in constant communication, proving as useful a source of information about the French literary scene as Bennett was for him about the English. In his *Journal* Gide recalls Bennett at this period, installed at *The Californie* with Valéry Larbaud: 'He earns around a thousand francs a day; he is paid at the rate of a shilling a word; he writes without stopping every day from 6 a.m. to 9 a.m., then gets into his bath and doesn't think of his work again until the next morning. . . .'[36] Bennett's prosperity was thus obvious to all. He was not at all clear, when he returned to England, of what his next plans were, but his expanding life style is noticeable in all his actions: he writes to Pinker to engage a secretary, he engages a chauffeur, in June he buys a yacht. Perhaps it's surprising, in view of all this, to find him settling modestly for some months in suburban Putney, at 14 St Simeon's Avenue, the home of his old friend Herbert Sharpe; climber though he was, Bennett always remained loyal to old friends, and they to him. This period with the Sharpes was to open a new stretch of intimacy with Herbert's son, the 'cellist, whom he had known since he was a small boy. A year later, on 27 June 1913, he went to a concert given by Cedric and noted: 'At the concert I seemed to see everyone I had ever known up to the age of 30. Vast air of a family party about it.'[37] Such continuity in a career as peripatetic and aspiring as Bennett's is very happy to note.

Of course, Bennett was not settling down in Putney for good. He had his eye on various other projects, one of which he accomplished in June, when he purchased the yacht *Velsa*. She was to be a great pride and joy to him for several years. He writes to tell Pinker that he had his eye on this particular boat for two years, but that she had been sold over his head – this time he managed to secure her for £550, telling Pinker somewhat improbably that he had beaten the owners down from twice the sum. Whatever the negotiations had been, the *Velsa* was now his. She was, he says, 'flat-bottomed with lee boards, and follows closely the lines of certain very picturesque Dutch fishing smacks . . .'; she had over six feet of headroom in the saloon and cabins, a bedroom fitted after his Cunard bedroom, and finally, triumphantly, 'she carries a piano and an encyclopedia'.[38] He kept her at Brightlingsea, and used to work on her often. He didn't get away for a voyage for some time, because he became ill again, with an abscess of the middle ear; his doctor forbade him to work and to sail. His mother also was both old and ill, so he spent some time with her in Brighton in August, at the Royal Albion Hotel. But gradually his health improved and in September he and Rickards set off for their first long trip to Holland, a trip which is recorded in articles written for *The Century* and republished in *From the Log of the Velsa*, with illustrations by Rickards. They saw plenty of Holland, from the small villages and towns, to dreary spots like 'stinking Schiedam . . . a suburban desolation', full of 'stagnation, tedium, provincialism', to the more elegant Marken, Hoorn and Haarlem. When it rained, Bennett stayed in the cabin and read Dostoevsky. He liked Amsterdam, 'the paradise of stomachs and the hell of feet', and admits to having visited a few museums, for 'when it's possible to step off a yacht clean into a museum and heavy rain is falling, the temptation to remain on board is not sufficiently powerful to keep you out of the museum. . . .'[39]

The *Velsa* was not the end of Bennett's material expansion. This was also the year in which he bought himself a country house, as he had promised he would do, years earlier. The house was in Essex, and it was beautiful. He did not move into it until February 1913, but the negotiations were completed in the autumn of 1912, and Bennett needed many alterations and improvements, with which Rickards helped him. The house was a Queen Anne house, in pale red brick, delightfully situated in a large garden in the country in a quiet corner of Essex. Even its address was perfect: it was Comarques, Thorpe-le-Soken, Essex. It is today an impressive and charming house. Bennett, when he could afford to pick and choose, chose well. He writes with some pride to his new American friend Mrs Herzog: 'We now possess an early Queen Anne house near the Essex coast, and in February are going to instal ourselves there definitely for everlasting; our deaths will one day cause a sensation in the village which we shall dominate, and the English villagers and landed gentry will wonder, as they stroll through the deserted house, why the madman had 3 bathrooms in a home so small; they will not know that it was due solely to a visit to the U.S.A. . . .'[40]

With all these interruptions, and with the continual pleas of his wife and doctor for him not to work too hard, Bennett really did very little work during 1912. As he says in his annual assessment on 31 December, it had been 'a material year', 'largely occupied with intestinal failure and worldly success'.[41] His income has risen to £16,000 during the year, 'which may be called success by any worldly-minded author. It is apparently about as much as I had earned during all the previous part of my life.'[42] But it had not been achieved without its price: as he complains luxuriously in a letter to Lee Mathews, it is 'no joke being a fashionable author'.[43] The strain of public attention, of constant unsolicited correspondence, is hard to imagine for those who have not endured it, and very hard to sympathize with, for it has usually been positively invoked. Nevertheless, it is real and it takes time to learn to deal with it. He was new to secretaries; between May and October he got through three. It is also hard not to sympathize in this year with Bennett's intestines. Reading through his journal, one would guess that his system was so disordered by constant travel in the autumn of 1911, so chilled by the return voyage to England, and so overcome by the attack of gastro-enteritis or typhoid in Cannes early in the year that he never really recovered. He had plenty of anxieties to keep him in a state of agitation: buying the yacht was fun, but buying a house is always a strain – Marguerite was to collapse herself with ill-health just after moving in, and in September of 1913, six months after, we find Bennett writing to Cedric Sharpe, who is just about to marry, not to buy 'any house on any system for a long time to come. You will be absolutely bound to regret it. . . .'[44] True, Cedric was proposing to buy expensively through a Building Society, but nevertheless there is a note of passion in Bennett's advice that seems founded in experience.

Characteristic of the annoyances of this period of time was a row that blew up between Bennett and the editor of *Everyman*, a new periodical backed by Dent, and founded and edited by Charles Sarolea. It was one of the rows that are strictly the price of fame but which a self-respecting author cannot simply swallow and let go by. Bennett was as calm and philosophical as any writer about adverse criticism, but Sarolea, in his article on Bennett, goes too far. The points that particularly enraged Bennett were that Bennett had 'deliberately chosen to suppress' his early autobiography, *The Truth about an Author*, that the subject of *The Old Wives' Tale* is the same as that of de Maupassant's *La Maison Tellier* (i.e. a brothel), that only the comic not the tragic aspects of humanity appeal to him, and that he wrote *Milestones* for money: in short that, as Sarolea said, he had 'sold his birthright as a man of genius for a mess of pottage'.[45] Bennett was righteously outraged. Far from disowning *The Truth about an Author*, which had it is true been published anonymously, he everywhere claimed it as his, and tried hard to get it republished; the difficulty was with the publishers, who would neither republish nor let it go, though Pinker finally managed to buy it back from Constable in November, and it was re-issued in 1914. Equally unfair are the attacks, thoroughly ill-conceived, on *The Old Wives' Tale*. Bennett was not in such a good position when he tried to claim that he did not write *Milestones* for money – why on earth should he not have done? – nor when he says that he has in fact suppressed his early plays, to his own financial loss –

for one at least of these early plays, *A Good Woman*, was to be revived, against Bennett's better judgement. Bennett says: 'though I have not suppressed my autobiography, I have suppressed my early plays, none of which has ever been performed. I have been told by pained experts in these markets that I have incidentally suppressed at a moderate computation some forty thousand pounds.'[46] This must have been in the nature of a boastful exaggeration of what Bennett knew to be the facts (whatever the so-called experts had said to him). But nevertheless, all in all, Bennett was right to feel indignant, and had a good case; his letter of self-defence was on the whole well judged.

Sarolea and Dent were evidently shaken by his attack and consulted Chesterton, who told them Bennett would never sue, the libel laws being what they were, and that their best bet was to try to make Bennett appear 'utterly foolish'. Consequently Bennett's letter, slightly changed in wording from its original form, appeared along with Sarolea's apology, in the issue of 1 November. Sarolea is obliged to apologize, and his attempts at irony over *The Truth about an Author* fall very far short of making Bennett look foolish. Indeed, a critic who had been guilty of such misrepresentation, if not of wilful malice, would have found it hard to answer back. His irony about Bennett's unmercenary nature and the sacrifice of the £40,000 is more effective, but Bennett emerges the victor from the battle.

Such were the irritations of fame, but Bennett was well equipped to survive them. He saw 1912 out in Paris, in the Hôtel du Rhin again, in a 'fine ground floor flat'. He met Doran and his family there, and negotiated a new contract over some serializations of old novels, a contract which he re-negotiated through Pinker, in a friendly way, behind Doran's back. He notes in his journal, 'Between April 1 and October 1 I did practically nothing.'[47] His word total had sunk to a mere 200,000. He was well on in his *Harper's* serial, *The Price of Love*. His income was enormous. *Milestones* was still running. He could afford to sit back for a while.

The principal event of 1913 was the removal to Comarques, the Bennetts' new country house. Marguerite travelled there on Monday, 24 February, and Arnold followed her the next day. After months of preparation the house, naturally, was not ready: the stair carpet wasn't laid until the end of March, and on 1 April fenders and fire-irons were still not complete. Shortly after the removal (and, it must be admitted, a lively dinner at the Café Royal) Marguerite fell ill, on 5 March, and had to be taken back from London to Comarques with an attendant nurse. Thus she missed the anniversary dinner to celebrate the opening, two years before, of *Milestones*; but she was up again for the opening night of Bennett's new play, *The Great Adventure*, which was directed by their old friend, Harley Granville Barker. It opened on 26 March, at the Kingsway, and was an immediate success: it ran until 7 November 1914. Rehearsals had not escaped the usual muddles and dramas characterizing all theatrical proceedings, the chief worry this time being the availability of the female lead, Miss Wish Wynne, a music hall and variety star. *The Great Adventure* was her first West End straight part, and after a few telegrams had flown backwards and forwards between Lee Matthews, her managers and the managers of the Kingsway, it was decided she was free to appear. Bennett notes in his journal that she was 'a genius', and certainly the critics and the public liked her. Her role, as Priam Farrl's wife (much younger in the stage version than in the novel), was an attractive one, and she made the most of it. The papers applauded the play, but declared that the chief honours were hers: *The Times* asked rhetorically 'Who is Miss Wish Wynne?' and concluded that she was not only an artiste, she was also an artist.

It was about this time that William Lee Mathews ceased to be Bennett's dramatic agent; all Bennett's dramatic work was now taken over by Pinker, except for pre-existing contracts. This may seem surprising, in view of Bennett's close friendship with Mathews and the soaring success of his theatrical affairs. But despite his friendship, he did not think highly of Mathews as a businessman, and had been planning to phase him out for at least a year. Also, it must be admitted that his affairs were now becoming so complex that there was much to be said in favour of keeping them all in one pair of hands. The severance was achieved, Bennett claims, 'with no unpleasantness at all'[48] and certainly the friendship was maintained: the two continued to see each other and to correspond for the rest of their lives, Lee Mathews taking an active part in theatrical affairs and introducing his friend, in 1925, to Komisarjevsky, the new Russian genius. Incidentally, Bennett's debt to Mathews was not only in the dramatic field: it was Mathews, not Pinker, who finally found for Bennett the perfect secretary, in the form of Miss Nerney, who came to Bennett on his recommendation at the end of 1912 and stayed with him until his death. It is amusing to find Bennett writing to Mathews in 1922 asking Mathews if he knows of a good secretary for H. G. Wells – Wells had clearly been pushing jobs off on to the competent Miss Nerney, and Bennett had perhaps decided it was time for him to look for himself.

As far as work goes, Bennett does not seem to have become much more industrious than he was in 1912: perhaps the lack of financial pressure affected his output. *The Great Adventure* was doing very nicely; money was coming in all the time. Bennett was distracted by messing about on his yacht, by the visit of his mother, by a constant flow of guests. Comarques was an excellent place to visit from London, for a lunch or a weekend, and Marguerite enjoyed being hostess. Lunch guests included Hugh de Selincourt, Vedrenne and Eadie after a play, J.C.Squire (very Jaegerish) and H.G. Wells; overnight guests included the Granville Barkers (also after a play), Knoblock, E.V.Lucas, Marriott, Pauline Smith, the Alcocks, Rickards and later in the year Ravel and Doran. There were also uninvited guests, such as the painter who came to do an oil sketch of Bennett: he annoyed Bennett by bringing a model girl with him ('damned cheek') and then failing to appreciate his surroundings. 'Comes into a 1700 AD house,' says Bennett indignantly, 'and asks you whether you have built it!'[49] Whether the interruptions were the cause of the slow progress of his *Harper's* serial or the other way round, we do not know: but certainly it was causing him, at this time, nothing but irritation, and work on the *Clayhanger* books was receding further into the distance.

In June, Bennett began to prepare the *Velsa* for a cruise of the Baltic with Rickards. In fact, as he admits in *From the Log of the Velsa*, he spent too long preparing her and working out interesting ways of getting to Denmark: his ingenuity led him astray. His intention was to send the *Velsa* and her crew well in advance to Esbjerg, and meet them there from the Harwich steamer: the result of this excess of 'wisdom and calculation' was that he and Rickards arrived in Esbjerg perfectly on time, after a twenty-two-hour crossing eating open sandwiches and sipping champagne, to find no sign of the *Velsa*, which had been badly delayed by the strong east winds. He and Rickards make the best of it. They stay in the Hôtel Spangsberg, hire an automobile, drive aimlessly around Jutland gazing at the tiresome Danish dogs and the lovely Danish girls, and finally have to be taken in hand by their headwaiter, who after days of waiting takes them to Germany himself, in person, to join the yacht, which is waiting for them in Friedrichstadt. As Bennett says, such a headwaiter is unique. After this bad start, the tour went more or less according to plan. They visited small towns in Denmark and big ports like Aarhus, where Bennett had the excitement of seeing that he was one of the authors performed at the Municipal Theatre: 'I had,' he says, 'a strange comic sensation of being world renowned....' Thence they sailed to Helsingor, and then to Copenhagen. Copenhagen is spectacular anyway, and to come upon it like that, from the sea, with the bridges opening, must have been a splendid experience: 'After all the monotonous tiny provincialism of the peninsula

left Virginia Woolf
right Aldous Huxley

Lord Birkenhead

left Miss Marie Tempest as 'Flora Lloyd'
in 'The Honeymoon'
right Miss Wish Wynne as 'Janet
Cannot' and Mr Henry Ainley as
'Ilam Carve' in 'The Great Adventure'

Miss Haidée Wright as 'Gertrude Rhead'
in 'Milestones'

Dorothy

Edith and Osbert Sitwell

Lord Beaverbrook arriving at Madrid
1924. Arnold Bennett is in the left background

and of the islands, it was sensational to find a vast capital at the far end of the farthest island.'[50] He and Rickards loved Copenhagen, with its cafés and its strange hotels and its curious art galleries; they had been told that it was dead in August, because everyone was at the seaside, but on the contrary, Bennett notes, the stylish Danish resorts were 'without exception far more dead than Copenhagen. In particular, Marienleyst, reputed to be the haunt of fashion and elegance, proved to be a very sad deserted strand. Copenhagen was not dead.'[51]

There is, perhaps, something comic to the world-weary about Bennett's passion for cities and for travel and for the new. But there is also something sublime. He is one of the best travel writers ever, for in him the spirit of inquiry never flags, and the ability to wonder and admire never dies. He is the least blasé of writers: he may criticize in a knowing way the service in a hotel, he may with maddening worldliness comment comparatively on tips and porters in every capital city in Europe, but he takes much pleasure in his knowledge, and his capacity for learning is amazing. He is not one of those seasoned travellers who move around in a cocoon of their own superiority: his plans go wrong, indeed he so arranges life that they are almost certain to go wrong; and he rises to the emergencies with a rare buoyancy. One would like to see Bennett, Rickards and the remarkable headwaiter of the Spangsberg Hôtel dining together on the train to Germany. One would like to see Bennett, offered a choice of cheese and cake in the Wiener Café in Copenhagen, demanding to see the cake, being refused, ordering cheese, and concluding gloriously: 'The Wiener Café ought to open a branch in London; it was the most English affair I have ever encountered out of England.'[52]

On his return to England, Bennett had to tackle *The Price of Love* again. He was reluctant; he wanted to get on with 'another sort of novel – much more autobiographical than I have yet written'.[53] But *The Price of Love* seemed 'goodish' as he reread it, and he finished it on 2 October, 'in a state of some exhaustion'. He was suffering from liver trouble, and was on a régime of sharp exercise and perspiration.

One cannot help wondering how Marguerite had been occupying herself, or was expected to occupy herself, during Arnold's absences. Did she have friends to stay while he was away? She was on good terms with most of his friends, and would lunch, for instance, with Jane Wells while in town. But how did she take to the life of a country gentlewoman? One answer is: she joined the golf club. Bennett despised the golf club for its mean architecture, its primness, its pettiness: did he also have to despise it for being less than wholly welcoming to his wife? Or did her social cachet, as the wife of a successful author, carry her through? For it must be remembered that Bennett, although successful, was also a Northerner, and said 'first class' to rhyme with 'gas': how many thousands a year, and how much glamour, does one need to live that down in an East Anglian golf club?

Marguerite, anyway, did not have to languish alone any more that year, for in October Arnold took her off to the Continent for a month's visit. They took the steamer from Harwich to Antwerp, where Bennett wasted a lot of time looking for a room which he had seen sixteen years before and never found: a typical novelist's pursuit. Then they went to Brussels, where they had news from New York that *The Great Adventure* had opened and was not the success that had been hoped. From Brussels they went to Paris, to the Hôtel du Rhin, which seemed to have become their favourite resting place. There they met many old friends – the Godebskis, Calvocoressi, Gide, Roy Devereux, Émile Martin, the Cornilliers, Ravel. Bennett went to see a nude Russian dancer with Calvo, and to buy a small Vuillard with Cipa Godebski (it cost £100). They returned to England in the first week of November. He was working on nothing but an idea for a new play, *Don Juan*, which had been in his mind ever since he had first written an outline of it in 1909 for Tree, and Tree had told Mathews that he hadn't 'enough dash to carry it off'. For the year, again, his output was to be low but his income high – he was obliged, on 31 December, to reckon the year in terms of books published (*The Regent, Paris Nights, The Plain Man and His Wife, The Great Adventure*) rather than in terms of works written (most of *The Price of Love, The Story-teller's Craft*, other articles, two short stories, one act of a play). Nor was the quality of what he had produced very high. *The Price of Love* is a workman-like novel, but little more: the struggle he had to write it, his doubts while writing it, and the fact that it was a serial, not a serious novel, indicate that it was not one of his most satisfying achievements.

The story, in fact, is for once better than what Bennett made of it: a proof of fatigue? It has a fine Jamesian complexity, or could have had. A forgetful old lady is left with nearly a thousand pounds cash in her house for the night; in the house also are her two grandnephews, one in trouble with his employer for fiddling with the petty cash, the other on his way to South Africa. Also her new young companion Rachel, who loves the petty cash crook, elegant Louis. During the night the money disappears. The old lady has a stroke, and dies. Rachel marries Louis. Where is the money? After several months cousin Julian returns from South Africa and confesses that he took half the money; he returns it. Louis starts to confess to his bride that he had taken the other half, but she turns on him and rejects his explanation in horror. Finally, it emerges that Rachel was responsible for the loss of Louis's money, for he had dropped it in the grate, and she had lit a fire in the grate. Penitent, she asks forgiveness. She knows that Louis is unreliable, a liar and a thief and a spendthrift, but she 'reconciled herself to the prospect of an everlasting vigil' – she loves him, she takes him on, weakness and all, for 'one tragedy alone could overthrow her – Louis' death'.[54] As for Louis, he knows that he has the upper hand, in his terms, for he knows he loves her less than she loves him. It is a neat little drama of love and suspicion, and in James's hands could have been left full of unspoken ambiguities and unresolved acts of faith; but that is not Bennett's way. He spells his characters out, as well as their actions – Julian is glum, blunt, self-accusing, and becomes a prey to remorse, Louis is idle, frivolous, shallow and winning, and Rachel is perfectly motivated by a quite indecorous selfish and corrupting sexual passion. It is not, really, nearly as well done as it could have been; some of the Five Towns scenes are good, such as the one where Louis seduces Rachel from her shopping into attending the cinema, and the one where Rachel visits Julian in his disgusting bedsitter, but on the whole the book is written down. This must have been partly the effect of writing for serialization: he felt obliged to aim lower than his theme demanded. James spotted this: while admiring the book to Pinker, he said that Bennett had 'rather declined in it on too easy a style', but at the same time he praised it highly, saying to Pinker, 'Oh, tell him if you will that I was greatly interested, and finished the book with great envy – envy of him and of his possession of such material. The two young men in it are perfectly realized, so salient and altogether so presented. I have no material like that, and I envy him that.'[55]

Despite tributes from such high quarters, Bennett was not convinced. An uncharacteristic note of far from false modesty comes into his tone whenever he discusses the work: writing to Pinker about Methuen's liking for it, he says: 'Everybody so far who has read this book seems to be very enthusiastic as to it, but no one has yet been able to inspire me with his enthusiasm.'[56] This glumness is accompanied, at much the same period, by a characteristically generous but somewhat depressed tribute to Conrad – he had written to Conrad towards the end of 1912, expressing deep admiration of *Nostromo*, *The Secret Agent* and *Under Western Eyes*, and now, in January 1914, reading *Chance*, he says in his journal: 'This is a discouraging book for a writer, because he damn well knows he can't write as well as this . . . simply superb.'[57] In the November before, he had said to himself as he sat reading history, 'I am 46. On the decline. Why fill my head with knowledge?'[58] He had sensibly repressed the thought, but it lingered.

His other work of 1913, *Don Juan de Marana*, which he finished on 31 January 1914, is not very reassuring either. He had had it on his mind since before he and Knoblock wrote *Milestones*, but he does not seem to have written it with much sense of joy, and despite various overtures and payments from various managements it was never performed. There is not much to be said about it: it is an unrealistic historical drama, with an ever-changing cast of dying ladies and hidalgoes, a few good jokes and a lot of nonsense. Don Juan, like Rachel in *The Price of Love*, staked all on his ideal of love, but alas, he is utterly uninteresting and unconvincing.

Artistically, then, this was a bad patch, but it had its human compensations. After Bennett's Paris trip in November, Ravel came to stay at Comarques for a few days. Bennett took him on a tour of the antique shops of Ipswich, where they bought 'a few things'. One wonders what Ravel made of Thorpe-le-Soken and Marguerite's involvement in golf clubs, parish concerts and village recreation clubs. Rickards and Doran came for Christmas. Meanwhile, Bennett was constantly being asked for articles – Squire was clearly keen to involve him in the *New Statesman*, of which he later became a director, and R.A.Scott-James wanted an article for his new periodical, *The New Weekly*. He was now so famous that even his oldest pieces were becoming saleable, and perhaps unwisely, in view of the line he had taken with Sarolea, he allowed one of his first plays, *A Good Woman*, to be produced in February in a mixed bill at the Palace Theatre: it appeared along with a one-acter called *L'Impresario*, about an escaped madman and a lady singing wild gipsy songs. *The Times* said it was an amusing little trifle, but Bennett did not think much of it. Nor did he allow his name to be put to an adaptation of *Helen with the High Hand*, by Richard Pryce, which opened at the Vaudeville on 17 February: wisely, for the critics did not much like the play and referred the audiences to the novel. Nothing could stop people from trying to jump on to the bandwagon, however; in July yet another hopeful adaptor was negotiating to put *The Grand Babylon Hotel* on the stage.

In the spring he escaped yet again from the 'crass inertia and stupidity'[59] of his neighbours by going on another yachting trip, this time efficiently taking with him car, wife and chauffeur as well. The *Velsa* went via the canals of France to Marseilles. Bennett and Marguerite went via Paris, where on 6 March they saw the Godebskis, Viñes, Fargue, and Calvo, and then on to Marseilles, where they joined the *Velsa* on 13 March. For the rest of March and for the whole of April they yachted off the coast of France and Italy, and drove inland, sight-seeing. As usual, he is breathtakingly and irresistibly

honest about his sight-seeing. For instance, he records: 'April 22. Orvieto....
Went to find very early church. S. Giovanni, *très* primitive. After we had
entered it and gone away, it occurred to me that we had not seen it at all,
but another quite ordinary church. So much for one's artistic education.
On gobe tout.'[60] For such remarks one loves the man. At Villino Chiaso they
called for tea on Max Beerbohm (who much admired Bennett's work); in
Fontainebleau on 3 May they prided themselves on having driven back from
Rome 'without killing even a fowl'. For the whole holiday, he had written
hardly a word, except for his journal. But work was waiting for him at
home.

Unfortunately but understandably, he did not feel much like it, after so
long a break. He must also have felt rather nervous, for it was no mere serial
or article lying in wait for him, but the third part of *Clayhanger*, which he
could not afford to botch. It was too earnestly and impatiently awaited. He
had had ideas on it before – that it should be autobiographical, that it should
reveal the daily intimacies of marriage. In a letter to Mrs Herzog he says:
'Wells's new novel, Marriage, of which I have just read the proofs, contains
more intimate conveyances of the *atmosphere* of married life than anybody
has ever achieved before. I am rather annoyed, as I am about to try to get the
same intimacy in my Clayhanger–Hilda book, entitled These Twain.'[61] But
in his immediate planning, in May 1914, he says: 'I seemed to get little
inspirational force for it.' He bridged the gap by playing tennis and sketching
with Rickards, and then got the final impulse merely from reading the
reviews, not even the book, of Mrs Parnell's *Life of Parnell*. There was a
full-page review in *The Times* of 19 May, and on 21 May another long piece
in *The Times Literary Supplement*, which Bennett read, and which em-
phasized the passionate nature of Parnell's love, which was 'fierce, hungry,
relentless, measureless, the love which made him hold her over the raging
waves and threaten to jump in with her . . . the love that made him tell her
it was hers "whether it be our heaven or our hell".'[62] For his book, he remembered, was to be about a heroic love. Yes, that was it, that was what he had
lost sight of, and the newspapers brought it back to him, in all its significance. Edwin's love for Hilda must also be relentless and measureless: he
had got it, he knew how he was going to do it, and at five to six in the
morning on 26 May he got up and began.

These Twain has been generally considered a falling off, a disappointment,
an unworthy successor to its two predecessors. Similarly, *Hilda Lessways*
has been considered inferior to *Clayhanger*. And so maybe they are, if one
must insist on marking books as though for an examination. But both these

latter two books have so much meaning that I cannot see them in comparative terms at all.

These Twain is the story of a marriage. It was written out of experience and disappointment, and out of a kind of triumph. Marriage is appalling, says Bennett, but it is worth it. And he was well qualified to make the statement. The book opens on tension. Hilda and Edwin, newly married, after many preceding dramas of bigamy and illness and separation, have come together again: and, it has not been enough remarked, they come together with the curious difference and apartness of the *Titanic* and the iceberg. (The *Titanic* sank in April 1912; Hardy commemorated the event in a poem called 'The Convergence of the Twain'.) The first two novels in the sequence, uniquely as far as I know, convey the impression of complete separateness and individuality of vision: so that the Edwin glimpsed by Hilda in *Hilda Lessways* is utterly different, utterly distinct from the Edwin who sees and puzzles over Hilda in *Clayhanger*. It is a stupendous effect. Edwin, to the reader, is a perplexed uncertain boy, afraid of his father, ashamed of his sisters, a compromiser, a coward; to Hilda, he is a profile in a window, 'tall, rather lanky, fair, with hair dishevelled, and a serious, studious, and magnanimous face . . .'; he is 'wistful, romantic, full of sad subtleties, of the unknown and the seductive, and of a latent benevolence . . . as recondite and as sympathetic as the town in which she had discovered him'.[63] To Hilda the ignorant, he is a hero. And to Edwin, she is at first an ugly young woman, and finally a heroine, mysterious, unpredictable, who can cry, after years of separation, dramatically, 'My heart never kissed any other man but you!'[64]

These Twain is the story of the conjunction of these two unlikely people, and of their discovery of one another in the state of marriage. They do not, of course, ever manage to discover or understand each other: they remain apart, baffled, flung emotionally from row to reconciliation to row again, in a perpetual battle. If Bennett's own marriage was like this – and one has good cause to suspect that it was worse, that the novel is an idealization, an attempt to come to terms with an even grimmer reality – then he must have been exhausted by it. Hilda and Edwin quarrel passionately – about his business, about her treatment of big James, about where she puts the furniture, about where to live. Hilda is much of the time distinctly unsympathetic – bad with servants, quarrelsome, petulant. Her cry 'Edwin never praises me!' was one of Marguerite's favourite cries about Arnold. And yet she is intensely alive, and the relationship is intensely real. With hardly an explicit word about sex, Bennett manages to convey her sensuality and their intimacy; and indeed, they disagree so much of the time about practical matters and about ideas that the reader slowly becomes aware that sex is their only bond. Despite the warfare of marriage, Bennett says, 'the heat of their kisses had not cooled; but to him at any rate the kisses often seemed intensely illogical; for, though he regarded himself as an improving expert in the science of life, he had not yet begun to perceive that those kisses were the only true logic of their joint career'.[65] This was a discovery that Bennett must have made years earlier about his own wife: was it going to prove enough? By this time he must, severely, have doubted; he must have been haunted, as Edwin was, by stories of divorces amongst friends and in the papers.

In view of the amount of personal feeling that Bennett clearly puts into the novel, it's amazing to see how solid and balanced it remains. It is, like its predecessors, a remarkable picture of the texture and conflicts and richness of provincial life. The events are commonplace in the extreme (with one exception, in the form of a visit to Dartmoor where Hilda glimpses her earlier lover, George Cannon – this extravagant piece of plot is exceptionally contrived, for Bennett in one of his serious works). There is a musical evening, a children's birthday party, a trip round Edwin's factory, a hospital scene. A musical factory inspector, a bachelor, turns out to have a mistress; Hilda despises Edwin's sister Clara and at the same time feels jealous of her; Edwin sees Janet Orgreaves and Hilda giggling together like children, though they are both forty; a servant gets pregnant; Hilda's son has bad eyesight. Out of such ordinary stuff Bennett creates real drama, real tension. The ageing of Janet Orgreaves, into the eternal spinster, is done superbly; so is the transformation of Clara from the pert little girl who loathes Auntie Hamps into the mother bowed down with maternity, sycophantic and domestic, vain and censorious, with no thoughts in her head except for her children. There is a marvellous, complicated scene at Bert Benbow's twelfth birthday party, where Hilda at first feels completely superior to Clara and all she possesses. She despises her furniture, she loathes her domesticity, she sees her husband as 'a stoutish, somewhat clay-dusted man' who looks rather ridiculous neglecting his business for his child's party. But she is forced by the power of the situation to join in, to try to do her bit, to fling her sovereigns about, to compete with Auntie Hamps's frightful generosity. This is what it is like, she says to herself, to marry a family. She sits there hating them for their bigotry and lack of feeling, their ignorance and self-conceit: 'They did not know what joy was, and they did not want anybody else to know what joy was.'[66] She thinks that she would prefer her own child to go to the devil, and herself to be thoroughly abandoned, to a life like Clara's. And then, in the middle of all this violent loathing, Clara's smallest child comes in, says a few words, climbs on her knee and falls asleep. Hilda watches: 'Clara smiled down at the child sleeping on her lap. She was happy. The child was happy. . . . Everybody gazed at the picture with secret and profound pleasure. Hilda wished once more that George was only two and a half years old again. . . . She was envious. . . . And yet a minute ago, she had been execrating the family life of the Benbows. The complexity of the tissue of existence was puzzling.'[67]

In such passages it seems to me that Bennett succeeds marvellously in catching the complexity, the minute fluctuations of thought and feeling that make up daily life. There are many more. The book is full of the ordinary efforts of fairly ordinary people to amuse themselves, to look after one another, to achieve joy in a limited environment. Hilda has a restless, envious, difficult nature, but she tries, and on the whole she succeeds. Edwin himself is difficult, and far more critically portrayed than the idealized middle-aged heroes of the later Bennett novels. Bennett's achievement in making the purchase of fish a romantic moment is amazing. Like Edwin and Hilda, he has to work hard, but he manages it.

Much of the inspiration of the novel, clearly, came from Bennett's own marriage, which had never been smooth and by this time was far from easy: the act of writing the book at all was an act of the will. But there were other sources as well as Marguerite. This was to be his last novel of the Five Towns: did he too feel moments of revulsion from the domestic life of his sisters at home, as Hilda feels from Clara? The ending of the novel was certainly affected by a major event in his own life, the death of his mother.

Mrs Bennett died on 23 November 1914, when he was two-thirds of the way through the novel. Two-thirds of the way through the novel, Auntie Hamps falls ill and dies. And that was the end of the Five Towns: he never wrote of them again, in any depth. Auntie Hamps was not of course modelled on Mrs Bennett, who was a much more quiet, retiring character, with more in common with the home-loving but independent Constance Povey of *The Old Wives' Tale*; but the circumstances of her death were used by Bennett nevertheless. In his journal for 20 November he notes the objects in his mother's bedroom, as he sat with her up in Burslem; some of the same objects are described again in the novel. Above all he noticed the 'damp chill' – Edwin feels that 'the terrible damp chill of the Five Towns winter hung in the bedroom like an invisible miasma',[68] and Bennett notes that the temperature in his dying mother's room is barely 60 degrees. Not much emotion enters his journal as he describes his mother's death: in the face of death and funeral arrangements he was as calm and reasonable as ever, refusing to allow the coffin to be taken 'the longest journey' to the cemetery, and saying, merely, of her death itself, that her condition was distressing, though less distressing than his father's, and 'it seemed strange that this should necessarily be the end of a life, that a life couldn't end more easily'.[69] (She died of arterial sclerosis and congestion of the lungs.) There was no reason why he should be unduly distressed over her death: she had reached a reasonable age – she was seventy-four – and he was conscious that he had looked after her to the best of his ability. She had chosen the coldness of the Five Towns; she preferred it up there. He had lured her down south on several occasions; a year earlier Walpole had met her at Comarques and described her, rather condescendingly, as Bennett's 'funny old Five Towns mother. She is obviously where he gets it all from. She sits beside him and keeps him in his place.'[70] But she could hardly have felt at home with people like Walpole, or with Marguerite for that matter. Like Constance, she preferred to die among her own furniture, however disagreeable that furniture might appear to her successful and discriminating son.

The death of Auntie Hamps is magnificently described: it is, as Bennett makes us well aware, the death of an era. Thrifty Auntie Hamps, who wore black silks, jet ornaments and seal-skins, had presented a glorious front to the world for years, but Edwin, in penetrating the defenceless fastness of her bedroom, finds all her 'squalid avaricious secrets'[71] revealed. Did he find his own mother's bedroom similarly squalid? Probably he did. Her appearance, her dying vagaries, her final meannesses about coal on the fire, her unwillingness to relinquish power, are all ruthlessly described: he has no pity on her. And even at the end, Edwin cannot help speculating on the conundrum at the heart of her being: did she really believe in her own hypocrisy or not? Did she actually believe in the God whose mottoes adorn her bedroom wall? Did those who spoke at her funeral actually believe that she was a saint, and an absolutely irreparable loss to the circuit? There is no answer. The secrets of the bedroom can be exposed, but not the secrets and duplicities of the Wesleyan Methodist heart.

Edwin refuses to have the burial service at the Wesleyan chapel, even though Clara points out that it would be heated. He has it at home instead. Like Bennett, he refuses to let his aunt take the longest journey. Like Bennett, he notices in the graveyard an inscription to a man who had outlived several young wives. Such immediate use of such intimate material is perhaps a little startling. But he knew that he would use it, now, and then bury it for good. He had been an exceptionally loyal son, but his dislike of the district he was born in was allowed to flourish after her death. Before her death he went back frequently to visit her. After it he hardly went back at all. It is a suitable irony that his first Five Towns novel, *Anna*, should have received its impetus partly from the death of his father, while his last, *These Twain*, was written over the last few months of his mother's life. With it, a whole period of his life and work was over.

10
Wartime

These Twain took him nearly a year to write. He finished it on 12 February 1915. *Clayhanger* had taken him only six months, and was longer. But then not only death but war intervened. The minor triumphs and irritations of July – an operation in Paris (did she not trust English doctors?) for Marguerite, a celebratory dinner for the 500th performance of *The Great Adventure* (guests including the Selwyns, Mimi Godebski, the Polish Joseph Retinger and his wife, Robert Loraine), a moment of satisfaction with the novel when he thinks of a new yacht – all these were swallowed up in the outbreak of war, on 5 August. Bennett was one of those who had not foreseen the war, and who prophesied that it would all be over in six months. How much he genuinely thought this, and how much he thought it was the right thing to say, it is hard to tell, for the war certainly showed Bennett as a responsible citizen, keenly aware of his role as a public figure. When war broke out, he had his nephews staying with him for their summer holidays, which must have heightened his anxiety, for they could hear firing over the Channel, although cross-Channel services from Harwich to the Hook were advertised as usual. The reality of war crept over him slowly – increases in the price of petrol and butter, the need for blackout, a fall in the value of his property, the loss of staff – and, more profoundly and tragically, the ruin of Belgium, which he had loved, and which had been to him a symbol of the Continent, his gateway to escape. On 21 August the fall of Brussels struck him as 'a great spectacular depressing fact',[1] however hard he tried to convince himself, along with millions of others, that the Allies knew what they were doing. His innate sense of humour and proportion gleam through his reports – he realizes that moving the boats inland at Brightlingsea isn't going to affect much, but that people have a need for action at such times, a need to hide their silver and their possessions. He himself was eager for news, and had telegrams sent direct from London with all the latest information by Central News; when he asks the local postmaster to use these war telegrams for public consumption by sticking them in the window of the Post Office, he is amused when his secretary Miss Nerney reports that people reading the telegram asked ' "Who is Arnold Bennett?" The reply was: "He's the War Minister." Then, in correction, "Oh no he isn't. He's the actor chap that lives down the road." '2

He embarked almost at once on a series of war articles for the *Daily News*, a fairly radical paper, which in the first days of the war carried pieces by Shaw, Wells and Galsworthy as well, though it was Bennett who settled down as their regular literary contributor. He had in fact a good connection with the paper: it began serializing *The Price of Love* on 4 August, though it had to suspend publication for lack of space four days later, and on 30 July it had carried a large interview in which Bennett had discussed the serial form, the risks of writing for the theatre, his own interest in the theatre and other such matters. Now he had to turn his attention to very different subjects.

His first article appeared on 24 August, and dealt with 'what the German conscript thinks' – evidently there had been a mass of journalistic speculation about whether or not the average German soldier was behind the war. Bennett says how dangerous it is to generalize about national characteristics – although he knows the French and their language and country well, he says, he wouldn't dare to generalize about their attitudes to war, so how could he do the same for Germany when all he knew of the country was a journey through Schleswig-Holstein and a trip by yacht through Kiel harbour? However, he decides it would be rash to consider the average German soldier uncommitted to the war. His second piece, on 1 September, dealt with the inadequacy of British soldiers' pay – 'Starvation is precisely the same thing for all classes. The way which we pay our defenders is ... a starvation wage. . . . To say that patriotism should be above money is mere impudence in the mouths of the elderly rich.' He was to return to this theme again and again, in pieces on the amateur administration of the Prince of Wales Fund, on inadequate relief for the families of soldiers, on the discrimination of family allowances – if illegitimate children, he says, are allowed to fight and die for their country, why shouldn't their mothers get state relief? Other subjects which he dealt with, in a more or less regular weekly Thursday page, were panic-buying and spy scares, the dangers of press censorship of news ('War News for Infants', runs one of his headlines), the rough treatment of keen recruits, the dangers of recruiting oratory, and conscription. Bennett was set against conscription, at this stage. These articles involved a good deal of work: by October he says he was spending a day and a half a week on war journalism. He comments, calmly, on the drop in his theatrical receipts, due to the war, and also to the drop in the commercial value of war stories abroad, due to the fact that the foreign market was flooded with distinguished war copy. He offers help, via Pinker, to authors in financial distress, and attends, on 3 September, a meeting of eminent authors, with Masterman in the chair; others present were Barrie, Wells, Chesterton, Hardy and Zangwill.

There wasn't really much for civilians to do, and people reacted differently to inertia. Bennett took the orthodox line, and in November became the military representative of the Thorpe Division Emergency Committee, a post which did not seem to carry many responsibilities, but which involved an impressive meeting with a Major-General Heath, who managed to persuade Bennett that it was the right thing to do. Marguerite, meanwhile, organized sales of work in aid of Belgian refugees, and encouraged people to make Red Cross shirts, with her usual energy. Miss Nerney took a part-time job in the local hospital. But such pursuits were not very satisfying, and most people felt a frustrated need for action. Wells, in August, had written to *The Times* urging the British public to organize itself against invasion, and to take to guerrilla warfare, if need be; this letter caused quite a stir, and he followed it up with another on 31 October, repudiating the stuffy military view that fighting was for the army, and saying: 'Let the expert have no illusions as to what we ordinary people are going to do if we find German soldiers in England one morning. We are going to fight. . . . Many men, and not a few women, will turn out to shoot. . . . If the experts attempt any pedantic interference, we will shoot the experts.'[3] Bennett clearly found this attitude somewhat irresponsible, as would many others less realistic than he; Major-General Heath, and all the army, naturally thought that Wells was crazy. On 3 December Bennett wrote to *The Times* saying that 'a civilian's spirit can only be properly shown in one way. That way is to enlist in the regular forces' . . . 'The military authorities absolutely discountenance any form of civilian fighting.'[4] Wells replied immediately, on 5 December, with a complete recantation, saying: 'Now let every man join something recognised and get his gun . . . my threat has completely served its purpose.'[5] It is hard not to take Bennett's side on this issue: what could have been more dangerous than a population of armed and paranoid and utterly gullible citizens? On the other hand, Wells too had his point, for on the day when his first letter was published *The Times* ran a column on 'War Preparation', and a major item reads: 'Instruct your keeper immediately to stop feeding your pheasants with maize or corn.' A certain amount of urgency had to be forced into the situation, and Wells helped to do it.

The intense patriotism, during the war years, of writers of Bennett's, Shaw's and Wells's generation has seemed strange to those reared on an anti-war diet of Wilfred Owen, Robert Graves and Siegfried Sassoon, but the fact remains that many sensible people, who certainly would not have called themselves patriots in peacetime, were so deeply affected by events that their emotion had to find some practical outlet. Henry James was so moved that he took British citizenship: Pinker was one of his sponsors. He followed the course of the war so closely that he, through Pinker, was one of Bennett's chief informants. Bennett, who had declared that he was not much of a man for committees, found himself on several. It is easy to dismiss the chrysanthemum shows and village concerts and soldiers' clubs as a frivolous waste of time, but people felt they had to do something: Wells in his letter to *The Times* said plaintively: 'We are not being used. We are made to feel out of it,'[6] and that was the general cry. It is hard now to imagine the confusion, the widespread fear of invasion, the uncertainty as to what to do if it occurred. Bennett found himself involved in a ridiculous drama of passwords and secret arrangements, and writes in his journal in exasperation, in December 1914, 'We haven't yet been able to get out of Headquarters what roads they will want if there is a raid, nor to settle with police what the signal will be.'[7] There was so little to be done, and so much to worry about. Bennett redrafted Major-General Heath's proclamation about sniping in the case of invasion: the affair of sniping, stirred up by Wells, was weighing heavy on Heath's mind. Bennett listened to the sound of guns, and counted the boats sunk, and caught the authorities out by deliberately taking maps into forbidden zones, and then writing them strong letters asking why they didn't stop him. Country life became more and more uncomfortable – the part-time cook drank, the chauffeur was suspected quite unjustly of being a German spy, another member of staff had to go off on an explosives course. It was not surprising that in 1915 Arnold Bennett found the lure of London, with its clubs and its committees and its gossip and its semblance of action, more attractive than the concerts of Thorpe. By this time, he was finding at least his middle-class neighbours too much for him: after a concert in December 1914, he says bleakly 'The ordeal is too much.'[8]

During the winter of 1914–15, he had his niece and nephew, Mary Kennerley (Tertia's daughter) and Richard Bennett (Frank's son) to stay, and livened himself up with an energetic and lengthy row by correspondence with Whigham of the *Metropolitan* magazine about a short story. In January, they had officers billeted on them, and forty horses in the yard. Early in February he finished *These Twain*, and thereafter spent most of his time till the end of March in London, engaged in committee work – principally for the Wounded Allies Relief Committee – and eating innumerable dinners and lunches in innumerable clubs. He had succumbed to a need universal at times of crisis, the need to talk. He saw all his old friends – Rickards, Pauline Smith, Alexander Webster (who was now married to Pauline's sister), Cedric Sharpe, his sisters Tertia and Emily, his brother Septimus, E.V.Lucas, Wells, Knoblock. Knoblock introduced a little diversion with schemes for filming some of Bennett's novels. He also made new friends over this period of intense club life, which was permanently to affect his social habits. He consolidated his acquaintance with Frank Swinnerton, who was now becoming one of his most intimate friends. They had met, briefly, in 1911: their first encounter was over lunch at the Authors' Club, a meeting which Swinnerton, then a young aspiring author and publisher, describes in his *Autobiography* (London, 1937): it had been slightly strained, and Swinnerton had been overawed and nervous, despite Bennett's praise of his novels. They didn't meet again till three years later, when they had lunch again, much more successfully, and Bennett invited Swinnerton to spend a weekend on the *Velsa*, which he did. In the autumn of 1914, however, Swinnerton was seriously ill and in bed for several months. To his surprise, Bennett kept the friendship up during this period, and in 1915, when, by his own account, they got to 'know each other really well', he emerged from his sickbed sporting a 'dramatic red beard'. They were to see a great deal of each other during the war years, and afterwards; both Bennett and Wells liked Swinnerton immensely, and were pleased to have found a protégé who responded so well to their paternal encouragements. Swinnerton, for his part, was very fond of Bennett, and sensitive to his problems: he very quickly picked up the sense that all was not quite well with Bennett's country house life.

Bennett was staying more and more in London. It was at this period, in 1915, that he transferred his allegiance from the Authors' Club to the Royal Yacht Club, which became his favourite refuge.

Other clubs which saw a great deal of him were the Reform, the Garrick, the National Sporting and the Automobile. In many ways, life went on much the same as usual for many people: the Bennetts visited concerts and the Royal Academy and went shopping; new plays opened. On 23 March Bennett went to the premiere of Barrie's *Rosie Rapture*, which was 'a frost, and most of it extremely poor',[9] but which nevertheless provided him with the public satisfaction of being 'greeted by cries in the pit of my name'.[10] On 25 March he agreed to become a director of the *New Statesman*; on 1 April he returned to Comarques, and on 2 April he began a new serial, intended for the *Strand* magazine, called *The Lion's Share*, which he says is 'light, and of intent not deeply imagined'.

During April and May he not only struggled with his new novel; he also had to brood over a new commitment. For while in London he had arranged, through the offices of G.H.Mair, to accompany Mair on a tour of the Western Front. On 17 April Pinker came to stay, unusually, to discuss negotiations for this journey, for it was a delicate business: it was not easy to get permits to visit France, and the fact that Bennett got one at all was a sign of the respect he commanded. Bennett wrote on 7 April to Pinker saying that the news that he was going must not get about in newspaper offices or 'the permission to go may be jeopardized, as there is a great deal of jealousy, etc.'. They got off all right, on 21 June, a couple of weeks later than they intended, but Bennett cannot have spent the intervening weeks in happy anticipation. The war was not going well: on 8 May came the news of the sinking of the *Lusitania*, which Bennett could hardly believe. Ironically, on the same day, Marguerite had gone early into Pauline Smith's room (she was staying at Comarques at the time) full of excitement about an article which she had written, and which had been accepted by a French magazine. Her news fell flat against Arnold's depression, and she had yet another reason for blaming him for her lack of artistic progress. For Marguerite, in her own way, was beginning to thrive on the war: she liked the officers and the concerts and the dances, she liked singing songs to the troops, though whether or not they liked it is another matter. Society in Thorpe was livelier, in some ways, than it had ever been: the tennis clubs 'flourish greatly because the officers belong to them'[11] and Marguerite had a patriotic excuse for giving dances herself. On the other hand, she was also nervous and agitated, obsessed by war rumours and stories about spies. Both Pauline Smith and Swinnerton noted, in their different ways, that her behaviour was odd, and on one occasion Bennett was driven from his usual reticence about her into whispering to Swinnerton, in the middle of a particularly long recitation to the officers, 'If that damned woman doesn't stop soon, we shall be late for dinner.'[12]

Until his departure, Bennett worked methodically on his new novel, only slightly ruffled by the news that *The Lion's Share*, intended for the *Metropolitan* in America and the *Strand* in Britain, had been the subject (before being read) of a committee meeting of the *Strand*: 'They held a meeting of directors and solemnly decided that the *Strand* could not print a suffragette serial. However, I think that I have reassured them.'[13] He was wrong; he had not. They would not touch such hot stuff, although Bennett's tone is far from militant, and although he promises in rather a cowardly fashion that suffragettism shall not triumph in his pages. Eventually the serial was published by the *Grand* magazine, and in book form by Cassells in 1916. It is, in fact, a very strange production, on one level quite ridiculous in its fanciful plot and detective-story atmosphere, and on another level a perfectly convincing and rather delicate picture of contrasting life-styles in Paris and elsewhere. One's chief complaint is that Bennett has put far too much in, and that the serious and the comic and the impossibly offhand are jumbled together in a most confusing fashion. The novel opens with the heroine, Audrey Moze, about to run away from home and her despotic father, in Ann Veronica manner. Home is the village of Moze, a seaside village in East Anglia, and thus the novel gives Bennett an excuse for loving and delightful descriptions of rivers, yachts, sunsets and seascapes. Within a few pages, Audrey's parents have both died, and she is left with an enormous fortune, which she wrests from a rival claimant on the will with unladylike determination. Then, disguised as a widow in order to have more fun, she sets off for Paris with a middle-aged feminist friend. In Paris the two ladies live at first on the Left Bank, in the Quartier, near Montparnasse, and mix with artistic society, thus providing Bennett with an excellent opportunity for descriptions of café life, of ladies' studios, of his old friends, his old homes (the rue d'Aumale appears, briefly), of artistic parties. Various characters are immediately recognizable: Ravel/Roussel appears in his midnight-blue suit, an artist called Miss Thomkins plays the role of Miss Thomasson who spent a couple of arduous hours ineffectually 'whipping up a mayonnaise for an impromptu lunch'.[14] This part of the novel is full of life: Audrey's excitement at the sight of her first café, with its heterogeneous population of men, women, girls, old men, children, billiard players, and its chromatic ices and coloured lobsters, is communicated with enthusiasm and was Bennett's own. Audrey, naturally, falls in love with a young violinist, about to be 'discovered', and less naturally gets herself involved with a militant group of suffragettes – but before she commits herself to the suffragette cause, she abandons the Left Bank faithlessly one day, on an impulse, and goes over to the Right Bank, where she hires a car and a chauffeur, takes a suite at the Hôtel de Danube, and buys a lot of expensive clothes. The contrast between the glamour of the Left Bank and the glamour of the Right Bank is done with considerable skill.

After this point, however, the novel begins to fall into the intricacies of its own plot. Audrey returns to London, gets mixed up with hiding a militant suffragette, gets chased by the police herself, escapes in a yacht, returns to Paris, arranges a concert for her pet violinist, quarrels with him, nearly marries somebody else, marries him. The mixture is too rich. Even Bennett's disagreeable Essex gardener Lockyer appears, under the name of Aguilar, and ends up by marrying a militant. It is in many ways a good read and a pure escape novel for both reader and writer – Bennett enjoyed writing about the charms of studio life, the delights of living on a yacht, the glamour of the Rue de la Paix, and all the more so as he was writing, in 1915, with some nostalgia, of things he might never see again. The yearning for luxury, and the lavish descriptions of it, which had been pure fantasy in early novels like *The Grand Babylon Hotel*, written when Bennett was working long hours for a few pounds a week, now have a solid reality. Bennett is familiar, now, with women whose handbags cost 1,200 francs, with the way that chauffeurs bully their underlings and demand breakfast in the best hotels; and his descriptions, though they have the same admiration for expense and quality, are also by now well informed and much more shrewd.

But the novel, as the *Strand* magazine suspected, does also have its more serious side, however overlaid it may be with frivolous side-issues. It was impossible not to treat of the suffragettes with some degree of seriousness. Bennett's heroine Audrey, not unlike Ann Veronica herself, is a fluctuating supporter of the cause: at one moment she is completely persuaded of its importance, and much moved by those who try to convert her, whereas at the next she is accusing one of the organizers of selfishness, bossiness and monomania. Interestingly, the middle- and upper-class suffragettes in the novel do emerge as self-interested bullies, more interested in personal power than in the cause itself, whereas the most sympathetic suffragette, Jane Foley, is a mill girl from Lancashire. Jane Foley is allowed her moment of conviction and tells the story of her labouring childhood and her subsequent imprisonments so affectingly and pleasantly that Audrey is convinced, momentarily, of the 'total futility of such matters as motor cars, fine raiment, beautiful boudoirs and correctness'.[15] But Audrey herself is no martyr: she wants a man, and she wants her own money, so she gets one and keeps the other. The tone of the novel would not have permitted her to do anything else, but nevertheless Bennett is able to use her as a vehicle for a considerable amount of serious reflection about the woman's role, and the alternative types he introduces all have a ring of conviction. There is Madame Piriac, Audrey's French cousin, who has a very French marriage with a much older and very important man who never seems to appear except occasionally in an opera box: she stands for the French attitude to Woman, sophisticated, worldly, feminine, expensive, full of duplicity and intelligence. There are the two American painter spinsters of indeterminate age: feminist, generous, independent, eccentric. One of them devotes herself to the cause; the other, very quietly, marries a wealthy man. There is Jane Foley, the working-class militant. There is Rosamund, the middle-class, middle-aged, gracious, vain, domineering suffragette organizer, who feeds on power and admiration. There is Miss Ingate, an eccentric muddled spinster whose enthusiasm for the cause is even more fluctuating than Audrey's own, and who is determined to stay out of prison at all costs. These are Audrey's models. What did Bennett himself feel about women's role, and the right of women to vote?

As we have seen, his own personal problems made it extremely difficult for him in real life to relate his feelings about women to his intellectual conceptions of them. His responses were thoroughly confused by the varying expectations of his class, his past background, his present background, and his own needs. At the same time, he wrote of women with more real understanding than most of his contemporaries, and his female characters are at least as memorable and central as his male. He could admire and catch the flavour and life-style of a Miss Thomkins, with her studio full of 'old easels, canvases, old frames, old costumes and multifarious other properties for pictures, trunks, lamps, boards, tables, and bric-à-brac bought at the Ham-and-Old-Iron Fair'[16] – Miss Thomkins made her own bed, and cleaned her own boots, and ate when she fancied at restaurants where she usually met a few friends, worked when she wanted, went out to a café when she got bored, and fell asleep amidst 'cups and saucers, lingerie, masterpieces and boots'.[17] There is no hint of masculine criticism or bias in this portrait: it is detailed, admiring, affectionate. He didn't like mess himself, but he liked other people to like it. He did not want all women to be like Madame Piriac, expensive well-organized sexual objects; but at the same time he wanted the Madame Piriacs to continue to exist. He liked difficult, independent, forthright women, and he approved of the determination of a minority to obtain political rights. On the other hand, being a sensible man, he also rightly foresaw what a disaster, in terms of progress, voting women would be. His answer to a questionnaire from the New Age about women's suffrage in 1911 is whole-hearted in its support, though he criticizes certain aspects of the campaign, particularly 'the behaviour of certain husbands of martyrs' – 'No hysterical male antics,' he says, 'would in the slightest degree weaken my own convinced support of the cause of women's suffrage; but then I am not lukewarm, while the electorate as a whole is either lukewarm or indifferent.'[18]

On militant methods, he is diplomatic. He says he can see no alternative, but does not give them unqualified approval, for he suggests they may be counter-productive: a fairly safe view, but certainly not antagonistic. In a series of articles on women which he wrote in 1920, published under the title *Our Women*, he says quite firmly that all girls should be professionally trained for a domestic or extra-domestic career, unless ill or feeble-minded, and foresees a future where women pilot aeroplanes, and take their husbands out to dinner because they are earning higher salaries. He is caustic about the life of idle luxury which had become a status symbol for the wives of successful men, and about the kind of men who find charm only in helpless, ignorant women – the charm of helplessness, he says, belongs only to the young, and 'in demanding it from modern women modern men can be convicted of an egotistical perversity somewhat akin to the perversity of the roué who will look at none but maids'.[19] This is well said; but he then goes on to assert, with an air of bravado, it is true, and with a thorough familiarity with the arguments on both sides, that most women are intellectually inferior to men, that they seem to be incapable of the highest artistic or scientific achievements, and that they love to be dominated. He says this in a friendly enough manner, and indeed concedes that things may change in a thousand years or so; Virginia Woolf, eight years later in *A Room of One's Own*, prophesied that change would take place not in a thousand years but in fifty. The fact that, fifty years later, the point can still be passionately disputed supports, in a way, both contenders. Certainly, feminists ought to have been grateful for the reasonable, encouraging, practical tone which Bennett adopts, and for his repudiation of the outworn concepts of femininity: he always defends the right of women to work, to earn, to achieve economic independence and fair pay, and attacks the 'economic slavery' of the married woman; his championship, in the eyes of a hostile public, was doubtless worth a great deal, for reactionaries read Bennett and listened to him and did not fear him, as they feared Wells and Shaw. He was a powerful ally, even when he muttered disrespectful things about Jane Austen, and wondered why women, who 'for ages have had every opportunity that education can furnish to shine creatively in painting and music'[20] have failed to do so. Women have wondered the same thing, it must be admitted.

But were the suffragettes grateful for his support? Did they see Bennett and Wells as defenders, or did they dismiss them as male chauvinists, as they might today? How did they receive *The Lion's Share*? They could have been forgiven for finding it a trivial dallying with a serious and indeed tragic theme: an important modern novelist who today chose race relations or the sufferings of the Third World as a piquant background for a light extra-vaganza might well be rejected as a serious supporter, even if he uttered impeccable sentiments at various intervals in his work.

On 21 June, after much messing about with passports and wrongly filled-in police passes, Mair and Bennett got off to France, via Boulogne. He was away till 13 July, but what he really made of his visit we shall never know. The records we have – his journal, and his articles for the *London Illustrated News* and *Saturday Evening Post*, collected in a volume under the title *Over There* – tell two different and equally incomplete stories. On the one hand, we have the technical calm and phlegm of the *Journals*, recording the emptiness of Paris, his meeting with Gide ('intellectually more than ever like an orchid'[21]), his reunion with the Godebskis and Ravel, who had only just been dissuaded from joining the 'aviation'; his tour of the countryside, Rheims, Château Thierry, Meaux, where champagne proprietors press champagne into his hands, and he sees 'wheat absolutely growing out of a German'. Then Paris again, where Lord Esher parades his fancy military costume. He records, calmly, the tremendous waste of ammunition, as shots pour around his ears on the road at Souchez. Nearest shot a hundred yards, he says. What he thought and felt, we cannot tell. His style is perfectly calculated to conceal emotion. He records the birds on the ramparts at Ypres, 'lustily enjoying odour of gas from shell',[22] but what he felt he does not record. One must deduce. One can deduce something, perhaps, from the fact that he never wrote, imaginatively, of what he had seen. The novels of his which touch on the war – *The Roll Call, Riceyman Steps* – show only the young volunteer about to depart, or the shell-shocked soldier returned. He wasted, one might say, the best copy of his life.

The reason might well be that he felt he could not divulge it. For, in contrast to his journal's bleak comments, we have his Front articles, patriotic, cheerful, false. It is easy to see, in terms of his character and the national situation, why he wrote them. He was above all a responsible man: he had been allowed out on a special errand, with special permission; and the last thing he wanted to do was to report truly on the desolation he had seen. Like a good citizen, he did not wish to spread alarm and despair. So his reports are diplomatic. It is easy to say that he should have told a different truth. What good would it have done? The truth was told later, by Graves and Owen. At the time, there was little to say. Would a few articles by Bennett have influenced the course of the war? Clearly not. Could they cheer up a few worried families? Possibly. So he chose the safer way. It is easy to say that he should have reported differently – Wells might have done.

But then, Wells did not go, and it does not take much democratic sense to see that Wells's criticisms of military authority had hardly proved constructive, whatever Wells might think of their effects. Bennett had accepted a role, and he played it. That he found it irksome might be inferred from his later silence on the matter. He was not a man to go about with his eyes shut, nor a man to spare the dead – he used his own father and mother to good advantage, after all. But he had the precaution to distinguish between a state of peace and a state of war, and did so. Another point might be added at this stage – Bennett was an exceptionally law-abiding citizen. Although he in no way sought promotion or office or even respectability – even his enemies had to admit that his attitude, in advocating less censorship, for example, was completely above reproach, intellectually – he had an innate horror of dishonesty, disloyalty, anti-social behaviour. In all his financial dealings, there is not the faintest shadow of sharp practice – no tax evasion, no over-quick investments. Intellectually and politically, his integrity was unquestioned. He was an honourable man. And as an honourable man, he felt that in an hour of need, as a public figure, his country could claim first of all his loyalty. He could snipe and agitate in private: he did. He and Wells sat together and planned a campaign against 'Yellow Pressism' and the unfair treatment of aliens. But when he reported back from the Front, he became a diplomat.

No wonder, then, that his reports are disappointing. It's not that they're unreadable, nor that they are positively dishonest; it's simply that one knows he is not telling the whole truth. Some of the observations and emotions he records are doubtless true enough, for he was skilled at salvaging what could be used from what could not: hence his feelings as he sees Paris, which he had so loved, do not ring false, nor does his rhetoric when, after praising her architecture, he concludes 'The city escaped. And the event seems vaster and more sublime than the mind can bear.'[23] He goes on to give the factual details recorded in his journal – the lack of autobuses and taxis, which are all at the Front, the trains manned by women, the shortage of salt and chicory – but already he is being forced into presenting an image, for he says 'supreme grief is omnipresent: but it is calm, cheerful, smiling'.[24] Amazing, if it were true. He is pledged to an image of the French as noble, stoic sufferers, of the Germans as brutal barbarians who open champagne bottles with sabres, burn holes in tablecloths with their cigars, ransack farm houses for fun, and lie as corpses beneath black crosses expressing 'the whole devilishness of the Prussian ideal'. He is also pledged to describe the English soldier as gay and cheerful, saluting his officers with a salute 'so proud, so eager it might have brought tears to the eyes', and praising his 75 as though it were 'a favourite sporting dog'. He is of necessity discreet when it comes to describing the trenches, but we can be sure they are fine places, where one can see 'a long line of men ... cheerfully ready to shoot ... a little further behind them gay young men seemed to be preparing food. Here and there were little resting places. . . .'[25] The uneasiness of Bennett's vocabulary suggests the violation he is doing to his memory, and to his suspicions of the truth. One almost admires the panache with which he declares, 'We had been to the very front of the front, and it was the most cheerful confident high-spirited place I had seen in France, or in England either.'[26]

His articles were not, of course, devoid of all content: his consistent ironic harping upon the falsity of Germany's claims to be fighting a defensive war is well done, and doubtless hammered the point home to a few readers. On this theme, indeed, he can safely let fly. He is no doubt sincere when he says: 'When you are walking through that which was Ypres, nothing arouses a stronger feeling – half contempt, half anger – than the thought of the mean, miserable silly childish and grotesque excuses which the wit of Germany has invented for her deliberately planned crimes.'[27] And one must remember, also, that he was a man who had genuinely loved Belgium, France, Holland; he had never liked Germany and on his Danish trip with Rickards he heaved a sigh of relief when leaving the 'military' waters of Germany. It was a pity that he, and so many of his countrymen, were so slow to grasp the direction in which that militarism was heading: no wonder he disliked Erskine Childers's *Riddle of the Sands*. It had too strong a flavour of 'I told you so'.

He returned to London on 14 July, and spent two nights at the Savoy; then went back to Comarques, and was in bed for days with an intestinal illness. Travel, which he enjoyed so much, did not agree with him. He found waiting for him the proofs of Wells's last novel, *Mr Britling Sees It Through*, which he corrected – his devotion in taking on the really dreary job of proof-reading out of friendship, which he did constantly for Wells, is amazing. Writing to Wells about the novel, he reveals some of his private feelings about the war – he says he finds some of Mr Britling's sentiments 'a bit Morning-Postish', and goes on to say: 'The spirit of Paris has not been good. The spirit of the Midi has been rotten. This I know of my own knowledge.'[28] When he was off the record, he had different comments to make. Then he settled down to write his articles, and to finish *The Lion's Share*. On 1 September he got back his first censored article from GHQ, which he kept as 'a curiosity'. Censorship in the First World War, it has been generally agreed, was ludicrously inadequate; in the Second World War, Wells's views on guerrilla warfare would never have found their way into print. But they had no need to worry about Bennett for he was playing their game, so he had a right to be amused at their dutiful excisions. While he was playing the game so efficiently he allowed his private irritations to break out, and reports angrily on 21 August, a year after the outbreak of war: 'In case of invasion, the military people have not yet got their transport in order.'[29]

Otherwise, it was back to the Wounded Allies Committee, and the articles for the *Daily News*, which he resumed in August. These articles, after his excursion to the Front, do perhaps show a slight increase in acrimony: his attacks on the War Office and its inefficiency and class prejudice are strongly worded. He criticizes public school officers, who played the same games and wore the same tie, and therefore think they know how to run a regiment. He describes the immense difficulties of 'indenting' for cups of tea or false teeth or trusses. When it comes to describing the Front, he is still patriotic – the French hospitals are praised for their 'humane, jolly spirit'. But at home, he is critical. He complains about the work conditions in munitions factories, and in one of his most interesting pieces, on the T.U.C. Congress (15 September 1915) he refutes criticisms of the workers' patriotism. 'We do not all live in the same Britain . . .,' he says, 'therefore, we are not all fighting for the same Britain. There is a Britain of country houses, gardens, foxes, hunt balls . . . fine wines, golf links . . . art and letters . . . [and] another Britain, of factories, workshops, dirt, bad air . . . small cottages, before-breakfast labour and union rules.'[30] No wonder, he says, the workers are resentful and suspicious; no wonder they do not respond more warmly to Lloyd George's 'theatrical manifestoes'.

At home, there was also a new excitement, in the form of Zeppelin scares. On 8 September there was a Zeppelin raid on London, the tenth fatal raid in England, which killed twenty and injured eighty-six – small figures by Second World War standards, but ominous enough. After this, there were endless scares in London and all over the country – Thorpe-le-Soken, exposed on the already-hit east coast, got its fair share. In October, Bennett went off for a few days to visit Wells: they walked in Little Easton in Warwick Park, watched the stags rutting, played hockey on a Sunday afternoon with sixteen others, and talked of taxing the rich. Bennett comments that Wells's home is 'like a large cottage made comfortable by people rich but capricious'.[31] What would they have said, Wells and Bennett, come the socialist revolution? Bennett still admired Wells's tremendous energy, which threw itself into physical games the moment that conversation flagged, and he comments that he 'drives a car very indifferent bad: but he enjoys driving'. On 26 October, Wells and his wife paid a return visit to Comarques. The friendship was solid, despite all their altercations in newspaper columns, and Wells could hardly complain of Bennett's white-washing of the authorities, for in *Mr Britling Sees It Through* he was shortly (in 1916) to publish one of the most sentimental patriotic lump-in-the-throat novels of the war.

1915 saw itself out with no marked change. Bennett finished *The Lion's Share* on 4 December and subsequently exhausted himself by organizing a 'high-class concert' at the Haymarket for 21 February for his Wounded Allies Committee. He quarrelled with both Methuen and Doran over designs for *These Twain*. The English edition he disliked because it showed Edwin 'half bald and beardless . . . with a grotesque waistcoat, a green suit, a low collar and a sailor's knot-necktie' and Hilda with 'eyebrows like a Chinese';[32] it was altered. The American edition he disapproved of less strongly and without effect, because it showed a 'scene in some small sleepy and clean old English town', and because the figures 'look as though they have had just a little bit too much to drink'.[33] He did not have to worry about the book, except aesthetically; it sold 13,350 copies in its first week when Methuen published it in January 1916. He also negotiated a contract to write a play from *Sacred and Profane Love* for the actress Doris Keane, whom he had seen (twice) and admired in Edward Sheldon's successful play, *Romance* – Sheldon, it will be remembered, had sat in on the first reading of *Milestones*, four years earlier, at Fontainebleau. The idea had been in Miss Keane's head for some time. Bennett travelled up to Glasgow to discuss the deal with Vedrenne. He wrote the play in 1916 but Miss Keane did not like it, and it was first produced by Basil Dean at the Aldwych in 1919.

Christmas was spent again at Comarques. In his end-of-year reckoning Bennett says that he wrote 272,000 words, 'had the best book and serial year I have ever had (though I didn't issue a single new novel), and by far the worst theatrical year since before *The Honeymoon*, I think. . .'.[34] The war had certainly damaged his theatrical income; but, although he was not to know it and maybe never realized it, his days of glory as a dramatist were over. Money continued to come in from the plays, of course; but the long West End runs of new plays were a thing of the past. His theatrical career closed, as it had begun, in a great deal of remunerative but otherwise unrewarded effort.

1916 was a dull year, of disillusion and friction, enlivened only by a brief holiday in Scotland and the beginning of a new novel. The war had been going on too long, no end seemed in sight, and it became increasingly difficult to get money for war charities out of an increasingly battered public. He writes plaintively to Mrs Herzog, relieved to turn to a sympathizer abroad: 'For we have now in England really begun to be at war',[35] and again: 'My own work has been practically stopped by the war . . . the war has turned me into a political writer.'[36] Mrs Herzog responded generously, with moral support and cheques, both for Arnold's Allies Relief Committee, and for Marguerite's Soldiers' Club; she set about selling her friend's pamphlets in the States, and doing what she could for the cause. The spring passed, with more clubs, chats with ministers, visits to Marriott and from Pauline Smith, and a big fair for the War Allies at the Caledonian Market, which, although it managed to coincide with the death of Kitchener (8 June) raised over £20,000. Bennett wrote his play of *Sacred and Profane Love*, which wasn't to be performed for three years, and installed a dictaphone. Then, in August, he and Marguerite went up to Scotland for their first holiday since the outbreak of war. They went to Glasgow, by one of the only trains still to possess a restaurant car, and visited Loch Lomond, Burns country, Culzean Castle and the Cairngorms, returning home via Edinburgh and York. On his return, Bennett saw war film of the Somme offensive – 'very instructive and salutary' – and wrote again to Mrs Herzog, again deploring the length of the war, and finally admitting: 'The war proves more and more that those who based their calculations on the ultimate resources of the combatants, and on nothing else, are going to be right.'[37] This conclusion was exceedingly depressing, particularly so to one of Bennett's rational convictions: for what could be more hopeless and irrational than the spectacle of two great nations fighting to the last bullet and the last man?

He turned, as so often, to watercolours and work: on 16 October he started to write the fourth *Clayhanger* novel, *The Roll Call*. November was to see a change in working habits which may have altered the future, for on 3 November he took, permanently, a flat at the Royal Yacht Club. Marguerite also found a flat in London at Thackeray Mansions, Oxford St, and although they often met for dinner or lunch when both were in London together, the fact that they had each a place of his and her own speaks for itself. On his third day of the new régime he writes in his journal: 'Rather like celibate life in Paris again. I dined at the Club and read Macready's diary; extraordinary sensation of having resumed a closed chapter of existence.'[38] The appeal of bachelor life and club life had proved too strong for him, and he returned to it doubtless with some relief. Marguerite must have realized that he was slipping away from her, for she made scenes (according to his letters) about his seeing so little of her, wanted him to lunch and dine with her more often when both were in town, and protested indignantly when he said that she did not understand what it was like to be a 'creative artist'. He writes to her, when she complains that he hasn't spent the night with her: 'The process of writing is so delicate, so easily thrown off-balance, that I have given up trying to explain it to you. But I can tell you that work begins immediately on waking . . . and that to wake up in a strange bed in strange surroundings . . . might well spoil a whole morning's work.'[39] One can take that as one likes: on one level it was no doubt a simple expression of the truth, which many writers would recognize. It is clear that by this stage Bennett liked life in the country and life with Marguerite only when he could escape from them as often as he wanted. He did not care much for her world of charities and officers' dances, though he put up with some of them with a good grace: such events as the Lord Mayor's Banquet at Frinton were not his idea of fun. Marguerite's character, far from mellowing with age, was becoming more difficult, and her quarrels over trivialities (concert tickets, the gardener Lockyer, the placing of the piano) were becoming more frequent and more violent. There was also another source of friction, over an issue which was not at all trivial. In 1916 she invited Frank Bennett's son Richard to stay at Comarques on a permanent basis (he had been a frequent visitor) and talked of adopting him, seeking from him the affection she felt that Bennett withheld, and seeking a substitute for the child she never had. The arrangement did not work out happily, though it may have begun well enough, and even from the beginning Bennett was doubtless aware of domestic frictions that he preferred to evade. He was very fond of Richard, and the offer to take the boy was motivated by some concern for his brother Frank and sister-in-law Florence, for Frank's business had failed and he was in great financial difficulties. Bennett sent Richard to Oundle, where Wells's boys went, and remained friendly with him for life. But Richard did not get on with Marguerite, and their relationship, through 1917, was a permanent source of family trouble. In anticipation of this, perhaps, Bennett set up on his own in London.

London, after all, was where things were happening, and Bennett was at the heart of them. His Wounded Allies Committees still needed him, and through such activities, and his newly extended club life, he was mixing with new people, many of them politicians, and many of them models for the aristocratic committee people that he was to portray in *The Pretty Lady*. It was a new experience for him, and more alluring than the world of the Tory ladies of Frinton. The war was a great social mixer, and it must take some of the blame for the increasing preponderance of lords and ladies in Bennett's serious fiction. It was also a time when unconventional behaviour became more acceptable: Wells, ever unconventional, was in the middle of his affair with Rebecca West, and Bennett saw a good deal of them both. The war saw, or helped to speed, the break-up of many marriages, including Bennett's own: the Granville Barkers for instance, whom Bennett had known for years, broke up and divorced in 1918. (Lillah McCarthy got married again in 1920, this time to Dr Frederick Keeble, an Oxford don, with whom she had been friendly for some time.) Bennett describes the first night of Granville Barker's play, *Vote by Ballot*, which he attended on 17 December 1917, and says 'Theatre packed. All the usual crowd. Wives and mistresses of the same men all mixed up and friendly together.'[40] He also comments on the amount of adultery in modern plays: 'The sensual appeal is really very marked everywhere, in both speech and action, on the stage. Adultery everywhere pictured as desirable, and copulation generally ditto.'[41] The social scene was changing considerably, and he wanted to see it happen. Also, London was where the work was: he was writing regularly for the *New Statesman*, for various other periodicals, and, as he said in a letter to Walpole, for 'three government departments': 'I came up to my beautiful Club yesterday and it is a solemn fact that I hadn't been here ten minutes before I had undertaken to write a government article for the *Strand* magazine in three days. A bit thick.'[42] He may complain that it is a bit thick, but he enjoyed the power and the pressure. London had claimed him. *These Twain* was to be his last novel of the Five Towns: thereafter, with varying and disputed degrees of success, he made London his subject matter and eventually his home.

Bennett's output during 1916 was, not surprisingly, low: a mere 127,600 words. He is obliged to reassure himself by reminding himself that in later years he has not been including his journal in his word total, a work the value of which he knows to be appreciating steadily, as he advises Pinker.[43] His low output may also have increased his enthusiasm for a plan of Swinnerton's to republish his Jacob Tonson articles, originally written for the *New Age*, in volume form. Swinnerton was working at Chatto & Windus, and he and Hugh Walpole enthused so much over the articles that Bennett agreed to the publication of a selection: it appeared later in 1917, under the title *Books and Persons*. There was some slight trouble with Orage, the editor of the *New Age*, whom they forgot to consult about the venture, but as Bennett had originally written for the *New Age* for eighteen months without payment, Orage was hardly in a strong position to object. The *New Statesman* articles, beginning in 1916 under the name Sardonyx, were also contributed free, as was Bennett's detailed help and advice to J.C.Squire, who was editing it in

Clifford Sharp's absence on military service – Bennett could be a hard enough bargainer, but he was also generous when the occasion seemed suitable and the periodical deserving.

Meanwhile, Bennett got on with *The Roll Call*, went to a spiritualist seance with Roger Fry and Yeats, lunched with his old hero George Moore, with Sickert, and with the Webbs. He liked the Webbs, but says 'they do not understand (what I call) life. Squire is an A.1. chap. But he is a vegetarian and he doesn't understand life either. And either he or his wife doesn't understand shirts.'[44] His enjoyment at being a man of the world among the high-living *New Statesman* people, and at being a socialist among the clubmen and yachtsmen, is evident. He had a way into every social circle, and felt the literary material available to him was increasing every year. *The Roll Call*, which he finished on 30 April 1917, after some trouble and bouts of ill-health and a certain lack of enthusiasm, deals with London life, his first serious novel to do so since *A Man from the North*, with which it has certain similarities, in that he tries to portray again the drab life of living in lodging houses, and to contrast it with a more successful fashionable world. The attempt is not very successful: there is something peculiarly dispiriting about the whole novel, which is hard to analyse.

The novel's hero is George Cannon, son of Hilda and stepson of Edwin Clayhanger; he is an aspiring architect (Bennett uses a good deal of information from Rickards) and he lives in London in rooms belonging to the clerk of his office. We are back on Marriott territory again – the studios, the struggling artists, the engravers, the oil lamps, the loneliness. He falls in love with his landlord's daughter, but it comes to nothing, because he cannot afford to marry her and she will not leave her father. He then moves into higher society, and finally marries a fashionable young woman who drives large cars badly and lives in Paris. His architectural career is modelled largely on Rickards – like Rickards he wins a big public competition for a big public building; like Rickards he then has ten years of struggle to establish himself; and he too regards architecture as 'the Cinderella of the professions' – there is a good scene where George goes up north to the opening of his grand new building, to find himself more or less totally ignored by all the town's dignitaries, who have no understanding of his work at all. It could have been an interesting novel – the sight of George achieving the ambitions his step-father had failed to fulfil could have been much better handled than it is. Bennett had resolutely turned his back on the Five Towns, for Edwin hardly appears – he sends his stepson a telegram, when he hears he has won the competition, saying, as Enoch Bennett was wont to say: 'It's better than a bat in the eye with a burnt stick', but apart from that there are very few mentions of him.

There is something curiously leaden about the working of the plot: the narrative is episodic, jumps years at random, and becomes heavy in its longer descriptions. Perhaps it is simply that there is too much unrelieved depression in the spectacle of George growing into such an ordinary person, with such dull worldly ambitions. The descriptions of his wife and children. compared with the descriptions of the little Benbows, or of George Cannon himself as a child, are vague in the extreme. At the end of the novel, under the pressure of history, and having seen his brother-in-law in uniform, George Cannon enlists. His motives for doing so are convincing and dispiriting in the extreme: he doesn't want to be less impressive than a man he doesn't really respect. There is a curious feeling of sell-out about the whole story. George Cannon isn't really a very nice person. At the beginning of the book he is young and silly; at the end he is thirty-three and a bore. One might well have expected Hilda's son to grow up just like this, but it's peculiarly disheartening to see him do it. It's even more gloomy to see him escape from the dingy lodgings into brighter drawing-rooms full of *objets d'art* than it was to leave Richard Larch, from that first novel, in the dark.

Nevertheless, the book has got one or two good things in it. For instance, when George is admiring a painting and finds out who painted it, Bennett says: 'Now that he knew the sketch to be the work of a woman he at once became more critical, perceiving in it imitative instead of original qualities.'[45] The painter of this picture, a friend of the forsaken landlord's daughter, is almost well done – aggressive, bohemian, a touch of lesbian. So is the land-lord's obstinate second marriage to his charlady. But the good moments are few and far between. Dullness prevails. The novel didn't appear till January 1919, and the reviews, though polite, were indecisive, like the book itself. *The Times Literary Supplement*, though praising Bennett's realism about the fashionable world where people 'are silly and ugly and do not know how to amuse themselves', is also very reasonably dissatisfied with the book's 'unfinished' aspect.[46] It simply wasn't a fitting ending to the *Clayhanger* trilogy, and the four books together don't feel like a quartet. The open ending, with George on his way to war, doesn't satisfy. Some critics demanded yet another sequel, but they weren't to get one. Bennett had finished with the Clayhangers.

Instead, he turned his mind to something quite different. His next idea came to him almost immediately, less than a week after finishing *The Roll Call*; and he was delighted with it. It restored all the enthusiasm that had been lacking for the last year. The novel was to be serious, contemporary and short, and it was to deal with an episode in the life of a French cocotte. He writes of his idea on 19 May, to Newman Flower, asking him not to tell anyone about it, and on 24 May 1917, with a feeling of more excitement than he had expressed for years, he sat down to write 'with gusto'. It was three days before his fiftieth birthday.

He expected *The Pretty Lady* to startle the public, and it did. Some of his most loyal admirers deserted him for ever on account of it. Bonar Law told him that 'his sister had been a very great and constant admirer', but that since this book she had 'done with' him.[47] Boots and Smiths refused to handle it, and Catholics were deeply offended by it. Inevitably, it's hard now to see what much of the fuss was about, because Bennett's handling of his theme was tactful enough, indeed excessively so: he prided himself on his ability to be realistic without being offensive, on his skill at dispensing with overt sexual descriptions. It was simply the theme that offended, and the public's shock provided him with yet another example of the hypocrisy and insularity of the English, compared with the French. The story deals with the affairs of a French cocotte in London during the war, against a background of Zeppelins and aristocratic ladies serving on committees or living it up in less public-spirited ways. The English ladies are clearly drawn very much from his own war experience and club gossip, but Christine is cast in a more familiar tradition. She reminds one of the Chichi of his early days in Paris, and doubtless some of the information about her daily life and habits had been remembered from years earlier. The novel had originally been planned as a Paris novel; the idea of setting it in London came later, as Bennett was talking about his plot to Wells. Bennett had always been interested in the subject of the courtesan and cocotte – his first lonely wanderings round the music halls of London as a lawyer's clerk had presented them to him as gay, cheerful, lively creatures, an impression which never left him, for prostitutes are never treated as squalid, fallen women in his books – they are always given qualities of courage, gaiety, and a kind of innocence. In this, he is in part following his French models – Balzac, in *Splendeurs et Misères des Courtesanes*, who is certainly no moralist on the topic; Zola, for whom courtesans like Nana were creatures of glory and wit as well as of wickedness; and de Maupassant, for whom they were usually simple, friendly, often motherly girls. Doubtless his own experiences, too, led him to see them in an agreeable light. One could accuse him of falling for the old myth of the tart with the heart of gold, but the myth has some truth in it and in *The Pretty Lady* Bennett is in part paying tribute to the kindness and sexual generosity of girls who understood and tried to help the inhibitions of a young man repressed from birth, who was quite incapable of coping sexually or socially with the sexually inexpert women of his own background. Perhaps he underestimated the profound prejudice that still existed against such subjects; he had himself for years moved in a much more free and unconventional world. But it is more likely that he knew exactly what he was doing, for he always showed himself in close touch with public opinion. He felt like being shocking. He had been good for a long time: serious and deep in *These Twain*, patriotic, finally, in *The Roll Call*, flippant and cheerful in *The Lion's Share*. The time had come to have a change, and to abandon the government-department atmosphere.

The Pretty Lady is only a partial success. Its heroine, Christine, is a cheerful, pretty, womanly French prostitute, who has fled from France and lives in great cosiness in a flat in Cork Street. She takes up with a middle-aged wealthy punctilious bachelor named G.J., who, like Bennett, works on war committees and mixes with titled ladies. At the end of the novel he finds a flat for Christine and puts her 'among her own furniture', which is her fondest dream. Her nature is simple and friendly; she knows how to look after a man, she is not at heart promiscuous, she is domesticated and wifely, and her greatest fear is of getting fat. She is contrasted – perhaps over-contrasted – with two 'modern women' – Concepcion, a young war widow, and Queenie, an aristocratic, committee-serving sensation-seeker, whose taste in furniture and manners is excessively contemporary. Bennett was fascinated by the type of nervous, highly strung, highly intelligent, heavy-smoking, expensive, upper-class girl, and these two portraits are attempts to work out his fascination. The book does not really work – the plot, with its air raids, its stray shell-shocked soldier, its melodramatic threats of suicide from the girls, its odd moments of committee sobriety, does not hang together, though it gives some picture of the mixture of frivolity and seriousness which made up the war in London. Its hero in particular does not convince – G.J., with his flat in the Albany and his passion for punctuality, is too like A.B. to be plausible, and the passion he inspires in both Christine and Lady Queenie is not at all likely. Nevertheless, its very disjointedness, its odd moments of hysteria and even of superstition, catch something of a wartime atmosphere that does not enter into any of his other books. It was published by Cassells in April 1918, and it sold well: 20,000 copies in a month. The fact that the press described it as pornographic and decadent no doubt helped. The *Sunday Chronicle* on 14 April said it was 'the last word in decadence', 'unsavoury', 'a damnable book' written by a man who had let 'his pen wallow in the slime of sensuality'. He has made vice attractive, says the reviewer, 'by the simple method of picturing the rosy or cosy side of it'.[48] This was excellent advertising. The book is not of course overtly shocking – it is discreet, as all of Bennett's are. But perhaps it does have shocking elements – the extreme calm with which both Christine, G.J. and the author accept her profession is unusual in English fiction, to say the least. To him, the prostitute was clearly a better wife than the average wife, which is a slightly disturbing notion. And Christine's devotion to the Catholic faith, together with one or two remarks about priests and confession, was certainly enough to upset all the Catholics. (The *Chronicle* objected even to her name.)

Shocking or not, the composition of *The Pretty Lady* was certainly a pleasure to Bennett, and it kept his spirits up during the depressing second half of 1917, when food rationing and war weariness had set in. It was a relief from war articles. It was also an opportunity to write about such things as air raids with genuine feeling, instead of with school-prefect patriotism. Air raids were becoming more and more tiresome, as the war dragged on, with no prospects of an ending. Marguerite was caught in one at Liverpool Street station and had to take refuge in the lavatory, and Bennett had to run from the Turkish baths to his club, impeded by a heavy overcoat. He must have been glad to be able to exorcize them in fiction. Characteristically, he shows no trace of personal fear, in his journal or letters, but says that Wells confessed he was afraid of going to pieces during a raid. He seems to have felt more curiosity than fear, and comments with interest on the way that the class war was carried down into the underground, which was used as air-raid shelters – the middle classes would criticize the working classes for not obeying the rules and say they ought not to be allowed down unless they did.

There was an air raid one night when the Galsworthys were dining, and the whole party had to retire to the basement; Bennett comments chiefly on the chivalry with which John treated the cook. (He was becoming increasingly fond of Galsworthy, after a sticky professional opening to their friendship and despite his enduring lack of respect for his novels – a year later, after a dinner with them, he writes 'Galsworthy very nice. Ada adorable.'[49]) Although social life carried on, indeed flourished, the pinch was felt in some quarters – at Comarques, bread was not put on the table as a matter of course with meals, and visitors had to ask for it. At Christmas 1917, only seven sat down to dinner, the smallest Christmas gathering they had ever had at Comarques, owing to difficulty of transport. Marguerite had tried to help the food situation by buying a pig, and on 11 January 1918 there is a fine outburst in his journal from Bennett who complains, 'it was only a small one, but we have been eating this damned animal ever since'.[50] He was finely abusive about pig's trotters, an over-rated food. A month later, he says that when people come to dinner, they are requested as a matter of course to bring some of their own food.

He continued to meet new friends – notably Sassoon, who was on the verge of the crisis which caused him to throw away his Military Cross, but who, when he met Bennett, was still thinking of returning to the Front. He also met the celebrated lawyer and attorney-general F.E.Smith (later Lord Birkenhead). Smith seems to have taken an instant liking to Bennett, and in November Bennett was welcomed by him at the highly select club which he had founded, the Other Club, to which Bennett had been elected without his knowledge – a different picture from the rather snide account which Compton Mackenzie gives of Bennett's election, through Robert Ross, to *The Reform*. Bennett found Smith lively but egotistic, and was amused when he rang him up on 13 December asking him to go on a secret mission with him to the United States – he declined the offer, which must, according to Smith's own account, have been made the very same day that Sir Edward Carson had put the proposition to Smith.[51] Bennett doubtless did not fancy the idea of travelling in a secretarial relationship to anyone, and travelling was by no means safe or pleasant at that time – anyway, he had done his share, by a journey to Ireland at the end of October and beginning of November undertaken at the request of the G.O.C. Ireland Intelligence Department.

This trip, which was to bring him at least one enduring friendship in the person of Thomas Bodkin, lawyer and art historian, seems to have been arranged in order to shed a little more light on the very over-heated Irish question. Bennett was the ideal reporter to choose for such a task – calm, fair, indignant with the English but not too indignant, sympathetic with the Irish but not too sympathetic. He went at a time of trouble: the Dublin Convention was sitting, attempting to sort out some kind of postwar future for Ireland, but it was making little progress, caught between two dismally familiar groups of extremists. Ever since the 1916 Rebellion (which Bennett said was mistakenly made to seem a trifle in the American press, for censorship reasons), anti-English feeling had been passionate, and the Convention had an impossible task. This ill-will had been stirred up afresh in September by the death in prison of a Sinn Fein hunger striker, Thomas Ashe, who had been forcibly fed in jail, and who died saying: 'Even though I die, I die in a good cause.' The inquest was accompanied by rage and riots, and stories were told about confiscation of arms and even of hurley sticks, about ill-treatment and victimization. This was the vexed situation which Bennett found when he arrived in Dublin.

He tried to hear views on all sides, visited Dublin Castle, was slightly surprised when he was allowed to inspect police reports at will, and not at all surprised when prominent Sinn Feiners, such as de Valera, Count Plunkett and John MacNeill, refused to see him. In the three pieces which he wrote about his experiences in the *Daily News* (8, 12 and 15 November), he says that he himself had always supported Home Rule, had sympathies with Sinn Fein because of its labour origins while doubting its political wisdom, and blames unimaginative British policy for the state of violence, while making it clear that he thinks Dublin Castle is not so much corrupt as aloof. 'Not only,' he says, 'is it unnecessarily silent, it unwisely suppresses . . . it has no popular mandate, and therefore no moral authority.' He also blames the Irish press, calling it 'extraordinarily and fantastically irresponsible'. In fact, he manages to make one feel that it is public communications that have gone wrong, and nothing much more serious – as was doubtless his intention. However, even he, moderate by policy, was alarmed by the Ulster Unionists – he visited Ulster, and reports: 'I went . . . with the object of meeting extremists, and I may say that I met them. Indeed, I have never met anybody like them. They would listen to nothing but their own case.'[52]

He tries to present a picture of an Ireland in which all sensible people want Home Rule: he prophesies that the Convention will recommend neither partition, nor sovereign status, but some kind of dominion status for a united Ireland. As so often, he could not quite comprehend the extent of the extremism of others. His views, published in both England and America, may have helped to quell some of the wilder and more inaccurate current rumours, but that was the most that could be hoped for. His tone is responsible, his opinions moderate, his research reliable. He had become a useful public man, and public affairs, for good or ill, were soon to overtake him.

It was also in November 1917 that he met for the first time the man who was to become one of his closest, most demanding and most influential friends, Lord Beaverbrook, who was responsible for introducing him to the world of active politics.

The two men met, at Beaverbrook's request, on 8 November. Both knew each other well by reputation, and Beaverbrook certainly knew that in Bennett he could not hope to purchase a tame and obliging journalist. Bennett's articles in the radical *Daily News* and *New Statesman* were well known, and on their first meeting Bennett presented Beaverbrook with a piece he was about to publish in which he had attacked him and his policies.

But Beaverbrook must have sensed that there was something there for him, as indeed there was. The two quickly became close friends: their feeling for one another was emotional and sincere. At their second meeting, after a lunch at Bennett's, they went together to an art gallery, where Beaverbrook impulsively bought a Rops etching for his new friend, and presented it to him. (G.J., in *The Pretty Lady*, admired Rops: Beaverbrook greatly admired *The Pretty Lady*.) Bennett, who came from a background where such gestures of immediate affection did not come easily, found him irresistible, and within five months we find him writing to Geoffrey Madan: 'I have become such firm friends with that other *bête noire* of the public, Beaverbrook, that I can't attack him.'[53] Not that he ever became an uncritical or silent admirer: that was not in him, and he continued to write for radical papers. But he loved the man. Beaverbrook had a great capacity for inspiring love, as well as hate; A.J.P.Taylor, his latest biographer, bears witness to this.

Beaverbrook and Bennett had much in common. Both started life in modest, hard-working homes, and perhaps both exaggerated, one directly, the other in fiction, the poverty of their background. Beaverbrook's father was a Church of Scotland minister in New Brunswick, Canada. He later, Beaverbrook alleges, began to lose his faith, took against preaching, and was happy to live in luxury on his son's wealth. Bennett found this a fine idea for a novel, for it must have struck a chord in his own family feeling. He says: 'Max gave me the history of the last 15 years of his father's life, beginning with the old man's phrase when he retired from the pastorate at the age of 70: "The evening mists are gathering" – meaning that doubts had come to him about the reality of the doctrines he had been preaching. He died at 85, and in his last years he spent 55,000 dollars of Max's money. It is a great subject for a novel.'[54] One can see exactly why this story appealed so much to Bennett: it goes straight to the heart of the conflict between spiritual and material prosperity.

Beaverbrook, like Bennett, started work as a clerk in a lawyer's office, and found it unsatisfactory. On his twenty-first birthday, in 1900, he said 'Now I'm going to make some money quickly', and he did. In seven years he was a dollar millionaire; by the time he came to England in 1910 he was worth far more. He achieved this by selling bonds, and rode high on the Canadian boom. But finance didn't satisfy him. He turned his attention to politics. He came to England as a financier, but, as A.J.P.Taylor has so admirably shown, a combination of circumstances turned his attention to politics, and he became the Unionist MP for Ashton-under-Lyne. He had important friends, a flair for publicity, and an understanding of the role of the press –

and by the time he met Bennett he had engineered the rise of Bonar Law, the fall of Asquith and the rise of Lloyd George, and had been made first of all a knight in the coronation honours of 1911, and then, reluctantly, a peer in 1917. He had also bought the *Daily Express*, and from this time onwards was to take an increasing interest in running his growing number of newspapers.

The power of the press lords was a subject which Bennett had touched on, however flippantly, in *What the Public Wants*. In the next play he wrote, *The Title*, his subject is the distribution and worthlessness of honours, and the comedy that arises when a man's wife insists on his accepting an honour he wished to refuse. It was a topical enough subject, after Lloyd George's largesse. (Beaverbrook's elevation had caused much indignation and was personally resisted by George V.) Bennett was irresistibly drawn towards the Beaverbrook world of intrigue and appearances and power and money, though he never showed any real interest himself in the kind of financial transactions which absorbed his friend – he liked earning money, but never had much interest in investing it, unlike some of Beaverbrook's political allies, who used him as a private adviser. Neither did Bennett wish for honours: he refused a knighthood when it was offered to him. He was an observer, not a participant, in these worldly games. But he could not help being drawn in, in some capacity.

Beaverbrook's first overture was to invite Bennett to sit on one of his committees – the Imperial War Memorial Committee. Beaverbrook, whose efforts to record and document the war properly were immensely far-sighted, wanted to commission artists to do war paintings and other works of art, and Bennett agreed to sit on the committee, with others like Masterman and Rothermere, to try, in his view, to keep out all the RAs by commissioning young painters of promise. It was an entertaining task and brought him in touch with new painters like Nash and old friends like Beerbohm.

Beaverbrook's next overture was rather more serious. He himself, having been disappointed in his hope of getting a cabinet position in 1916–17 (he had expected, apparently, the Board of Trade), was finally, amid storms of public protest and objections from the king, made minister of an entirely new Ministry of Information in February 1918. His friend and rival, Northcliffe, was made director of enemy propaganda. Beaverbrook rode the protests and refused to resign, and then had to set about forming his ministry. He chose an odd collection of people, mostly from his personal friends, and one of the men he chose was Arnold Bennett.

He wanted Bennett to be director of propaganda in France, and asked him on 11 April if he would undertake the post. Bennett was amused to find that he was considered an expert in French psychology on the basis of *The Pretty Lady*, which Beaverbrook admired greatly. Three days later Bennett wrote and accepted. He was due to take up his duties on 9 May; before that he finished his play, *The Title*. Beaverbrook had dramatically altered the course of his friend's career. He had also, indirectly, put him on the Army Reserve List; Lloyd George, who had become prime minister partly through his machinations, introduced his Manpower Bill in April 1918, and Bennett, a month before his fifty-first birthday, was just young enough to be in the reserve. Wells, a few months older, was too old. Luckily his military services were not to be called upon. But the Ministry was to keep him busy for the rest of the war.

His first day in the office was, he says, 'rather a lark', but he soon found that he could do no other work, apart from his journalism. The post was without pay, and he put in an eight-hour day five days a week, travelling to Comarques on Saturday evenings and back to London early on Monday morning. A.J.P.Taylor says that Bennett was the most successful of Beaverbrook's appointments, and that he showed considerable flair for administration, but unfortunately there is no official record of the Ministry's achievements, so it's very difficult to know what he actually did. It's easier to know what the Ministry failed to do: as we've seen, Beaverbrook himself was highly unpopular in many quarters from the beginning, and kept up a running feud with the Foreign Office about areas of responsibility and access to documents. He also tried to involve his Ministry, without success, in the censoring of German radio (the department of the Press Bureau), in persuading the Americans to put the Allied case in Ireland, and in rousing anti-bolshevik feeling. The one clear lesson to be drawn from Beaverbrook's brief period of power was the need for more co-ordinated information, more planning of propaganda, and less inter-departmental squabbling, but unfortunately, when the Second World War came round, most of the Ministry's records seemed to be lost somewhere between the Foreign Office and the Record Office, so his experiences were largely wasted. H.V.Rhodes, given in 1938 the job of exploring the nature of German propaganda during the First World War, assumed at first that there must be some experts somewhere who remembered how things had been done, and that there must be some records still around, but in the end he drew such a blank that he had to resort to an article on propaganda in the *Encyclopedia Britannica*.[55]

The record of Bennett's activities is nearly as blank. In his journal, characteristically, he relates only his political and diplomatic mistakes, such as a misunderstanding over the king's attendance at France's Day at

Westminster Abbey, and a pro-French article in the *Observer* which inspired a minute of censure from the War Office, which in turn inspired the wrath of Beaverbrook, and eventually an apology from Lloyd George. He lunched with foreign journalists, wrote contributions for Allied Overseas broadcasts, investigated the problem of the hostility of the French press, and presumably had dealings with men such as the character in *Lord Raingo*, who devotes himself to writing articles about the English garden, in an attempt to persuade the French that they have no right to despise it: 'They don't know,' says this amazing character, 'that England possessed some of the very finest specimens of formal gardens in the world, and I intend to enlighten them upon this point.'[56] When his minister expresses some doubt about the utility of bombarding a nation at war with propaganda about formal gardens, he replies that anything that increases the respect of the French intelligentsia for the British could not but be useful.

Whether or not this is a direct portrait of one of the members of his staff, it is fair to say that the Ministry contained some curious people, and brought Bennett into contact with others. Ford Madox Ford, for instance, wrote a piece on the Armistice for Bennett, and never forgave him for censoring parts of it. It proved the end of their long friendship. D. H. Lawrence, in desperate financial straits at this time, and embarrassingly married to a German baroness, applied to him for work, which sensibly enough he could not find; but, with characteristic generosity, he gave money to Pinker, to be given anonymously to Lawrence. He seems to have managed to avoid any major rows; unlike Beaverbrook, he was basically a tactful, diplomatic and easy-going man, able to get on with a great range of people, and able to state his case to Beaverbrook himself quite forcefully without losing his friendship. A letter from Bennett to Beaverbrook, written in October 1918, about the general hostility which the Ministry aroused, is quite outspoken about the fact that much of the hostility is directed against Beaverbrook himself, and yet it is so phrased that the two men were able to remain on good terms.

This new way of life kept Bennett too busy to attend many of the rehearsals of his new play, *The Title*, which opened at the Royalty on 20 July. He didn't go to the first night, but took an interest in the production, dropped in when he had time, and was pleased with its apparent success – it ran for 285 performances. He continued to attend official dinners in the evenings, and some less official ones – on 2 July he dined at the Savoy with Beaverbrook, the Edwin Montagus and Diana Manners (Lady Diana Cooper) and the conversation turned, embarrassingly, to whether or not Diana Manners was the original of Queenie in *The Pretty Lady*. The two had not met before, and Bennett knew of her and her reputation only through gossip and the gossip columns, which acclaimed her as 'the Duke and Duchess of Rutland's charming and ubiquitous daughter', as 'one of the prettiest and most popular of the younger generation in society',[57] and which delighted to show her at dances, house parties, bazaars, hunt balls and taking part in amateur theatricals. It was the Countess of Chell situation all over again; clearly, on one level, Bennett could repudiate the charge, as he didn't know her personally, but equally clearly he had caught something of her character through hearsay. Lady Diana herself could see the resemblance, and reports the uncanny experience of living through incidents similar to those in the novel, which Bennett could not have known from anyone. They were on the same wavelength, and Bennett had picked up enough from gossip and the papers to be able to get close to her without having met her. She was a very close friend of Beaverbrook's; she was young, beautiful, talented, aristocratic, and fitted very much Bennett's descriptions of Queenie and Concepcion. Concepcion had worked in a factory on the Clyde; Lady Diana worked at Guy's Hospital. Both appeared in charity performances; Lady Diana was a gifted and successful actress. But it was the style of her set that Bennett had captured, and which fascinated him. She herself, writing in her autobiography *The Rainbow Comes and Goes*, describes how she and her circle, 'the Grenfells, the Listers, the Asquiths, Horners, Trees, Charterises, Tennants and Herberts', called themselves the Corrupt Coterie – 'There was amongst us a reverberation of the Yellow Book and Aubrey Beardsley.... Swinburne often got recited. Our pride was to be unafraid of words, unshocked by drink and unashamed of "decadence" and gambling – Unlike-Other-People, I'm afraid. Our peak of unpopularity was certainly 1914–1915.'[58] At the period when she met Bennett, however, disapproval (which was an emotion he very rarely felt, and certainly would not have felt for her) was swallowed up, even in the public imagination, by the more serious matter of war; the war efforts of the Coterie, silly as some of them may have looked (Bennett certainly makes fun of them in *The Pretty Lady*), were taken as a sign of grace.

Bennett was impressed by Lady Diana, and she liked him. After the dinner, they returned with Beaverbrook to Beaverbrook's rooms at the Hyde Park Hotel, and Bennett and she sat on the windowsill looking at the view and talking of life and women, thus beginning what was to be a lasting friendship. He thought her unhappy (like Queenie and Concepcion) but perhaps, like them, she liked to be thought unhappy: it was part of the Swinburne–*Yellow Book* pose. This was the famous occasion on which

Bennett noted (in the privacy of his journal) that Beaverbrook's pyjamas were second-rate. The remark has so often been quoted as a sign of Bennett's snobbery and vulgarity that it is perhaps necessary to point out that he admired Beaverbrook immensely, and commented on his pyjamas as a friendly joke. It amused him to see a multi-millionaire cabinet minister sitting in bed in second-rate pyjamas, just as it amused him to sit on a windowsill with a very beautiful and aristocratic young woman who thought he had put her in a novel.

The war news improved during the summer, but Bennett's work did not diminish. On the contrary, Beaverbrook was so pleased with him that he increased his duties, and at the end of September Bennett writes to J.C. Squire that 'I have only been at the Ministry of Information five months, and have risen to be the head of it, with supreme authority over all departments, under Beaverbrook, who leaves decisions to me. . . . It is my fatal gift for inspiring confidence and never saying anything that lands me into these messes.'[59] One of the reasons for Beaverbrook's reliance upon his friend was that he himself was a sick man. He managed to conceal the seriousness of his illness for some time, but he was worse than even Bennett noticed, and on 21 October he resigned. During his period of office he threatened to resign many times – indeed, he threatened to resign before he was even officially appointed – and had had constant rows with the Foreign Office. He had been publicly attacked by the Liberals again and again, and accused of introducing corruptible businessmen as heads of departments, and of using the Ministry as an instrument of party politics. But in fact he stuck it out until the war was more or less over; he could see, and Bennett could see, that the days of his Ministry were numbered, that there would be no need for it once the armistice was signed, and that it was a waste of time to think in terms of long-term plans or reorganizations. On 15 October Bennett is commenting on the 'air of unreality' in his plans, and thought of resigning with Beaverbrook, but he was asked to stay on until the Ministry was broken up. He visited Beaverbrook frequently during his illness; he had had an operation on a glandular swelling in his neck, and recovered temporarily, only to fall ill again next year with actinomycosis. Although depressed, he was already doubtless looking ahead, to the next elections, to the future of the *Daily Express* and what he could do with it.

The disbanding of the temporary wartime ministries and departments seems to have been handled with a singular absence of tact. Bennett received his dismissal in a Roneo-ed war cabinet minute, and he says that many others were treated in the same way. His resignation took effect from 14 November, though he spent some time winding up his affairs there. It is difficult to say precisely what the experience had meant to him. He had clearly found some of the work interesting, he had liked the flavour of public life, and, as he noted in mid-career, he had acquired 'the most marvellous material for a book';[60] the book was to be *Lord Raingo*. But he had no real feeling for power, just as he had no real feeling for finance. He knew that he was probably more effective as a private journalist than he would ever be as a politician or a committee member, and he had constant proof of the respect with which he was regarded by men in public life: an article of his in the *Daily News* on 21 November, blaming Liberal leadership, produced from Asquith himself 'a polite letter of self-justification'. He was, in many ways, much happier with his freedom to print what he liked than with the discretions of office. He had no patience with those who jockeyed for honours and appointments, and when he himself was offered a knighthood, along with Wells, in 1919 (through Beaverbrook's instigation, of course), he turned it down. He had to: his play attacking the distribution and the corruption of honours was still fresh in the public memory, and he was not a man to change his views to fit the moment. One wonders if Marguerite regretted his decision, as does the wife in *The Title*. There is an interesting conversation recorded with Beaverbrook, on 21 November 1918 – Bennett says: 'I had tea with Max yesterday. He wanted to compare my desire to express myself and make money with the political desire to get titles; but he failed.'[61] Max clearly felt slightly uneasy in the face of his friend's noble disregard, and cannot have believed in it entirely, or he would not have pressed Lloyd George the following year.

So the war and the Ministry came to an end, leaving Bennett free to turn his mind to other things. He had done no creative writing for half a year, and his mind was already beginning to turn towards the theatre – a weekend meeting with the importunate Lillah McCarthy in November, and an invitation to join the board of directors of the Lyric Hammersmith, as Chairman, had set his imagination to work. The Ministry of Information disappeared completely, and its work, as A.J.P. Taylor says, 'vanished beyond recall'.[62] The episode served Bennett in two ways: it provided him with some valuable material for fiction, and it cemented his friendship with Beaverbrook: their mutual esteem increased during this association, and was not impaired by the messy, confused disbanding–resignation operation at the end of it. Beaverbrook wrote a letter of warm thanks and appreciation to Bennett for his services saying: 'I am sorry in a way that it is all over. My association with you in the Ministry will always be a memorable incident in my life, and I feel sure that our personal friendship will survive the mere dissolution of official ties.'[63] And so it did. Dorothy Cheston Bennett said to me once that perhaps it would have been 'a good thing if Arnold had never met Max', and one can see what she means: Beaverbrook's powerful personality pulled Bennett increasingly into a world of journalism and public affairs which he enjoyed, but which may well have sapped his energy (he was growing older – he was fifty-one when the war ended) and prevented him from concentrating on his more serious fiction. Also, Beaverbrook set a high standard of expense and luxury which Bennett was to find, in the end, dispiriting. On the other hand, both gained, in personal terms, tremendously from the friendship. And it provided the background for at least one extremely interesting novel.

The war ended, for Bennett, with very little sense of euphoria or abandon. While society friends were smashing glasses, dancing on tables and letting their hair down at the Carlton, and soldiers and secretaries were making bonfires from billboards in Leicester Square, Bennett was sitting quietly in his Ministry tidying up his papers. The weather was bad that autumn: it rained constantly, damping the Armistice celebrations. Bennett had neuralgia and was over-tired, Beaverbrook was depressed and ill in bed, Masterman had a bad cold, and the country was suffering from a major flu epidemic – *The Times* reported 7,000 died of flu in the first week of November, and another 7,500 the following week. Cinemas and public places were closed for health reasons, there were queues for bread and potatoes, the food controller was appealing for economy in milk consumption, and the newly unemployed munitions workers were on the march, foreshadowing the labour troubles of the 1920s.

Bennett was too old and too disillusioned to get up and dance. The spectacle of two great nations bleeding each other to death had not been edifying, and Bennett was far too much of a realist to hope for a radical change in human nature. It is true that the war hadn't affected him as closely as it had some of his friends – he had no sons to worry about, his nephews were too young to be involved, and the nearest he had come to bereavement was when two of his ex-gardeners were killed at the Front. Compared with a slightly younger generation, he had been relatively detached: Katherine Mansfield, for instance, had lost her brother and many of her close friends. It was her generation that became hysterical with relief. Bennett must have felt relief, but he didn't manifest it much. He had personal worries still hanging over him: his relationship with Marguerite had clearly deteriorated throughout the war. He had found many aspects of the war intensely interesting, and had enjoyed the sensation of being a man of influence, deferred to by Asquith, consulted by Beaverbrook, listened to by the nation. He had met a wider range of people, in the vast social mix-up that the war produced, than he would have otherwise have encountered, and he loved contrasts and variety. He positively enjoyed the spectacle of the archetypal gentleman, Galsworthy, offering chocolates to the cook during an air raid. But on the whole, the war had depressed him. In his own way, he was to enter into the spirit of the 1920s, approving some of its manifestations more than others – he came to like dancing, but always disapproved of the cocktail habit – but he was depressed by the universal silliness that the war produced. On 23 October, as the war ground to a halt, he went to the Pavilion to see a review called *As You Were* – not surprisingly, at this time the theatres of London were full of musical comedies, reviews and mediocre war plays – and commented bleakly to his journal: 'A few fair jokes (verbal). As a whole terribly mediocre. Every scene turned on adultery, or mere copulation. Even in the primeval forest scene, an adultery among gorillas was shown.'[64]

A new world, in many respects more silly than brave, was born, and Bennett was not to be its greatest chronicler. Evelyn Waugh, Noël Coward, Aldous Huxley, Michael Arlen and William Gerhardi were waiting to catch it. Bennett, who had never been a Bright Young Thing even when he was young, was now distinctly cast in the role of Grand Old Man.

11

Postwar Troubles

At the end of the war, however, Bennett was by no means out-dated. He was more in demand than ever, and particularly in the theatre. His most lasting contribution was probably not through his own plays, but through his backing of the Lyric, Hammersmith, which offered some of the finest productions and some of the best plays of the period, all warmly supported by Bennett. *The Beggar's Opera*, lavishly designed by Lovat Fraser, was a spectacular success, but there were many others, all of them a tribute to the management, which continued to produce plays of real quality in an age when frivolity in entertainment was most in demand.

Bennett's own plays were less fortunate, but he threw himself into writing them with enthusiasm. His first postwar undertaking was the long-requested play for Lillah Macarthy, whose divorce from Granville Barker had taken place in June 1918. (Another sign of the times was the colossal increase in the divorce rate – the annual rate rose from a prewar average of 965 to a postwar average of 4,874.) Lillah Macarthy had known Bennett well for years, and had been begging him for a play, without success, for at least a decade; she had renewed the attack on 8 November, and managed to get hold of him for the weekend of 7 and 8 December, which they both spent with her future husband, Dr Frederick Keeble, the biologist. Bennett promised to write her a piece on the biblical subject of Judith. Perhaps he was influenced by the country house atmosphere; perhaps he was sorry for Lillah, whose marriage had been foundering for years, and who needed work to cheer herself up. (In the same spirit, Shaw had written *Annajanska* for her, in which she had appeared at the Coliseum the year before; despite the loyalty of such influential friends, her successful and brilliant career was in fact more or less ended with her marriage.) Having once aroused Bennett's interest, Lillah did not let the moment slip, and within a week he had committed himself to her and to the producer, John Drinkwater, and had agreed to finish the play by the end of January. He had also vaguely promised plays to three other managements. The sense of release from war work and war anxieties must have gone to his head. He had already arranged to write the book *Our Women*, which was to appear at the end of 1919. But *Judith* was the proposition which attracted him most, for he began it in January, as he had promised, and finished it by 28 January 1919.

It is a strange play, and it did not succeed. Like *Don Juan de Marana*, it is a historical piece, a mixture of comedy and seriousness, and this was not his happiest medium. The language is intermittently archaic and modern, and the jokes are heavy-handed. It's not surprising, however, that Lillah McCarthy saw in it a suitable vehicle for herself as an actress. The play required her to appear at first in sackcloth, which she then took off in an unveiling scene. It required her to loll around on leopard skins in a tent, seduce Holofernes, and stab him in the back. It was strong, sexy, dramatic stuff; and she resolved to appear half-naked. Bennett was immensely impressed by her appearance. The first night in April was in that stronghold of respectability, Eastbourne, and Lillah appeared thus: 'Above a line drawn $\frac{1}{2}$ inch or 1 inch about the "mont de Venus" she wore nothing except a 4 in band of black velvet round the body hiding the breasts and a similar perpendicular band of velvet starting from between the breasts and going down to the skirt and so hiding the navel. Two thin shoulder straps held this contrivance in position . . . the skirt was slit everywhere and showed her legs up to the top of the thigh. . . . She looked a magnificent picture thus, but a police prosecution would not have surprised me at all.'[1] The Eastbourne audience, however, received the play with 'immense enthusiasm', and a local critic considered Lillah's performance as 'almost perfect'.[2] So there were great hopes for its West End opening. It opened at the Kingsway on 30 April, and Bennett, by now an experienced barometer of theatrical response, could tell at once that things were not as they should be – for one thing, 'the interested friendly applause was too insistent',[3] always a bad sign. The reviews, though mixed, were on the whole bad: most papers praised Lillah's 'much-daring costume', 'her excessively daring costume', and liked the 'gorgeous pageantry' and 'rich pictures', but had little to say for Bennett's script. The *Telegraph* found that his dialogue did not 'rise above the modest level of the libretto of pageantry', the *Evening Standard* complained rather stuffily that he had laid profane hands on a sacred and familiar tale and, more justifiably, that the play had no action and no character-drawing. The *Daily Express* said the play was intellectually provocative, and would offend 'a great many sensitive folk'. Bennett was greatly disappointed, partly because he had paid the play unusual attention, to the extent of braving the first night, and partly for the sake of Lillah and Marguerite, who were good friends, and had had such faith in it. As the audiences and the receipts fell, Bennett comforted himself, a little unjustifiably, with the thought that the play had been too true and difficult to please the public, but Marguerite took the failure as 'a bombshell'. And relations with Marguerite at this time could hardly bear any extra strain.

There were many things troubling them. The war had divided them, without a doubt. Marguerite's enthusiasm for officers and dancing was not one he could share; they had set up different establishments in London; he had been extremely busy and preoccupied for many months; and Marguerite, for reasons of her own, had begun to make excuses to get out of accompanying him – for instance, she refused a weekend at the Wells's at the end of 1918 because she said she could not leave the dogs – the second time, Bennett comments impassively, that she had made such an excuse. Their relationship is difficult to chart, for it was full of ups and downs right to the very last week – they dined together in company, celebrated their eleventh wedding anniversary at the Café Royal on 4 July 1918, visited together, spent a much-needed holiday in Somerset in September 1918. But a sense of strain was beginning to tell. Richard Bennett, the adopted nephew, was a source of friction as well as of pleasure; he was still living with them, and indeed accompanied them to the first night of *Judith*. His uncle was deeply interested in his progress – in March 1918 he and Marguerite had spent the weekend at his school, Oundle, staying with the headmaster, Sanderson, and there are constant references to Richard's scientific interests. Bennett even complains on one occasion of having smoked too much because of the excuse of providing ash for Richard's scientific experiments. He accompanied him to Cambridge, in October 1920, when Richard went up to Clare College, and Richard was a constant guest in later years. In fact, Arnold and Richard got on well – Arnold was never very relaxed with children but he was good with adolescents, and his correspondence with Richard shows that he was a careful and understanding guardian.

But Marguerite was another matter. Richard did not like her, and the less he liked her, the more demanding and difficult and rejected she became. There was no reason why he should like her. She came from an alien culture, and she demanded the kind of response that a boy from the Potteries would not know how to give. Their whole relationship was an extension of the problems of Marguerite's first meeting with Arnold's sisters. Marguerite, a

Frenchwoman, had been ready to embrace her new sisters-in-law, but she met with a cold welcome. Women in Stoke-on-Trent are not lavish with their kisses. Similarly, she doubtless had an idea that she would find in Richard a loving, demonstrative, docile child, who would supply some of the admiration and attention that she needed. The story of their fraught relationship has been admirably told by Dudley Barker in *Writer by Trade*.*[4] Marguerite, foolishly, tried to win Richard's affection by making communication with his real parents, Frank and Florence Bennett, more and more difficult. She complained about Florence's letters to her son, and persuaded Bennett to write to his brother that he must look upon Richard as 'not your son, but ours for all mortal purposes. He will be your nephew.'[5] Bennett also said, apologetically, that the difference between the French and English attitudes on such matters was rather pronounced. It is easy to guess how distressed Florence and Frank must have been by this problem. Frank was in personal and financial difficulties (he was an alcoholic) and had moved into a small house in Rochdale, which was not large enough to receive Marguerite as a guest. Richard, in the grandeur of Comarques, and missing his father and mother, must have felt a traitor. Marguerite's attitude and behaviour over this issue were very strange. She wanted to adopt the child legally and refused to understand even the legal objections, let alone the emotional ones. She also wanted to change his name to Arnold, a crazy notion which Bennett firmly resisted, and when she realized that his refusal was absolute she became very agitated and wrote him a letter saying that henceforth she had no more interest in the boy.[6] It is possible that she desperately wanted, or thought she wanted, a child of her own, as she says in this letter, but the ill-tempered unreasonable tone of her correspondence together with her lack of real affection or concern for Richard make it seem unlikely. She wanted power and 'victory'. Richard must have felt increasingly uneasy, a pawn in some incomprehensible adult game, and finally, in the summer of 1919, when his uncle was away in Ireland on holiday, he could stand it no longer. He and Marguerite quarrelled, irretrievably, over some trivial domestic issue, as the result of which he wrote her a note (they were a great family for writing internal post) saying that he had never been 'really fond of her', and that 'when Uncle is away I feel unhappy and not free'.[7] She could not forgive him for this rejection. He was packed off home, and she cut herself off from him completely. Arnold reproached him for his rudeness, but he must have understood its causes all too well. He continued to pay his bills, to invite him to his yacht and to visit him

* A biography of A.B., with particular emphasis on the story of Richard.

at Cambridge, and he wrote to him frequently for the rest of his life.

Such were the domestic rows that were brewing up over these years; the incident with Richard illustrates their relationship all too clearly. Marguerite had a violent temper, and her emotional, inconsistent behaviour showed itself at its most dangerous when dealing with a child. One might argue that a child of her own might have changed her, but Bennett had good cause to fear her heredity, as well as his own. Indeed, this is the reason he offers for his decision not to have children. In one of the notes that flew between them during these years, he says that he doesn't object to the idea of having children because of his work (as she had evidently claimed), but because his own father had died of softening of the brain, and two of her family were mentally abnormal. 'These things are apt to jump a generation,'[8] he says. One can't tell whether this is his real reason or not; whatever his other objections to children, he had good cause not to see in her an ideal mother, and was at this point so depressed by his marriage that the last thing he can have wanted to do was to perpetuate it. To be fair to Marguerite, she was reaching a difficult age, when childlessness can become a peculiar torment, and perhaps he was not sufficiently aware of this, or sympathetic to it. But one cannot blame him for being too tired to cope. Friends such as Swinnerton were well aware of his domestic unhappiness, and watched him withdraw more and more into his own world.

In July 1919, he took up a more permanent residence in London: he left his rooms at the Yacht Club and moved into a flat in George Street, Hanover Square. There was room here for Marguerite as well, so she let her Oxford Street flat, and they would stay in London together. This may have been an attempt of a kind at reconciliation, for Bennett was not a man to give up easily. He had plenty of work to distract him from marriage problems; he was working on a new play, and was also much involved with the affairs of the Lyric, Hammersmith, which he had persuaded Beaverbrook to back. The commercial and artistic success of this enterprise delighted him, and was some compensation for the struggles he had over his own plays.

The Lyric was only one of many ventures that claimed his time and advice over this period; he was now a rich and established literary figure, and his name and backing were in great demand. He was as generous as ever, offering help to young writers, both known and unknown. He found time to write long encouraging letters to Walpole, Pauline Smith and Swinnerton, discussing their work in attentive detail. He had recommended T.S. Eliot to the War Office in 1918, and continued to praise his poetry and his periodical, the *Criterion*. He recommended Robert Graves for a university post in

Cairo; Graves remembers he was 'the first critic who spoke out strongly for my poems in the daily press' (*Goodbye To All That*).[9] John Rothenstein, whose father, William, Bennett had met ten years earlier, was another of those whom he encouraged. Rothenstein recalls: 'I look back with particular affection and gratitude to Arnold Bennett ... the readiness of Bennett to discuss with me the technicalities of his profession, his assumption that I would be a writer, and his apparent conviction that my writings offered some degree of promise, gave me pleasure and confidence, as well as cause for surprise. ... I was deeply touched that he should perceive in it a gleam of something worthy of cultivation.'[10] Such tributes were widespread and deserved, for Bennett's generosity was remarkable, as was his lack of jealousy and fear in the face of rising generations of new writers.

Bennett's help wasn't confined to writers, either. He also took a great interest in young painters, writing a preface to the Catalogue of the First Exhibition of Paul Nash (April 1918), and writing to Mrs Herzog to ask her to find someone to look after the asthmatic and 'extremely lonely' Ben Nicholson, who had been sent to California to look after his health. In 1918 and 1919 he was approached to back two periodicals, one devoted to the graphic arts, which Paul Nash would edit, and the other an already established quarterly called *Art and Letters*. He showed himself interested in both, and agreed to stand 'all the loss, which I am fairly sure will be considerable'[11] for four numbers of the Paul Nash project. He got Swinnerton and Chatto & Windus to take an interest too, but nothing came of it. Perhaps his sensible financial warnings frightened Paul Nash off. *Art and Letters* was a distinguished illustrated periodical, edited by Frank Rutter, with a dazzling list of contributors – it published work by T.S.Eliot, Herbert Read, Modigliani, Gaudier-Brzeska, Wyndham Lewis, Ezra Pound, Dorothy Richardson and Aldous Huxley. Bennett's real contact with it was through Osbert Sitwell, whom he admired, and he agreed, in September 1918, to stand the quarterly's losses, up to a certain well-defined limit. He liked the Sitwell circle, perhaps surprisingly – he records a dinner with Osbert at his house in Swan Walk, Chelsea, in June 1919, at which he met Aldous Huxley, Sassoon, W.H.Davies, Leonard Woolf and Herbert Read: Bennett liked both the guests and the dinner. (He and Huxley were in fact to become close friends, again perhaps surprisingly, in view of Bennett's distrust of hereditary intellectuals.) The Sitwells shared Bennett's enthusiasm for modern painting, and Bennett wrote an introduction for the catalogue of an exhibition which they organized at the Mansard Gallery in August 1919. It included paintings by Fournier, Dufy, Soutine, Vlaminck, Utrillo, Matisse,

Picasso and Modigliani. Bennett recognized the Modiglianis as masterpieces and bought one. He was continuing faithfully in his role of popularizer of high art and educator of public taste; not the slightest sign of reactionary hardening was overtaking him. He says, of the exhibition, that it ought to 'do as much good as the lately departed Russian ballet. It is an education to the islanders; and of course it is equally a joy.'[12] And in November of the same year he writes to Paul Nash for paintings for an exhibition of modern art in the Five Towns, which he is helping the Fine Art section of the Ceramic Society to organize. 'In this district of 250,000 people,' he says, 'there has never been a picture show.'[13] Last time I was there, in 1972, the Art Gallery contained a collection of sculptures by Henry Moore. He would have liked that.

Another friend who encouraged his enthusiasm for art was Dr Thomas Bodkin, the Irish lawyer and art historian, whom he had met in Dublin on his official visit in 1917. He went to visit him again in August 1919, after a holiday in Scotland with Beaverbrook. They went to the National Gallery together, of which Bodkin was later to be director, and also round the antique shops, where Bodkin saved Bennett from buying a fake Poussin. He met George Russell, James Stephens, a friend of Marie Bashkirtseff called Miss Purser. He went to the races, drank stout, got his feet wet and worried about the feckless style of the Irish, who managed to cut a dash on very ordinary incomes. Then he went back to Liverpool, for the first night of his play, *Sacred and Profane Love*, which opened on 15 September, with Iris Hoey in the lead. He writes back to Bodkin that it was 'a furious success',[14] and so indeed it seemed to be, for he had to take two curtain calls as the author, which he had never done before. Still, he knew well enough that a London audience was another matter. The play opened at the Aldwych on 10 November, and ran for just over a hundred performances. This was a respectable but not a brilliant success. On the other hand, financially Bennett was doing very nicely, for the same play went on tour in the United States in February 1920 and took 25,000 dollars in the first two weeks. The same year he sold the film rights for £1,500. The theatre was still offering bright rewards; which was just as well, for Bennett had three commissioned plays yet to write.

That autumn he did very little work, by his own standards, and leaves no record of his yearly output in words and income in cash. He was, it is true, planning his plays, and looking hard – too hard – for ideas. He had finished his book on women in June. He was not working on a novel, though he was toying with the idea of one about Beaverbrook's father. He was not exactly idle – he went to the theatre, discussed Squire's new *London Mercury* at great length, prided himself on the success of the exhibition of war paintings that resulted from his and Masterman's commissions for the War Memorial Committee. But he was not working. At one point he writes to Beaverbrook declining a dinner because of ill-health, and writes to Walpole on 12 December that 'I am still doing no work, – haven't done any for 3½ months. I could work; but I won't.' Later in the letter he says 'Marguerite is very well. She is just now flaunting over London a fur cloak whose existence in her wardrobe is due to the cardinal fact that I must either earn money or spend it. At present I am not earning it.'[15] Would one be right to suppose that trouble with Marguerite was preventing him from working? Or did he not feel he had to? His income was safe enough: he could command a high price for journalism, his plays brought in an income from provincial and foreign tours, many of his books were in print. *Our Women* was still in hand, *Sacred and Profane Love* might run for years. Still, it wasn't like Bennett to relax too much. Inactivity in him was a bad sign.

At the end of January 1920, Arnold Bennett and Frank Swinnerton set off together for a holiday in Portugal. Their friendship had become closer during the last few years, and was unruffled by such minor dissensions as Swinnerton's coolness (in print in the *Daily Telegraph*) about *Sacred and Profane Love*. Bennett had always supported his friend, defending him from the carping of the *London Mercury*, writing detailed and encouraging criticisms of his books, and a foreword for Swinnerton's extremely successful novel, *Nocturne*, and inviting him for many a weekend to Comarques, where they enjoyed literary gossip. The holiday was a success. Bennett, naturally, wrote it up and illustrated it and managed to sell 'Impressions of Portugal' to *Harper's*, who published them in 1922. He also wrote several letters from Portugal to his nephew Richard, describing the weather, the bad roads and the casino, and concluding 'I have never enjoyed a holiday more'.[16]

On his return, Bennett declined an invitation from Hearst newspapers to go to Russia for them and began his new play, *The Bright Island*. He was encouraged by the success of *Sacred and Profane Love* in the United States, but nevertheless was not surprised when the finished play, three months later, was turned down by Basil Dean, who had commissioned it. He comments that the Lyric accepted it with enthusiasm, and that the year before the Lyric had rejected *Sacred and Profane Love*, which Basil Dean had accepted with enthusiasm. But despite its initial alacrity, the Lyric also let its option lapse, and the play was not produced until February 1925, when the Stage

Society put it on, directed by Komisarjevsky. This, for Bennett, was in itself an admission that he knew the play was uncommercial (though he had picked up £500 in lapsed options, he claims) – he writes to Hubert Griffith in February 1925: 'My opinion of the thing remains what it was. I showed what I thought of it by asking the Stage Society to produce it. I consider that bits of it are undramatic, but otherwise I do not blush for it.'[17]

He ought, however, perhaps, to have blushed for it a little: it is a curiously unreal piece, set on an imaginary island, with two British characters, and the rest characters from the Commedia del' Arte, such as Pantaloon, Harlequin, Columbine, etc. The play flirts with a few political and social ideas – that men should have two wives and wives two husbands, for instance – and has a few good jokes about bribery, British justice and the British ruling classes, but Bennett completely lacks Shaw's abstract brilliance, and cannot master the serious paradox. He is not at all at home in an abstract setting; he has wit and irony, but they always spring from detail and observation. Wells, drawing a comparison between his own development and Bennett's, notes this point: he says 'He increased in precision and his generalizations weakened; I lost precision and my generalizations grew wider and stronger.'[18] It was because of this weakness that Bennett's plays are on the whole so unsatisfactory.

Body and Soul, his next play, which he wrote in May 1920 and which was performed in 1922, is a much less ambitious, much sillier play, and its plot too is pure fantasy, but it is more amusing to read. It is a slight comedy, dealing with a plot by the society heroine Lady Mab Infold to pass off herself as a secretary, and a typewriter saleswoman as herself. The stock figures are there – the typewriter woman is a homely but clever girl from Lancashire; there is a scene with the Mayor and Mayoress of Bursley; there is a phoney hypnotist and spiritualist, and a wicked Marquis. Lady Mab herself is an exaggerated portrait of the idle, rich, gossip-column types that he had drawn more seriously in *The Pretty Lady*; like Diana Manners's set, Lady Mab wears outrageous pyjamas, makes shocking remarks, believes that she and her friends can make or break an opera, and takes a keen interest in her own plentiful press cuttings. There is nothing serious in the play at all, but it is quite well done. However, it did not run. Bennett thought Viola Tree, in the role of Lady Mab, was excellent, but it came off in less than a month. He seems to have taken it seriously himself, and wrote to Harriet Cohen that it might 'with luck be understood of the people in 20 years time as Shaw's plays will,'[19] but it is hard to see what of its content he found difficult or controversial.

249

Certainly, at this stage in his life, although he was well able to take the abuse of the critics, he did seem to be growing incapable of perceiving the slightness of his own work, particularly in the theatre; moreover, he took exception to the suggestion that he did not take his plays seriously, and wrote at length rebuking W.J.Turner, who had dared to suggest that *Sacred and Profane Love* could not have been regarded by its author as 'a contribution to dramatic literature'. Perhaps the accusation that he wrote plays for money had enough truth in it to hurt, and made him all the more careful to defend his integrity.

It was hard for him to stay away from the theatre: his plays were clamoured for, at least in advance, and the new film world was making overtures. The Lyric, Hammersmith, also needed his attention, and in May 1920 he helped with the adaptation of *The Beggar's Opera*, which was to be one of the Lyric's greatest artistic and commercial successes and ran for three years. *The Bright Island, Body and Soul* and another slight play called *The Love Match* were all written between mid-March and the end of July. *The Love Match* is a play about a millionaire, adultery, divorce and an extravagant wife who insists on moving furniture around against her husband's will and sacking his staff: and it reflects, in however trivial a way, Bennett's own pre-occupations. It too earned the same rebuke as *Sacred and Profane Love*, for *The Times* critic wrote: 'If we cannot take this play very seriously, it is because Mr Bennett himself has not been very serious about it.'[20] This comment must have annoyed Bennett; but he cannot claim to have wasted much time over it. It took him a month to write, he thought as he finished it that Eadie might well refuse to take up his £200 option (he did refuse), and he hardly fulfils his promise to conclude the play 'with something very fine about love'. The ending is banal: the old master–slave, man–woman relation-ship theme, handled with a mere fraction of the force that produced *Hilda Lessways*.

Still, whatever the quality of his work, he was back to prewar productivity, and prewar diversions. He wanted a new yacht. The *Velsa* had been a war casualty: he lent her to the Admiralty in 1916, and after the war she was sold. He now wanted something bigger and better, and in August he set about finding it. He went to Southampton, and gazed longingly at the Duke of Westminster's £35,000 yacht *Belem*. He negotiated for a sixty-year-old yacht called the *Wanderer*, but the deal fell through on the surveyor's report. Then he wandered around East Anglia with Swinnerton on a (hired) yacht, the *Zoraïda*; played tennis and croquet when at home, and pondered on an idea for a film script. The summer was marred by an expected tragedy: on

29 August, after a long illness, Rickards died of tuberculous meningitis, leaving a widow of twenty-six. He had been suffering from tuberculosis, aggravated by army conditions – at one point in the war Bennett had tried to get his friend some more suitable employment, but without success. Bennett had been to see him in May, in Bournemouth, and had found him very ill, exiled to 'a world of sickness and tragedy'.[21] Characteristically, he says little of his own grief at the loss of one of his oldest and closest friends, just as earlier he had hardly commented on the death of Schwob. He went to the funeral, deserting Gide who was staying with him at Comarques, found it a distressing experience, and later devoted himself to compiling a memorial volume for his friend, a task both of sentiment and practical help for Rickards's widow. One might assume, from his lack of emotive comment in the journal, that the two friends had been seeing less of one another, but this was not so: during the war, particularly, they had been constantly together. His 'Personal Sketch', which prefaces the memorial volume, *The Art of A.E.Rickards*, pays tribute to his professional skill, his disregard of 'certificates, degrees, distinctions', his attention to both the practical and the ideal, and to his personal qualities, which made him 'a marvellous travelling companion'. He was, Bennett says, 'an artist before everything. I have never met with the artistic temperament ... more completely developed,' and concludes that 'The two most interesting, provocative and stimulating men I have yet encountered are H.G.Wells and A.E.Rickards.'[22]

After a few more days cruising with Swinnerton (who went off to get married on 8 September), Bennett visited Scotland for a week or two with his nephew Richard. They went to Glasgow, Inverness, Dornoch, where they saw the northern lights, and Golspie, where Bennett bought a new yacht, the *Hoyden*, which he later re-christened the *Marie Marguerite*, a compliment to his wife which was shortly to become an embarrassment. This yacht was a much more impressive affair than the 103-ton *Velsa* – in fact, writing to Richard a month later, he says proudly 'She's not a yacht, she's a ship.'[23] One can't help wondering if Richard really enjoyed his holiday with his uncle: on their return he received a long jocular reprimand for his extreme taciturnity. One remembers Pauline Smith, bullied into making conversation. Bennett, however, enjoyed himself. They returned to London at the beginning of October, and Bennett saw Richard into Cambridge, which he describes as 'most beautiful'. He had no son of his own, and had missed university himself. It was a pleasure to him to be able to help his nephew, though their correspondence continues to be marked by sound advice about work, drink, clothes and money.

251

Bennett then began work on his first novel for some time, *Mr Prohack*. He worked hard, writing 14,500 words in less than a month, before the end of October. It was just as well that he made a good start, for November was full of interruptions; some pleasant, such as the work on his new yacht, now at Brightlingsea, and a new revival of *Milestones*; some distracting, such as plans for a new film; and some painful, like a long and almost daily series of dental appointments. For nearly a month he was in the dentist's hands, suffering from pyorrhoea, having injections and extractions. This sensible, practical man's teeth must have been horribly neglected. They had never been attractive – Swinnerton in particular comments constantly on his 'ugly teeth' – but one wouldn't have expected such a hypochondriac to let them get into such poor condition. It was also in November that Marguerite went off on an extraordinary expedition, reciting Baudelaire in Scotland, under the auspices of the Anglo-French Society. She records that Arnold saw her off on the station, in the extreme cold, and said to her 'Do you realise that you have undertaken to do the most astounding thing? It requires nerve! Not even Baudelaire could have foreseen that his poems would be recited in Scotland!'[24] Her war work over, she had turned her attention to more dangerous fields.

The Anglo-French Poetry Society was a body (set up in 1920) which had Bennett for president, and a committee composed of Marguerite, Edith Sitwell and Edith Sitwell's friend Helen Rootham. It seems to have existed principally to organize recitals for Marguerite, and incidentally introduced her to the man who was to play a large part in breaking up the Bennett marriage.

This man was a Frenchman, Pierre Legros, who lectured in French at Bedford College, where Marguerite gave a recital. He was also the tenant of her flat in Thackeray Mansions. He was introduced to the Bennetts by Robert Nichols, the poet, and they seem to have met in 1920; there are several references to him in Bennett's journal. He was much younger than she was: he was thirty, she was forty-six. He and the Bennetts met socially – he knew the Wells's and others of their friends – and Marguerite's interest in him must soon have become marked. She would walk with him alone in Hyde Park, visit him alone in his flat, and talk to him of poetry and love affairs. George and Jean Beardmore, who have documented this relationship in *Arnold Bennett in Love*, suggest that it may have been partly to get her away from Legros that Bennett encouraged her to go off to Scotland. Whatever his hopes of the trip to Glasgow, Edinburgh and Aberdeen, it merely postponed the *dénouement*. There was plenty of trouble in store.

Although Bennett might have been able to see it coming, he didn't yet let it interfere with his work. He shelved *Mr Prohack* for a while in December in order to turn his attention to his first original screen play, *The Wedding Dress*, which he finished on 11 December. There was big money in films already, and Bennett had his eye on it: there was a rumour that Shaw had been offered '£10,000 per original film',[25] which whetted the appetite. Also, Bennett could not resist trying his hand at something new.

The Wedding Dress was never made. At this point there is something curiously depressing about Bennett's literary output, however good the reasons for his new directions. And what is equally curious at this point is Bennett's continuing good judgement about the work of others. He may have over-rated Walpole: he was a friend. But his recognition of D.H. Lawrence, for instance, was immediate, generous and whole-hearted. He read *The Lost Girl* at the end of November, just when he was himself most deeply engaged in trivia, and immediately recognized it as 'the work of a genius', Lawrence as 'far and away the best of the younger school'.[26] This was particularly perceptive in view of the fact that *The Lost Girl* is in many ways an ironic and critical comment on *The Old Wives' Tale* or *Anna of the Five Towns* – its heroine, too, is the daughter of a draper, and she too makes her escape from the drab, ruined world of the Midlands into a new country, in her case the mountains of Italy. Lawrence said of Bennett: 'I hate Bennett's resignation. Tragedy ought really to be a great kick at misery. But *Anna of the Five Towns* seems like an acceptance....'[27] We are back with Frank Harris, who thought that Sophia had the soul of a muck-rake.

It is interesting that both Harris and Lawrence had an excessive interest in sex and women, and could not conceive of salvation without sex. Bennett could, and did. Sophia endures and Anna endures, whereas Lawrence's heroine escapes in the arms of an Italian lover, in a subjugation that many modern women (see Kate Millett's striking analysis of Lawrence[28]) would consider a fate worse than death. How interesting it is that Bennett, who could write with dull banality about masters and slaves and submission, should have made all his true heroines fight till the end, with an inner indestructible core, whereas Lawrence's women find themselves only in submission and destruction. As Millett quotes, Lawrence used to bang his wife against the wall and yell at her, 'I am the master', and she would reply, cuttingly, 'You can be the master as much as you like. I don't care.'[29] Lawrence's attitude might well come out of one of Bennett's worst pieces, though never would he treat it in so sombre a tone.

But in reality, Bennett respected the indestructible selfness of others: his passion for justice was greater than his desire for mastery. His fairness to Marguerite's difficult self lasts till the end. He may have quarrelled over furniture and gardeners, but he did not try to destroy her; neither did he ever suppose that a woman could not exist without a man. And his sense of justice extends into his assessment of Lawrence. He knew Lawrence was great, and he said so. He had been on his side for years: in 1915 he and May Sinclair had been the only two writers to protest publicly about the banning of *The Rainbow*. There was nothing in such protests for Bennett: he himself would never write a book that would be banned; he enjoyed his own public popularity, and freedom of speech was then an unpopular cause. He knew he would not get Lawrence's artistic support, though he helped the younger man himself financially as well as in his criticisms. But Bennett, unlike Lawrence, had a sense of fairness, which left his judgements unclouded. It is a dull quality, maybe, but a great one. It is not easy even for the great and wealthy to see new movements rise to tread them down, and it is as well to remember that Bennett's background was as insecure as Lawrence's own. He too might have descended to petty spite, as Lawrence did to Wells and the writers he disliked and envied. He must have known that *The Lost Girl* was a different class of novel from *Mr Prohack*. But one looks in vain in his works and actions for the least sign of resentment – anxiety, perhaps, but no resentment.

Towards the end of December, Bennett went back to *Mr Prohack*. He finished it on 17 June 1921, over a period when he was troubled with re-writes of his film and what he calls 'conjugal worries'. The novel had already been sold as a serial to *The Delineator* in America, and as the proofs began to arrive in April for the first instalments, he must have been under some pressure to finish it. Christmas 1920 was spent at Claridge's, and the New Year at the Savoy. Bennett says that he made notes for his novel on these events, as though to justify the lack of domesticity. Which of them could not face Comarques, Arnold or Marguerite? Marguerite was much absorbed in her recital plans: she was taking her new career seriously. Was this a relief to him, or an added embarrassment? As we have seen, he was far from en-chanted by the kind of artistic nonsense indulged in at times by the Stage Society, which, despite its excellent support of Ibsen and Shaw, did also have a tendency to put on verse plays, Irish, Greek and indigenous – such plays, one imagines, as the one written by William Rodney, in Virginia Woolf's *Night and Day*, who reads his work aloud to the heroine, Katharine, and produces in her 'a chill stupour . . . as the lines flowed on, sometimes long and sometimes short, but always delivered with the same lilt of the voice, which seemed to nail each line more firmly on to the same spot in the hearer's brain'.[30] Bennett did not like this kind of thing, and made fun of it in *The Regent*. (On the other hand, he liked and admired the Sitwells, who were much given to dramatic recitations.) Marguerite's poetry readings, at this point, were of course also associated in his mind with Legros and notions of infidelity, which must have made them even more irritating, assuming a basic lack of sympathy with the genre. If he did admire his wife's readings (and there is no public moment at which he shows a lack of loyalty, one must admit), it is curious that he never uses them dramatically in any of his novels: a scene with a recital at an evening party would have been a suitable incident in many of his books, and he uses concerts, plays, rehearsals, charity balls, private views and other such social events frequently. But the nearest he gets to using a dramatic recitation is the moment in *The Pretty Lady* when a young prostitute, Alice, recites at a night club, when slightly drunk, the poem

> Helen, thy beauty is to me
> Like those Nicean barks of yore.

Despite the fact that she is a silly young girl, she recites 'with a surprisingly correct and sure pronunciation of difficult words to show that she had, in fact, received some training'.[31] Recitations are thus hardly shown in a very favourable light. In contrast, Bennett's later novels, written after he and Marguerite are separated, contain several sympathetic portraits of straight actresses, of successful actresses, of struggling not-so-young actresses. The world of the theatre, though it caused him many a headache, attracted him much more than its poetic and pseudo-poetic fringes, and was to prove as much a bond as a source of friction in his next partnership.

Christmas at Claridge's, the New Year at the Savoy. Life was certainly expensive. Bennett was finding that one can pay dearly, in cash as well as in emotion, for domestic friction: he tells Marguerite at one point that he is not a machine for making money. She may have been demanding, but she wasn't the only one to blame. He had led her to think of him as a prodigious earner; in some ways he had encouraged her extravagances. He was proud of his ability to buy her whatever she wanted – a car, a fur coat, a holiday. A scene which recurs again and again in his novels and his journals is a scene in which a room, masculine in essence, is adorned by cast-off women's dresses lying decoratively on the furniture; the day in Cannes, in 1911, when Marguerite and her friend Mrs Selwyn had been trying on dresses in his hotel apartment is described with much feeling. It symbolized for him, perhaps, the union of sex, purchasing power and beauty. A man who is sexually insecure may well feel that he has to buy his wife, as the Beardmores rather crudely put it in their account of his relationship with Marguerite. This is a very false view of his total attitude to his wife, but there was perhaps an element of it at work. And of course, apart from her demands, he was himself extravagant, and liked the best. He wasn't a saver. He had worked himself into a strange position. A novelist who chooses to write a novel about a rich man, as he did in *Mr Prohack*, and then finds himself obliged to spend Christmas and the New Year doing research in expensive hotels, to the tune of £27 a dinner (prewar prices), might well be said to have caught himself in a trap of his own making.

12

Separation

1921 was the year that saw the separation of Bennett and his wife. They parted in October, and a deed of separation was drawn up and the two parts of it formally exchanged on 23 November. Bennett writes in his journal on that day, 'The matter is complete.'[1] And the marriage was indeed over, though not as tidily as he would have wished: it still contained much future trouble.

There was nothing particularly clear-cut about their growing estrangement. Many things had separated them – his work, his bachelor habits, his liking of club life, her temper, her loneliness and resentment, the rows over Richard, their different tastes in amusement – but right to the end they continued to spend time together, both in public and in private. They went out to concerts, weddings, theatres and dances, and according to Bennett she asked him to take her to a concert the day after she had confirmed with their lawyer that she wanted a legal separation. Their relationship had evolved in a *laissez-faire* manner, and she did not recognize when the game was over. It was not simply their increasing incompatibility that drew them apart: the trouble over Legros got worse, not better. Marguerite seems to have been indignant about the fact that Bennett seemed jealous of her spending so much time with Legros, and accuses him of being jealous even of her dogs; but Bennett in turn claimed that he was not jealous, that he allowed her an unusual degree of freedom, that he did not care whom she visited or when, and that he trusted her. On the other hand, he does accuse her of being rude and peevish to him in private and public.[2] They struggled hard to come to some kind of agreement, discussing when to see each other, which days she should spend alone, etc. – it seems that she, who had complained that Bennett ignored her, was now demanding her own privacy. The conclusion must be that she was having an affair with Legros, and was possibly even slightly annoyed that Bennett did not get more annoyed about it.

She was financially totally dependent on her husband, and what really seems to have upset Bennett, in the end, was the notion that he was expected to keep his wife's lover. Marguerite was much older than Legros, and Bennett doubtless thought that she was being exploited by him. This put him in a very unpleasant position. He had always been generous to her, but saw no reason why he should keep Legros as well.

Towards the end of March, Marguerite went off to Frascati, ostensibly alone, ostensibly for a solitary holiday. A week or so later she was joined by Legros. She wrote several letters to Bennett (published in *Arnold Bennett in Love*) describing her holiday in the most naïve terms – describing the food, the wine, the sun, the scenery. She had clearly told Bennett that Legros was coming to see her with his mistress, to which Bennett replies caustically 'I have become rather friendly with Marjorie Gordon, a young musical comedy actress. But it is improbable that she will bring a young man with her to meet me in Timbuctoo by accident. . . . Let us hope that at the last moment poor Legros's mistress hasn't been prevented from going with him to Italy! You will be very kind if you will let me have a description of her when you see her. She intrigues me.'[3] Marguerite and Legros stayed together in Frascati for a fortnight, and letters between her and Bennett become increasingly emotional: she accuses him of exaggerating an innocent situation; he says that Legros, whom he has always treated with courtesy, has been rude and deceitful, that he will pay for no more holidays, that Marguerite is infatuated. Yet he is still trying to be fair, still trying to salvage the situation, still expressing a rather sad affection – he addresses her as 'my poor one' and 'my ingenuous wife'. Ingenuous towards Legros and his intentions she may have been, but her treatment towards her husband is full of a calculated duplicity. Her travel plans had been carefully concealed (though her departure, possibly through guilt, had been stormy) and there is something very irritating in the way she tries to present Legros as a poor neurasthenic war victim whom she is cherishing out of pure goodness of heart. She cannot seriously have expected her husband to tolerate such a situation. But then, she was an unorthodox woman, her judgements and sense of reality had always been eccentric, and at that period, in the 1920s, she was surrounded with unorthodoxy. Certainly, when she returned home on 23 April, she expected to be received home and welcomed. And, for a while, she was.

As ever in such cases, it's difficult to unravel cause and effect. Did she behave like this because Bennett neglected her? Was he possibly having an affair with Marjorie Gordon, or some other of the attractive girlfriends with whom he used to go dancing, or is the suggestion that he might be, simply a defensive piece of provocation? There is no proof at all that he was ever unfaithful to Marguerite (unless one counts the story that he slept with a call girl in order to check the facts in *The Pretty Lady*[4]), but he certainly had plenty of cause to be so, had he wished, and plenty of opportunity. He did neglect her, in some ways: his yachting voyages, which she clearly resented, always left her out, as she did not like yachting, and one suspects he did not like to take her. After the dramas of spring, Bennett spent most of the summer of 1921 on the *Marie Marguerite*, a fine expensive toy, with its crew of eight. He writes to Galsworthy in August:

> 'I have been cruising now for $3\frac{1}{2}$ months, and shall cruise for one more month. (But I have a study on board, and have already written 50,000 words therein.) I believe my wife still exists. She spent a few days on the yacht at the start, and we shall end up together in a blaze of glory at Ostend; but otherwise I see little of her during this cruising craze. She hates yachting.'[5]

It could be true that Arnold, in cruel disregard of his wife's inclinations, left her languishing while he went off for month after month; it could also be true that he fled to his yacht as a refuge. When he did call back at Comarques, during this yachting phase, he found her 'holding a court'. Perhaps she preferred it without him. Perhaps he threw her into the arms of a lover by his constant preoccupations and neglect. Certainly she was technically the guilty party. But that is never the whole story.

He at least must have foreseen the conclusion for some time, though she thought to the end that she might be able to have it both ways. Fortunately he was able to finish *Mr Prohack* in June, and then he escaped to his yacht, where he worked on nothing more serious than articles for the *Sunday Pictorial* about such subjects as 'Marriage and the Modern Girl', in which ironically he declares that the modern girl ought to be 'a better and more realistic judge of men'.[6] He also wrote some light pieces for the *Strand*. The project for a new serious non-serial novel about Beaverbrook's father was still in his mind, but in the event it was shelved for ever.

It was as well that he had nothing very weighty to work on, because the business of separation, and of explaining himself to their friends, was painful and exhausting. Some friends were clearly aware of the trouble, and were informed at once: his letter to Beaverbrook is frank, and permits a note of relief – 'Henceforth,' he says, 'I shall be decidedly more free,'[7] and immediately accepts an invitation for a weekend at Cherkley. To others, he explains that he feels deeply sorry for his wife, and knows she will regret her decision, but could do no other. A long letter to Marie Belloc Lowndes, written in February 1922, protests in detail that Marguerite and Legros had 'become the scandal of my household and staff and even the scandal of restaurants. In the last two years preceding our separation Marguerite had £2,500 from me for her own various private purposes (in addition to an excessive sum for housekeeping) and yet she was always complaining that I was stingy with money and kept her poor. There can be no doubt that much of her money went to Legros. Indeed I know it did.'[8] Marguerite, at the age of forty-seven, was a different woman from the thrifty managing French housewife he had admired at thirty-three.

Bennett insists that she had several times asked for a separation in order to live with Legros, and that her resentment after the separation sprang from her lack of foresight about what it would actually involve. She had sacrificed a great deal of status and a famous husband for a man whom most of their circle despised. Financially, she did not suffer: in an over-chivalrous gesture, Bennett made her a very generous settlement, giving her £2,000 a year, provided that this sum should prove to be not more than a quarter of his net income, £5,000 capital at his death, and an income for life of two-thirds of his estate after this £5,000 had been paid. Clearly he did not at this point anticipate re-marriage or the other events of the future: he wanted to demonstrate that he was not, as she had said, mean. £2,000 a year, in those days, was a very handsome income, which enabled her to live in style. She had been much influenced, in the last few months of their marriage, by her aunt and uncle, Hélène and Georges Bion, who had been to visit her at Comarques, and who had pointed out to her that she owned nothing of her own – a bit of partisan family argument that had led her to ask Arnold to give her Comarques, and to express astonishment and indignation when he refused. In the settlement, Bennett tried hard to rid himself of the accusation of meanness, which had been so unfairly levelled against him: the accusations must have wounded him immensely, because he had always been generous to a fault, both materially and emotionally.

In these days of women's rights, when there is much discussion about ownership and shares in the matrimonial home, Marguerite's position might technically seem more reasonable, because it was true that she was completely dependent on her husband's gifts and goodwill, and although she had no children, she was of an age where it would be difficult to earn her living. But the goodwill had never been known to fail, in financial terms at least. No court of law would have awarded her so much, which was doubtless one of the reasons why she so bitterly resisted the idea of divorce, though as

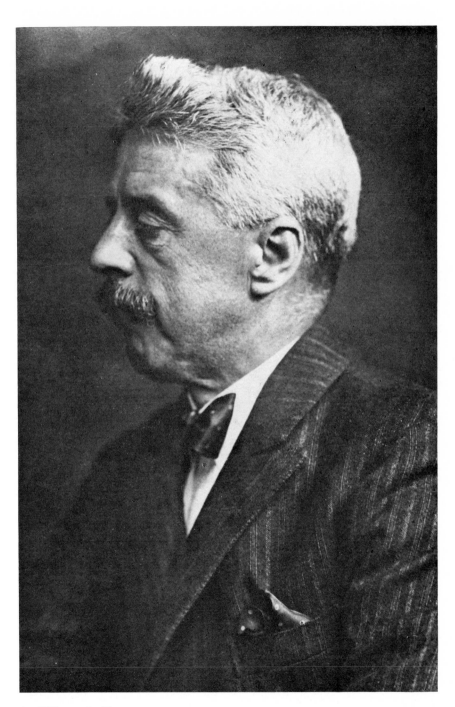

Arnold Bennett in old age

Alec Guiness in 'The Card'

below A scene from Joyce Cheeseman's adaptation of *The Old Wives' Tale* at the Victoria Theatre, Stoke
right A scene from 'Clayhanger' at the Victoria Theatre, Stoke

Bennett's gravestone

Virginia with her husband and family

usual she was to cloak her motives with a more respectable and naïve inter-
pretation. She very much disliked the idea of being blamed, and after the
separation seems to have been startled by the hostility she had aroused in
some quarters; she tried to whitewash herself and vilify her husband, and
succeeded in persuading some old friends, like Mrs Belloc Lowndes, that
she had been very badly treated.

The gossip surrounding the separation must have hurt Bennett. He did
not like to attack Marguerite, but equally did not like to hear his own name
blackened. Having suspected that he had been joked about for his tolerance
of an unfaithful wife, he now had to put up with being blamed for deserting
her. Still, at least the pretence was over. At the end of October, Comarques
was put up for sale – Marguerite went off with a lot of possessions, including
some papers, such as the 1906 journal, which she thought would be safer
in her own hands. Much of the furniture, originally purchased in France by
Bennett, ended up back there, in Marguerite's final home near her birthplace.
The whole French chapter was over. Legros was never to appear on the scene
again, and nobody knows what happened to him. Marguerite, however, was
to reappear constantly. Bennett, worn out by these legal and emotional
troubles, escaped, at the end of November, to a yacht, this time the
Amaryllis, which belonged to his friend Herbert Sullivan.

The yacht was at Nice, the weather was glorious, he was a free man. He
must have recovered rapidly, for he began to write a new novel – not the one
he had planned but a short piece for serialization, *Lilian*, about a secretary.
At first, as the novel opens, one hopes he is going to use more of the material
of those early years on *Woman*, when he had sympathized so much with the
pale office girls and thin spinsters who lived on buns and 'half a meat pie':
the first scene is set at night, in a typewriting bureau which makes the proud
claim of being open twenty-four hours a day. Lilian, alone, is staffing it.
Lilian had been brought up to better things. Her father, an art master in
Putney who adored her, had died leaving her almost penniless and completely uneducated and alone in the world, thereby demonstrating the point
that Bennett makes so plainly in *Our Women* – 'The loving, adored father had
in effect abandoned a beautiful idolized daughter to the alternatives of
starvation or prostitution. He had shackled her wrists behind her back and
hobbled her feet and bequeathed her to the wolves.'[9] So far so good, and still
good when the greying, quizzical owner of the establishment, Mr Grig,
comes in to visit her and finds her crying because she has been frightened
by a night watchman. Unfortunately from this point the story degenerates
somewhat, for we learn that Lilian is extremely beautiful and adored by all,

even by the handsome Lord Mackworth who happens to call in with a late-night bit of typing, and whose negligence in paying his bill gets Lilian the sack. Lilian spends her remaining few pounds on her clothes, is invited out to dinner by Mr Grig, who declares himself in love with her (though an old widower) and whisks her off to the South of France, where she becomes pregnant and marries him just before he dies of pneumonia. She then returns to London to lord it over the typewriting establishment, having managed to get herself married in time by the skin of her teeth. In fact, of the two alternatives prostitution and starvation, she chose prostitution.

The novel is short, slight and hurried, and contains ridiculous incidents like the handsome Lord Mackworth episode; but it also contains some very interesting things, which shed some light on Bennett himself. Not least interesting is the portrait of Mr Grig, a man of about Bennett's own age, and the somewhat perverse delight that Lilian, 'a nice girl', takes in being seen with him dancing and at the Casino. Grig gives Lilian a long speech about how 'a middle-aged man who has already had experience of marriage and marries a girl young enough to be his daughter is either a coward or a fool or without taste ... when romance comes that way, it wants the sauce of secrecy and plotting – the double life, and so on. The feeling of naughtiness . . . perversity, doing society in the eye. It's a continual excitement.'[10] Was this Bennett persuading himself that he deserved a little fun? That he was still attractive to women, although not free? He must have been much pursued, particularly at Cannes and Nice and Monte Carlo, where he wrote this novel, by pleasure-seekers intent not on marriage but a good time. There were plenty of much younger girls around, on the look-out for just such men. And Grig, rather endearingly, shares Bennett's feeble constitution; he is always fussing poor Lilian about the cold, reminding her to take her furs, and complaining ominously about the treacherous climate of the Riviera. Is there a certain amount of self-mockery in this? In the event, Mr Grig's fears are justified: Lilian insists on taking a car up into the mountains at night, the window breaks, and Mr Grig gets double pneumonia.

Not only is the situation between Mr Grig and Lilian interesting: there are also at least two very fine touches in the novel, buried in the trivia, that deserve resurrection. The first occurs when Lilian, worried that Mr Grig is ill and will need brandy during the night, ventures out into the corridor of the hotel, and encounters a gambling prostitute, who lends her the brandy and declines thanks on the grounds that 'us girls ought to stand by each other, that's what I think'. Lilian, at the sound of the phrase 'us girls', feels 'as if the entire hotel had trembled under her feet'.[11] This whole scene between the two girls is finely done, better than the scene between Sophia and the courtesans in *The Old Wives' Tale*. At the end of the scene, while her lover lies dying, Lilian asks the other girl how she 'stains her skin that lovely Spanish colour' and receives full instructions and the materials to do it with. This was the age of jazz and perversity, and even nice little English typists from Putney felt its impact.

The other fine touch is at the end of the novel: Lilian, seven months' pregnant, returns to England to take over the home of her dead husband, and is greeted coldly by the proper parlourmaid and the spinster sister. She is full of hope and, braced by their defiance, determined to battle for her rights and indeed looking forward to the conflict, she goes up to her husband's bedroom, which she has never seen and will never share; and there she is shaken by the sight of his suits, hanging in the wardrobe, and drawers full of neckties.

> 'Could one man have possessed so many neckties? She picked up a necktie at random, striped in violent colours. . . . She did not know, and could not have known, that the colours were those of a famous school club. She was entirely ignorant of the immense, the unparalleled prestige of club colours in the organised life of the ruling classes. Mechanically again, she put the necktie to her mouth, nibbled at it, bit it passionately, voluptuously; the feel of the woven stuff thrilled her; and that club necktie was understood, comprehended, realised. . . . Lilian sobbed like a child. The parlourmaid entered with the tea and the nice bread and butter, and saw the child munching the necktie, and was shaken. . . .'[12]

The thrill of this, its mixture of eroticism and childish need for oral comfort, the startling use of the word 'munching', is something special and authentic, which makes its way through the easiness and unaspiring style so dominant in the novel, and indeed so noticeable even in this passage. Bennett could write lazily, he could aim low on purpose, but he couldn't write a really conventional book. His training from the French masters and his own innate originality of perception cannot help but show themselves.

Lilian was not particularly well received, with some reason: Doran in America thought it was too short and wanted a longer and different ending, Cassells objected to the phrases 'I am going to have a baby' and 'I am seven months gone', and the *Daily Express* called it a pot-boiler. The last is the most serious accusation. Bennett, as usual, assumed that it could not be a pot-boiler because it had shocked the bourgeoisie (like *The Pretty Lady*) and as usual claimed that he could have written a much more remunerative novel if he had stooped to sentimentality and conventional morality. This may be true: there are degrees of pot-boiling, as of virtue and crime, and it is true that he never compromised his sense of truth. But then as now, shocking pot-boilers succeeded. *Lilian* was not a great success, financially; the critics who attacked it probably had more in mind its slightness and the signs of rapid execution that it shows, than its shock value. He could hardly claim to have worked on it very diligently: it took him less than two months to write, and those two months were full of distractions, as well as covering a period of convalescence from his broken marriage.

The distractions of the South of France are well described through Lilian's eyes in the novel, and through Bennett's in his journal. During the whole period he was staying on the *Amaryllis*, moored variously at Nice, Cannes, Monte Carlo and Monaco. He notes at one point that Nice is 'very provincial at this season', with no well-dressed women about, but nevertheless he and his friends managed to enjoy a daunting round of operas, casinos, theatres. Bennett danced every day. They celebrated Christmas Day by 'a rather showy dinner' at the Reserve, and spent the evening at the casino. The days of the country squire with his family table at Comarques were well and truly over, and Comarques stood empty. In January the gay life continued: he saw and envied splendid yachts, watched gamblers and grand duchesses, had tea with Beaverbrook's mother and a dull conversation with Baroness Orczy. He watched the new manners of the 1920s, danced to the new jazz, and like Lilian listened to conversations at neighbouring tables, most of them in English, and found they were all about 'gambling, dancing, golf, lawn tennis, polo, cards, racing, trains de luxe, clothes, hotels, prices and women'. How much did he feel himself one of these wealthy English holiday-makers, and how much did he still regard himself as an observer and a recorder? He found the spectacle of such luxury fascinating, and puts into the mouth of Mr Grig a defence of it – Grig says 'You must remember there's nothing new in this. It's been going on in the Mediterranean for thousands of years, and it's likely to go on for thousands of years more. It's what human nature *is*. What are you going to do about it?'[13]

What indeed? At the very least, Bennett intended to watch what was happening, and history had certainly provided him with one of the most fascinating and dramatic periods of social change one could imagine. The girls of the 1920s were almost a different species from the over-dressed turn-of-the-century girls of Burslem. For the first time in history they showed their legs, and wore wicked flesh-coloured stockings instead of proper black or white ones; it was an absurdly leg-conscious age. Underwear was for the first time coloured, instead of virginal white, and it was advertised in respectable papers as 'amusing' or 'fascinating' (though in 1921 the lord chamberlain was still deleting the word 'chemise' from West End plays). Girls had begun to smoke and cut off their hair and powder their noses, though lipstick was still more or less taboo. Dancing had changed out of all recognition: it was still obligatory for gentlemen to wear gloves to do it, but they could now dance cheek-to-cheek and body-to-body with strangers, and the new American ragtime, which had begun to creep in before the war, was now everywhere. Jazz flourished not only in the wicked South of France, but even in Claridge's, the Savoy, the Criterion, the Piccadilly. Bennett had to have dancing lessons later on in the 1920s to catch up with the rapid changes – but he seems always to have been ready to try. The new vogue which he deplored most was the cocktail vogue: he was always careful about alcohol, advised his nephew Richard never to touch spirits, and was highly critical of modern girls who would down dry martinis instead of cups of tea. He was also critical of too many late nights and too many drugs, the drugs in question being aspirins, but in this region as well as others he didn't always follow his own sensible advice. The spectacle was too interesting, and he couldn't stay away: four years later, true to form, we find him attending the first night of the 'most magnificent dance club in the world', the Kitcat, which became wildly popular with the smart set, and commenting that the sight of the crowded floors and balconies, the cramped dancers swaying to 'Vincent Lopez £1,100 a week band from New York, and the other lower noises – gave you the impression that the bottom had fallen out of civilization.'[14]

Seeing it fall was quite an experience, and although Bennett had bouts of moralizing (he was to lecture Dorothy Cheston Bennett on the evils of cocktails and gambling) he was at least as much intrigued as appalled. His novels of this period, *Mr Prohack* and *Lilian*, bear witness to his interest, though, perhaps significantly, his most successful later novel had no connection with the smart world at all. The material was all there, but Bennett never found quite the style with which to attack it, and *Lilian* bears witness to his failure.

He finished *Lilian* on 24 January, and suffered his usual bout of post-novel ill-health, made worse by wet weather. He recovered after a few more sessions at the casino, and returned to England by the de luxe train on 8 February 1922. He returned to a world of theatrical anxieties – two plays of his were about to be produced – and to the disastrous news of the death of Pinker. His last letter to Pinker, written from Cannes, was a long discussion about the chequered career and constant re-writes of his screenplay *The Wedding Dress*: Pinker was just about to depart for New York, and Bennett tells him firmly what he can say to Lasky, the director of the film company, Famous Players. Pinker left England at the end of January and died, like Bennett's last hero Mr Grig, of pneumonia in New York on 8 February, the day that Bennett left the South of France. Bennett, though he had never been very intimate with Pinker, was deeply shocked, for he knew that he had lost not only an old friend, but also an invaluable ally, and the best agent in London. They had been associated for twenty years, and Pinker had acted as banker, creditor, financial adviser, peace-maker and salesman. He had seen Bennett through family crises, through a broken engagement, a marriage and a separation. He knew every detail of Bennett's financial affairs and through them, inevitably, a good deal of his personal affairs, for the two impinged; and it was always to Pinker that Bennett applied for help. Even on holiday they would write each other long business letters. Bennett was not the kind of writer who goes off leaving no address, forgets to answer his post, and has to be reminded to deliver copy. Their relationship was professional, but it was very close. Many of Bennett's friends have said that Bennett, despite his pose of being a good businessman, was not really very practical about money, and was essentially uninterested in it for its own sake – unlike, for instance, his friend Beaverbrook. What Bennett valued was his own earning capacity, and the continual surprise of being a wealthy man. Subsequent events seem to indicate that this view of him is correct. He had been nursed and protected by Pinker, and he knew it. Writing to his nephew Richard shortly after Pinker's death, he says that he might lose by it thousands a year – this might seem a cool comment, out of context, but in terms of their relationship it was a considerable tribute.

From various points of view, Pinker's death hit him at a bad time. His financial arrangements, owing to his separation from Marguerite, were delicate. Bennett had of course confided the details to Pinker in October, as soon as he was sure of the situation, and had trusted in his discretion. He had also had a very expensive year. The yacht had not been cheap, and it had a crew of eight. There was a town flat and a nephew at Cambridge to maintain full time; he had disposed of the extra expense of Comarques as soon as he could. Bennett was not short of money, but he was certainly not living cheaply or simply. Added to these problems, he was just about to run into a spell of unusually intense theatrical and film complications. Eric Pinker, J. B. Pinker's nephew and successor, took over Bennett's affairs, but Bennett clearly did not trust him as thoroughly as he had trusted Pinker: his tone in letters is at times brusque and dictatorial, as though he is determined to teach the younger man his business.

The first worry was the production of *The Love Match*, which opened at the Strand on 21 March. Bennett was unhappy about the performance of the leading actor, Bourchier, who was to play the wife-reforming millionaire Russ, and wrote him a long letter on the day of the first night accusing him of playing to the gallery; for which, had it been true, Bourchier could hardly have been blamed. Few actors would take such last-moment admonitions from anyone other than the director at all kindly, and indeed a not very friendly dispute about the play arose between Bennett and the director, his old friend Frank Vernon, who had directed *Milestones*. Vernon wanted the play changed; Bennett stuck to it and accused the public and the performers. The play, as has been said, got poor notices, lost money, and came off within a month. With it also failed a project to revive *The Great Adventure* with Bourchier in the lead, though this play was revived with some success two years later.

Bennett's morale must have been cheered, however, by the success of *Mr Prohack*, which was published in May, Bennett's last novel to be published by Methuen. Despite some haggling over advertising and some suspicion of 'the unanimous enthusiasm' with which it was received, he must have been pleased to find it so popular, for it was a novel written to please. It is a curious mixture of realism and fantasy, at first sight simply an indulgence in the familiar fantasy of sudden, unexpected, almost unlimited wealth, but on closer inspection a fairly searching analysis of the use and nature of riches. It is written in Bennett's 'easy' style, but it has some interesting things in it, and grips in a way that many of his light novels don't.

Mr Prohack, at the beginning of the book, is a civil servant, a conscientious, middle-income, middle-class civil servant, discussing how to cut down his expenditure: should he give up one of his clubs, should his daughter give up her new dress, can they manage with fewer servants? Within a chapter or two he has in the most unlikely manner inherited £100,000 from a profiteering rogue who made money out of the war, to whom he had once lent a hundred pounds. (Mr Prohack had lost money through the war – he had saved the Treasury millions, by his sound financial sense, and seen his own fixed income dwindle in purchasing power.) Prohack accepts this disreputable inheritance, invests it, multiplies it, and finds he cannot spend it. Arduously he slogs from tailor to shirtmaker to Turkish bath to first night; he is obliged to rent a magnificent new house in Manchester Square, and finds himself perpetually threatened by boredom, nervous exhaustion and hypochondria. His daughter turns out to be an economical girl, who enjoys scrimping and saving and living on nothing; his son, on the contrary, becomes a wild financial speculator, who goes in for big money, yachts and risks. His wife, like most of the women in Bennett's lighter novels, is extravagant, foolish and snobbish, though these qualities are presented as endearing. The novel, in fact, presents a variety of attitudes to wealth and luxury, which lead one inevitably to speculate on Bennett's own. He too, like Mr Prohack, frequented expensive shirtmakers and Turkish baths; he too stayed in grand hotels and applied himself diligently to spending his money, almost as though spending were an art: for Prohack, spending is a therapy, prescribed by a doctor as a cure for his nervous ailments. And yet the novel stresses again and again the dirty origins of Prohack's money, the irresponsibility and unreality of his son's investments, the sycophancy which the rich encounter, and the boredom which afflicts them. At the end of the novel Prohack, having tried various ways of coping with his fairytale inheritance, decides to go into business, and buys a paper-making business. He tells his wife: 'I've got a sort of idea that some one ought to be economic and productive. It may kill me, but I'll die producing, anyhow.'[15] This is a good Northern working-class Methodist solution to the problem. And Bennett, after all, was in the very peculiar position of being a wealthy man who had earned every penny he ever spent. Surrounded, now, by those who had inherited wealth or made it by profitable investments and business speculations, he must have felt that the sources of his own income were unusually pure. He obeyed the work ethic of his childhood by working exceptionally hard; he did not sit back and live modestly on a modicum of royalties, as he could have chosen to do. What he spent, he had earned by his own labour. He had a perfect right to it. And yet Mr Prohack, like so many of the later novels, does manifest a certain uneasiness.

Mr Prohack's success produced renewed invitations from Lasky, the film man from Famous Players, but Bennett was becoming wary of the film world, and considered he hadn't been paid anything like well enough for his three months' work on *The Wedding Dress*. The film business was expanding rapidly – there were 266 cinemas in London in 1921 – but it was still in its infancy as far as contracts and negotiations were concerned. Neither agents nor writers knew exactly what they ought to demand, film-makers could not predict profits, there were no screen writer's unions, and already there were suspicions of sharp practice and exploitation. In his collection of essays, *The Savour of Life*, possibly to dispel the impression that he was making a fortune out of films, Bennett gives an account of his negotiations with Lasky and Hugh Ford, and states that in film rights from books and plays he made precisely £6,400 (from six titles) – a satisfactory supplement, but by no means a fortune. Various films were made, notably *The Card* and *The Old Wives' Tale*, but Bennett was not satisfied with any of the productions. Despite disasters, he felt more at home with the theatre, and in June he went off on his yacht with Knoblock, to try to repeat the success of *Milestones*.

The new play, *London Life*, was written during the month of June, and finished by the beginning of July. It wasn't produced until two years later, in June 1924, and yet again critics were to accuse Bennett of provincialism and false modernity, their favourite complaints. The play is remarkable largely for its large cast and lavish changes of scenery: the action shifts from Burslem to the White Horse in Ipswich, from a country house to the Terrace of the House of Commons, from a society lady's indoor party to a garden party (complete with fireworks) in the country home of a Jewish financier and newspaper proprietor. The characters are stereotyped, as usual: there is the rising politician, the country lady who yearns for town, the smart young daughter, the clever newspaper reporter, the chorus girl who makes good. The plot is somewhat involved, spans twelve years and involves details of a financial deal reminiscent of stories Bennett must have been told by Beaverbrook, about profiteering cabinet ministers. The attempt to portray an ambitious man who is prepared to sacrifice more or less everything to his own career, who will manipulate newspapers and women and politicians to his own ends, and yet remains convinced that he is a jolly nice good chap at heart is not successful, and critics simply saw in the play an expression of Bennett's worship of success. The elaborate scene changes and ambitious cast list must have owed something to Knoblock; Bennett's own plays are much more modest in their demands on the director. One can sympathize with the critics who heaved a sigh of despair as yet another curtain rose on a solicitor's office in Burslem, peopled by tough bluff men talking about smoke control: after all, the play had been called *London Life*. But they were not appeased by the removal to the Terrace of the House of Commons. One wonders what Beaverbrook made of his friend's use of his material. Did he have cause to regret indiscretions?

Life on board the *Marie Marguerite* was not, however, all work. Bennett enjoyed himself, and stayed afloat, cruising up and down the south coast of England and the north coast of France until the end of September. He had a varying collection of guests. After Knoblock's departure, he was visited by various friends, including his two nieces Mary Kennerley and Margaret

Beardmore, his nephew Richard, Sir Denison Ross, the oriental scholar, and his wife and, principally, Harriet Cohen. Harriet Cohen, then a young and brilliant pianist, was a new friend and protégée. Bennett had heard her play the year before, and had admired her. They had become close friends, writing one another frequent letters in a tone of teasing affection. Bennett was now a man on his own, and he liked female companionship, particularly young, admiring, handsome female companionship: their friendship did not develop into an affair, but it had a spirited, slightly provocative quality that is missing from his relations with, for instance, Pauline Smith. Harriet was not shy; on the contrary, she was an extremely dashing, flamboyant, stylish character. She was exceptionally beautiful: photographs of her at this age show her as slim, dark, elegant, dramatic. She was tubercular and had to look after her health, taking frequent visits abroad, but, as many tubercular patients are said to be, she was also a flirt, and fancied everybody to be madly in love with her. Many people doubtless were, but Bennett reproaches her on several occasions for her manner. She took his criticism in good part. In London he used to take her to first nights and concerts, and dine with her at the Savoy Grill. She recalls in her autobiography, *A Bundle of Time*, that people used to whisper that she was an 'old man's darling', but this seems merely to have amused her. Through him and with him, she met many of his friends – the Wells's, the Huxleys, the Sitwells, Beaverbrook, Gerhardi, Shaw, Somerset Maugham. (Shaw said, of a particularly sexy photograph of Harriet, 'Men have been divorced for less.')

She visited Bennett on his yacht several times, and enjoyed his company greatly. Her attractions for him were obvious. But she wasn't the only eligible young lady to go yachting with him. In his letters to her he alludes, provocatively, to several others, including 'one war widow, one war virgin (very blonde)'. He clearly liked to surround himself with attractive female satellites, as a natural response to the loss of Marguerite. Indeed, before he had decided that there must be a separation, he had already started to raise his morale with girlfriends. His new enthusiasm for dancing (one doesn't think of him as a dancing man, but as an amusing chatter-up of sitting-out girls) must date from his realization that there was a need to look elsewhere, and every possibility of doing so. This does not imply that he would find it easy to provide himself with an attractive young replacement. There were plenty of girls like Lilian waiting for an attractive Lord Mackworth or a wealthy Mr Grig, but Bennett, no matter what allegations were raised against him, was the last person to want to buy affection. He was sensitive and diffident. Indeed, Raymond Mortimer convincingly suggested in a recent review of *Arnold Bennett in Love* that one of the reasons why he had tolerated Marguerite's eccentricities for so long was that he had a deep dislike of casual affairs, and relied upon her for sexual satisfaction. Finally, the irritations had outweighed the gains, and he had let her go. But he was still energetic, emotional, in the prime of life. Men from Burslem, even after more than thirty years in the outside world, do not readily embark on illicit affairs. Free love was eagerly pursued in the 1920s, but not by Bennett. What was he to do next?

13
Bennett and Dorothy

His next love was his last. She was an actress, but not the musical comedy star Marjorie Gordon whom he had mentioned to Marguerite in an effort to prove his independence. Her name was Dorothy Cheston, and she was a straight actress. He first met her in the spring of 1922; he had glimpsed her briefly in a drawing-room play but wasn't introduced, and their first real meeting took place in Liverpool, where she was appearing, romantically and appropriately, in Nigel Playfair's production of his own play, *Body and Soul*. He had been separated from Marguerite for six months.

Dorothy struck him at once: she was extremely attractive, with the short blonde hair of the 1920s, delicate, very English in her appearance, quite unlike the dark dramatic Marguerite. She had been on the stage for some years, and was capable of playing a wide variety of character roles, though one imagines from her appearance that she was more of an *ingénue* at heart than a *femme fatale* (like the character in Bennett's late story, *Venus Rising from the Sea*, who keeps getting herself miscast as a wicked woman). Her family were not theatrical, but respectable middle-class, though they must have had artistic interests, as her brother was a talented watercolourist. She had had a good academic education at Queen's College, Harley Street, a school which Katherine Mansfield had also attended. There's no record that she had any opportunity to express her interest in the stage there. In those days it still took character for a middle-class girl to become an actress, but Dorothy had plenty of character.

Her first meeting with Bennett was a success. She describes it in her excellent account of their relationship, *A Portrait Done at Home*. She recalls his courtesy and sensitivity towards her, his interest in her conversation and his ability to put her at her ease. She was much younger than he (she was thirty, and looked younger) and very much aware that he was a famous author on a tour of inspection. So she was pleased and flattered when he insisted on sitting between her and the other leading actress, Viola Lyall, at the dinner that followed the performance. They talked of Dreiser and Dostoevsky. Bennett must have been delighted to find an actress who was intelligent, well-read, and aware of his own interests. They got on so well that it drew attention, and Bourchier, the director, who had travelled up with Bennett, whispered meaningfully to Dorothy that he supposed she knew that Bennett's marriage had come to an end. Naturally she did not wish to question anyone about this, as her curiosity would have seemed indelicate; but she equally naturally assumed Bourchier to mean that Bennett was divorced. Why else should he have bothered to inform her? She knew nothing about his history, as she did not move in gossipy literary London; so she accepted the fact that he was a free and divorced man.

The next time they met was in April, when he invited her to visit him on the day of the boat race. She went to tea in his flat in George Street, where she admired his curving baroque decor and his Aubusson rug, impressed by his style as Marguerite had been years earlier. Bennett told her that he was off to spend the summer on his yacht, and that he would contact her as soon as he got back. He must have thought of her, during the summer, because he kept his promise to get in touch on his return. He could not in fact do so immediately, as he had to deal with the disastrous London production of *Body and Soul*, which opened on 11 September at the Euston Theatre, with Viola Tree in the lead. But on 1 November he fulfilled his promise to Dorothy Cheston by writing to invite her to come and have 'food and drink in a Sabbatic manner'[1] with him the following Sunday. She accepted. And thus they embarked on a relationship that was to change both their lives.

The sabbatical supper was followed up with many other invitations. They dined together at Claridge's the following week, went out together in public, dined quietly at home, played piano duets. She invited him to tea in her flat in Church Street. It is interesting to note that the ritual of making tea, which Dorothy records in her portrait of him, assumed for him a distinct significance, for he uses it in several of the novels and stories written after their meeting, and always as a setting for romance or romantic speculation. Just as he had associated illness and nursing with Marguerite, he must have associated tea-making with his first love for Dorothy. Their relationship became increasingly close. He introduced her to his friends, worried over her travel arrangements (she was off on tour at the beginning of 1923, in a play by Sudermann with Mrs Pat Campbell), and wrote to her when she was away, in letters that at first begin politely with 'My dear Dorothy Cheston', or 'dear Lady' and within four months are prefaced by 'My dearest Dorothea'. (As ever, he liked to embellish a name, turning Dorothy into Dorothea as he had turned Eleanor Green into Eleanora.) He would sign himself, 'your devoted A'. Once again, he was in love. She responded with letters, telegrams and growing affection. His feeling for her is soon clear from his correspondence: his letters do not have the sparring note that one finds in his letters to Harriet Cohen, but a more protective, anxious, serious tone. He concerned himself over her career, as well as her travel arrangements; he missed her when she was away, tried to keep her touring spirits up (a difficult task, when she was in Oldham and Blackburn) and made elaborate arrangements for getting her back.

How soon did they both realize it was a serious matter, and that what had started as a series of gallant invitations had turned into something different? Arnold Bennett was no trifler, and Dorothy was no vamp. She was well brought up and unsuspicious. They were both, as she says, very shy. She remarks: 'Two shy people together possess more than double the quota of shyness which each possesses',[2] which is a shrewd observation. He, with his inhibitions and speech difficulties, must have found it agonizingly embarrassing and difficult to discuss his own past and his intentions; she, quiet, sensitive, unassuming, was the last person to interrogate him, or even to hint at a need for explanation. So it's not surprising that they drifted together, without making their position clear.

Their pleasure in each other's company increased. Dorothy records that one night he kissed her with a solemn emotion, at the end of a duet they had been playing. She trusted him, quite rightly, completely. He must have known that she did. He loved her and needed her, and yet he knew that he was not free to marry her – and that she might well be expecting an offer of marriage. He had plenty of time to think, while she was away on tour. She left at the beginning of February for Brighton, where he went to see the play, then toured the North of England. She returned to London for a weekend in late February, at his persuasion, and spent Sunday with him; this was the occasion that he declared his love for her. It was not an easy declaration to make, for it involved revealing his marital situation, of which Dorothy knew nothing. He told her of his unhappy marriage, of his reluctance to go through the divorce courts, his lavish financial settlements. She cannot have been quite sure whether he was proposing an open or a secret liaison, but he certainly spoke as though society would accept them as a couple, if she would accept what he had to offer, and he talked seriously in terms of a life-long association. He was caught in the dilemma of all second loves: how can one convince the second woman that one will love her and cherish her for ever, having abandoned the first, to whom the same vows were made? He made a good case for his leaving of Marguerite, explaining that she had often threatened to leave him and that, finally, to her surprise, he had taken her at her word; and also saying, no doubt with much sincerity, that he could not have left a woman 'with whom he had spent so many of her younger and middle years, had he felt that her life would be empty and devoid of other interests'.[3] Dorothy was not to worry that he had left Marguerite alone, poor and unfriended, in order to find a younger woman. Of one thing at least Dorothy was convinced: Arnold persuaded her that his marriage had never been a success, and that it had indeed been a hopeless project from the very beginning. He said to her often that there had been 'nothing in it for him' after the first few days, and when one looks back at the way he drifted into marriage, his state of shock after his engagement to Eleanor Green, and Marguerite's demanding attitude, one can well believe that he really meant it. Even the idyllic-seeming days at Fontainebleau had been marked with discord, as Pauline Smith noticed, and things had gone from the tolerable to the intolerable. Their natures had proved incompatible, and as Bennett told Dorothy, all too accurately, 'Marguerite will make as much trouble as she can'.

Dorothy was persuaded by his description of the failure of his first marriage, and never had any reason to doubt it: indeed, events confirmed Bennett's gloomy account of his wife's character. But she still did not know how to take his proposals. She was afraid, justifiably, of unforeseen social complications, and his view of the permissiveness of the world they lived in seemed to her naïve. She was acutely aware of how she would look in the eyes of the world, if she lived with a wealthy and famous man. Most of the people who lived together without marriage seemed to her to be either insincere and self-indulgent, or else fanatical and unloving social reformers, doing it for the sake of a cause. She was neither. She was a high-principled and sincere girl, independent, enthusiastic about her career, valuing her integrity, and probably on the defensive in her career and morals because of her background. She was no crusader. On the other hand, she was lonely: after the Great War there was an acute shortage of men in her age group, and the knowledgeable, authoritative, confident friendship, let alone the love, of a man like Bennett must have been very valuable to her. She could rely on him. His interest in her was not selfish: he genuinely seemed to want to help her in her career, a rare attribute in a husband or lover in those days as in these. He was also, as she knew, in a position to do so. But how could she embark on an unorthodox liaison without misgivings? Marriage seemed out of the question, as Marguerite not only did not wish to divorce, she actually threatened to return. Arnold had decided that this was quite impossible, but he shrank from disturbing the *status quo* by new legal overtures. Divorce negotiations would be lengthy, worrying, costly, embarrassing and possibly unsuccessful. He could not face the upheaval and Dorothy sympathized with his reluctance. It was easy to see how deeply his first marriage had wounded him, and although at first she took his comments on Marguerite's hysterical and unstable temper as exaggerations, caused by pain, she soon found that they were grounded in reality. Marguerite was not a reasonable, civilized woman, who would willingly wish her husband a new life and happiness once it became clear that he wanted and needed his freedom. She remained difficult to the end; as Bennett told Dorothy, she was 'wrong in the head'.

So Dorothy and Arnold remained undecided about their future, wondering what form it should take. The uncertainty cannot have been (to him at least) too oppressive, for during this period, before the moment that brought them to decision, he found the energy to move flats, from George Street with its associations with the past, to 75 Cadogan Square, 'a rather fine thing in houses', which he moved into in December. And during this time he also wrote one of the finest novels of his later years, *Riceyman Steps*. A new resurgence of vitality, after the low ebb represented by his last few plays and the short and sketchy *Lilian*, had taken place in him: no wonder he did not want to disturb the flow by reopening old troubles. He may well have sensed that he had not many years of creative life left and he wished to make the most of them. Dorothy, modestly disclaiming the view that his new energy was connected with his discovery of her, thought rather that it sprang from sheer relief at having got rid of Marguerite, which sounds equally plausible. He must have been quietly and hopelessly unhappy for years, and at the possibility of turning to new work and a new life, with no more rows and struggles and pretences, was seized with eagerness.

Riceyman Steps is the finest justification of Bennett's decision to turn to London for his settings. As we have seen, his first few London novels had been marked by a kind of triviality and unease; amusing though some of them are, they all bear marks of the strain (a great moral strain, as well as an artistic one) of trying to encompass the luxury of Bond Street and the deprivations of servants in the same novel. The gulf between the two was too great to cross, particularly for an avowed socialist, and Bennett's defences of luxury are always punctured by himself, which lends a book like *Mr Prohack* its fascinating ambivalence. But in *Riceyman Steps* he returns, firmly, to the dingy world glimpsed in his first novel – also a London novel – *A Man from the North*. Only here there is no man from the North. All the characters are Londoners. He also returns to his old writing habits, embarking for the first time for some years on some serious research. The research for *Lilian, The Pretty Lady* and *Mr Prohack*, had been done in Claridge's, in the South of France and in the drawing-rooms of modern socialites, but for *Riceyman Steps* Bennett turned to less attractive sources. He had always been interested in both antiquarian booksellers and in misers; and his new hero, Mr Earlforward, is both. His interest in misers had already demonstrated itself in *Anna of the Five Towns* and *Helen With The High Hand*, and had its roots both in real memories and in French realist fiction: French literature, ever since Molière's *L'Avare*, had shown a pronounced interest in the phenomenon. English literature too has its *Silas Marner*, but on the whole has done the subject less justice. (Bennett's own curiosity about misers, who represent an extreme case of Methodist thrift and frugality, a virtue become a sin, must be connected with his attitudes towards the positive virtue of spending and extravagance – an attempt to escape a morbid anally-fixated inheritance, perhaps? Earlforward's fury when his wife has his house cleaned by vacuum cleaner, and realizes that his own dirt is being stolen from him, is full of Freudian undertones.) The conception of this particular novel was probably sparked off by the discovery, in an old Southampton book shop, T. James and Co., of 34 Bernard Street, of a curious old book called *Lives and Anecdotes of Misers*, by F. Sommer Merryweather (1850). Bennett bought it in 1921 on one of his yachting expeditions, read it and used it. But his interest in the subject long preceded the purchase of the book.

He not only studied misers; he also studied the district of Clerkenwell, where he was to set the novel. He visited it in person many times, on one occasion taking Harriet Cohen with him, and giving her dinner after their explorations at St Pancras Station. His enthusiasm for his new project was obvious, she says. And he read up the history of Clerkenwell, from a book on the subject by W. J. Pinks, which he used extensively, taking, for instance, Pink's account of the collapse of the tunnel which was being excavated for the underground near Clerkenwell Green in 1862. He got to know the district thoroughly, both in its history and in its reality; few of his later novels have so precise a sense of location. It is not that his evocations of, for instance, the dining-room of the Savoy are lacking in conviction: he is adept at describing a sense of glamour, glitter and waste; he is good on the manners of waiters and the dresses of women. But his descriptions of these things become increasingly generalized and uniform, his nouns more abstract, his exclamations more frequent. One hotel restaurant is after all much like another. Perhaps it was the shock of returning, in *Riceyman Steps*, to an utterly different setting that makes his writing so much more careful. He can take no short cuts: his readers will have to be told, in detail, what to see, if they are to imagine the life of Mrs Arb in her little shop and Mr Earlforward in his. Their manners and morals are strange and foreign, they must be described, not assumed.

One might think that the more heavily a novelist leans on research, the less deeply felt and original his work will be. With Bennett, precisely the reverse seems to be true, and in this he is very much part of the tradition he admired – Zola's novels have the same quality. Documentary reinforced by indignant emotion is his forte, and I at times find his protests about social conditions more moving than Dickens's, and his irony more delicately judged. There is a superb passage in *Riceyman Steps*, at the beginning of chapter 11, when he describes the problems of living in an over-crowded house in a slum – the mixture of observation, documentation (he read widely about working-class life in the district) and insight is very fine, as fine as his adaptations of the Old Potter's account of his childhood in *Clayhanger*. The house he describes has, he says:

'. . . a full, but not an extraordinary share of experience of human life. There were three floors of it. On the ground floor lived a meat salesman, his wife and three children, the eldest of whom was five years of age. The meat salesman shouted and bawled cheap bits of meat in an open-fronted shop in Exmouth Street during a sixty hour week which ended at midnight on Saturday. He possessed enormous vocal power. All the children out of naughtiness had rickets. On the first floor lived a french-polisher, his wife and two children, the eldest of whom was two years of age . . . he worked only forty-four hours a week. His fingers were always the colour of rosewood, and he emitted an odour which often competed not unsuccessfully with the characteristic house odour of stale soap suds. Out of ill-will for mankind he had an everlasting cough. On the second floor lived a middle-aged dressmaker, alone . . . the adult inhabitants of the house were always unhappy save when drinking alcohol or making love . . . they had failed to cultivate the virtue of Christian resignation. They permitted trifles to annoy them. On the previous day the wife of the meat salesman had been upset because her "copper" leaked, and because she could never for a moment be free of her own children, and because it was rather difficult to turn her perambulator through the kitchen doorway into an entrance hall three feet wide, and because she had to take all three children with her to market. . . .'⁴

And so on, and so on. How did Mr Bennett of Cadogan Square know about turning the perambulator? Had he watched? Did he remember from the crowded days of Hope Street? Wherever he got it from, he put it down better than any other writer of his age. His descriptions of working-class trials and virtues, particularly from the woman's point of view, are unequalled. Perhaps he simply felt it in his bones. Whatever way, this is not mere documentary, it is creative imagination at its most powerful.

The plot of the novel is simple enough. Mr Earlforward has an antiquarian book shop and he is a miser. He has a charwoman called Elsie, who has a shell-shocked lover called Joe. Earlforward marries, near the beginning of the novel, a neat, economical-seeming little widow, Mrs Arb, who has moved into a neighbouring shop. They celebrate their wedding by visiting Madame Tussaud's, a visit which recalls the visit to the Louvre which the wedding party makes in Zola's *L'Assommoir*, yet more proof that Bennett was returning back to his first exemplars. The conflict in Earlforward between miserliness, ill-health, and a genuine wish to do the right thing by his bride is very finely done. They live together, and she is increasingly horrified by his increasing meanness. They both fall ill, are nursed by the devoted Elsie, and both, in grim circumstances, die. That is all there is to it. What makes it so remarkable is its accuracy, its compassion, its feeling for the quality of working-class life and morality, its physical detail. There is nothing in it that had much bearing on Bennett's own personal life: it is objective, and yet done with a fine sympathy. He even manages to make Earlforward's excesses of meanness perfectly understandable: his mixture of fussiness and laziness, his untidiness, his willingness to give an expensive book to charity rather than a very small sum of money, his curious mixture of professional expertise and incompetence are completely convincing, and rather awe-inspiring. The setting is drab, the characters are neurotic rather than tragic, and yet the novel isn't depressing. There is something wonderful about it. How amazing, how various and odd, one says to oneself on finishing it. How very interesting, one thinks. Bennett had fulfilled one of his earliest maxims, expressed decades earlier in his little book on *Journalism for Women* – he had revealed the extraordinary in the ordinary, he had revealed the drama that lies in all things.

It's true that some have found this book deeply depressing, as they have found others of his works: I used to think *The Old Wives' Tale*, for instance, one of the saddest books I had ever read, and tended to concur with John Wain's judgement: Wain, another writer from the Potteries, said: 'His melancholy was not the reaction of a man who is "disturbed" by life, but of one who was, if anything, frozen by it into a semi-paralytic suffering, of which the obverse is his frequently jarring jauntiness . . .' and went on to remark, 'Defoe is fascinated by life, by the variety of things that can happen to a man; Bennett is numbed at the ultimate monotony of the pattern.'[5] But after longer consideration, I feel this isn't so. Bennett is really gripped by the peculiarities of the ordinary. They exhilarate him. The pattern isn't monotonous, it is immensely varied, if inspected closely enough with a trained eye, and Bennett had trained his eye superbly. The lives of his characters may seem appalling, but the curiosity with which Bennett observes them is passionate, and a work so full of the writer's interest cannot leave the reader entirely in gloom. Often, stuck on a railway station, waiting in a queue, or simply bored by social events, one can think of Bennett and redeem the situation. The dullest things spoke to him; they woke him up, rather than freezing him into suffering.

Bennett finished *Riceyman Steps* on 17 March 1923, and he knew that it was good. Harriet Cohen says that he hadn't been so excited by anything for twenty years.[6] He writes to tell Gide, modestly, that it is 'rather better than some of my novels',[7] and it was immediately recognized as being so by critics and friends. Since then, it has been admired as the best of his later novels. It was in a mood of triumph, therefore, that he set off to Paris for a week's holiday at the end of March, with a friend whom he had met on his visit to America in 1911 – appropriately enough a bibliophile, Dr Rosenbach. One wonders if Bennett discussed *Riceyman Steps* with him, or drew on his attitudes for the portrait in the novel of an American collector, Mr Bauersch, who is so irritated by Earlforward's 'cursed indifference', yet has to own himself 'spiritually beaten by it' because after all, however lazy and disorganized and mean Earlforward might be, he still has the goods. Bennett and Rosenbach had a week of 'violent entertainments', visiting friends, authors, publishers, going to concerts and giving a dinner for Ravel. Bennett wrote to describe his visit to Dorothy Cheston, who was playing in Eastbourne at the time. He wrote to her at least three times in the week, asking her in capital letters about the date of her return to London. And when he got back, and saw her again, he decided to make another visit to Paris, this time in her company.

They went in the third week of April, and stayed for a week. Dorothy had decided, as she relates in *A Portrait Done at Home*, that the only way to get to know each other better, and to decide how serious their affection was, would be to go away together, away from the distractions of London. He obviously had been pressing her to take a holiday with him, and with Paris still fresh in his mind it seemed the obvious place to go. Even though the journey was straightforward, she was impressed, and possibly a little daunted, by her first encounter with his complicated machinery of travel arrangements. She had little taste herself for elaborate domestic arrangements, or for his rituals of timetables; she preferred to live simply and unencumbered. But underneath the highly organized man of the world she saw something quite different. She relates that every morning he used to call for her at her hotel, to embark on the day's activities, and would bring her a bunch of white flowers. 'He carried these flowers tightly, holding his arm rather high up and rather rigidly. His gesture reminded me of the King of Hearts in a pack of cards.'[8] She says that it was not only his awkwardness, 'due to emotion', that touched her – it was also the fact that the flower-seller had always managed to sell him some flowers that were not quite fresh, for the flower-seller had spotted in him 'a large minded and perhaps simple minded Englishman who would never haggle nor look for a breach of good faith....'[9] As we have seen, Bennett considered himself quite an effective haggler, but there is something in Dorothy Cheston's story that rings absolutely true. She was captivated more by wilting flowers than she would have been by fresh ones; she saw in them that he was vulnerable and human, despite his worldly façade and his greater age. The image haunted her: the incident bound them together. It reveals her in all her seriousness of nature. She did not want the public Bennett, she wanted the private one.

Another advantage of Paris was that it contained friends who would welcome Dorothy with open minds: she met the Godebskis and liked them. Perhaps their easy acceptance and friendship, which contained no hint of criticism or surprise, encouraged her to brave the social scenes in London. She had convinced herself that if Arnold had been free, she would have married him, and as she believed in the spirit, not the forms, of marriage she found the courage to enter into a relationship which was to last until his death. She took the decision, she says, in late May, a month after their return to London. It was difficult, at times, even in a sophisticated social circle; her own temperament was not frivolous, and her background was upper middle class, respectable and quiet, rather than aristocratic and nonchalant. On the other hand, she was an actress, a career woman, and had already broken away from home into a life of her own. Most of Arnold's friends greeted her with enthusiasm. Some of them, like Harriet Cohen and Marjorie Gordon, the actress, she knew already, and she soon became accepted by most of his older friends, though there was continual friction with various members of his ultra-respectable family, who, having quarrelled with Marguerite, were now prepared to take Marguerite's side against Dorothy simply on grounds of legality and propriety. Arnold, whose generosity towards his family had been remarkable, might well have hoped to meet a little more tolerance. Dorothy found this painful, but there were plenty of compensations, and she did not have to dwell on the problems.

She and Arnold did not live together until three years later when their daughter was born. They lived in separate establishments, visited and wrote notes constantly, and had what many would think of as an ideal mutual existence. Bennett did not have his domestic arrangements disturbed by a woman in the house; Dorothy did not have to organize his meals and his servants. She was able to get used to him slowly. As Marguerite had found before her (and she came to have some sympathy with Marguerite), he was a difficult man, exacting, often ill, often miserably depressed. Their arrangement allowed them time to breathe. They shared their good times, and drew apart when he was feeling bad. At first she thought that so much circumspection and separation meant that he did not feel for her as deeply as he claimed – it took time for her to realize that his nature could not let itself go, was always on guard, would always be tense, and that this was no reflection on his love for her.

They played a curious game, over these years. That June, as usual, Bennett had arranged to go yachting; this was before Dorothy had agreed to become his mistress. His arrangements were unalterable, despite his new-found love. So off he went. Dorothy visited him on the yacht constantly, spending most weekends on board, but there were always others on board, out of respect for the conventions. One feels that Dorothy, having made her position quite clear in her own eyes and the eyes of the world, may have found such deference to the conventions superfluous, slightly indelicate, and even offensive. There were problems at times finding suitable men – there is an amusing letter from Arnold to Harriet Cohen (another guest) in which he accepts her suggestion of Eric Gillett as an extra man, but says he couldn't have Osbert Sitwell (another suggestion) as he was too tall for the bed, or Max Beaverbrook because it would be too dreadful to be cooped up on a yacht with Beaverbrook if anything went wrong. Surely, he suggests, Harriet must know plenty of suitable docile young men who wouldn't mind sleeping in a small bed in a poor cabin. Luckily, on this occasion, Eric Gillett accepted, and he, Dorothy and Harriet got on well.

Bennett was on the yacht throughout June, July and August, sailing off the south coast of England and visiting Cowes, Brighton, Southampton and the north coasts of France, Holland and Belgium. He was not working on anything substantial: he mentions some short stories, in a letter to Gide, but little else. Intellectually, he seems to have been most concerned with the affairs of Middleton Murry's new periodical, the *Adelphi*. He took a great interest in this, as he had in the first issues of J.C.Squire's *London Mercury*, and was free with his advice: he thinks Lawrence is getting wild, though still magnificent, doesn't like Murry's layout and advertising (the *Adelphi* carried small ads for books, liners, typewriters and milk chocolate). He pushed his old friend Pauline Smith, as it turned out most successfully: short stories by her were published in August and October 1923, and in April and July 1924. She had found a suitable niche. He himself wrote contributions on the Sitwells and Shelley. Most daringly, and perhaps most usefully, he criticized Middleton Murry's editorials about his late wife Katherine Mansfield. This was a brave thing to do: Murry had been much shocked by his wife's death on 9 January of that year, when she was only thirty-four and at the height of her talents, and although it was natural that he should use the *Adelphi* as a vehicle for publishing her short stories, poems and extracts from her journal, readers were less happy when he described, very emotionally, his reactions to her death in his editorial of the July issue (the second issue). He describes how, after she died, 'for a fortnight I lived in a dream. Then I awoke. I was alone. But absolutely alone, as perhaps only a man who has known what it is not to be alone can know loneliness. And suddenly I knew that all the friends whom I loved were nothing to me. . . .'[10] The September issue continued to make admiring references to her style, and every issue carried a good deal of original work by her. Bennett's letters about this problem are a model of tact, and show his essential good-feeling. He knows he is on highly dangerous ground, but knows at the same time that somebody has got to say something – no doubt his literary friends had been urging him to speak up. After advising Murry to leave the appreciation of Katherine Mansfield to others, he says: 'My dear fellow, I realise that you are entitled to describe the above as an enormity. . . . My sympathy is yours, whether you want it or not. . . . If you resent this letter I shall not complain, nor shall I allow anything adverse that you may say to alter my deep good will towards you.'[11] His advice was heeded: the *Adelphi* went on publishing Katherine Mansfield, but Middleton Murry devoted his editorials to safer subjects, such as Tolstoy, T.S Eliot and Shaw's *Saint Joan*. The only subsequent lapse in taste on the Mansfield theme was a very bad unsigned memorial poem, which appeared complete with black funeral edges in January 1924 to mark the anniversary of her death: Murry continued to get over-excited about other matters, but left his wife in peace.

Bennett stayed on the *Marie Marguerite* until the end of August. In the third week of August he visited his old friend Eden Phillpotts and his wife Emily in Torquay. He hadn't seen them for years. He had once admired Phillpotts's country house; now Phillpotts could admire his yacht. Another old friend also visited him on board: Pauline Smith had been with him earlier in the summer, for a trip from Poole to the Isle of Wight, and returned towards the end of August. On her first visit, Bennett had wrested from her a first short story, 'The Pain', which the *Adelphi* published, and also wrote off to Jonathan Cape suggesting that he should suggest that she should write a full-length novel. On her second visit he made her sketch the plot of the novel she intended to write, which was later in fact to be published by Cape in 1926 under the title *The Beadle*. As before at Fontainebleau, she found his attentions a mixture of torment and pleasure: he made her work, he ignored her protests about her health and her dislike of the ship's motion, and told her she must finish her novel if it killed her, and then would cheer her up by a few words of praise. He enjoyed organizing her business affairs, and taught her to write businesslike letters to editors and publishers. His reward was her attention, which was highly discriminating. While she was on board the yacht in August, the proofs of *Riceyman Steps* arrived. She read them, tucked up under rugs in the deck house on 'a wild grey day', and they made her weep.

At the beginning of September, he let his yacht and returned to London. It was a London of dinners, parties and jazz. Bennett entertained and was entertained, read and wrote about Mark Rutherford, wrote some articles for the *Royal* magazine and enjoyed the publication, in October, of *Riceyman Steps*, which was immediately recognized by reviewers as an important work, and placed in the same class as *Clayhanger* and *The Old Wives' Tale*. Even J.B.Priestley, a less than wholly admiring critic, wrote a long piece in the *London Mercury* describing it as 'undoubtedly Mr Bennett's greatest achievement as a pure craftsman, and . . . perhaps the best example of his disguised romantic method, of the romance that fights its way through reality when all the gates of easy appeal have been barred'.[12] He was to win the James Tait Black Memorial Prize for this novel: the prize money was £141 and Bennett comments: 'This is the first prize for a book I ever had.'[13]

He spent a weekend at Beaverbrook's that autumn, discussing with him the image of the *Evening Standard,* Beaverbrook's new paper, with which Bennett was later to become closely associated. Bennett urged him to make it sophisticated and prestigious, which proved sound advice: till the end of his life Beaverbrook defended the *Standard* as the only sophisticated evening paper in England.

Bennett also returned to his theatrical interests, while being careful to avoid the overtures of film magnates. A revival of *The Great Adventure* was planned, Basil Dean was nibbling at *London Life,* and Bennett was adapting *Mr Prohack* for the stage. The Lyric, Hammersmith was flourishing; in December 1925 he was to attend the last performance of *The Beggar's Opera,* which had run for three years and 1,469 performances (it was revived for sixty more in 1926). And there was now another connection with the stage, through Dorothy. She says that shortly after his return to London that autumn he met the director Ronald Calthrop, who was planning to put on a couple of productions at the Kingsway; Bennett spoke to him about Dorothy, with the result that Dorothy was engaged to play Viola in *Twelfth Night,* with Viola Tree (who had appeared in *The Love Match*) as Olivia. The production itself wasn't a great success, but it brought Dorothy some good notices and her next part: she was engaged to play the role of Honoria Looe the following year in the revival of *The Great Adventure.* So Bennett had remained loyal to his promise to help her. Ironically, Dorothy, who had been an independent actress for years, now found herself accused by rivals of being 'the author's friend' – Arnold's help could have its disadvantages.

The end of 1923 was celebrated in appropriate style, at the Chelsea Arts Ball with Dorothy. The next morning, Bennett felt listless and made a New Year's Resolution to go out less. He did not keep it. He could not resist his own popularity. He was invited everywhere: high-brow teas, dinners at the Savoy, clubs, first nights and concerts followed one another at an alarming pace. *Riceyman Steps* had brought him new prestige; it was read by lords and barbers, and Conrad was reported to say that it showed 'Bennett victorious'. It was difficult, in this atmosphere of frantic social life, to get much serious work done. George Doran was over in England in January (while Swinnerton was touring the United States) and he had to be entertained. A new success, *The Way of the World,* opened in February at the Lyric, which gave him much satisfaction: Edith Evans starred in it, and it was 'the finest comic show I ever saw on any stage in the wide world',[14] writes Bennett to Swinnerton. The Lyric was booming and fashionable: everybody went to the first night, and the slums of Hammersmith were thronged with 'the cars of the high-brows'.[15] In the midst of all this, Bennett managed to write a long short story (about 20,000 words) called 'Elsie and the Child', which was to be the backbone of a new collection of short stories.

Bennett's feelings about this story were very mixed. The idea for it had come not from himself, but from Newman Flower. Flower had noticed that Elsie, the heroine of *Riceyman Steps*, was a tremendous success with the public, and he wished to exploit this success. Bennett allowed himself to be persuaded, but he was not entirely happy about it. A great deal of the public enthusiasm for *Riceyman Steps*, as he noted, sprang from the fact that Elsie was a good-hearted charwoman, sympathetic, unselfish and chaste. Bennett did not deceive himself into believing that people liked her and the book through a natural love of goodness. They liked her because she represented what they believed the working classes ought to be. In a letter of much shrewdness, written to Gide, he says of Elsie: 'She is a domestique, and all London and New York is wishing that it could find devoted servants like her! "*Psychologies des Foules!*" '[16] The condescension and sentimentality at the heart of his book's success depressed him – had nobody noticed that he had done the best portrait of a miser since Balzac, if not even a better one than Balzac's own? But success on any terms was pleasant, and it gave him the courage to tell Gide that he had been attacked by 'les jeunes' and was considered as a back number in high-brow circles.

He certainly felt a slight sense of self-betrayal in using Elsie as a bait for more sympathy and praise. The story, in fact, is not too bad; and appears all the better for being a companion piece to a volume of stories about yachts and dinner parties. It relates Elsie's efforts to become a proper maid-servant and to wear the right clothes and say the right things and wait at table at Dr Raste's, as she had aspired to do in *Riceyman Steps*. But the plot hinges on Dr Raste's daughter's passion for Elsie, and her reluctance to leave her to go away to boarding school, and it is fundamentally false. It does not ring true. *Riceyman Steps* was a freshly observed novel, involving research and inquiry: 'Elsie and the Child' is loosely written and artificial. He did do some research on it – he revisited Clerkenwell, interrogated his doctor about the daily lives of panel doctors, and quotes some rather unpleasant bits of medical evidence. And there are, as ever, some interesting social observations – for instance the description of the school Eva attends in Lloyd Square. Eva goes to a small class held by a semi-retired mistress, 'for some of the more select families with small girls in crowded Clerkenwell were as hard put to it for a school as pioneers in an undeveloped country, and they had to club together and organise themselves'.[17] This could be a description of the educational situation in 1960 in neighbouring Barnsbury (which Bennett also visited, admiring the sphinxes of Richmond Avenue). But these observations are attached to a poor structure. Although Bennett as usual received praise of the story gracefully, he must have been aware that in it he was giving the public what it wanted, to use his own phrase.

He was in a very difficult position with regard to the public, in these years. The difficulty consisted in the unusual fact that he found it remarkably easy to address it. Unlike most writers, who cannot hit the popular tone if they try, and who sneer at best-sellers while uneasily afraid that they could never write one however much of their intelligence they devoted to market research, Bennett found it all too easy to be popular. It was both a strength and a weakness, as the contrast between *Riceyman Steps* and 'Elsie and the Child' shows. His popular manuals on *Literary Taste, How to Live on Twenty-four Hours a Day* and so on are extremely well done, and reached an audience which did not read books as a matter of course, in itself a considerable achievement. At the same time, this aspect of his work, as well as his evident enjoyment of the fruits of his labours, made him a very easy target for the young and envious. He was an established and powerful figure, leading a public life which attracted attention, and some of the attention that he began to receive during this period was distinctly hostile. He had expected that it would be: he was too shrewd to expect to escape attack. His reactions to the attack, when it came, show one of the most admirable sides of his character.

As we have seen, he genuinely admired many younger writers, and showed an open mind as well as fine taste and generosity in his praise of them. He warmly defended Joyce, Proust and Lawrence from their critics and would-be censors; he admired E.M.Forster, Aldous Huxley and the Sitwells (though he confessed that he could not understand a word of Gertrude Stein). He was prepared to describe himself and his work as old fashioned, and as early as 1910 he had recounted in the *New Age* his reaction to the post-impressionists' paintings, his sense of their excellence and originality, and the accompanying doubt that his own writing, like old-fashioned painting, might be a little photographic in technique. 'Supposing,' he says there, 'a young writer turned up and forced me, and some of my contemporaries – us who fancy ourselves a bit – to admit that we had been concerning ourselves unduly with (in)essentials, that we had been worrying ourselves to achieve infantile realisms?' Well, that day would be a great and disturbing day – for us.'[18] His mind was open to criticism, but at the same time he was determined not to forsake his own old loyalties in the face of fashionable disdain, or to see his old heroes attacked. He tried to preserve a balance. When Middleton Murry attacked George Moore in an editorial of the *Adelphi* in April 1924, he wrote a very strong letter of protest, and rightly: Murry's piece, 'Wrap me up in my Aubusson Carpet', had been a characteristically emotional and unbalanced attack on Moore, referring to his 'senile indecency', his 'spluttering of venom', his 'senile bleat', etc. – and all this because Moore, himself an old man, had dared to be rude to Hardy, another old man. Murry had concluded: 'Of all men of letters of his age today, Mr Moore is the least respected. Those who recognise talent are contemptuous of the man.'[19] Bennett would not stand for this: Moore was old and far from wealthy, and the attack was far too personal in tone to be acceptable.

It was not that Bennett's own views on fiction had remained static, for to the end of his life he continued not only to read and admire new books, but also to re-assess his first loves, such as Balzac, whom he begins to doubt: in May 1926 he finds him 'thin and tedious', says he will try *Splendeurs et Misères des Courtisanes* again, and 'if that won't pass, I'll try *Cousine Bette*, which I think is the finest Balzac, and if that won't pass I shall have to denounce Balzac as a back number, to my extreme regret'.[20] But he knew that he was too old to change his own ways: writing to Murry, he said: 'My life is an immense romance. It shall continue to be a romance. But I can only keep it so in my own way, and that way will not be by joining "les jeunes"!'[21]

He could not have joined them even if he had wanted to. He was too old, and he belonged to another world. Even Wells, who was less traditional than Bennett, was regarded by younger writers as a back number. Bennett tried to keep in touch, and succeeded more than most; he was obviously regarded as a sympathetic critic by many, or the Sitwells, Paul Nash, Sassoon, Eliot and Graves, to name but a few of those he helped, wouldn't have turned to him. But there were others who were less well disposed towards him: a whole generation of younger reviewers was waiting to get him.

On the whole, as we've seen, he responded calmly to criticism, only taking issue on specific points, as he did with Sarolea in the Everyman affair. He was annoyed by misapprehensions: he writes to L.G.Johnson, who had written a critical book called *Arnold Bennett of the Five Towns*, taking him to task for over-rating *Sacred and Profane Love* and under-rating *The Pretty Lady*: he was annoyed with Capes for misquoting his enthusiasm for Joyce in an advertisement for *Portrait of the Artist as a Young Man*. He was annoyed by some of Priestley's comments in *The Mercury* (February 1924), as he notes in his journal, but six months later when Priestley sent him the article, now included in a book of essays, Bennett wrote back in the most friendly fashion, saying he thought it 'very able' but admitting that, 'like all authors, I feel deeply convinced that I am not understood as completely as my amazing merits deserve. An editor who wanted a free article from me once came along and said: "You are the greatest writer that ever lived – or *could* live." That is the kind of nourishment we require.'[22] A man capable of such extreme good nature and wit at his own expense is hardly likely to be in danger of paranoia.

Nevertheless, Bennett was by now a target for satire, and he knew it. This was in part the price of fame, and he had deliberately courted publicity and made himself into a 'character' – partly, perhaps, through shyness. But he had too much sense of justice to complain when the publicity turned against him. Throughout the 1920s he was a popular cartoon character, turning up in various guises – at first nights, in the barber's, and most significantly in Beerbohm's fine cartoon, which he himself approved, depicting the young Bennett and the old Bennett together, the older man saying with satisfaction, 'All gone according to plan, you see' and the younger saying with equally deep satisfaction, '*My* plan, you know.' Like his own character Lord Raingo, Bennett recognized that all publicity was good publicity, and that it was good to let the press and the cartoonists find something to seize upon. The eccentricities of his dress at this period – his very fine lace shirts, his quiff of hair, his fob – were both an identity and a disguise. (One wonders how consciously he modelled himself on his old hero Balzac, who also had a dual need for invisibility and publicity, and who also dressed strangely and affected distinctive decorations, such as his turquoise-headed cane.)

Not all the satire, however, was friendly. Younger writers were jealous of his wealth, and therefore critical of his materialism. Lawrence, who had written begging letters to Pinker suggesting that Bennett might be able to help him (which he did), naturally didn't enjoy charity and referred to Bennett as 'a pig in clover',[23] an image which is not in fact as offensive as perhaps it was meant to be. Ezra Pound, in his poem 'Mr Nixon', writes in most unflattering terms of a character recognizable as Bennett 'in the cream gilded cabin of his steam yacht' advising the younger writer, Pound, on how to make money:

> 'I was as poor as you are;
> When I began I got, of course,
> Advance on royalties, fifty at first' said Mr Nixon,
> 'Follow me, and take a column
> Even if you have to work free.

Butter reviewers. From fifty to three hundred
I rose in eighteen months;
The hardest nut I had to crack
Was Dr Dundas.

I never mentioned a man but with the view
Of selling my own works.
The tip's a good one, as for literature
It gives no man a sinecure.

And no one knows, at sight, a masterpiece
And give up verse, my boy,
There's nothing in it.'[24]

Another writer who attacked Bennett (significantly, a close friend of Pound's) was Wyndham Lewis. In a novel called *The Roaring Queen*, which had to wait for publication until 1973, though it was written in the thirties, Lewis paints an unmistakable portrait of Bennett under the name of Samuel Shodbutt. It was in fact a posthumous attack, written after Bennett was dead – the book wasn't published when scheduled, in 1936, for other reasons, because it libelled many other identifiable literary characters – but it gives us a very good picture of the qualities Bennett was popularly supposed to possess, and the reasons why Lewis disliked them. Shodbutt (known as S.S., as Bennett was known as A.B., and Priestley as J.B.) is a powerful reviewer, fond of the French language and Gaboriau, possessor of a magnificent dressing gown, fond of his food and comforts, an expert traveller and incredibly vain, particularly about his own power as a critic. Wyndham Lewis describes him:

'Samuel Shodbutt's richly-tailored embonpoint was regal. Literature was the richer for Samuel Shodbutt's appearance, and S.S. was the richer for Literature. A lock of sallow leaden silver oppressed his right-hand temple – he had the constant frown of Power – the frown of the Power-of-the-pen – to make and to mar, of course: the great critic's frown in excelsis. For this was a Literary Emperor. Or was not Shodbutt the dream of a literary emperor (or of a French literary pontiff) by a mid-Victorian haberdasher.'[25]

Bennett, Lewis suggests, has turned literature into a saleable commodity, with Book-of-the-Week prizes handed out more or less at random to satisfy his own sense of power – a clear reference to Bennett's later *Evening Standard* articles. The portrait, although unfair, is funny enough, catching Bennett's catch phrases – 'It's the goods', 'first-rate', 'I take my hat off', 'I stake my critical reputation on it', etc. – and the book as a whole has some fine comic moments at the expense of the literary establishment of the 1920s. But the tone is sour; even Bennett's generosity to other writers is turned into a mockery, and of course there is the usual snob dismissal of his 'grocer' origins. What had Lewis got against him? Was it simply envy, or did he really think that Bennett had degraded literature by associating it with money, and by trying to sell his own books, and books he admired?

Walter Allen, in his preface to *The Roaring Queen*, suggests that there was a personal animosity, and that Lewis thought Bennett had 'done him down over the years'. They had first met, it seems, at a dinner at Osbert Sitwell's: Sickert was there, who insisted on talking about a book by Lewis, which, Lewis said, offended Bennett, for 'Naturally it was aggravating of Sickert to make Bennett talk about a "young author's" book for half an hour. For I saw only too well that as an old hand he had resented this ordeal. So much irresponsible jealousy had been more than he could stomach. . . . Bennett had an age complex as big as a house.'[26] Whether or not Bennett really disliked Lewis we don't know; nor do we know whether it was jealousy that caused his dislike. He could have had many other reasons, as Wyndham Lewis was not the most likeable of men, and generosity, which he found so funny in Bennett, was certainly not his strong point.

Bennett, in fact, was remarkably free, at least in practice, of an age complex. But others weren't. Another younger writer who attacked him was Virginia Woolf (she also features in *The Roaring Queen* as Rhoda Hyman, the Empress of high-brow London, a lanky and sickly lady in Victorian muslins with a drooping, intellect-ravaged exterior);[27] sadly perhaps, as she herself suffered agonies when criticized by other writers, and would have been deeply hurt, for instance, by her caricature in Lewis's satire. She was a more serious and sensitive opponent than Pound or Lewis, and the history of her relationship with Bennett throws some light on both of them. It began in print.

Bennett, in March 1923, had published a short article in *Cassell's Weekly*, called 'Is the Novel Decaying?' (a theme clearly as popular then as it is now); in it he had said, reasonably enough, that it is hard to spot the great writers of the future, and ridiculous to assume that they don't exist simply because one doesn't recognize them oneself. He goes on to state his own faith that novels cannot really survive and achieve greatness unless the characters are real and convincing, for 'the foundation of good fiction is character-creating and nothing else'. (This view may seem ludicrously old-fashioned to some, but it is seriously upheld even today by others; John Bayley, the distinguished modern critic, agrees with Arnold Bennett, and very convincingly criticizes Virginia Woolf herself for the decay of fiction through the plotless, characterless claustrophobic monologue. And one must also remember that Bennett's tone, in a popular periodical like *Cassell's Weekly*, was intentionally provocative.) He then, after his remarks about character-drawing, devotes one short paragraph to Virginia Woolf, in which he says: 'I have seldom read a cleverer book than *Jacob's Room*, a novel which has made a great stir in a small world. It is packed and bursting with originality, and it is exquisitely written. But the characters do not vitally survive in the mind because the author has been obsessed by details of originality and cleverness.'[28] This is just about all he says on Virginia Woolf. She took the criticism very seriously – indeed, she over-reacted. She replied in *The Criterion* in July 1924, in a paper which was originally read to the Heretic Society at Cambridge, and which later appeared as a pamphlet entitled *Mr Bennett and Mrs Brown*. It's an interesting essay, aggressive and polemical in tone, accusing Bennett (and Wells and Galsworthy) of materialism, of lack of interest in the soul, of thinking they could create character by describing external facts such as clothes, houses, incomes. In September 1924, T. S. Eliot, editor of *The Criterion*, asked Bennett if he would write a reply. Bennett liked Eliot, had long admired his poetry, appreciated his appreciation of Pauline Smith, and therefore agreed to oblige. He was still toying with the idea in January 1925, but never bothered to finish his piece, which shows he was not burning with indignation and reproof. In fact, he took Virginia Woolf's criticisms very calmly, more or less ignoring them on all their appearances. She had clearly been deeply hurt by his assertion that she couldn't create memorable characters, just as she was offended by his views on women. (See her *Writer's Diary*, 26 September 1920.) She attacked; he didn't bother to defend. The strange thing about her pamphlet is that it seems to me to accuse Bennett of lacking the qualities which he most possessed. Odd, too, that she most attacks *Hilda Lessways*, and attacks it for its dull materialism and endless descriptions of houses and furniture, when it is in fact a book of almost morbid intensity, clearly written under the invigorating influence of the Russians (particularly Dostoevsky). It is also a feminist novel, but not in terms that she could perceive, perhaps. The North was a foreign country to her, and she did not recognize its signals. The blindness is a common one.

To jump forward a little in time, one could hardly find a more interesting juxtaposition of their two characters than the encounter described by Virginia

Woolf in her diary for 2 December 1930. Their literary sparring was by this time common knowledge, and it was determined that the two should become friends. Bennett himself did not like having enemies. They had missed an opportunity for 'scrapping' a few years earlier, at dinner with the Wells's in November 1926. Shaw had been there and had monopolized the talk over dinner, and after dinner Shaw, Dorothy, Virginia Woolf and Wells himself had 'formed a group and never moved'.[29] On the next occasion, in 1930, they talked for a long time, in Ethel Sands's 'little back room'; characteristically, she mocks his stammer and his accent, in true Bloomsbury style, even calling in Lord David Cecil to help in the mockery, but in true Virginia Woolf style has to admit 'I like the old creature. I do my best, as a writer, to detect signs of genius in his smoky brown eyes: I certainly see sensuality, power, I suppose. . . .' Bennett praised George Moore, and allowed her to tease him about his clothes and baths and beds and yacht, then went off saying, 'Now I must go home. I have to write one thousand words tomorrow morning.'[30]

Virginia Woolf complains that the encounter left her with only the scrag end of the evening, and no strength to write a word the morning after; though, with fascinating self-confession, she then adds in a footnote to the day's entry: 'Reflection: It is presumably a bad thing to look through articles, reviews, etc. to find one's own name. Yet I often do.'[31] And that same week, she is agonizing over 'one slight snub' in *The Times Literary Supplement*. She, who had attacked Bennett with the full force of her wit and intellect: an ageing lion, as he was. Which of them was worldly, which unworldly, Bennett with his yacht and his well-cut suit, Virginia with her snobbery and her migraines? Did she suspect the physical tension that had made Bennett suffer for most of his life, and did she in any way connect it with her own physical manifestations of neurosis? Both of them were highly strung, but his was the sensitivity of a deprived working-class child, not of an upper-class aesthete. Both were melancholic. How could Virginia Woolf have seen him as 'coarse . . . glutted with success . . . a shopkeeper's view of literature . . . yet with the rudiments of sensibility. . . .'[32] (I quote selectively, from her rather splendid epitaph.) How could one ascribe to a man who had been rendered *inarticulate* by sensibility merely the rudiments of it? His stammer embodied, physically and unmistakably, his response to life, but she was incapable, through class, of seeing it as anything other than an impediment to his rather dull discourse. Despite herself, and no doubt a little charmed by his evident goodwill towards her, she liked him, but the victory of generosity was his. It was not easy to get on with the younger generation, particularly when they came armed to the teeth. She never learned to. But he had far more humility and modesty than she ever had, and had learned to accept defeat and failures and bad reviews with equanimity. This was not insensitivity: it was modesty, the last quality publicly ascribed to him. He had seen other writers better than himself savaged: why should he escape?

The most curious thing about their relationship, perhaps, is the fact that their works are oddly similar. Not, it is true, in technique, but in import. She accuses him of being interested only in the externals of daily life: in fact he writes magnificently of the little movements of the spirit in its daily routine, just as she does, of the soul within a drab housemaid's exterior. He accuses her of failing to invent character, but her characters – Mrs Dalloway, Mrs Ramsay, Eleanor Pargiter – are as distinctive and enduring as his own. They both wrote of the inner dramas of ordinary events – a holiday, a marriage, a child's sufferings in an adult world; they were both adept at social comedy. But there was something in her, some really fundamental recoil from grocers and shops, that blinded her appreciation both of his subject matter and of his meaning. Her recoil was an involuntary movement of class. She did not like the *nouveau riche*. The sensitivity manifested in a stammer, in insomnia, in gastric disorders, was something she could not translate into her own terms.

During 1924 and early 1925, Bennett found more opportunities to exercise his capacity for taking failure well. Failure, as usual, came in the form of unsuccessful theatrical ventures. He didn't let it get him down too much, and managed to enjoy the usual round of holidays and yacht trips – in April 1924 he went to Spain in a large party organized by Beaverbrook, and joined Dorothy later in the Basque country. (It was Beaverbrook's principle never to invite married couples on his excursions.) He sailed through a great deal of the summer on the *Marie Marguerite*, entertaining and visiting old friends and relations. Nevertheless, he must have been disappointed by the failure, this summer, of one of his more ambitious and hopeful enterprises, *London Life*.

He and Knoblock obviously hoped to repeat the success of *Milestones*, and must have been particularly disheartened when they didn't because so many of their friends were doing well. It was an exciting time in the theatre: Shaw's *Saint Joan* opened with Sybil Thorndike in the lead, and Beaverbrook declared that it was 'the greatest play I ever saw'. *The Way of the World* launched Edith Evans at the Lyric, Hammersmith upon her dazzling career. Eden Phillpotts scored a huge success with *The Farmer's Wife*, which was put on at the Court, after a false start years earlier in Birmingham, and ran for years: it played for 1,320 performances. There were, it is true, less happy omens: Dorothy's run of *Twelfth Night* closed on 9 December, and their friend Marjorie Gordon opened at the same theatre in a new musical called *Kate*, which ran for thirty performances only. It deserved to be a flop, in Bennett's view; he disliked the book intensely. He obviously didn't care much for Shaw's *Back to Methuselah*, either, as he fell asleep during it. Dorothy, more enthusiastic, kept Shaw's programme, which he gave her as a souvenir. But on the whole, it was a time of high expectations, and *London Life* seemed assured the kind of production which would give it every chance.

It had originally been written for the Queen's Theatre, which had never put it on. Basil Dean, who had directed Bennett's *The Honeymoon* and *Sacred and Profane Love*, was looking desperately for a play for Drury Lane, of which he was the new director; his thoughts naturally turned to Bennett. Bennett and Knoblock did a little re-writing for him in February, and Dean was delighted. He liked the play and hoped to make a big splash with it. But things didn't work out as they planned. Dean did his best to make the piece spectacular, but nevertheless the *Daily Telegraph* complained that there were 'no horse races, no burning houses, or falling roofs, no sea voyages' – as the traditions of Drury Lane had led them to expect. The play, which opened on 3 June, ran for only five weeks. Bennett had been particularly interested in the production; Basil Dean, in his autobiography *Seven Ages* (1970), recalls that Bennett liked very much to be involved in rehearsals and contributed a piece for the programme entitled (somewhat fraudulently, in view of the fact that the play had originally been written for the Queen's) 'writing for Drury Lane'. (He actually withdrew this article when the management refused him three extra free stalls for the first night.)

Bennett was unsure of the reasons for the play's failure. He cannot have been taken by surprise, as he complained during rehearsals of the selfishness and stupidity of some of the actors, and wrote to Wells before the opening that all the board of the theatre except Basil Dean disliked the play, and that one of them had even resigned in protest. He consoled himself, as we have seen, by telling himself that it was above the heads of his audience, but he was well aware that a long run at Drury Lane would have been extremely profitable. However, he had another consolation, in the form of a successful revival of *The Great Adventure*, which opened at the Haymarket, with Dorothy in the role of Honoria Looe. As usual, Bennett meddled a little, trying to dissuade his principal actor from upstaging Dorothy during her big speech, complaining that one of the other actors had completely mis-understood the actual plot. But the papers welcomed the play, describing it as a 'happy revival', so Bennett was able to retire to his yacht, leaving Dorothy on stage, with some peace of mind. He returned in August, after a summer on board, and took up his life with her – they used to meet at Ciro's after her performance several nights a week.

Dorothy's new success on the stage had revived all her old enthusiasm: she was full of ideas for cabarets, and appeared on a Sunday night at a soirée of the beautiful Elsa Lanchester and Harold Scott in a short piece directed and translated by herself. It was the golden age of revue; oddly enough Bennett seems never to have turned his hand to revue-writing, though he had a go at nearly everything else. All seemed to be going well, when a bombshell from the past fell on him, in the form of a very unwelcome reminder of Marguerite. This extraordinary woman had written a memoir of her husband, and had offered it for sale to the *Daily Express*, through the agents Curtis, Brown. This in itself perhaps would not have been so extraordinary, for literary figures are in a sense fair game for their ex-wives, ex-mistresses, ex-lovers, children and relations, and the records would be a lot duller and more inaccurate without some of their effusions. The most amazing thing is that throughout her memoir, Marguerite nowhere mentions that she and her husband are separated. The whole thing is written as by a loyal wife, in a tone of smug propriety – the last sentence, it is true, does have a certain amount of ambiguity, for after describing her own artistic flair, and her desire to settle down in her old age in 'beautiful scenery, not too far from a village', she goes on to say: 'Up to the present my life has been very interest-ing. At times I find it thrilling, for I love to study human nature and to enjoy all that life offers – like my famous husband, Arnold Bennett.'[33]

Bennett no doubt thought that she should have owned up to the fact that life offered her more thrills than those of being his wife. The first he heard of the memoir's existence was when Max Beaverbrook rang him up on the night of 25 September, asking Bennett what to do. Beaverbrook assured him that it was 'unadulterated praise', which it was, and Bennett decided that as he had no power to stop publication, he might as well have it published by a friend as by an enemy, and he gave the *Express* permission to go ahead with it. He recognized that Marguerite would never understand 'the awful bad taste of the whole thing', and was only anxious not to appear party to a piece of vulgar self-advertisement. Beaverbrook promised to solve that by putting in a note explaining that the Bennetts had been separated for some time. In fact the first instalment, which appeared on 19 November 1924, was preceded by a large front-page announcement explaining the situation. 'Two years ago,' the *Express* declares, 'Mr and Mrs Bennett separated. It was a legal separation by deed, and it was complete. And now, in her position of remembered intimacy, Mrs Arnold Bennett . . . herself an expressionist and rebellious thinker, has written the story of her married life. . . . Should this private life be told in public? The *Daily Express*, without expressing approval or disapproval of Mrs Bennett's departure from tradition, has decided to publish it. . . .'[34] The *Express*'s neutral tone is familiar.

Bennett was puzzled by the piece for other reasons. He was not only surprised by her having written it at all; he was surprised that she had managed to write it. He was scornful about her naïve pride in herself for having written 15,000 words of articles on him. Certainly the book has no literary merit, and is unreliable as a documentary: it describes their first meeting in Paris, his working habits, his travels, his hobbies, his love of luxury. There is a naïve touch of self-importance throughout it: her interest in his trip to Denmark with Rickards, for instance, focuses on her image of herself waiting at Harwich to greet his return: 'It was very windy that day; my pink muslin frock and white shawl were floating in the wind. . . . My signal was seen; also the woman whom, to her great annoyance, they had left behind. . . .'[35] Despite its intrinsic lack of merit, however, the book was snapped up: Bennett was a big name, and people wanted to read about him. (Photographs of the interior of his house in Cadogan Square appeared in the September 1924 issue of *Vogue* – he was gossip-column news in a big way.) Those in the know about his situation must have found an added piquancy, but most people did not know. (Was it a relief to have it out in the open?) Bennett wrote to George Doran at once, anticipating that the book would be offered and published in America, and asking him as a friend to explain the circumstances: a letter which contrasts sadly with his previous request to Doran, when Marguerite visited the States in the spring of 1923 intending to give some recitals, asking him to 'deal sweetly with her. The very last thing I desire is that she should feel anything against her old friends.'[36] The change was of her own making. And her actions over this matter may well have encouraged him to express some of his resentments, however obliquely and discreetly, in his next novel. She had forfeited the right, at last, to his consideration. As he told Beaverbrook, it was not as though she needed the money.

The storm blew over: the last instalment of what he referred to jokingly to Dorothy as 'My Daily Wife' appeared on 29 November, and although there were still book versions to come (by Philpot in England, 1925, and

Greenberg in America) it was not like Bennett to waste unnecessary time over something that could not be helped. One may wonder if he tried as hard as he might have done to prevent publication, but his efforts would have been in all likelihood unsuccessful, and as we have seen he was afraid of his wife's ill-nature. So he diverted himself by plunging headlong into a new but interesting smallscope theatrical disaster. *The Great Adventure* had closed at the end of October, after a respectable run, and Dorothy went off to Italy for a holiday with their friend Mrs Atkins, leaving Bennett planning to re-write *The Bright Island* for production early in 1925. He was also working on an adaptation of *Mr Prohack*: the theatre kept its hold.

The Bright Island was put on by the Stage Society on 15 February 1925, at the Aldwych. It was directed by the distinguished Russian director Komisarjevsky. Komisarjevsky had been introduced to Bennett by his old friend Lee Mathews. They met on 26 January, for dinner, and Bennet was impressed by Komisarjevsky's stories of life in the theatre in Russia, which he had left partly because of the drudgery of producing propaganda plays. Nobody had great hopes of *The Bright Island*: it had already been turned down by several managements, and when it appeared it was duly slated. One critic called it 'the worst play written by a celebrated man for a long time past'. The *Telegraph* would have preferred it to be a 'political squib' not a play, and complained of the author's sense of confusion, lack of direction, and labyrinthine plot, and the *Standard* said flatly that it was 'flat and un-inspired'. Bennett took this in good part, as usual, and in no time at all was condoling with Shaw for some awful performances of *Man and Superman* at the Chelsea Palace, also in February. Shaw had prophesied that *The Bright Island* would never do because people cannot stand 'unrelieved scoffing'. Thus they protected one another from the public and the vicissitudes of theatrical life. *The Bright Island*'s most permanent appearance was in 1924, in an attractive limited de luxe edition of two hundred copies printed by the Golden Cockerel Press for the Vine Book series of Bookman's *Journal*. It was thereafter forgotten.

Before the production of *The Bright Island*, at the end of 1924, Bennett went off for another holiday with Dorothy; she'd been in Italy since November, and they spent a happy month together in Naples and Genoa. Both enjoyed travelling, and the next six years were punctuated by constant trips abroad – when things went wrong they would go abroad to cheer them-selves up, when things were going well they would go to celebrate. They seem to have had a good agreement about the way they would spend their time together, though Dorothy perhaps was slightly less enthusiastic about social life in London than Bennett, and liked to get him to herself. But she was an independent woman, and had no objection to spending time without him. On this occasion she stayed in Italy for a month longer than he did, returning to London in the third week of February to the usual busy social round – the Colefaxes, the Barries, John Barrymore, Thomas Bodkin, Max Beerbohm, Noël Coward, Beverley Nichols, *No, No, Nanette*, *The Cherry Orchard*. It's impossible to catalogue the diversity of Bennett's friends and interests: reading his journal, and the journals of his contemporaries, one gets the impression that he knew everybody and went to everything. It's not surprising that Dorothy wanted at times to whip him off to the country, and occasionally succeeded in doing so.

One wonders how he found the strength for his social life, and why he bothered to keep so much of it up. Some have claimed that his constant theatre-going was influenced by Dorothy, but he had been deeply committed to the theatre long before he met her. He was getting older, and naturally he fell asleep sometimes during dull performances, but that's no proof that he didn't want to go. He has been accused, during these years, of snobbery – indeed, the popular image of Bennett is of a social climber who sought high society. There is very little truth in it. For instance, his interest in royalty and titles was minimal; and he made no attempt to make his way into really aristocratic circles. It is true that he was himself something of a social catch, a literary lion, and as such he was constantly invited to fashionable gatherings, and as constantly responding, but one cannot help feeling that he responded largely out of curiosity. His popularity socially can be measured by the constant attentions of Lady Colefax, who made overtures to all successful people – over this period she was also pursuing Virginia Woolf, whose biographer, Quentin Bell, describes her as 'a sensitive barometer of fame'.[37] Virginia Woolf, like Bennett, succumbed to her charm, and Beverley Nichols, one of her protégés, writes a loyal and amusing account of her social activities in his book, *The Sweet and Twenties*. He says she was 'the greatest lion-hunter of them all. She was, of course, a snob, but she was a snob for brains . . . her address book was not compiled from Burke nor the Almanach de Gotha; she was more drawn to *Who's Who* and *The Artists' and Writers' Year Book* . . . dark, sharp-featured, beady eyed . . . six luncheon parties a week . . . a perpetual cascade of Christian names. . . .'[38]

Perhaps the idea that Bennett himself was a snob springs more from the snobbish remarks that people continued to make about him than from his own behaviour – he did have a Northern accent, he was blunt in his manner, he did dress flamboyantly, if expensively. There are various anecdotes by those who considered themselves his social superiors, demonstrating his vulgarity, such as those by Clive Bell and Sir Gerald Kelly, and Compton Mackenzie's description of Bennett's first appearance, with cigar and braces and red and yellow waistcoat, at the Reform Club.[39] But these hardly reflect on himself: in fact the reverse. He liked clubs because he could see there a variety of important people, and observe them with curiosity; he liked to meet politicians, ministers, self-made millionaires, lawyers, bankers. He liked to see how they behaved. But he had very little of the social disease of pursuing purely social distinction, which the most surprising people catch. The social type – Sybil Colefax, Ottoline Morrell, Diana Manners – interested him, but no more than other types, such as musical comedy actresses and intellectual high-brows like Huxley. Ottoline Morrell, in fact, whose Tuesday evenings were attended by a glittering array of social and intellectual aspirants, far from despising him, seems to have liked him, and to have been upset when he would put her in her place, mistaking her, so she says, for 'what he most disliked', a high-brow.[40] She also comments that Bertrand Russell 'took such a violent dislike to him that he said he couldn't be in the same room with him. I never understood why, except that he said he was so "vulgar", which was not accurate. He was superficially showy, but not vulgar, indeed he had a very great sense of delicacy in his life, and an exquisite love of craftsmanship.'[41] It seems that Bennett, far from seeking the grand, was constantly solicited by it, and determined to reject the bits of it that he didn't like; in turn, to the end of his life there were some who judged him harshly largely for his social origins. He himself was remarkably free of prejudice: indeed, one of his most profound aims was to be so. All that one can say about his extremely full social life is that he was too interested in what was going on to be able to turn down invitations, which is hardly a definition of snobbery. His real personal friends cut across class, though it might be true to say that most of his closest friends were, like himself, from fairly ordinary backgrounds – Swinnerton, Rickards, Wells, Beaverbrook, had all had to make their own way in life.

He was seeing much of Beaverbrook in the spring of 1925, not only through friendship, but for a purpose. He was consulting him about his next novel. This was not, as one might have expected, the long-projected piece about Beaverbrook's father: it was a quite different subject, drawn from more recent experience. The novel, *Lord Raingo*, was to be about politics, and its debt to Beaverbrook's experiences, as well as to Bennett's own, is apparent throughout. Bennett began writing the novel on 13 May; he had already had several consultations with Beaverbrook, who, he said 'has exactly the right sort of imagination, and a very powerful and accurate one'. Beaverbrook's own ideas on writing creative literature were naïve, and he had often amused Bennett by his strange comments, such as his outburst over *St Joan* – 'Arnold, I've come to the conclusion that there's a technique for playwriting'[42] – but he knew the stuff, and he knew, when prompted, how to deliver it.

Lord Raingo was written between 13 May 1925 and 26 January 1926. It is a longish book – 130,000 words – and Bennett wrote it over a period of travel and distractions. It involved a good deal of hard work, and was in itself ambitious – a plot involving a prime minister and cabinet ministers had to be tactful and accurate. Beaverbrook vetted all the politics, finding only two or three small slips in the entire novel, which is a tribute to his briefing and to Bennett's attention. The novel, inevitably, aroused immense interest. Its hero is a millionaire, who at the beginning of the novel (set in wartime) is appointed minister of records, a job which evidently had much in common with Beaverbrook's appointment as minister of information. Like Bennett, Raingo was appointed at the end of the war, and does not have long in office. The plot covers Raingo's machinations at the ministry, his relations with the prime minister, who happens to be an old childhood friend from the North, and his relations with other members of the war cabinet, which contains portraits of characters clearly based on real people, such as that of Tom Hogarth, which was readily acknowledged after publication by Churchill. In order to become a minister, Raingo receives a peerage – again, Beaverbrook's help about the social thrills and embarrassments of this elevation was invaluable. Raingo's satisfaction in his rank and power is painted deliberately as being positively childish: he sees the war as a 'game of bloody football', he enjoys the inter-departmental strife and one-upmanship, and wants the war to go on for ever so he can continue to enjoy his position. At first, one thinks that Bennett's interest in the man beneath the robes, the child within the man, is in itself rather juvenile, and that his picture of cabinet ministers quarrelling and drinking and joking like schoolboys is a somewhat wilful attempt to cut people down to size, an almost irresponsible bit of schoolboy satire and humour, by the plain man from the Five Towns determined to expose the essential human childishness of the great. One thinks this partly because Bennett himself had written so much about his own surprise at finding himself a middle-aged man, his own naïve satisfaction in being treated with respect by the famous, and one assumes that he sympathizes with Raingo's pompous and slightly ridiculous pleasure in buying robes and having his photograph taken, in being caricatured by the press, in being immensely popular with the newspaper-reading public, in receiving clothes baskets full of press cuttings when he falls ill. And Bennett does in a way sympathize, but he does not identify. Raingo is very much a man in his own right, and not a very likeable one at times. Bennett, after all, had refused a title, and was at liberty to comment on the aspirations of those who accepted or angled for them.

Nevertheless, Bennett takes the opportunity of exorcizing a few of his own wartime ghosts. Like Bennett in war, Raingo is unhappily married at the beginning of the novel, and leaves his wife a great deal of the time in a country house in Essex; presumably unlike Bennett, he keeps a mistress, Delphine, in a little flat in Orange Street. The wife, Adela, is not at all like Marguerite: she is cold, English, clumsy, uncomfortable. Yet she is also ambitious: her first question when she learns that her husband is to become a peer is to ask whether she will have to wear a coronet. When she kills herself in a car crash halfway through the book, Raingo is relieved. As a result of his inconvenient marriage, Raingo spends a good deal of his time not only with his mistress, but in clubs, and Bennett very subtly makes the point that he is not popular there – he is a personality, he is popular with the public, but he is not really accepted by his contemporaries, he is not at ease in company. He comes from a cold home, and his manner towards others is cold and uneasy: he has a childish desire to compensate for his uncertainties with robes and deference and power. The portrait, though uneven, is convincing: this self-made millionaire is much more realistic than the joke-card millionaires of the fantasies and light novels. The lonely millionaire is a cliché, but Bennett demonstrates Raingo's loneliness with conviction: he wanders from the club to the ministry to the Savoy, always pretending to be busy, but really, outside the context of work, at a loss.

Except, of course, with his mistress Delphine, who again is a cliché – dark, magnificent, warm, womanly, domestic, devoted, always waiting for her lover. Or is she? At first one dismisses her as a stock piece of character-drawing, rather as one dismisses Raingo as yet another of Bennett's middle-aged heroes, and indeed the character is not particularly well done. But it has its surprises. What really makes this novel a success is not so much its political setting, interesting though that must have been when it was published: it is the skill with which Bennett has drawn the depths of self-deception of which people are capable, when surrounded by all the apparatus of pomp and wealth and ceremony to support them in their illusions. He has chosen two sides of Raingo's predicament to illustrate this, and interwoven them with great skill – what a pity it is that he allowed his style to become so relaxed and popular (as Henry James remarked on his style in *The Price of*

Love) when he had such good material and such insights to hand. Raingo is deceived on two fronts – about his mistress, and about his health. From the very beginning of the novel, he is a sick man with a weak heart; he makes use of his weakness to obtain the peerage, suggesting that his health would never stand the strain of standing for the House of Commons. We believe he is weak, but not very weak. Similarly, his relationship with Delphine shows weakness – he has reason to suspect her of hiding things from him, he sees her dining with a strange man in the Savoy, she is out at strange times. We think, again, that there is not much wrong with him: he is merely a suspicious, jealous, elderly lover, a hypochondriac about his love and his health.

But in fact, both his fears are justified. Delphine commits suicide when her former fiancé is killed in France. He himself contracts pneumonia and suffers a prolonged illness, at the end of which he dies. What is superbly done in this novel is the vacillation of the man's will, when it is beset by fears and suspicions. The Delphine scene, it is true, is marred by theatrical Ouida-like touches, and by the introduction of an improbably beautiful younger sister who improbably enough seems to fall in love with Raingo's improbably escaped prisoner-of-war son (who improbably arrives home on the day of his mother's funeral) – but beneath this dross there is some fine observation. And the progress of Raingo's illness, from its suspiciously mild, almost imperceptible inception, to its final conclusion, is magnificent. The relationships with the doctors, both local and national, the nurses, the need for reassurance, the constant doubt and hope, the looking for portents, the vain and pathetic attempts to take an interest in business, the easy tears, the physical and mental decline, the relief of pretending to be delirious and the reality into which the pretence merges, the length of the nights, the touch of the pillows, the colour of the dawn – all these have rarely been bettered. There are few if any more realistic deathbed scenes in fiction. The disciple of de Maupassant and Flaubert had lived up to expectation. One could almost peel away the popular irrelevancies from this story, and leave it intact. As a narrative, it is gripping (one is as surprised by each stage of Raingo's illness as he is himself, and yet, like himself, as deeply suspicious of anything said by the doctors and nurses) – and as a psychological study it is first-class. Did Bennett recall it during his own final and surprisingly similar illness? He must have done, because he must have been, in a sense, imagining his own death. He could well have looked back on it with satisfaction, for he was more stoical than Raingo.

This ambitious novel was written against a background of constant activity and movement. Visits to Torquay, Oxford, Covent Garden and his yacht follow one another thick and fast. In Torquay, patching up an old friendship, he and Phillpotts decided to collaborate on a comic libretto. It was perhaps to escape from all these diversions that he and Dorothy decided to go off on a working holiday to Austria. They let the *Marie Marguerite* and went to Salzburg, where, in thirty-three days, he wrote 21,500 words of his novel, 11,000 words of his journal and two articles of 1,600 words each for the *Sunday Pictorial*. They left Salzburg on 11 August, Dorothy to start rehearsals for a Pirandello play for the Lyric with Nigel Playfair, and Bennett to finish *Raingo* on his yacht. The yacht sailed the canals of Holland, with his brother Septimus and the Keebles as guests. Bennett wrote, and worried about Septimus, who was depressed and silent, and suffering from tuberculosis – he died the next spring, in Wales, on 9 March 1926.

Doubtless Bennett imagined that he had achieved by this stage a permanent balance in his life, between work, private life, social life. He was fifty-nine, happy, successful, wealthy. The relationship with Dorothy seemed ideal: she had her own career, which didn't interfere with his. When they were together, they could work well, as his output at Salzburg demonstrates. When they were apart, they wrote each other long, almost daily, intimate letters about their adventures. He had love and companionship, a house and a yacht, and a fair degree of independence; his three years with Dorothy had been full and they had both learned to adapt to separation and closeness. Things could have gone on like that for ever, and they probably both hoped that they would. Neither of them expected the next stage in their relationship, which was to have such far-reaching consequences.

At the end of August, Bennett received from Dorothy the news that she was expecting a baby. She had been trying to contact him for days, but the yacht had been elusive. He must have been amazed, but his reply was perfect: as soon as he heard, he cabled to her: 'Very sorry. Very glad. Shall catch boat Hook of Holland, be with you tomorrow.'[43]

14
In the Thick of Things

It was an unexpected development. Bennett responded with enthusiasm, confusion and warm support. He didn't, as he had at first suggested, rush straight home: he decided that he'd better put his prior commitments first, as usual (he hated to have his timetables upset, and was unfailingly courteous), and so he stayed on board to receive Knoblock and the Rosses, whom he was expecting as guests. But he wrote to Dorothy, expressing his love for her, his delight at the prospect of becoming a father, his apprehension about 'the extreme difficulty of the father, who will be in his 60th year, doing his full duty by the child. When the child is ten, I shall be seventy.'[1] It was characteristic that worry about others should be uppermost in his mind. He saw at once that a baby would change his life tremendously, in practical terms, but says in his letter to her: 'I have a curious feeling of elation, of response to a challenge from destiny.'[2] Perhaps he did welcome the challenge: he had always liked the difficult, and life had been growing rather easy of late.

At first, Dorothy seems to have wanted to go abroad to have the baby, as she might have been conventionally expected to do: Katherine Mansfield in the same situation had disappeared, some years earlier, to the privacy of a Bavarian spa. But Bennett believed in meeting difficulties more directly, and wanted her to stay in London. He took full responsibility for the child from his first letter, talking already of money and wills, and more romantically of a beautiful peasant costume which he had just bought her in Middleburg, 'high-waisted.... I was much struck by the lovely effect of it on young women with child. Of course this was before I had the least idea of your condition. It makes them look like 15th or 16th cent. madonnas.'[3] When he returned to London, a day or two later, he and Dorothy began to look forward to the baby with interest. She had clearly been much fortified by his reaction to her somewhat startling news.

Like many prospective mothers, she began to take a new interest in other people's babies, talked about what her own would be like, and amused herself by taking the unborn child to picture galleries, speculating on his (she always thought of the baby as masculine at this stage) emotions, and worrying about whether he was receiving the right influences. Bennett listened to all this with sympathy, and, more practically, altered his will, in October, arranging to leave to Dorothy everything except what he had earmarked for Marguerite. The new situation necessitated some family adjustments, as Bennett had no intention of keeping the baby's arrival quiet. He met Dorothy's mother: Dorothy met Tertia. On the surface at least, all was smiles and acceptance, though there must have been strong undercurrents of emotion in some quarters. The gynaecologist said all was well: Bennett wrote to Jane Wells accepting her congratulations, saying that Dorothy 'is 34, and a very hefty wench'.[4] She was not in fact as hefty as she seemed to him, and her sensitivity, acute at all times, was strained by her expectations: what can Bennett have made of it when she remarked one evening, as they were eating fried roes on toast, 'We're eating "young"!'[5] But for the time being, she was healthy enough, and Bennett was able to continue his work on *Lord Raingo*.

The shock of finding himself a father-to-be naturally did not hinder his work schedule. As well as *Raingo*, he managed to write a few short stories that autumn, a couple of articles on religion for the *Daily Express*, and to finish his libretto with Phillpotts. (It was called *Vallombrosa*, and was never performed.) Then, on 14 December, he and Dorothy set off together for a long stay abroad. They spent a couple of months in the Hôtel de Russie in Rome, where, on 26 January, he finished *Lord Raingo*; less than a fortnight later he began a new novel, *The Strange Vanguard*, which was to be in contrast 'sensational, comical, moralistic, larkish'.[6] After Raingo's gloomy death-bed, no wonder he felt in need of some light relief. Dorothy enjoyed the art and architecture, and tried her hand at writing. In February they left Rome, and travelled slowly home via Nice, Marseilles, Avignon and Paris, a leisurely and luxurious journey punctuated by visits to friends. Dorothy was by now considerably pregnant, but does not seem to have suffered from the journey, and the only inconvenience and delay caused by her condition was right at the end, when they reached Calais in March. They were expecting to cross straight over the Channel, but the weather was so rough that they didn't like to risk it, so they put up in a hotel and waited for a calm crossing. They were held up for three days, and during this period Bennett wandered round the town, seeing all there was to see. He wrote a sketch of Calais, later published in the collection *The Savour of Life*, which captures perfectly the authentic thrill of discovering a new strange place. It is typical of Bennett that he writes best of such places: he had just returned from three months amidst some of the finest scenery of Europe, but he never describes it as well as he describes the dullness of Calais. Such subjects are peculiarly his own: as Philip Larkin writes evocatively in middle age of the forgotten boredom of a suburban childhood, so one feels those long days at Burslem inspired Bennett at sixty with a peculiar nostalgic poetry which Rome could never provide. 'The day is Sunday,' he says. 'The fantastic *ennui* of the provinces beats down upon you, worse than the wind. You walk, you walk. Calais does exist. Towers, spires, public buildings with some style . . .'[7] – and also Rodin's *Burghers*, which he came upon with much satisfaction in the Place d'Armes. If there was anything interesting to find, Bennett would surely find it. Italy was in a sense too easy for him, much as he loved it. It is in Calais that one sees him at his best, fulfilling his earliest principles of life, the principle of finding interest in dullness.

They got away from Calais on 24 March, and returned not to Cadogan Square but to Claridge's, where Bennett had for some reason decided it would be more convenient to wait for Dorothy's confinement. Now that the baby was practically with them, the threat to his domestic routines was evidently enormous. He had received Dorothy in Cadogan Square before their travels, even allowing her to remove one of his curly ornate clocks because the sight of it gave her nausea (and we know how irritable he was about other people rearranging his furniture) but the reorganizations due to a baby are worse than those imposed by any woman.

What did he think about babies? He had known plenty – nieces, nephews, offspring of friends. He had taken a sympathetic interest in his butler Fred Harvey's small daughter, Winifred. He had written about them with feeling, sometimes with sentiment, sometimes with savagery. He had both mocked and admired parental passion. Clara Benbow, the young sister of Clayhanger, is shown again and again foolishly doting on her children: children are seen as greedy monsters in the marvellous comic birthday party scene in *The Old Wives' Tale*, where the young host Cyril snatches cake from his guest and crams it, weeping, into his mouth. On the other hand, the young baby Cyril, lying on a shawl while immense events take place over his head, is seen with amazing empathy, as though Bennett really remembered what it was like to lie by the fire and play with 'an india-rubber ball, an india-rubber doll, a rattle, and Fan',[8] and Clayhanger's feelings for his stepson George are done with real tenderness. Bennett was a domestic writer, and he knew what domestic life was like, no matter how far he had moved into a grander world of hotels and yachts. The yacht had had to go: one cannot, he wisely re-marked, afford both a yacht and a baby. Nor can one avoid the reality of a baby by moving into Claridge's.

He seems to have regarded the great event with his usual real or affected calm, taking an interest in all the side-issues, such as the conversations and manners of the nurses in the nursing home where Dorothy moved. It was at 27 Welbeck Street, and Dorothy went there in anticipation a day or two early. Bennett called on her, took her out to dinner the first day, and for a short walk the next, and listened to her gossip. He spent the evening of 12 April, when she was already in labour, at the nursing home, and was much struck by the sight of the already waiting bassinette and baby clothes. The next morning, 13 April 1926, his daughter Virginia was born.

She was a large, healthy baby: Bennett saw her when she was three hours old and reported that she weighed 8 lb. 1 oz. and had a large head. His secretary, Miss Nerney, declared more enthusiastically that the other babies in the home were monkeys compared to her. Dorothy was thrilled, though at first slightly disappointed, he says, that the baby was not a boy. His own response varies from the worldly ('it is getting less repulsive every day') to the profound – 'If I hadn't been [a father],' he wrote to Harriet Cohen, 'I should never have known what an ass I should have been not to have been one.'[9]

The response of their friends was on the whole warm and enthusiastic, and flowers and messages of congratulations showered upon them. The Wells's, Swinnerton and Harriet Cohen (in Switzerland for her health), had been loyal throughout. Other friends had to be informed more tactfully: some of the family did not take the news particularly well. Dorothy had by this time changed her name to Dorothy Cheston Bennett by deed poll (she had done it in September 1925, as soon as the expected baby began to seem a reality) but that was not enough to satisfy them. One of the problems was that Marguerite had, since the separation, been cultivating various people from the past, telling her version of the story: she had called on the Kennerleys in Putney, and also on Frederick Marriott. Her behaviour, not surprisingly, aroused ill-will that lingered on for years.

However, Bennett was sufficiently well protected from her gossip to be able to enjoy the experience of fatherhood. Dorothy stayed in the Welbeck Street Clinic for some time, until 9 May. Bennett had abandoned his intention of staying at Claridge's till the end of April, and had moved back home to Cadogan Square. He visited Dorothy daily, and was caught nursing the baby by Knoblock on one occasion. The rest of the time he spent on his new novel, walking around looking for ideas, dining at the club, and going to theatres and concerts, including the Sitwells' *Façade* and Komisarjevsky's production of *The Inspector General*. His complaint to Harriet Cohen (13 May 1926), that it was Dorothy's return to social life which involved him in a new course of 'hated theatre-going', looks a little thin when one sees how often he went without her while she was out of action.

Dorothy and Virginia returned to Cadogan Square in style on 9 May; they were received 'in state' by the servants. However, Dorothy did not have to face too much of the role of lady of the house, which she had always rather dreaded, for towards the end of May they all went to Amberley for a few weeks, taking a nurse with them. They stayed in a rented house, which belonged to a painter Fred Stratton, whose work Bennett describes as 'filthy'. There Bennett worked on his novel, read Dreiser and Balzac, listened to the songs of the birds and 'the infant squalling like a devil', and diverted himself with country walks and village cricket matches. It was not as idyllic as it might have been, in several ways. For one thing, the General Strike was hanging over them. It began on 4 May; Bennett had been at first content to note the high spirits which any crisis calls forth, but he had gradually got gloomier along with everyone else, and by 11 May he was calling the strike 'a political crime that must be paid for'.[10] He did not join the overdogs who were keen to beat the strike, though many of his friends were doing so; but his support of the underdog was far less marked than usual. Had the combination of fatherhood and materialism exerted its famed pressure towards the right? There are few people more instinctively set against revolution than parents of small children.

On 9 May a cabled article by him appeared in the *New York Herald Tribune*: there's a front-page photograph of him, and a large headline saying 'Labour's Strike Policy Suicidal in Opinion of Arnold Bennett', which is a tribute to the respect paid to his views on the other side of the Atlantic. His views are in fact not particularly extreme – he claims there is solidarity on both sides of the dispute, but that the Labour leaders lack common sense and 'political sagacity'. He plays down rumours of violence, and paints a rosy picture of the morale of the man in the street, just as he had diplomatically painted a rosy picture of the morale of the British soldier during the war, says that the strike has made an unpopular government 'amazingly popular', and claims that 'all non-strikers and quite half of the strikers are very strongly in sympathy with it. The mine-owners were always unpopular and they still are.'[11] Later in the article, he states what was doubtless his own feeling, diplomacy apart – 'What thoughtful people fear is not any success for the strike but that failure of the strike may lead to a very violent and ultimately anti-labour reaction.'[12] One may well wish that he'd shown a little more sympathy with and faith in the strikers, but he wasn't by any means the only left-wing sympathizer to pursue this line.

Another, more personal matter was oppressing him. Once again, Marguerite had refused a divorce. No doubt he and Dorothy had hoped that once the child was born, she would perceive the seriousness of their intentions and the hopelessness of her own case, but she would not shift her attitude. Jealousy must have caused some of her obstinacy. Dorothy had the baby that she and Arnold had denied themselves, and Dorothy was still young and good-looking. It is at this point that Marguerite's attitude can only be described as vindictive. She might once have wanted the status of being Bennett's wife rather than his ex-wife; but what status attached to being his wife when he was openly and happily living with another woman and her child? She wanted her revenge, and she was never to relent. Her stated reason for refusing to divorce him was that she felt a 'still-continuing affection' for him. He could hardly have much confidence in such professions. Nor did he like the constant pressure from well- or ill-meaning friends and relations (particularly her relations) who urged him to return to her. He had no wish whatsoever to return to her, or even to see her again. And whatever respect for her he once had must have been diminishing rapidly. For she was not only vindictive: she was also mercenary. She was well aware that the terms of settlement of their separation were more favourable to her than any judge would grant her in a divorce, and was heard to say several times that there was no point in getting divorced, she was better off as she was. Her attitude to the settlement had been grasping, and was to remain so until long after Bennett's death: she had made extravagant claims for herself, so extravagant that a lawyer had pointed out to her that if they were conceded Bennett might be left with no income at all for himself, whereupon she said: 'What if it did not? He could always rely on *me* to make *him* an allowance' (a comment of which Bennett said to Dorothy, 'This was almost the most wonderful remark she ever did make.'[13]) One could hardly expect such a woman, happy in the possession of what Bennett himself described as an absurd agreement in her favour, to turn generous, or even to act fairly in a crisis. She was too far gone for that.

However, the summer was not completely overcast. He and Dorothy went for long walks, he found that he enjoyed nursing the baby, the baby learned to enjoy making noises. They had visitors – John Cowper Powys, Aldous and Julian Huxley, a mysterious uninvited photographer who had tracked him down at his country retreat. He finished *The Strange Vanguard* on 8 July, saying that he had never worked so easily as during the preceding six weeks; it was published in the autumn of 1927 in America, and in January 1928 by Cassells in England. It is an extremely frivolous piece of work, one of the silliest of all his fantasies, about a businessman who is kidnapped in the Bay of Naples and carried off to Rome on the yacht of a Five Towns millionaire. Nothing is missing: intrigue, comedy, romance, pathos and some fine descriptions of Rome approached from the Tiber. Few of his novels have been so obviously and crudely written for serialization: there is an absurd cliff-hanger at the end of every chapter. And yet, silly though it is, it's not dull: it can still be read as it was written, for amusement. He simply couldn't help doing this kind of thing rather well. Did he look back, as he wrote it, to the sensational serials which had started his career so many years ago, when he thought he was doing well if he could earn three guineas a day from such stuff? He must have done, as it happened, for at exactly the same period he discovered to his amused surprise that the *Nouvelle Revue Française*, a very high-brow periodical, had chosen to launch his work upon the French public with a translation of his long-forgotten fantasy, *The Ghost*, a work which he had so thoroughly forgotten that he had to write off to London for a copy to see what it was like. It was satisfying to find there was life in the old books yet, but rather daunting to find that the *Nouvelle Revue Française* viewed him in such a light. Later, Gide intervened in this matter on his behalf, and persuaded the editors that Bennett might be more suitably represented by other works.

The summer passed away pleasantly and productively: he and Dorothy played duets on the piano, and called on his sister Tertia and her family who were staying in Bognor. In July they returned to Cadogan Square, dinner parties, lunches and theatres. Dorothy spent a little time sleeping at her old flat while Bennett's house was prepared and re-arranged for herself, nurse and baby: she was not too well, suffering from what he describes as muscular pains and hay fever – an illness which later developed into pleurisy. She moved into Cadogan Square 'definitely' on 22 July, with most of her furniture, and slept in her own bedroom next to Bennett's. He, meanwhile, was well, industrious and energetic. He was writing a good deal of journalism, and thanked Hornibrook's *Culture of the Abdomen* for his new-found vigour. This little book was amazingly popular – first published in 1924, it reached over forty editions, and was republished in 1956 by Penguin. Its popularity was partly due to Bennett's praise of it – he wrote a piece in the *Sunday*

311

Pictorial, which was used in advertisements in later editions, claiming that with seven minutes of Hornibrook exercises a day he had managed to lose thirty pounds of weight and get rid of his dyspepsia. One can see why the book appealed to him – it was written for sufferers from obesity and constipation, and its tone at times is positively Lutheran in its exhortations. 'One cannot live over a cesspit in good health,' says Hornibrook. 'How much more difficult to remain well if we carry our cesspit about inside us. . . .'[14] The exercises he recommends were certainly sensible enough – Hornibrook examines the superior muscle control of other nations, criticizes modern diets and modern posture, and sets out to restore the muscular balance. It was a much more useful approach than some that Bennett tried – for a man who prided himself on his common sense, he certainly had some strange attitudes to health: on two occasions during the past two years he had purchased and taken tablets which he knew to be worthless, and which on one occasion were positively dangerous – the first lot, which he took in October 1924, were simply yeast pills, and he swallowed them to the comment that an indestructible faith in quack medicine advertisements was a very interesting and perhaps a universal trait. The second lot, however, were anti-fat pills, which made his heart thump and caused such perspiration that he sent for his doctor, Griffin, in a panic. Griffin told him off, understandably, but Bennett's comment was: 'It is perfectly staggering the idiotic things even a wise man will do.'[15] His interest in health cures was in fact incurable. He tried hypnotism for his stammer, but without success. He was interested in régimes and exercises, and wrote at length on his insomnia in the *Evening Standard*. And yet he does not seem to have been very observant about Dorothy's health.

In a way, his interest in new health theories can be seen simply as part of his unbounded desire to improve himself in every way. He was interested in every accomplishment, in every form of knowledge. In 1924, to Dorothy's amusement, he had started to take dancing lessons; now, in July 1926, he started to go to art lectures at the Tate, almost by accident. He went to the Tate, as he sometimes went to Victoria Station or the Victoria and Albert or to walk in Hyde Park in search of ideas for short stories, and got gripped by lectures on Romney or nineteenth-century French painting. Dorothy, meanwhile, he says, was 'going on all right', and at the end of August they set off together for a fortnight in Venice. They enjoyed their holiday, but when Bennett left on 12 September he left Dorothy behind ill with pleurisy. He clearly expected her to be well enough to travel in a day or two (which she did), and found himself too busy to go and meet her – he was preoccupied

with the forthcoming serialization of *Lord Raingo*, a projected Berlin production of *The Great Adventure*, and with taking Pauline Smith to the first
night of Margaret Kennedy and Basil Dean's *Constant Nymph*, a show which
received triumphant applause.

In October, he and Dorothy went down to Cherkley for lunch with
Beaverbrook, and Beaverbrook asked him if he would like to do a weekly
article on books for the *Evening Standard*. Bennett didn't commit himself at
once, but on 2 November he agreed. His series, which became duly celebrated, began on 18 November 1926, and continued until his death. It was an
extremely readable and entertaining series. Bennett didn't confine himself
simply to reviewing new books, but would chat on about the state of
literature in general, about old books that he wished to be remembered,
about favourite authors and grievances. It was read eagerly and had the
reputation of being the best 'selling' book column in print. Bennett still
had the flair he had had in the old days on the *New Age*. He imparted
enthusiasm; people actually went off and bought the books he praised, and
a good review by him could sell thousands. He made the reputation of Lion
Feuchtwanger's *Jew Süss*, for instance, almost single-handed, boosted such
unknown writers as Faulkner, and continued to praise Gerhardi, Pauline
Smith and Lawrence.

The second weekend in November was spent at Easton Glebe with the
Wells's. Bennett had demonstrated his loyalty to Wells and his opposition
to *les jeunes* over the publication, that autumn, of Wells's *The World of
William Clissold*. Although Bennett had reservations about the book, he had
enjoyed it, and had at once written to tell his friend so; and he became very
annoyed with the niggling criticisms of younger writers, particularly of
D.H.Lawrence, who reviewed the novel in the *Calendar* of October 1926,
in a piece which Bennett says shows his 'childish and spiteful disposition'.[16]
The review is indeed both very harsh in its judgement and very disrespectful
in tone. Lawrence starts off arrogantly enough by saying the book is 'simply
not good enough to be called a novel', and goes on to criticize Wells for dullness, for bad character-drawing, for losing his story in 'a vast grey drizzle of
words'. He concludes that the novel is 'the effusion of a peeved elderly
gentleman', 'all chewed-up newspaper and chewed-up scientific reports,
like a mouse's nest'.[17] Bennett may well have had some sympathy with
Lawrence's criticisms, but he objected strongly to his literary manners.
(Nevertheless, like many others who objected with good reason to Lawrence's
rudeness, he could not cast Lawrence as a writer out of his mind – the following February he was writing warmly about a wonderful description of his in

the *Nation* of a thunder and hail storm – 'He can do it sometimes. In fact he can damned well do it sometimes!'[18]) Bennett and Wells, who had supported each other through their early struggles as unknown and poor young men, now supported each other against that other struggle, the fight against the rising hungry generations. Their loyalty was unbroken. Dorothy still remembers Jane's kindness, and both Jane and Wells warmly encouraged Bennett in his new ménage. Bennett was delighted to receive, on 26 October, a 'great letter' from Wells in praise of *Raingo*, Dorothy and the new régime.

It has been suggested by one of Wells's biographers, Lovat Dickson, that Bennett had a vulgar, lascivious attitude towards sex, which Wells lapsed into under his encouragement. Dickson constantly refers to Bennett as being vulgar, a man of common mould, shallow, and describes his *Journals* as being merely 'gossipy'. The idea that Wells and Bennett used to spend most of their time together talking about sex and girls, as Dickson says, is ridiculous; so is the suggestion that it was their lower-class origins that engaged them in these discussions. The notion that Wells was in any way corrupted by Bennett is also ridiculous, for if anything the reverse would have been true. Bennett, in sexual matters, was on the whole discreet, fastidious, and chivalrous towards the opposite sex. His journal is a model of tact rather than of gossip; he records much, but the note of malicious nosy society gossip which marks many memoirs is entirely lacking. It is true that he was tolerant of the indiscretions of others, and never sounds the note of moral indignation. He listened to Wells's problems over the Ann Veronica affair, he met him constantly during the war in the company of Rebecca West, and in February 1927 he visited him, with Dorothy, at his establishment with Odette Keun in Grasse. But it is hard to imagine where Dickson got the idea that his attitude was low or vulgar. On the contrary, Bennett made great efforts to demonstrate his continued affection for Jane throughout these tribulations, and Jane in her turn was devoted to him, and relied on him. Lovat Dickson's surprise that Jane should have liked Bennett so much is comic, and is based on a complete misreading of Bennett's character and attitudes. Of the two men, Wells was the irresponsible and unorthodox, Bennett the restrained and inhibited. Unorthodoxy had, as it were, been thrust upon him, whereas Wells embraced it again and again, with fervour, and with a carelessness of consequence which is at times rather unattractive. One cannot imagine Bennett seducing the daughters of his colleagues and nonchalantly producing illegitimate children. However, he valued Wells and his friendship, and he and Dorothy were glad of his support. In the new permissive world they were creating, the Wells's were old campaigners, and the Bennetts mere novices. It's a tribute to the four of them that they could get on so well together, enjoying domestic weekends at Easton Glebe, with ball games, apple pie, conversation and Schubert on the gramophone.

November was a full month. Bennett was planning his new novel, *Accident*, correcting his article on Phillpotts, planning plays for the Lyric, attending rehearsals for Michael Morton's adaptation of *Riceyman Steps* at the Ambassadors (Gwen Ffrangcon-Davies, who impressed him as an actress and as a woman, played Violet), and, above all, receiving the uproar of praise and blame that greeted the publication of *Lord Raingo*. This was a time-consuming business, for his old friend F.E. Smith (by now Lord Birkenhead) had attacked him in the *Daily Mail* on 23 November, in a long interview called 'Trifling with Reputations'. Birkenhead, in the same article, also attacked Wells, Lady Oxford, and a writer called Hesketh Pearson who was subsequently tried for trying to publish a book of fake political memoirs. Bennett rose to the attack in a piece advertised as 'Novelist's Slashing Reply', in which he declared that, contrary to Birkenhead's suggestion, Raingo was not modelled on any statesman, alive or dead. He also defends Wells and William Clissold, and asks: 'When statesmen pass half their days in being rude to each other . . . why should novelists, though their brains are obviously inferior to those of statesmen, be debarred from the same joyous pastime?'[19] On 29 November Birkenhead wrote again, with a little apology but more of an attack, this time criticizing him for the way he allowed the *Standard* and *Express* to advertise the book. The *Express* had written: 'The book is the story of the life of an ex-cabinet minister . . . the woman in the case was well known at the time in the popular dining rooms and fashionable dance clubs which she visited nearly every night.' Why didn't Bennett, an employee of the *Standard*, put an end to this kind of suggestion?

Bennett's final retort appeared on 30 November. He took strong exception, naturally, to being described as an employee, and said, rather disingenuously, that it was not his place to take any interest in the advertising of his works. His job ended with the writing of the book. (We have seen that he could well take the opposite line when it suited him.) He also counter-attacks, saying that it ill-befitted Birkenhead, himself the author of much profitable journalism, to sneer about the pecuniary motives of other authors. Birkenhead was silenced, retired gracefully, and the dispute was over – probably both enjoyed it, for they remained good friends (though Bennett was critical of some of Birkenhead's reactionary views) and met at dinner at the Savoy on 2 December. It was an amicable dinner, with much chat and

315

speculation about *Raingo* throughout the evening. Later, Beaverbrook divulged that Birkenhead had once asked him whether or not Raingo was modelled on himself, Birkenhead. Many consciences must have been made uneasy by the gossip that *Raingo* aroused, and Birkenhead's reaction may well have been one of premature self-defence. Bennett was astonished to find how many statesmen had mistresses and had assumed for that reason alone that Raingo was a portrait of themselves. The one man who seems to have kept well out of all the fuss was Beaverbrook himself, who was, of course, responsible for most of Bennett's inside information.

Christmas 1926 was organized by Dorothy. It was her first Christmas in charge of a household, and one does not envy her the task of suiting Bennett's exacting standards. She seems, however, to have been more pliable and conciliatory than Marguerite, and to have been able to avoid rows with servants. And there were plenty of servants: she never had to devote all her attention to the baby, and was free to go where she pleased. They set off in the new year for a holiday in Austria and Italy, where they spent most of their time in the Hôtel Savoy at Cortina, where they were deprived of their sitting-room by the Duke of Genoa, but were otherwise comfortable. Aldous Huxley and his wife Maria had rented a house nearby, and they picnicked, dined, talked or skied together nearly every day – Bennett was the only one who didn't ski.

The Huxleys enjoyed themselves as much as the Bennetts – Aldous, writing to his father on 31 December 1926, says he is looking forward to the arrival of 'no less a personage than the great Arnold Bennett, who is always very good company'. In February he writes again, saying 'the chief amusement of the last weeks has consisted of Arnold Bennett, whom we have seen every day and who has been in excellent form'.[20] It was in some ways an unlikely friendship – at the same period, the Huxleys were also maintaining a relationship in the same district with Frieda and D.H.Lawrence, which seems a more likely conjunction. Huxley made fun of both of them – there are echoes of Bennett in his novels, as well as his well-known portrait of Lawrence in *Point Counter Point* – but he didn't offend either. However, he kept them apart in Cortina. One can't imagine what an evening with the six of them would have been like. Lawrence, encouraged by Maria Huxley, was at this time painting the nude canvases that were to cause him trouble with the police, so different from Bennett's polite watercolours.

Bennett was thoroughly enjoying his new life. The responsibilities of fatherhood hadn't proved too onerous. He was not working too hard, though of course he couldn't stop altogether – he corrected the proofs of *The Strange*

Vanguard, continued with his *Standard* articles, and was amused by the irritation caused by his provocative pieces on the dearth of young imaginative writers, which he had written with the express purpose of stirring things up a little. His first piece on the theme, which appeared in the 'Books and Persons' column for 25 November 1926, was called 'Plain Words to Our Younger Novelists': in it, Bennett attacks a successful new novel by a writer called Mary Borden, which contained 'thousands of acres of speechifying', complains of the lack of grammar and errors of taste even in talented writers like Edward Sackville-West, who could write such a sentence as ' "He *literally* pulled his eyes away and fixed them upon the piece of cake in his hand." My italics' and concludes: 'I am very interested in young writers and rather gloomy about them.' He conceded that the war had killed 50 per cent of aspiring writers, but the others 'promise too little'. Their elders, such as E.M.Forster and D.H.Lawrence, can knock 'the stuffing out of the boys and girls',[21] he says. He followed this attack the next week with another piece in which he again criticizes Virginia Woolf for her defects of character-drawing, construction, and her serious lack of vitality. Perhaps he does show a slight sense of pique here, for he says 'she alone . . . came forward and attacked the old', while at the same time he claims not to have read her *Mr Bennett and Mrs Brown*. He also says that Margaret Kennedy's *Constant Nymph*, which he admired, sagged in the middle, which was the kind of remark that Wyndham Lewis was to pick up in *The Roaring Queen*: Shodbutt says to his wife, 'The middle of anything is *always* a bore. . . . The middle cannot be anything but a bore. . . . It all lies in *the last page*. . . . I *never* read more than the last page. Balzac said he knew what a book was like without even opening it. I can't say that. That's more than I can claim – I take my hat off to Balzac. He was a *genius*! No. I have to open them. But I never need go farther than the last page.'[22]

The only writer whom Bennett doesn't attack is Pauline Smith: she continues to receive his unqualified approval. But it's interesting to note that, despite all his fame as a selling reviewer, she never became popular, and never attained more than a prestige success, which she owed largely to him. So much for the view that he sold books like butter. He was always careful not to attack the frail; he never praised books that he did not believe to be good. His provocation of the young was not ill-natured, but generous: he wanted to cause a stir, and why not?

On 9 February he read in the paper news that turned his mind from the future to the past. His old friend George Sturt was dead. He notes the fact with a more than superficial calm; Sturt had been ill for many years, Bennett had not seen him for about sixteen years and their last meeting had been strained. Sturt had become increasingly and deliberately provincial, Bennett increasingly cosmopolitan. Bennett thought his work had declined in quality. He remembers that it was through his example that Sturt had started to keep a journal, says that his death produced 'no effect of sadness', and does not mention him again. Unlike his friendships with Rickards, Wells, or even Marriott, this one had not stood the test of time and the trial of one party's greatly superior worldly success. When, later that year, he started to reread his correspondence with Sturt, with a view to writing an introduction to a posthumous collection (an act of characteristic generosity), he found that they made him 'feel sad, somehow; because I saw in them a reflection in commentary of the history of my literary life – over thirty years'.[23]

Over thirty years. It had been a long stretch, and Bennett had achieved more, surely, than he could ever have hoped for. Dictator of taste, friend of the famous, with a row of solid books behind him, and a delightful baby before him. No wonder he felt slightly sad about Sturt, who had acquired none of these things. He would have appreciated the quirk of literary history which led Leavis, another dictator of taste, to write Bennett off in a sentence or two, and which was to re-instate Sturt, albeit with a highly minority audience, as a serious writer.

Bennett and Dorothy returned to London in March, via Wells in Grasse and Maurice Baring in Paris. They found Virginia 'quite grown up' – she was nearly one year old, could say dada 'like hell', had six teeth, was very well and active, and in her father's eyes as beautiful as ever, though he comments in his journal, somewhat comically, that Dorothy thought she was growing plainer. Dorothy herself was not too well: she had to have an operation for haemorrhoids towards the end of the month. Bennett, meanwhile, threw himself enthusiastically back to work, partly with the intention of liberating his conscience for a proposed forthcoming all-male trip to the Aegean, in the Duke of Westminster's yacht, the *Flying Cloud*, which his friend Otto Kahn had hired. So Bennett, returned from a domestic holiday, contemplating a bachelor one, supporting two wives, a baby and two nurses, quite apart from his regular domestic staff, had to put in some work. He wrote his articles for the *Standard*, and returned to his new novel – not a very serious one, but not a fantasy either. He himself described it, a little defensively, as old-fashioned, which it certainly is. It is not Bennett at his best, though it is readable enough.

It is called *Accident*, and is distantly based on Bennett's memory of an accident in which he was involved in France years earlier in 1911: the plot, such as it is, deals with Alan Frith-Walter, cultured businessman, who at the beginning of the novel is setting off on a *train de luxe* for Italy, where he is to join his wife for the New Year. He is alone, relaxed, pleased with himself, and reading his Wordsworth. But gradually things begin to go wrong – he meets his runaway daughter-in-law, discovers his son has turned socialist, and the train crashes. The story line is ridiculous, showing Bennett yet again at the impossible task of reconciling luxury and conscience, but nevertheless the novel has a considerable charm. Nearly all of it is set on the train itself, and the journey is charted in great and loving detail: every little stop, every nuance of comfort or discomfort in the *wagon-lits*, the meals, the service, is described with a lively traveller's addiction. Bennett the solitary voyager really lets himself go, and there is nothing tedious about his obsession to any reader who has ever shared his passion. The sense of gathering menace, the ridiculous arguments between passengers about whether accidents on French railways really do go in twos and threes, the superstitions and hysteria, the haphazard inconsequence of the accident itself, the contrast between the luxury train and the hard wooden-seated third-class Swiss train in which they have to finish the journey – all these things are noted with his usual imaginative accuracy. And there is also a very fine pair of characters. Frith-Walter himself is a rather nebulous, typical Bennett middle-aged successful hero, and his children and wife are mere ciphers. The best characterization is reserved for a subsidiary pair of travellers, the Lucasses, an elderly married couple whose constant strife is evident to the whole train. She is an ageing provincial beauty, a hag, with 'thin dyed hair at the top of her forehead, and wild eyes set too closely together'; she knits frantically, and she and her husband live 'in a state of acute emotion'. Lucass later explains to Frith-Walter that her nerves have gone to pieces because of many operations and extreme ill-health. He loves her, can see no wrong in her, although he is aware that she is an embarrassing spectacle to all beholders. Frith-Walter, talking to her alone over tea in the train, is amazed by the charm that is after all left in her: she was provincial, wore no powder, despised the 'minor weapons of warfare', and yet was intensely alive in her neurosis, still profoundly sexual in her manner. Frith-Walter, who had been reflecting for most of the journey on his good luck in having a placid unhysterical wife, is unsettled by her attractions; and in Bennett's prose we find echoes of the feeling of *The Old Wives' Tale*. 'What a woman!' Frith-Walter reflects. 'What a woman now, and what a woman she must have been a quarter of a century earlier! Youth and beauty and bodily strength had been stripped from her. Her empire had been narrowed down to one old man. But she was not defeated. . . .'[24] Her intense, punishing relationship with her husband is beautifully done: the novel is worth reading for that alone.

Accident had been started in November 1926, before the Swiss holiday: he finished the first draft in April 1927. Despite Dorothy's operation, and constant social engagements with the Colefaxes, the Beaverbrooks, the Wells's, the Shaws, the Maughams, Bennett found it a good spring for working, though most of the work was journalistic. He grappled with relativity for the *Standard* '(Einstein for the Tired)', wrote on 'Summer Time' and 'Modern Youth' for the *Sunday Pictorial*, wrote a few short stories, and was able to write to his Irish friend, Thomas Bodkin, on 9 April that he had already that year written 115,000 words. From his journal he sounds during this period both vigorous and happy: there are few complaints about his health, a great deal of pride in his productivity, and evidence of great pleasure and relaxation in his new domestic life. At this time, he seems confident of rising to the challenge of his household, and even of enjoying the new claims on his energy. He bought a new Rolls in March, which excited both of them. His interest in the outside world manifests itself not only in club life and society life, but in bus rides, visits to art galleries, and plans for new big novels – principally for the novel that had haunted him for years, his big hotel novel, which was to appear, finally, as *Imperial Palace*.

On 5 April he set off from Victoria Station to Rome, having arranged to meet Otto Kahn and his party some days later in Sicily. He travelled alone, by train, noting the Fascist Englishwoman (a card-carrying one) who unsuccessfully tried to engage him in conversation at lunch on the train, the alcoholic waiter, the beautiful sunset and other such things, and reading *The Brothers Karamazov* for the fourth time. In Rome he slept well, did some churches, took some notes, wrote some letters, had lunch in a *trattoria*, and caught the six o'clock train to Naples. As ever, when reading his travel notes, travel journals, or memoirs (this trip was to reappear later as *Mediterranean Scenes*) one cannot help but comment on his happiness. It is a happiness that rouses no envy, for it is solid, unecstatic, almost attainable: the fine balance of interests, internal, external, sensual, intellectual, the self-reliant, self-contained, yet in no way introverted good faith of the hopeful voyager, represent at least a possible image of unselfish yet independent well-being. It is a kind of ideal, and rarely achieved, I suppose, but it looks democratic rather than exclusive. Though what could be more exclusive than the Duke of Westminster's yacht? Perhaps one finds Bennett so cheering and reassuring simply because he existed, because he got there, because he enjoyed it. Out of all those millions in the Potteries, one of them managed to take a train to Taormina, sail the Aegean, and enjoy every minute of it. What would he have said of the package tour, the £25 weekend in Sicily from Gatwick, the coach trips? He would surely have approved. One cannot imagine his deploring the quality of tourist one meets abroad these days. He liked his luxury, but he didn't mind sharing it.

He met up with his yacht party on the evening of 19 April, in Taormina: there were three old friends in the group whom he hadn't seen for fifteen years, and he didn't recognize any of them – Jo Davidson the sculptor, Dougherty the painter and Frank Brownishields. There were other members of the party who were new to him – all male. None of them had yet been on the yacht – they found her in the port at Syracuse on the morning of the twenty-first. Bennett thought she was magnificent, thrilling, highly satis-factory, beautiful (in that order). And so was the whole voyage. They 'did' the Aegean: Milo, Crete, Athens, Piraeus, the Dardanelles, Constantinople, Corfu, and back to Venice. It was all up to expectation: it exceeded expecta-tion. His appreciation was enormous. The only pleasure which he failed to appreciate was the games of cards which went on nightly: Ralph Kommer (the Austrian director) almost convinced him of the beauties of the game of bridge, and insisted he would be a good learner, having no vanity, but Bennett did not learn.

In Vienna, he was joined by Dorothy on 25 May. She had travelled out with Iris Tree and Diana Cooper, who were bound for Budapest. They spent a week in Vienna, and then returned to home and work – work for both of them, for Dorothy was eager to resume her career. But after a long period of resting – Dorothy hadn't worked since her role in *The Great Adventure*, two years earlier, before Virginia's birth – it isn't easy to walk back into the theatre, and find directors waiting with offers of parts, for directors have extremely short memories. There seems to have been some scheme afoot for putting on *Don Juan* at last, for Dorothy and the actor-manager Maurice Browne spent much time during June rehearsing the play in Bennett's drawing-room, but the scheme came to nothing. There was talk of Ivor Novello appearing in the title role, but he was reluctant to tour the provinces. Dorothy also kept in touch with other theatrical friends – Noël Coward came to tea and offered advice, Mrs Pat Campbell came to lunch in July, was 'magnificent with the baby',[25] and backed up Arnold's advice that she should certainly not return to the stage in small parts. So what was she to do? Wait for a big opportunity to present itself? She had been long enough in the theatre and was realistic enough to know that in such a situation one might well wait for ever.

However, while waiting, life was not exactly empty or dull. There were dinners, first nights, trips to Knole, quiet evenings playing duets on the piano, plans for a summer holiday, the baby, and the success of Bennett's latest book, *The Woman Who Stole Everything*, which appeared in June. (Bennett had seen a placard announcing its publication in Cassell's *Storyteller* magazine on Victoria Station just before his departure for Sicily in April.) The stories are a mixed collection, most of them set in the world of yachts, foreign travel and first nights, though there is one Five Towns story using the old characters, and one fantasy re-using the fantasy Five Towns millionaire, Lord Furber, from *The Strange Vanguard*. The title story is the most ambitious, and the longest: it's another attempt to capture the modern young woman, who, as usual, is juxtaposed with a middle-aged contrast, in this case a bachelor uncle. But all the stories are readable, though slight – there's an interesting one set in Venice, in which two old boys of Oundle (where Richard and the Wells boys went) meet, deplore the death of Sanderson, the headmaster (who was the real headmaster), and discuss why one of them is down-and-out. The down-and-out old boy is called Byatt, which, one recalls, was the name of the ex-headmaster of both Wells and Bennett. His technique with names is really extremely strange. One could interpret this whole story as a comment on Bennett's feelings about the contrast between his own schooling and his nephew's, if one had the energy to follow up and analyse the clues.

The collection was well received: the reviewers liked it, his friends liked it, and it sold extremely well. Meanwhile, Bennett was working hard on a re-write of *Accident*, using much of the refreshed memory of train travel that he had just acquired. He was also putting together a collection of essays, later printed as *The Savour of Life*, and Miss Nerney was typing out his *Florentine Journal* with a view to its publication (Miss Nerney said that she '*loved* copying it')[26] – it is noticeable that Bennett often comments on her judgements on his work, and is increasingly cheered by her enthusiasm or cast down by her coolness, which is a tribute to their continuing good working relationship. The *Standard* articles were pouring out, and in July he took on a new assignment, which was to begin in November, of articles for *The World Today*, in which he resolved to take 'politics more seriously'. (He was to use his friend Thomas Bodkin, the art historian from Dublin, as his source of information about Irish affairs; he brooded over the Irish article which appeared in April 1928 for nearly a year beforehand.) For a man who is sometimes accused of having gone soft intellectually, he was extraordinarily active and indeed expansionist in his interests.

And yet his modesty remains: there is a characteristic letter to Eliot, dated 3 June, in which he discusses the new *Criterion*, now become a monthly, promises to boost it in the *Standard* when he can, and then says 'I should like to send you a contribution, but I am really afraid of doing so. I should have to take so much care over it! My articles, especially those about books, are rather slapdash. I am also handicapped by an intense ignorance. Indeed my life-long regret is that I have no exact knowledge of any subject on earth. I always envy scholars.'[27] Here again we see the older writer threatened by the younger, as well as the self-educated provincial threatened by the scholar. Bennett could be cocky enough when he pleased, but he recognized that there was a kind of excellence represented by the *Criterion* which he could hardly claim as his own. On the other hand, the *Criterion* in turn had the sense to recognize the quality of Bennett's *Journals*, and published extracts from them in 1927 and 1928: respect, one hopes, was mutual.

In the summer, the Bennetts went off to the seaside, to St Leonards on Sea. Bennett spent his time walking on the beach, visiting friends in the neighbourhood, and contemplating the past through re-reading his long correspondence with Sturt. He was thinking of editing and publishing the letters, but the experience of reading through them again depressed him, partly because they recorded thirty years of work. He had good enough cause to feel complacent about the results of those thirty years of labour, and might have seemed so at times to the outside world, but, as those who knew him well noted, complacency was never his forte. He set himself high standards to the end. Did he wonder, re-reading his early views on Flaubert and Zola, whether he had lived up to his own expectations of himself? Did he doubt his final place in English literature? He was near the end of the course, and it may well be that this renewed contact with his earliest ambitions convinced him that he must make a final assault on grand-scale fame.

They returned from the country on 4 September, to a scene of intense activity: on the fifth Dorothy and Arnold dined with Beaverbrook at his office, and five days later Bennett left on an excursion to Berlin with Beaverbrook, Castlerosse, Diana Cooper and Venetia Montagu. Before he went he found time to correct the proofs of *The Strange Vanguard*, and to organize the Court Theatre's production of *Mr Prohack*. This production was an important one. It was directed by Komisarjevsky, and managed by Sidney Bernstein, then described by Bennett as 'all right, *sympathique*, young, some artistic perceptions and some artistic blindnesses'.[28] It also marked Dorothy's return to the stage; she received good notices in the role of Lady Massulam. And it launched the successful career of Charles

Laughton, then aged twenty-eight, who was passed by Bennett as a 'possible Prohack' in a lightning five-minute interview on 8 September. (Laughton married their friend Elsa Lanchester, the red-haired night-club beauty.) The play was put on by Sloane Productions Ltd, of which Bennett was a shareholder, and which also produced a play by Merezhkowski, again with Dorothy and Charles Laughton. *Paul I* opened on 1 October, *Prohack* opened on 16 November, and in the middle of October Bennett was still re-writing. They were both desperately busy. Dorothy was rehearsing *Paul I* while Bennett was away in Berlin, eating German sausages, betting on the tonnage of ships, sleeping in a double state room, visiting theatres and galleries, and comparing Venetia and Diana in letters home (both witty, but Diana kinder with it). The trio had no purpose other than pleasure, and Bennett seems to have found Max's pace exhausting. 'Max a handful,' he writes at one point to Dorothy.

He was away less than a fortnight, and returned to the trials of the theatre, and the sorrow of the death of Jane Wells. She had been ill since April, and constantly visited by the Bennetts, both of whom were much attached to her; Bennett had even tried, uselessly, to find medical help. They had visited her on their way to Winchelsea in the early summer and found her unable to do more than walk a few steps. Their last visit was on 25 September, when she was too ill to come downstairs at all. She died on 6 October 1927, of cancer, and Bennett attended her funeral on 10 October, remarking on the great number of people there, how few of them were in mourning (she had expressly requested that they should not be) and how few of them were official A1 people from 'the great world'.[29]

Most of October was taken up with rehearsals and re-writes of *Mr Prohack*, with a quick excursion up to Manchester to see the first and only production of his 1925 play, *Flora*, in a theatre at Rusholme which had once been the stables of the Tramway Company in its horse-drawn days. *Flora*, despite lengthy negotiations at the end of the year with Mrs Patrick Campbell, was never given a London production. The prospects of *Mr Prohack*, on the other hand, looked favourable. *Paul I*, although an exceedingly gloomy play, was doing well, rehearsals were going well, and Charles Laughton was a potential star. Bennett, who had decided not to attend his own first night, spent the evening of 16 November quietly entertaining friends at the Yacht Club and trying to forget the Court. When he made his way over there, later in the evening, the curtain had just fallen, and everyone seemed very pleased, particularly Laughton, who had scored a personal triumph. Bennett, Dorothy, and the Board of Sloane Productions Ltd read all the notices the next day and found them satisfactory. *Paul I* was a prestige success, *Mr Prohack* a popular success, and it played to good houses with sound returns, insofar as the size of the theatre permitted. The advance bookings were not good in November, but by December had improved greatly. The only problem was that the lease of the Court expired at the end of December, and a new theatre would have to be found. Bennett, who could see that the play would do well, had every confidence that there would be no problem in finding one – nor would there have been, but unfortunately at the forced end of the run Laughton went off on holiday, saying (through his agent) that he could not wait for more than four weeks for a transfer, as he had been offered another leading role in Ben Levy's adaptation of Hugh Walpole's novel, *A Man with Red Hair*. The four weeks expired the day before Dennis Eadie, who wanted the play, was able to offer his own theatre, the Royalty, and thus Laughton, who was still away on holiday, was lost. Without Laughton, the play could not transfer. If Laughton had been there to make the decision himself, he might have made it differently, but either way he did no damage to his own career. The Walpole play only ran for a couple of months, but his subsequent triumphs on stage and screen need no recalling. It was Bennett and Dorothy who lost: Dorothy the opportunity of being in a solid West End run, and Bennett the income from such a run.

The *Prohack* transfer problems didn't depress Bennett unduly: he seems to have been more upset by the death of Gladys Beaverbrook, which he emotionally described in his journal (1 December) as a 'damned shame', and by the complications ensuing from the death, in November, of Charles Masterman. Before his death, Masterman had turned extremely odd, and left his wife and three children very badly off. His relationship with Bennett was of long standing, and Bennett had been increasingly worried by the spectacle of his decay, so it is not surprising that he took it upon himself to organize a trust fund for the education of his children, and wrote round to his friends raising money and finding trustees, as well as contributing generously himself. On 2 January, when he took Masterman's widow Lucy out to dinner in a new restaurant in Jermyn Street, she told him: 'Charles always said: "If you're really in a hole, go to A.B. He's the one." '[30] And so he was.

Another death, more expected and less tragic, was that of Hardy, who died on 11 January. Bennett gave expression to his admiration and sense of loss by writing an article for the *Standard* recalling his last meeting with him in London, when 'Hardy was nearly eighty, a spare man, very young and active and cheerful indeed for his age, who chatted and chattered away quite cheerfully. . . . I remember thinking, "This man is all right." No nonsense about him. No secret but apparent preoccupation with the fact that he was the biggest living thing in English literature.'[31] He also kicked up a row about the way tickets had been distributed for the funeral in the Abbey. He, naturally, was invited. Galsworthy was a pall-bearer. It was an impressive occasion, but Bennett wrote with fury to the *Express* asking why so few writers had been asked, and why no members of the Royal Family attended. It was not only Hardy himself who concerned him. Hardy, after all, was dead. It was the status of the profession. He was a good campaigner on behalf of others, as well as on his own behalf. Activity was his way of expressing himself. His activities often annoyed other people a good deal – he writes to his nephew Richard about the Abbey affair, saying that he received an anonymous letter saying 'Arnold Bennett, tripe! Thomas Hardy, gentleman!'[32] Such matters amused him. But it wasn't so amusing to reach an age where friends and wives of friends would die off more and more frequently around him.

The final crunch over *Prohack* came on 1 February 1928. It disturbed Dorothy more than it disturbed Bennett, for she had in a way more at stake. His last financial year had been the best for 'many years', and his prospects were good. She, however, was determined to make a go of her own career, and was prepared to try to raise capital to keep *Mr Prohack* on: but it was not capital that was needed, but Laughton and a theatre, and Laughton was lost. When they heard on 1 February that the Royalty would have been available, Bennett conceded that it was 'great tragic news' and 'really bad luck', but continued to be slightly nervous about Dorothy's ambitions. He seemed relieved to hear Shaw advising her three days later that if she was determined to go in for theatrical management and acting, then a 'divorce' would be 'the first preliminary!'[33] In this attitude, he was not being wholly honest: he had promised her at the outset of their relationship that she should be free to pursue her career. She was talented, he believed in her talent. Perhaps he was simply nervous of the domestic upheavals that the theatre creates – the odd hours, the endless crises, the wasted emotions, the emotional and financial speculation. If this was so, he was being unfair: he had known Dorothy to be an independent and career-minded woman before he started living with her. It might have been possible for Dorothy to stay away from the theatre if she had been able to live away from London – but it would have been impossibly difficult to be so nearly connected, and yet unable to take part. His attitude to her work was, at best, ambivalent: like most husbands, perhaps, he both wanted and did not want her to succeed in her own right.

It may have been in some recognition of this difficulty that Dorothy went off on her own, at the end of February, to the South of France, for a month to herself: whither Bennett wrote her the most charming letters, full of details about Virginia's accomplishments, adorned with smudges from her fingers, reassuring Dorothy about his love for her and his happiness with her. She expected a great deal from life, he said, and although he makes it clear that this was not to him a fault, it was clearly a problem.

He, meanwhile, was planning a new play, a new film, and a new novel. The new play, which he began on 17 February, was *The Return Journey*: it opened on 1 September at the St James's. The film, *Piccadilly*, was written in May, filmed in the summer, and first shown in January 1929. The novel, his last and longest, wasn't begun till September 1929, but it had already become sufficiently real to him as his next novel for him to reject other suggestions. He knew it would be his next serious work. *The Return Journey*, which he finished in June, was serious in its way: it was based on the Faust theme, and dealt with the adventures of a Cambridge don, Dr Henry Fausting, who is discovered at the beginning of the first act about to commit suicide through boredom. He is dissuaded from this course of action by a Professor Satollyon from Warsaw and a young undergraduate called Margaret. The play includes Bennett's usual hymns to luxury and fine living.

At the end of June, before the production of *The Return Journey*, Bennett, Dorothy and Virginia went off to France, to Le Touquet, for a family holiday, with the Swinnertons established in a nearby hotel, but before a week was out Bennett was recalled to London by du Maurier to do some re-writing. He agreed to alter the second act, went back to Le Touquet, and did it. He revisited London on 19 July, to attend a rehearsal, discuss costumes, etc.

The rest of the summer was spent in walks, picnics, articles, buying hats for and going to the races with Dorothy, and reading. Dorothy herself was not idle: she had been working on a translation of a successful French play by Bourdet, *Vient de Paraître*. *Accident* began to appear as a serial in the *Express* on 16 July, under the title *Train de Luxe*: it didn't appear in volume form until the following January. On 14 August they returned to London, and to the play, which still lacked a title: by 21 August, by rummaging through the Bible and Shakespeare concordance, he had found eleven, of which *The Return Journey* was finally chosen. As usual, he found the period of rehearsals rather trying, dealing, as he told Pinero at the Garrick Club, with 'a lot of hypersensitive and sometimes conceited persons'. Nor had he much faith in the play's success with a popular audience. Luckily he had plenty to divert him – *Lady Chatterley's Lover*, for instance, which obliged him to concede that Lawrence was the most original novelist writing, except Joyce. There was also an entertaining scandal over the publication of Radclyffe Hall's lesbian novel, *The Well of Loneliness*, which was much talked over in the clubs and discussed in the papers. E. M. Forster got up a campaign to defend the book when it was prosecuted by the police, and Bennett as ever spoke out against censorship, describing the book in the *Standard* as 'courageous', but he managed to offend its author nevertheless by quite properly maintaining that although she had every right to publish it, it was nevertheless badly written.

The first night of *The Return Journey*, the last of his plays to be performed, was on 1 September. He didn't attend it, but turned up afterwards for the champagne and the post mortem. The notices were poor: *The Times* thought it was 'disappointing', 'painful', 'a mockery'; the *Mail* called it clever but dull; the *Standard* praised du Maurier's 'immaculate ease and charm' but thought the play wasn't very profound and didn't fulfil its promise. All the reviews agreed that the idea was good, but that it wasn't carried off, and that the play didn't live up to its prologue. Du Maurier clearly felt there was still hope, however, and was still asking for re-writes in the middle of October, but Bennett had had enough, and said du Maurier could re-write it himself if he wanted to. The play ran for nearly three months, until 24 November – a respectable run, in view of the notices. After the first night, Dorothy and Bennett departed again for another holiday, this time to Annecy, where they were unexpectedly joined by Diana and Duff Cooper, who were also staying there. Bennett liked the hotel and the Coopers, and enjoyed meeting their party (Lady Diana recalls introducing Bennett to Lady Horner in Lake Annecy, as both were treading water in their swimsuits – both in their sixties). But the scenery, Bennett thought, was second-rate, and said that Noël Coward, who had described one particular spot with special enthusiasm to Dorothy, must have been 'in love, some hot August'[34] when he saw it.

They returned to England in the middle of September, to the usual round of theatres and invitations, and to an unusual social event in the form of a tennis match with Wells in Cadogan Square on 3 October, to celebrate Wells's sixty-second birthday. They were ageing but fit, Bennett and Wells, and not wholly displeased when a press photographer who had heard of the sporting and literary event wanted to turn up to record it. Bennett notes that he is still only sixty-one. (The press man turned up anyway to watch, but took no pictures. One would have liked to have seen some.) Bennett, at this period, was employed with a film called *Punch and Judy* and a book about

God, and Dorothy, still hopeful about her Bourdet adaptation, was offered a part in a new play.

The play, by Alisia Ramsay, was about Byron, and it was suggested that Dorothy should play Lady Byron. Esmé Percy, who also directed the play, took the role of Byron. It opened on 22 January 1929, at the Lyric, after a week in Portsmouth. Bennett was from the beginning far from happy with the production, the play, and some of the actors, and wrote a long letter to Esmé Percy to tell him so. The reviewers agreed with Bennett: they praised Percy, allowed Dorothy and some of the others their good moments, but agreed that the play was poor – the *Telegraph* described it as 'stagey and crude to the last degree', full of 'windy suspirations of forced breath'. Clearly it wasn't going to run: in fact it came off on 22 February.

Dorothy and *Byron* weren't Bennett's only theatrical worries. He also had on his mind the forthcoming production (25 June 1929, Covent Garden) of Eugene Goossens's one-act opera, *Judith*, for which he had written the libretto; the first showing of his film *Piccadilly*, on 30 January; and his new film script, *Punch and Judy*, which had proved heavy-going, especially towards the end. In January he met Hitchcock, who was to direct the film, and they discussed it. Bennett clearly thought he had the better of the argument, but equally clearly Hitchcock was not satisfied with Bennett's version, and by the middle of March there was complete disagreement. One of the points at stake was whether the film should be a talkie or a silent film: Bennett had been contracted for a silent film, and talk of turning it into a talkie annoyed him greatly. He considered himself contracted to supply a story and not dialogue. Hitchcock did not apparently impress him. He was still an unknown director, several years away from fame, and Bennett saw no reason to listen to him. The discussions of contract obligations were to drag on into July, but in March the Bennetts wisely decided to cut their losses and anxieties and get out. They went off, on 26 March, to Antibes, for a holiday. (It was already their second trip abroad in 1929: they had snatched a quick weekend in Paris early in February, after the collapse of *Byron*.) The weather was not good to begin with, the sands at Juan les Pins were dirty, and their car crushed the petrol tank of a German car in front of them, but apart from these minor disasters and disappointments they had a good time. Bennett's religious booklet had just appeared in print, and he enjoyed refuting its critics. Unfortunately, during this period, his journal becomes more formal, more written for publication: as indeed it was. *Life and Letters* had published extracts in January and February 1929, the *Criterion* had published extracts from the *Florentine Journal* in January and

329

February 1928, and the *Daily Telegraph* and *Harper's* were both after more. The journal which he kept during 1929, and which Cassells published in 1930, as a whole volume,[35] is both more discreet and more self-conscious than his earlier notes. There was, evidently, much that did not appear in print, but the very fact of writing for an audience seems to have altered the tone of his thinking to himself.

They returned to Cadogan Square towards the end of April, to more rows about the *Punch and Judy* film with British International. He never seems to have been happy with the film as a medium, or with film people: an article of his in the early film magazine, *Close Up*,[36] betrays a very entrenched novelist's view of the art, and he confessed himself mystified by the success of such famous pieces as Sam Goldwyn's *Bulldog Drummond*. Film as an art form and film as a popular medium defeated him. He was also working to no avail on a new play, thereby breaking a promise he had made to himself to meddle with the theatre no more. He also broke another self-imposed vow, not to attend any more of his own first nights, by going to Covent Garden on 25 June to see Goossens's opera, *Judith*, with his own libretto; he was able to console himself by reflecting that Goossens was far more exposed conducting his orchestra than he was hiding in his box. The reception, in fact, was polite: Goossens was well established as a conductor and the critics were keen to encourage any new British composer, but they had to agree that, despite Bennett's efforts with the story and the Russian ballet's efforts in the chorus, the music was a little monotonous.

At the end of June, he and Dorothy took off again, to France and Italy, for six weeks. They went to Lake Garda, making many excursions to the surrounding beauty spots, and then driving to the Riviera, via Turin. It was presumably on this holiday that they visited Somerset Maugham, who was living in style near Cannes, and took part in a long and magnificent picnic on an outlying island, the Isle Sainte Marguerite, which they had reached by motor launch. Bennett tells the story in his journal, and recounts how the weather got worse as the day went on, and how the guests began to wonder whether it would be safe to sail home again, or whether it would be wiser to stay on the island for the night. He himself was all for sticking to the scheduled departure hour, but others of the sixteen guests were too nervous to leave, and some were so deep in a game of bridge and a game of baccarat that they did not want to leave. The captain of the motor launch seemed one of the nervous party, unwilling to trust the weather, but finally the storm dropped sufficiently for them to leave, and they arrived back in Cannes in the small hours of the morning, and went to a nightclub where they were able to cheer themselves up by eating and listening to a deafening saxophone. Bennett, throughout, had been of the party that had believed in sticking to schedule, whatever the advice of the captain or conditions of the weather. Mrs Cheston Bennett, recalling this episode very vividly, says that he didn't like to think that anybody knew more about boats than he did, and that possibly he was slightly put out by the spectacle of his old friend (and junior's) worldly success. It's an interesting case of a moment at which his methodical, rigidly planning nature did, in particular circumstances, become positively foolhardy. Had the motor launch and the guests been his, however, one guesses that he might have behaved differently. And his own account of the episode certainly does not lack self-awareness.

There is, amusingly enough, yet a third account of this incident from the host, Somerset Maugham himself, who describes the party: 'The women wore pyjamas and the men tennis shirts, ducks and espadrilles but Arnold, refusing to permit himself such *sans gêne*, was dressed in a check suit with a sort of mustard colour, fancy shoes, fancy socks, a striped shirt, a starched collar and a foulard tie.' During the panic about the mistral, according to Maugham, Bennett 'remained dignified, self-possessed, good-tempered and interested. When at six in the morning, bedraggled and unshaven, we at last got home, he looked as dapper and as well-groomed as he had looked eighteen hours before.'[37]

After the Riviera, the Bennetts drove up through France, revisiting Blois and Fontainebleau, which drew from him some caustic comments on the guided tour; and to show a distinct failing of enthusiasm for the Empire style, which penury had obliged him to admire so many years earlier. The end of July they spent in a hotel in Brittany, the Celtic Hotel at St Cast. Bennett left Dorothy and Virginia there, and went back to England alone in August, for he was planning another trip with Beaverbrook, this time to new territory – to Russia. His appetite for travel was insatiable: he had been on the move more or less continually for over a month, averaging during one part of the trip one hundred and seventy miles a day. He spent a few days in London, preparing for his new excursion, worrying about the expense of doing up his house in Cadogan Square, lunching with George Doran (who was having considerable problems, after the amalgamation of his firm with Doubledays, and under the shadow of the approaching depression), and attending a Memorial Service for the actor Leslie Fabian. All of which left him, understandably, a little gloomy.

The party set off on the R.M.S.P. *Arcadian* on 10 August. According to Beaverbrook's usual practice, there were no married couples in the party, though there were women – Lady Louis Mountbatten, Venetia Montagu again, and Jean Norton. A new note seems to be creeping into Bennett's observations at this point – that of financial anxiety. The extreme wealth of some of the party worried him slightly: he writes to Dorothy that he feels 'more than ever like a pauper'.[38] Anxiety about the renewal of the lease of the house, and his talks with Doran, were hanging over him. The voyage was spent with the usual games of cards – some of the players played for fairly large sums, but Bennett was no gambler. He tried to work, but found it hard to concentrate and was annoyed when other passengers rudely recognized him. (As there were five hundred passengers on board it's not surprising that some of them did.) The boat sailed via Danzig and Oslo, arriving on the nineteenth; they visited Leningrad and Moscow, and set off home again, via Copenhagen, which they reached on the twenty-sixth.

Bennett's impressions of Russia were published in the *Daily Express*, in four instalments, starting on 4 September.[39] At first he found it 'thrilling', but his enthusiasm seems gradually to have waned during the visit. The first article is devoted to Leningrad – they were on the first British ship to enter the port of Leningrad since the war, and he describes the regulations 'of forged steel' and the war-like atmosphere that filled the place. He describes the vast squares and the wide streets, and then comments on the fact that all the streets are up, all the cobbles loose, the buildings are shabby and forlorn, with chipped stucco and worn paint . . . imagine, he says, Holborn after an explosion, indefinitely abandoned by city surveyors. It is a vivid picture. Moscow, in his next article, he describes as being more human, on a smaller scale, more densely populated, but Moscow too was shabby: it seemed unfashionable to be smart. 'A perambulation of the streets,' he says, 'was as agreeable as eating a dust sandwich.' He went to the ballet, to see an appalling modern propaganda piece called *The Red Poppy*, and an excellent old-style production of Rimsky-Korsakov's *Sadki*, 'exquisitely sung and acted'.

The next two articles he devotes to Soviet propaganda and the Soviet régime: he finds the propaganda irritating, the guides ill-informed, the Russian attitude to the English paranoid, and the prices their own worst advertisement – 'fantastic, outrageous, extortionate'. He concludes, finally, that the Communist Party is 'an autocracy – that is, a tyranny – far more complete than that of the Czars', and notes with dismay that while he was there *Pravda* reported the execution of a railway official for an unnamed crime. Such things can happen in five minutes, he says. He is by no means resolutely anti-Soviet: he agrees that the children play cheerfully on the steps of the old palaces, that there are no serious signs of depression or hardship, any more than there are in the East End. He agrees that the peasants are undeniably better off than they were. But he left feeling 'disappointed and disturbed' by the fate of what he calls the most 'arduous, the most daring political experiment in all history'. It was based on a great ideal, he says, but vitiated by prodigious lying. He was not the first or last visitor to respond in this way. He was upset by the sight of the food queues, and the champagne for visitors at £4 a bottle, while 'Communist officials have rooms at five shillings a month....' His last words must sum up many a guest's experience: 'I departed from Russia with relief,' he says, 'Russia had got on my nerves.'

His enthusiasm may have been tempered in part by his own worries: Dorothy, left behind in Brittany, was not well. She had an abscess, and was in low spirits. Being alone in the hotel with the baby was not pleasant: she did not like the other guests. She returned home four days early, to have her abscess attended to, and her letters to Arnold were necessarily not very cheerful. She too had caught the anxiety about money. There were other problems – Richard Bennett, his nephew, was causing trouble of some kind; another old acquaintance, the writer Geoffrey Scott, had died; and above all, his new big novel was hanging over him like a cloud. He had been planning this novel for years. It was going to be long – he had written, that month, to Gide, that he could not write serious short novels, that it had to be a long one. Was he wondering whether he still had the stamina or the desire to write a long, sustained work? For years now younger critics had been accusing him of lack of seriousness, of having sold his soul for money, and so on; he had conceived a scheme to re-establish himself and refute his critics. But had he still got the will and the power to carry it off? He needed Dorothy's support more than ever, he wrote to her.

He returned to London at the end of August, and began *Imperial Palace* on 25 September at 3.30 p.m. His comments in his journal, like his letters from Russia to Dorothy, show a distinct fear of the blight of long novels, 'an ultimately supervening creative fatigue'.[40] He was much older than he had been when he wrote *The Old Wives' Tale* and *Clayhanger*, and he was moreover writing not in the relative peace of Fontainebleau, but in the middle of a busy social life in London, where the claims on his time, as an important public figure, were endless. He had faith in his theme, which he says had been haunting him for thirty years, but distrusted his ability to do it justice: perhaps he thought that by voicing these fears, he would exorcize them.

He settled down to work, seriously, and finished the novel in July 1930; it turned out even longer than he had intended. During the period of composition he did not, however, cut himself off from all other activities. He was concerned with the French translations of his novels (which Gide was supervising), with de luxe English editions of *The Old Wives' Tale* and various short stories, with his regular *Evening Standard* reviewing, with the publication of his 1929 *Journal* (some of which upset old friends who found themselves therein), with Goossens's plans for a new opera, possibly from *Don Juan*, and he still found time to attend first nights at theatres and cinemas. He even found time to be as courteous and helpful as ever to old friends, reading through, for instance, William Rothenstein's *Men and Memories* in typescript, with many encouraging and critical comments; he answered the correspondence of completely unknown younger writers, such as James Hanley. And as well as these daily professional preoccupations, there were two new big events: the finding of a new house, and Dorothy's revival of *Milestones*.

They had known for some time that the lease of 75 Cadogan Square was expiring, and that they would have to move. There was much discussion about their new home, and some disagreement. A large new block of flats, Chiltern Court, had just been built at Baker Street. H. G. Wells had acquired one, and Bennett went to see the block with the architect. Dorothy had her doubts from the first: the flats were too small, they would have to take two and convert them into one; there was noise from the building works, and the district was not as quiet as Belgravia. The architect assured them that there would be no noise once the block was finished. The conversion, she thought, would prove expensive, and their finances were not as healthy as they wished. Bennett seems to have made up his mind to accept the flat in a hurried, somewhat irrational manner, against her advice. By the end of March he was writing to William Rothenstein, who knew they were house-hunting, that he had definitely decided to take the Chiltern Court flat, which would, when converted, provide an abode '185 feet' in total length. Perhaps he was simply tired of looking for other places: house-hunting is a time-consuming and depressing job, and he simply could not be bothered with it. He had to finish his novel, and he took a snap decision to clear his mind of the problem. As they didn't move into the flat until November 1930, a good deal of conversion work must have been necessary, but he seems to have left it to the architect.

Dorothy's venture with a revival of *Milestones* was connected with her anxiety about money. She had hopes of helping the Bennett finances, and relieving the increasingly obvious pressure on Bennett's mind, by organizing a successful tour and run of what had been a very successful play. As we have seen, Bennett's attitude towards her theatrical ventures was ambivalent: at one moment encouraging her to find bigger projects, at the next warning her about the fickleness and unreliability of the public. Dorothy resolved at least to try. It was quite a while since she had worked – not since the Byron play in February 1929, a year earlier. She had a little money of her own, and she decided to invest it in a new production of *Milestones*, which opened at the Criterion on 28 January. It was well received: the *Telegraph* said it revived extremely well, and seemed to be not at all out of tune with the post-war world: the *Express* described it as a brilliant play, 'as charming, as humorous, as beautiful and challenging' as it had seemed in 1912; the *Standard* called it a welcome revival. But good notices don't necessarily mean a long run, and the play closed in the second week of April. Dorothy, as with *Mr Prohack*, did not wish to concede defeat, and took the play on tour to Birmingham and Southampton. She lost money. Bennett wrote to her: 'You will never in the end make money by play-producing on your own. You may make a bit on one production, but you will lose it on the next. Money is not to be made in the theatre. This is the universal experience. Still, I believe in your going on....'[41] He does not reproach her: why should he, after all? The money was hers to lose, and he was hardly in a position to pontificate about the need to resist the lure of the theatre, having just succumbed to it, yet again, with yet another play himself. He had written more than twenty plays, many of which had never been put on, several of which had failed, and he still couldn't stop. They understood one another on this score. They had known each other from the beginning on a basis of mutual understanding. Bennett might have found her independent ambitions trying at times, and expressed his impatience – he was not an easy man to live with, from day to day, as both Marguerite and Dorothy bear witness – but nevertheless he and Dorothy were in the game together. They both liked the sense of adventure – after the first night of *Mr Prohack*, Dorothy said to him 'You and I are great adventurers' – and they could hardly with any consistency reproach one another for seeking it.

Those who have chosen to interpret Bennett's impatience with Dorothy's theatrical ventures more seriously, surely do it against the evidence, for they were both hooked. It's easy enough to get annoyed with somebody for having a completely unreasonable and dotty obsession (might the reciting of Baudelaire and Ronsard finally have appeared in this light?), but not so easy if one shares it. Bennett was too logical a man, despite his rigid thinking, not to recognize this. His anxieties, towards the end of his life, were of another order. So were hers.

15
The End

Bennett, when he finished *Imperial Palace* in July 1930, was sixty-three years old. His father, the long forgotten Enoch, had died at the age of fifty-eight. His brother Frank was a failure and an alcoholic. His youngest brother Septimus was dead. His sister Emily was distinctly odd. Arnold Bennett had travelled far to escape the family ghost, but perhaps, under the pressure of writing an immense work, it haunted him a little. In his journal there are several comments that indicate his sense of distance from the past, coupled with his fear of it – on his return journey from Manchester to see the first production of *Flora*, he passed through the Potteries, and says: 'I took the 12.5 back to London, which went through the Potteries. The sight of this district gave me a shudder.'[1] On 2 February 1928 he notes that a visit from relatives whom one does not often see is 'rather wearing . . . in fact, desolating.'[2] Was he wearing out? What man does not think of the death of his father on the appropriate day, and count subsequent days as free gifts? Dorothy certainly felt that he was anxious about his health, knew that he was worried that his father's illness might overtake him, and worried herself on his account. With her encouragement, he agreed to have medical checks, from which he emerged cheerful and encouraged, saying that the doctors had ascribed him the arteries of a forty-year-old and blood pressure below normal. All seemed well, and might well have been so.

But Dorothy, at least, was still worried. His abruptness over the decision to buy the Chiltern Court flat might have been a symptom of strain and overwork on the new long novel. Perhaps, this time, he had seriously over-taxed and overstretched himself. If the results were disappointing, if the book was not successful and well received, if he found he could not fulfil his original grandiose conceptions, what depressions might not ensue? It was not only a question of internal depression, either. In America, the book trade, like everything else, was going badly. George Doran, who had looked after Bennett's interests so well for so many years, and who had been such a good friend to him on his visit there in 1911, was not in such a happy or influential position since joining Doubledays in 1927. Bennett has grown suspicious of him, and warns Ralph Pinker to examine his accounts with the greatest care as he has been told they are 'very unreliable'.[3] Doran, in his new position, had been less accommodating than before to old friends and profit-makers, such as Swinnerton and Bennett, declining to publish *Mediterranean Scenes*, which sold well in England. There were several reasons for these changes, the strongest of which was the general decline of trade, but Doran was also having personal difficulties: his marriage had broken up, and so had the marriage of his daughter to Stanley Rinehart, another publisher, who had left Doubledays in order to set up an independent firm.

In 1930, at exactly the period when Bennett was trying to negotiate a contract for *Imperial Palace*, Doran moved yet again, from Doubledays to a lavishly paid job for Hearst, his job being to build up a list for Hearst's Cosmopolitan Book Corporation, a short-lived venture. This was unsettling for Bennett, who did not know what to do for the best for himself, and who clearly did not quite trust Doran, despite his continuing affection for him. At the same time, he felt no particular affection for or obligation to Doubledays, either. It was Doubledays, in fact, who acquired and published the book, but the whole Doran affair was dispiriting. Doran was in London throughout the autumn and Bennett saw him often, and felt through him, no doubt, the cold chill of the future. *Imperial Palace* was to flourish, but the book trade as a whole during the 1930s suffered severely. Doran's mood was restless and he spread unease. Dorothy did not care for him, and Bennett warned her against him: writing to Eric Pinker in January 1931, Bennett describes him as a 'pathetic spectacle'. Even so, his fate was not as pathetic as that of some of his associates: the Depression, which Bennett was spared, ruined the Pinker firm, and many other old friends.

Imperial Palace, with its theme of luxury, was both appropriate and inappropriate at such a time. It was a monument both in form and subject to the past, and was read avidly by those who feared lean times ahead. At the same time, it was attacked by others as being socially irresponsible and obtuse. It is a strange and impressive novel, despite its faults, and despite the fact that it is not in the *Clayhanger* class. It is a completely different kind of success, a tribute to an obsession, which happily for Bennett was a common, human one, and one he of all people could communicate. Dorothy recalls that when Bennett gave her the first pages of the book to read, she

337

had a moment of real fear, during which she thought that his obsessions had got out of hand, and that he had lost his critical faculty. And one can see what she felt. The novel, with its odd obsessive lists and numbers, its details about cutlery and carpets and leaking taps, its comprehensive view of the staff problems and relations of a massive hotel, its trips to meat markets and furniture workrooms, is an extraordinary enterprise. It is so methodical, so factual, and yet at the same time it surely overestimates the romantic attractions of its hero, hotel director Evelyn Orcham. The heroines, Gracie Savott and Violet Powler, are made to accord to Evelyn's hotel the kind of awestruck deference and reverence which might conceivably have been more appropriate if bestowed upon a great work of art – an architect's creation, or a sculptor's, or even a novelist's. Here are Evelyn and Gracie, walking at night in the rain. Gracie suddenly spots the hotel, and exclaims: 'That's marvellous, especially on a night like this. I do admire you for that. You're a poet.' What she had seen was: 'beyond the forest, high in the invisible firmament, the flood-lit tower of the Imperial Palace, poking itself brilliantly up to the skies. There was nothing in all London, then, but that commanding great column of white light.'[4] Strange enthusiasm, one might think.

Psychologically, *Imperial Palace* is a fascinating puzzle. In it, Bennett seems to be working out some of his problems, past and present, more overtly than usual, and for the last time. Its hero, Evelyn Orcham, has much in common with the typical late-Bennett hero: he is a man of the world, efficient, masterly, not to say domineering, fussy about his clothes, good with cigars and food, a light drinker, proud, self-contained, middle-aged. He is also long-widowed and celibate. And, like his creator, he has funny teeth, teeth which rouse one of his girlfriends to transports of delight. He is sexually naïve and diffident: one is allowed to think of him as being naïve. His first, brief marriage, which had ended in a fatal childbirth, had been a disaster, and since then Evelyn had kept away from women, living alone in his secret flat in the Palace, tended, of course, by his faithful valet. Everybody in the entire novel admires or is in awe of Evelyn. Here is a fantasy worked out on an impressive scale. Not only do most of the characters admire him; they are actually employed by him, so their admiration is secure and inviolable. If any hotel employee misbehaves or swerves in loyalty for a moment, however innocently, he or she is instantly and mercilessly dismissed. Moreover, Evelyn takes pleasure in telling his female employees what to wear, how to make up, and how to comport themselves. Violet Powler, whom he raises from an obscure post in the laundry to the post of head housekeeper, and finally marries, receives instructions on how to appear in the smart world of the Palace. She enjoys it, in a submissive, excited, sexual way, just as he enjoys doing it. And yet she is portrayed as a sturdy, sensible, tactful, but obstinate woman, who is the only one of Evelyn's staff who dares to oppose him. (Of course, she apologizes for it in the end.) There is nothing unrealistic in this: it is a frank account of many a sexual relationship, and Bennett knew what he was doing. When Evelyn tells Violet to wear powder and rouge – which he does in a light tone, so as not to offend her – she flushes and, Bennett says, 'the flush amused and pleased him. She had no caprices, no moods, no nerves. Yet the flush!'[5]

Violet Powler, the ideal submissive yet sensible woman, the ideal housekeeper–wife, with her instinctive taste and tact, is all too obviously a picture of the woman whom Bennett never found and could never have had. He would not have wanted her if he had got her: he would have found her dull. He wanted to dominate, as his letters to Marguerite demonstrate, but he also wanted resistance. He wanted a housekeeper, but he wanted (like Evelyn) to be the supreme housekeeper himself. And his sexual needs could not be fulfilled simply by the enjoyment of dominating, as an employer: he wanted equality, provocation, adventure. Why else should the three women with whom he became most deeply involved, Eleanor Green, Marguerite and Dorothy, have been such high-spirited and independent creatures? Perhaps in the *cocottes* of Paris, to whom he was always so courteous in his journals and his fiction, he found a good blend of submission and adventurous impropriety and independence, a blend which did not allow the more destructive elements of his dominating impulse to get out of hand. In Marguerite, perhaps he thought he had found the same mixture – and had indeed found some of it. But the mixture was slightly wrong, and it turned against him. Whatever he sought, one cannot accuse him, in any of his choices, of taking the easy way, as Evelyn did. He rose to higher challenges. He is critical of Evelyn, and this is one of the most interesting things about the novel, for those other middle-aged heroes, in *Accident*, in *Lilian*, in *Mr Prohack*, in *Lord Raingo*, even in fantasies like *The Strange Vanguard*, get off very lightly.

The other woman in the novel, Gracie Savott, is the source of most of the criticism of Evelyn and his way of life. She, again, is a type which he had attempted before – in *The Pretty Lady*, in *The Strange Vanguard*, in various plays. She is the modern woman, the girl of the twenties – sophisticated, talented, wealthy, unconventional. She smokes, drinks, wears a good deal of makeup, and seeks sensation. Her origins are complex, for Bennett had come to know many such young women – Diana Manners, Harriet Cohen,

Venetia Montagu, and many of the actresses he had met through his connection with the theatre and through Dorothy. Evelyn, who meets Gracie at the beginning of the novel, senses at once that she is dangerous, and tries to avoid her, but without avail. She hunts him down, declares her passion for him, and gets him into bed, which is quite an accomplishment. His diffidence and reluctance and embarrassment on this occasion are most objectively drawn. The only thing that is not quite convincing is the fact that Gracie should have nourished such a passion for a director of a hotel in the first place: her enthusiasm for him as a man of affairs rings a little false. But, on another level, the fact that she wanted him because he was so obviously inaccessible and unwilling is quite plausibly pointed out. Bennett, in this novel at least, is seriously attempting to come to terms with the type, for Gracie is not painted as being entirely endearing, any more than Evelyn is: she is capricious, selfish, a liar, and she is moreover not a virgin. She is not meant to please the many. Her intellectual notions – she writes a book, quotes the Psalms, and talks about electrons – are not given any particular dignity. One feels that in this territory Bennett is halfway between trying to make her sound really interesting and intriguing, and making her sound like a conventionally 'interesting' but pretentious affected dilettante. Perhaps years of popularizing Einstein had confused him about the nature of his audience in this area: he simply did not know how far he could go. Certainly Gracie does not possess a quarter of the true unconventionality of Hilda Lessways, but one need not necessarily put this down to Bennett's own softening or desire to placate. For Gracie rings true: she is simply an inferior type. The qualities which Bennett lends her to render her sympathetic are conventional enough – she is, for instance, excessively generous to her pregnant maid – but then the way in which she is generous has a certain perversity. She is, in fact, perverse in many ways, and so is Evelyn, and the novel comes near to coming to terms with the matter.

It fails, however; Gracie and Evelyn separate, Evelyn returns to the arms of the docile Violet, and Gracie marries an old admirer. One could read Gracie's seduction and rejection of Evelyn as a very belated attempt to explain and come to terms with Eleanor's rejection of Bennett in 1906. One could also read Evelyn's failure to love Gracie and give himself to her when she wants him as an attempt to understand Bennett's own inadequacies, both with Eleanor and Marguerite. Certainly these were subjects he had hardly attempted before. The success of These Twain, which is about marital discord, rests in its constraint, its discretion, its perseverance, all Northern qualities, and manifested in that novel at a point in time when

Bennett still believed that his marriage could through sheer will-power be salvaged. It could not and was not: some other kind of post mortem was necessary. In the relaxed climate of the 1920s, another kind of novel could be written. Bennett had read his Joyce and his Lawrence: he knew the possibilities. What kind of novel was struggling to get out when Bennett started to describe Gracie in her pyjamas, in her camisole, in her bath? When he begins to use words like 'knickers'? When he shows Evelyn fleeing from all this sexuality, and rushing out to buy newspapers and chocolate, to bolster himself up with the world again? When he describes the sexual effect of Gracie wearing cheap clothes from a department store, compared with the expensive couture clothes which she wears daily? Above all, when he describes the jilted Evelyn thinking that he ought, to keep her in order, have beaten her – 'A whip might keep her in order. It's the only thing that would. And I never thought of it. What I ought to do is to go back with a cane and rip everything off her, and give her a hiding till she fainted away, and then when she came to, make her kneel down and beg my pardon for being thrashed.'[6]

This was another novel, and Bennett wasn't going to write it. He couldn't, just as E.M. Forster, for similar reasons of social inhibition, couldn't write a good book on the theme of *Maurice*, even when it was not intended for publication. No matter how secret and private the intentions, certain things cannot even be put down on paper, as Bennett found when he was trying to write two journals, one about sex and one about life. The gap between the self and the written word is too great. This, surely, is the real explanation of why Bennett's Five Town novels are on the whole so superior to his later ones, whatever the charms of the later ones: their subjects are more not less repressed than their creator, therefore they can be described, delicately, through constraint and implication, by a writer who understands them and their means of expression better than they do themselves. Forster could create no convincing positive social future for Maurice and his lover because there was none that he could admit: he could not admit the current practical reality because of his upbringing. Lawrence and Joyce could admit the lot, but Bennett and Forster had to work by analogy and restraint. Both attempted to come to terms with the present, their own present, and both failed. One might say that Bennett had less reason for failure than Forster – a novel about the sexual eccentricities consequent upon having been brought up in Burslem by a dominating father in a hypocritical Methodist climate would have been more acceptable in the twenties or thirties than a novel about practising homosexuality and its problems – but to say such a thing would be grossly to underestimate the pressures that had formed Bennett as a man, and to misunderstand the nature of his achievement. He achieved out of himself, not against himself; rather like Forster, he was a man who wished to live in society and to make sense of it and work through it, rather than a natural rebel. Bennett's finest novels are concerned with the restrictions within which men flourish. His best London novel, *Riceyman Steps*, is set in a most impoverished and rigid constraint. Even in *Imperial Palace*, which is a large book tackling an enormous number of scenes and characters, as well as new themes, he works very obviously to a schedule, as though the mere reiteration of room numbers and prosaic details were necessary to shore up his intentions. And yet his own life had proved unpredictable, confusing, startling even.

After his separation from Marguerite, he could have written a sequel to *These Twain*, in which Edwin and Hilda parted. Or he could have written of the birth of his child. He did neither of these things: he hardly hinted at them, even indirectly. Perhaps he had lost the energy to deal creatively with new shocks and revelations. Or perhaps, simply, like Forster, he had no positive language to encompass them.

Imperial Palace, however one may regard it as his last monument, was a fine achievement. It was a very long novel: it had grown during composition, and ended up even longer than he had intended. (When he was accused by a reviewer of writing long novels in order to keep up with J. B. Priestley, he quite rightly retorted that he had been writing long novels before Priestley had set pen to paper.) It shows no signs of lack of firmness of purpose, or of creative fatigue, at least in its execution. But about its conception one must have grave doubts. It is not in the same class as his earlier masterpieces, and that is partly because its subject matter is not in the same class. Its subject matter remains trivial. He could make it superbly interesting, he could carry with him thousands of readers, but he could not disguise the fact that for him the luxury hotel was something of a private obsession, deeply rooted in his own provincialism, his own early deprivations, his own claustrophobia in the cloying domestic scene. In his life, perhaps, he was at peace with this obsession, but in artistic terms, however hard he tried, he could come up with no real answer to the gulf between the rich and the poor, the joys of luxury and the slavery on which they depend. He does not avoid the issue – on the contrary, he returns to it relentlessly, in novel after novel, in *Mr Prohack*, in *Lilian*, in *Accident*, indeed in all his later books. He describes the decadence of luxury, in such scenes as the one set in the nightclub Caligula in *Imperial Palace*, with an observant eye. Like a good realist, he draws contrasted scenes of luxury, simplicity, squalor, poverty, decadence, all within the one book, all set against one another. But he lacks Zola's moral fervour: or does he perhaps lack his dishonesty? Zola, the hero of Bennett's youth, painted decadent Paris in glowing terms of fury, encompassing the whole social scale, from laundress and courtesan to banker and aristocrat, and his zeal never slackened. He is hard on his characters, they pay the price of sin and die bad deaths. But Zola, like Bennett, made good; like Bennett, he furnished his house with ornate furniture, the provincial's delight, and enjoyed his own wealth, while punishing the inhabitants of his fiction. He is a greater writer, but Bennett is perhaps the more honest man. Bennett said of himself that he lacked the capacity for righteous indignation, and this was so. He saw so much of it in his childhood that he had to repudiate it: it was so profoundly hypocritical, so complacent, and worst of all it took delight in the woes of others. Bennett always and steadfastly refuses himself this corrupt pleasure. Perhaps he goes too far in the other direction, tolerating too much, regarding too blandly. And yet one feels at times, even in his weaker novels, with their private indulgences and fantasies, that he is on the brink of some real discovery about the nature of human happiness, about the possibility of a good life for the many. That he cared deeply about the many – as deeply as Zola – is evident from his recurrent themes, from the shaping of his novels. *Imperial Palace*, unlike *The Grand Babylon Hotel*, is a serious novel, but he cannot quite bring it off, partly because of his own sexual doubts, manifested in the Evelyn/Gracie/Violet relationship, and partly because he can never answer his own underlying question: how is it that men can enjoy themselves in great comfort and luxury while their fellow men are toiling on inadequate wages to provide that luxury? He does not allow himself the simple answer, which is that such men are morally obtuse, dead in their souls, and wicked. He could see, as so few of the morally outraged seem able to see, that such an answer would condemn not only himself but also most of the things that give life any value. He was looking for a more complex answer, which he never found. Had he been Wells or the Webbs, he might have found it in politics, but their faith in their politics was something which he could not accept. So he remains an observer and a questioner, pondering, as did so many in the eighteenth and nineteenth centuries, the right use of riches. He was accused often, towards the end of his life, by younger critics, of having sold his soul for a yacht and a motor-car, and one could indeed see his novels as a process of justification for having acquired the yacht and the motor-car. But it would be an untrue response to them. *Imperial Palace* is not a celebration of or an apology for luxury and power and exclusivity: it is an account of them. It is trivial only in its failure to make sense of them, a demand which one would not make of many writers. This is what makes it superficial. It remains a brave attempt, in more ways than one. Would one really have respected Bennett more, as a writer, if he had ignored his own inquiries about contemporary life, and continued to write successful historical provincial pieces like *Clayhanger*?

When the novel was finished, the Bennetts went off to Cornwall for a six-week holiday in July and August. Dorothy recalls this as a happy time: there was little to worry him except for minor rows about forthcoming publicity for the novel (focused mainly upon trying to prevent his publishers and well-meaning friends such as Walpole from identifying the Savoy too obviously as his source); and compared with the composing of the novel itself, such disputes were a luxury. He had certainly earned some time off. At the end of August, he went off for a few days for a brief cruise with his old friend Alfred Mason, off the south coast, in his yacht the *Sea Flower*. Dorothy had had premonitions of danger about the trip, but he writes constantly to reassure her, telling her that the beds are '*utterly* comfortable',[7] that the food is plain but good, that the boat and the skipper are thoroughly safe and reliable and that it is 'dead calm – damn it',[8] and that his only complaint is the lack of sweets at dinner. He returned to London in the middle of September, to more negotiations about the novel, to new plans from Goossens about *Don Juan*, to Somerset Maugham's *Cakes and Ale*, which he admired, and Lawrence's *The Virgin and the Gipsy*, which he admired even more. He also returned, alas, to the dentist: he had had all his top teeth removed, and was having problems with his false ones, problems which he describes in a letter to Harriet Cohen, who was playing in Chicago – and who wished, incidentally, to claim a little of Gracie Savott for herself.

There was also the removal. This took place in November, and was a big upheaval. Bennett had started a new novel, *The Dream of Destiny*, which he was never to finish, and he says in his letter to Harriet Cohen[9] that he was writing it in the intervals of helping Dorothy to organize the move. But knowing his reluctance to allow anybody else to organize anything, the matter no doubt preoccupied him considerably. They finally moved on 9 November, when Dorothy herself was already busy rehearsing for her part in a new play, a revival of *The Man from Blankley's*, which opened at the Fortune Theatre on 26 November. Dorothy played Cecilia Flinders. The play was the opening production of a new company, The People's Theatre, and it was well received – it ran till 18 December. So Dorothy was busy during this period. It may have been partly her own professional commitments, as well as her initial reluctance to take the flat, that darkened the change for her. Also, looking back, the move must have seemed even more final and tragic in retrospect. But the truth is that she never liked Chiltern Court: she found the converted flat inconvenient and noisy (the noise from the tube trains below was apparently appalling, despite the architect's protestations that they would hear nothing), the district was less suitable for family life, the change was in no way for the better. There is little evidence that Bennett was any more pleased. He suspected he had made a mistake, though, with his usual rigidity, he was determined to stick to it. He was pleased, perhaps, with his new modern study, with its hundreds of yards of modern steel shelving; he had moved far away from the old Empire style, and now his study was in delicate shades of pale beige, silver grey, yellow and grey-brown, a scheme designed by Marion Dorn. The furniture, by E.A. Brown, was contemporary, and the carpets were designed by E. McKnight Kauffer, a friend and artist, who had also illustrated de luxe editions of T.S. Eliot's poetry and Bennett's short story, 'Venus Rising from the Sea'.

The flat, in architecture and furnishings, was very much of the twentieth century. Having been obliged to leave Cadogan Square, he had not tried to repeat its style. But he must have had his doubts about it. He strained himself transferring his thousands of books from the house to the flat, and was tired and irritable. But Dorothy's doubts seem only to have strengthened his resolve to stay: she says he had become 'adamant and brittle'. The noisiness of the place must have made itself apparent to him immediately, and he, who would go to great trouble to find himself quiet rooms in a hotel, and who was a chronically bad sleeper, found himself condemned to sleep in a perpetual racket. It is useless to speculate how long it would have taken him to change his mind and move out. At the end of 1930, he was in no mood for changing his mind. He and Dorothy were both tired. She noted in him a 'curious rigidity' which was new to her, and which was 'almost physical'.[10] Was this the beginning of something serious, or was it simply a phase, brought on by work and worry and upheaval, which their usual remedy of a short trip abroad would cure?

On 29 December 1930 they went to Paris, to the Hôtel Matignon. They stayed in France for three weeks, and visited the American sculptor Jo Davidson, an old friend (he had been on the Otto Kahn Mediterranean cruise) who was doing a bust of Bennett: indeed, he was doing busts of several literary figures, having been commissioned to do so for Doubledays by George Doran. The expense of this scheme precipitated Doran's departure from Doubledays, and some of the busts remained unfinished. Bennett tried to persuade George Moore to sit, but Moore was old, ill and in a nursing home, and refused. Dorothy thought that Bennett was still behaving un-characteristically: during their week's visit to Davidson, she had herself been unwell and in bed with pleurisy, and she noted one night that the bottle of Evian water by his bedside was nearly finished. She meant to bring him her own from her own room, but forgot. In the morning, she found he had filled his carafe from the tap and drunk the tap water. 'You didn't drink that!' she exclaimed, when she saw it, reproaching herself for having forgotten the Evian water the night before, and he turned on her and said aggressively and defiantly, 'I did!' It was so unlike him to be careless about such matters – he, the devotee of *The Culture of the Abdomen*, the pioneer of hygiene and the hotel bathroom. His rigidity and defiance were still very evident, unappeased by a change of climate: was he still brooding over the problem of the flat and the objections she had raised?

They went back to Paris, and met old friends such as Gide and Valéry Larbaud. Gide's concern over the French translation of *The Old Wives' Tale* was nearly over (it appeared, as *Un Conte des Bonnes Femmes*, in a version done by Marcel de Coppet, with emendations and improvements by R.M. du Gard and Gide himself), and Bennett was very grateful and much impressed by the time he had spent on it. All he had been able to do in return was to reassure Gide about the quality of his own English translator, Mme Bussy, who was a sister of Lytton Strachey and in Bennett's view second only to Scott-Moncrieff. The disinterest which these two utterly dissimilar writers took in each other's works is a pleasant literary incident. It was on this visit that Bennett met for the first time James Joyce, whose work he had defended. Bennett noted that Mrs Joyce must have 'a terrible time' stopping Joyce drinking. What Joyce thought of Bennett, we do not know.

Again, in Paris, the story of the water was repeated. Dorothy and Bennett were sitting in the restaurant of the hotel, when Bennett helped himself to water from the carafe. The waiter, seeing what he had done, reproached him, saying: 'Ah, ce n'est pas sage, Monsieur, ce n'est pas sage.' He did not defend himself to the waiter, as he had done to Dorothy: he seemed to accept the reproof. And on the way back to London, in the third week of January, he began to feel ill.

At first he thought his shivering fits were simply an attack of influenza. He went to bed when he got home, and tried to work at his new novel, *The Dream of Destiny*, but found he couldn't get on with it. He never finished it; he had written a third of it before he went to France, and this fragment was published posthumously the following year. It is a strange piece, for a last testament. Unusually for him, he had turned again to the supernatural, or

346

at least to the world of the immaterial, for the first time since *The Glimpse* – there are some odd moments in other books, like the one in *The Pretty Lady* where Christine hears a voice calling her, but he had never built a whole plot around one of them. Oddly enough, this plot, like that of *The Glimpse*, had originated in a short story – on this occasion 'The Dream', which appeared in *The Night Visitors*, also in 1932. One might well hold a theory that these two short ideas, once he had had them, haunted him and insisted on being made into full-length novels.

The story of *Dream of Destiny* is simple, as far as it goes – its hero, another middle-aged bachelor, has a dream that he marries a girl, who dies in child-birth. Later, he meets the girl, an American actress, and tries to avoid her, fearing that the dream will come true, but fails. The book goes no farther. Its heroine, Phoebe Friar, finds acting a nervous strain, as Dorothy did; and Dorothy, it must be remembered, had suffered from a bad prophetic dream about Arnold the autumn before. She says, in an article in *John o'London's Weekly*, that he talked the novel over with her because it was 'in her line' – whether he meant her line as an actress, or her line as a picker-up of psychic messages, she does not say. He had been reading, she said, J. W. Dunne's *Experiment with Time* – also Einstein and Addington.[11] One can only speculate as to why certain ideas which had not formerly interested him had begun to absorb him – one could see it simply as a symptom of mental decline, or one could interpret it more positively in the terms of one of Doris Lessing's latest short stories, 'The Temptation of Jack Orkney'. In this story, Doris Lessing describes the experiences of a hardened thirties atheist materialist socialist after attending the deathbed of his father: he begins to dream. He has to dream. Thoughts of the spirit that had never troubled him rise up in him and confuse all his old allegiances. Had Bennett begun to dream also?

Certainly, even if he had, *Dream of Destiny* is not a very profound ex-pression, as it stands, of any new discoveries about life. It is superficial, glossy, too easily written. Its most interesting feature is not its dream plot, but the fact that the hero, Roland Layne-Smith, is the controlling manager of a large block of industrial flats. Flats were on Bennett's mind: the search for a new one had been exhausting. The novel contrasts the spaciousness of the Boltons, where the opening scenes take place, with the cramped quarters, long narrow corridors, and asphalt atmosphere of Thames Court, the working-class block which Roland administers. The rooms in the flats are too small, too odorous, the sitting-rooms and kitchenettes of which he tries to feel proud are like those in a doll's house. Why had Bennett chosen to write in this way about housing? Was it an oblique recognition of the fact that his own irritations about Chiltern Court were mere peevishness, and that other people are much worse off, all the time, with inevitable noise, and no space to move about in either? It would have been very like him, if this had been his motive: a last apology for having more than others.

He was unable to work at the novel, but on 26 January he made himself get up again, saying he felt a little better. He lunched once at the Reform, went to Newman Flower's son's wedding reception at the Savoy, and wrote his last article for *Books and Persons*. But after a few days he was feeling wretchedly ill again. He said he was all right, but after the wedding reception on 3 February, followed by a concert, he felt so bad that he went to bed and called in a specialist.

This time, the illness was diagnosed as typhoid. Sir William Willcox, who attended him, said that it was probable that he had also suffered from typhoid in 1912, when he was so ill in the South of France after his trip to the States. Dorothy's fears had been realized. For the next few weeks he lay in a state of increasing weakness, conscious sometimes, delirious sometimes, and desperately ill. It was a long period to nurse a difficult and famous patient, and circumstances did not make things any easier for Dorothy. Some friends, of course, were helpful and sympathetic – she remembers particularly Aldous Huxley and Somerset Maugham – but there were problems from the past. For one thing, Marguerite, who had been forbidden to come near him, and whose overtures he had rejected several times during his years with Dorothy, turned up at Chiltern Court when she heard that Bennett was ill. She was not allowed near him (it was a condition of her allowance that she should not set foot in his home), but she sat downstairs in the foyer, speaking to people as they passed, and Dorothy had the misery of knowing that there was a hostile, alien ghost from the past threatening her position and spreading ill-will. Marguerite was doubtless recalling her own excellence in the role of nurse. The fact that she had first become intimate with him when he was an invalid seems to have made a profound impression on her, and her later letters, after their separation, are marked by a fantasy that he would need her again as a nurse. That the time had now come, and she was not needed, may well have made her very bitter.

Then there was also Bennett's own family, a difficult lot at the best of times. Dorothy and Bennett had conscientiously tried to remain on good terms with as many of them as possible, but Dorothy's role in this particular scene was almost unplayable. Frank Beardmore, his brother-in-law, refused to go near Chiltern Court, but his wife Sissie, Bennett's sister (and the mother of George Beardmore), turned up and refused to move. She was an alarming woman, terrifying even to her own children (according to George), one of the first women JPs, and she was a formidable and not particularly cheerful presence. After her death in 1939, her children worked out that she had held sixteen public offices. She must have had the air of a public examiner, as she sat there, day after day. Tertia had always been the most sympathetic of his sisters, but she was a very different kind of woman from Dorothy. The situation was full of friction and potential trouble. Dorothy recalls that on one occasion the sisters were bearing down on Bennett's bedroom, where she knew him to be asleep, and when she tried to ward them off into another room to explain to them that it was not a good time to disturb him, they took it as an affront.

There was also the question of medical advice. It was rumoured at the time that Bennett had wished to call in Sir Thomas Horder, the King's physician, but had not liked to do so because of professional etiquette and the fear of offending Sir William Willcox, but Dorothy maintains that he was perfectly satisfied with the treatment he received. Indeed, on one occasion, when he made a point of sending the nurses out of the room so that he could be alone with Dorothy and Sir William, Sir William assumed that he was about to raise some such problem, and assured Bennett that he must not hesitate to call in anyone he wanted. Bennett replied that he had no such intention, that he was 'well satisfied' and that he had simply sent the nurses away in order to enjoy a little conversation with his equals. 'Nurses, you know, poor things!' he said.

Whatever attentions he received, nothing could be done for him. Straw was laid down on the streets outside to stop the terrible roar of the traffic, but it was ineffectual. He became increasingly delirious. Dorothy notes that she went out one evening to a concert, and when she came in she went to speak to him. She said she had been listening to Brahms, and he turned on her quite blankly and said 'Brahms? Who is Brahms?' At other times, he was lucid, and it was in one of his lucid moments that he took hold of her arm and said 'Everything is going wrong, my girl.' He was right, whatever he meant by the phrase. On 26 March, after an illness of two months, he died.

After so long an illness, the event was hardly a surprise. It had been awaited. The newspapers had carried bulletins on Bennett's sinking health, as they had done for his own character, *Lord Raingo*. But it was nonetheless felt as a tragedy, both by his near friends who had loyally stayed by him, and by the nation who admired him. People like Pauline Smith, who had visited his flat during his sickness, to play with Virginia and wait for news, and Beaverbrook, who had gazed at him through an open door as he lay delirious in bed, were never to find such a friend again. (According to A.J.P.Taylor, Beaverbrook became increasingly solitary after his death.) Dorothy and Virginia (now nearly five) were left to struggle through a particularly grim decade alone. He was to be desperately missed. Virginia Woolf, who had contended with him in his lifetime, wrote in her diary a moving epitaph, showing her quality as well as his:

> 'Arnold Bennett died last night, which leaves me sadder than I should have supposed. A lovable genuine man: impeded, somehow a little awkward in life; well meaning; ponderous; kindly; coarse; knowing he was coarse; dimly floundering and feeling for something else; glutted with success; wounded in his feelings. . . . Some real understanding power, as well as gigantic absorbing power. Queer how one regrets the dispersal of anybody who seemed – as I say – genuine: who had direct contact with life – for he abused me; and yet I rather wished him to go on abusing me; and me abusing him. An element in life – even in mine that was so remote – taken away. This is what one minds.'[12]

Her immediate and genuine emotion contrasts oddly with the memorial of Hugh Walpole, an old friend and protégé who had been much helped by Bennett; and who was later that year to unveil a memorial plaque to him in Thorpe-le-Soken, where he had received so much hospitality. Walpole writes that he was 'very jealous and critical of me in the last years', that 'he had his picture of himself as he wanted to be, and you had to play up to that. He was very kind, very generous, so long as you didn't pierce that armour or damage that picture.' He goes on to catalogue the people that Bennett never forgave – Priestley, Frank Harris, Rebecca West, Virginia Woolf, 'and some of the young, and I myself doubtless said something on one of my American tours (faithfully reported by Swinnerton) that he never quite got over'.[13] Was it guilt that spoke? Walpole seemed to regard Bennett as a thoroughgoing materialist, whose view was bounded by bricks and mortar; perhaps Bennett and Virginia Woolf understood one another better than he understood either.

The papers were full of public tributes: his death was headline news. *The Times*, in over two full columns, stressed the hard struggle he had to achieve success, his practical wisdom, his lack of conceit, his enjoyment of life, his 'unwearing wonder at life's variety'. There is a long appraisal of *The Old Wives' Tale*, granting it classic status: 'To write it – one might say –

Bennett grew wings; the wings dropped off again, but while they lasted, he flew.' His qualities, the obituary says, 'would have made him a first class administrator – as those who knew him at the Ministry of Information believe – had his life taken a different turn'. The *Telegraph*, in a long piece written by Rebecca West, which Walpole describes as 'catty', praises above all his fearlessness in the fight against prudery and censorship, but she also criticizes his championship of materialism, 'of a hard and unsympathetic democracy, of liberty and equality without much fraternity, and the sworn foe of tradition, convention and sentiment, good or bad'. There speaks another critic of materialism who had never known poverty, and who could not discern Bennett's passionate yearning for fraternity and joy and opportunity for all. The *News Chronicle* said that London would be a duller place without him – and described, as did all the other papers, the 'tilt of his hat and the curve of his forelock'. He had made himself into a personality: he was, says the *Chronicle*, his own greatest character. And this was true. Rebecca West describes his appearance – the stiff movements, the carriage of the head, the crest of hair, the 'cumbrous and ornate style of dress; all the devices, in fact, by which a shy man had converted the oddities of which he was sensitive into a baroque exterior behind which he could hide'. She went on to say, 'All London will miss him, and some Londoners will miss him very bitterly. For he abounded in kindliness; and it was to be noted that some of his closest friends were men who had no other friends. His rich understanding of human nature enabled him to bridge gulfs that others could not.' This was well said: he would have appreciated such a tribute, for it bears witness to a very rare quality, which even Rebecca West, a less than wholly admiring judge, could not fail to notice.

There were no more novels to come, and his persuasively honest and amiable presence had departed. His work has been neglected in some ways from that day to this, though he has always had constant admirers, and of late there has been considerable evidence of renewed interest, both here and in the United States. New editions are being published. His *Journals*, republished by Penguin, have reached and impressed a whole new audience, and his better-known novels and short stories have been constantly in print in both prestige and popular versions. Even his lesser-known novels are reappearing: Hamish Hamilton reprinted *A Man from the North* in 1973, its first appearance for many years. Successful television adaptations have been made of *Imperial Palace* and *The Price of Love*. Extravaganzas such as *Mr Prohack* have proved popular as radio serials. In Stoke-on-Trent, Peter Cheeseman, the director of the Victoria Theatre, and his wife Joyce, have made several successful adaptations of his work – *Jock-on-the-go*, adapted from *Jock-at-a-Venture*, and a version of *Anna of the Five Towns* were outstandingly good, and reached a large local audience. Peter and Joyce Cheeseman were warned, when they first started to think of adapting Bennett, that they wouldn't get an audience, as he was very unpopular locally, but they persevered, and found that on the contrary audiences were highly enthusiastic, despite the fact that the local newspapers still caustically refer to Fenton, every time it is mentioned, as 'the town that Bennett forgot'. *The Card*, which has always been popular, and was filmed in 1951 with Alec Guiness in the lead, was scheduled for two more productions – one at Stoke in 1973; one, a musical version, was done by Val May in 1973 at Bristol, and reached the West End. So Bennett is still well remembered, and there is every sign that he will take and maintain his proper place as one of the most readable and versatile of major novelists, a writer much more honest and lasting than Galsworthy, and more perceptive, in many areas, than Wells.

Immediately after his death, however, things looked bad. There was gossip about how little money he had left – the kind of gossip which, while he was alive, had been kept in check by his personality, was now free to flourish. He had been considered to be an immensely rich man, partly because he himself was proud of his own earning capacity and often mentioned it with bravado, and partly because he had always lived in style. As we have seen, he had been unfailingly generous to friends, relations, good causes, protégés, his wife, his employees and his own family. It was speculated that he would leave a very large sum: the London Diarist of the *Standard*, when it was discovered that he had left less than was expected, had to explain that although he was highly paid (sums of £5,000 a year for his *Standard* column, £2,000 for the *Express* serial of *Accident* were mentioned) and although he sold well – 100,000 copies of *Imperial Palace* in the United States – he had never produced a gold mine in the form of a steady big seller like H. G. Wells's *Outline of History*.

In fact, Bennett left £36,600, securities valued at £7,900, copyrights at £4,225, and manuscripts at £7,500 – a sizable but not a vast estate. He had, it was true, earned large amounts, but he had also spent large amounts. And, as he realized very vividly on his last trip with Beaverbrook, as far as wealth went, he was simply not in the Beaverbrook class. However much he had written about financiers (they had featured more and more in his later novels), he did not himself care for or understand high finance; he had no grasp of investments, insurance policies, stocks and shares. £36,600 is not of course a negligible sum of money; he was very far from the hardship which some maliciously suggested, nor had his earning capacity dropped. But much of it was committed to Marguerite. At their separation, he had left her £5,000 out of his capital when he should die, plus the income during her lifetime of two-thirds of his estate once the £5,000 had been paid, a short-sighted and over-generous commitment. In the last years of his life, in January and October 1927, and in December 1928, he had tried to secure Dorothy's future by making over to her the royalties and copyright in eleven of his plays, and by presenting her, in front of witnesses (Swinnerton, his solicitor Geoffrey Russell and Miss Nerney), with forty-seven volumes of manuscripts, and the rights in his unpublished journals. In 1934 Marguerite, who must have been doing very well anyway, disputed the will, claiming that Bennett had had no right to 'divest himself of his possessions during his lifetime' as he had covenanted previously to leave her 'a portion of that of which he died possessed'. After an appeal, which turned on whether or not an unfinished journal could be given as a gift or whether it remained in essence part of the estate, Marguerite lost, and his evident wishes were upheld.

Even so, the estate was not as great as Bennett himself must have expected, because, whatever his fears of the Depression, and whatever the gloom spread by George Doran, he could not have predicted the overwhelming slump in the book trade. Royalties dropped severely. Projected films were never made. There were some new posthumous publications – *Dream of Destiny* and some short stories were published in 1932, and the *Journals*, edited by Newman Flower, began to appear. But compared with Bennett's full working income, these were small matters.

The *Evening Standard*, naturally, reported Bennett's illness, death, funeral and memorial service at St Clement Dane in great detail. It had lost one of its most popular contributors. (Harold Nicolson started a new series of *Books and Persons* on 26 March, the day of his death.) He was cremated at Golders Green Crematorium. The hymn sung was 'Rock of Ages', which Hilda Lessways had so fervently admired when it was sung at the Sunday School centenary in *Clayhanger*. The ashes were later carried up to Burslem by his brother Frank in a third-class railway carriage, and interred in Burslem Cemetery. At this point in the scene Marguerite reappears, reinstated at least with the Bennett family, as she had never been with Bennett himself. Photographs of the interment show her and Mrs Beardmore marching vigorously along in black robes and curious funereal hats, looking indomitable, while Frank looks worried and faded. It is a strange fact that

353

Marguerite managed to persuade some of the Bennett family and many of the people of the Five Towns that she was a wronged widow, deserving of respect: she was to haunt the district long after his death.

The ashes now lie in the Bennett family grave in Burslem cemetery, covered by a most unattractive grey granite obelisk, on which the day of his death is incorrectly inscribed. The cemetery itself, where the lovers used to walk before the parks were built, is attractive enough, and behind it rises the old slag heap, now gently flattened and rounded, and covered in grass.

For weeks after his death, the 'Londoner's Diary' in the *Standard* was full of details about Bennett, about his American obituaries, about the dangers of drinking water in Paris. His fate was treated as an awful warning for travellers. Viscount Castlerosse wrote a long personal memoir, which was published on 27 March, describing his shyness, his peacock clothes, his good humour, his friendship with Beaverbrook. The flags of the Five Towns were flown at half-mast on the day of his death, and his ashes ended up there, but it was in London that he was most missed. 'All London will miss him,' said Rebecca West. And it did.

Nevertheless, his death was followed by rumours, and his literary reputation, in the following years, declined. Some of his old friends, like Wells, managed in future years to give an impression of estrangement, which a close study of the last years of their friendship does not support. In his *Experiment in Autobiography*, published in 1934, Wells is peculiarly cool and analytic about Bennett, and says that their paths diverged in later life. Why he said this, it is hard to imagine: perhaps it is simply a reflection of Wells's own increasing and general disillusion. He speaks warmly of few, analytically of all. And one must remember that this too was Bennett's pose, when speaking of those he loved. The deaths of Jane Wells and Rickards had brought from him no warmth or eloquence in his journal. Instead, he had commented on the 'world of sickness and tragedy' that Rickards lived in, and the lack of A1 people at Jane Wells's funeral. Wells, in fact, when asked for a tribute to Bennett for the occasion of the unveiling of a plaque on Bennett's birthplace in Hope Street in 1932, wrote to the *Staffordshire Sentinel*: 'I find it difficult to send you a message.' He was, Wells says, one of his most intimate and reliable friends, and 'his death had left a permanent gap in my life. I feel it far too acutely to write fine things about it.' (Shaw, on the same occasion, sent in a warm appraisal of Bennett as one of the first writers to appreciate provincial life.)

Another friend who managed to show signs of coldness was George Doran. They had been growing apart during the last year or two of Bennett's life,

Doran's career was insecure, and he was an influential, busy gossip. He may well have spread rumours about Bennett's last years. There was also Marguerite, who had by no means abandoned the cause of proving her devotion to her husband, and her rights in him, even though he was now dead. She wanted to play the role of Veuve Arnold Bennett, and she did. Bennett had left plenty of problems behind him; even Swinnerton, one of his closest friends, was to become involved in a dispute about his will.

In literary terms, it was almost inevitable that his reputation should decline. He had been a popular writer: his popularity was certain to turn against him.

Dorothy was left alone, with anxieties about the future and the present. She comforted herself by telling herself that Bennett had at least been spared the slow decline which he had feared, which had killed his father, and which was to kill two of his sisters. She was a woman of strength and character, and she and Virginia survived, courageously, through what must have been a very difficult period. Some of their old friends she kept in touch with; others, like Wells and Doran, she no longer trusted. She went to America for some time, and now lives in Chelsea. Virginia, married with three children, lives in France. She married a Frenchman, continuing the Bennett enthusiasm for the country. Marguerite, after her husband's death, returned to France, to her country house at Lolière, near her birthplace of Négrepelisse, where she lived till old age, talking to the end of her famous English husband who had so foolishly quarrelled with her. The house was furnished with the spoils of Comarques, and there she would write poetry, give poetry recitals and entertain neighbours and visitors – oddly enough, she seems to have been much visited by younger members of the Bennett family, who would go off to see Tante Marguerite, partly out of sympathy perhaps, and partly out of curiosity. Or perhaps they were simply displaying respectable Bennett solidarity with the legitimate widow. It is hard to tell. She died in 1960, thus finishing half a lifetime of ambiguous devotion.

Even today, more than forty years after his death, memories of those old conflicts still flourish. In the Five Towns, which were his own creation, Bennett's reputation has been mixed. Was he not an unfaithful husband? No matter how great the provocation, such a fact weighs heavily in the balance, even against a great local author. A mixture of pride and disrespect still lingers. He would have understood it perfectly: he had been reared in this world of harsh moral judgements, and a few years before his death, when he took his sister Sissie to see a play by Galsworthy, he comments on her 'complete confusion between moral and artistic perceptions',[14] and her

355

inability to enjoy a play wherein anyone did anything wrong, such as drink (she was a teetotaller), because she couldn't 'like' the characters. Just as Mrs Bennett didn't 'like' Carmen, so her neighbours felt they couldn't really 'like' Bennett. Compared with the lives of many of his contemporaries, Bennett's life was blameless and honourable in the extreme. It was his ill-luck that his family and his native town should judge him by a rigorous standard which he had himself criticized many times, but which had in its turn formed his character and made him what he was.

Probably he would not have minded; probably he would have been amused. He had, in his living, escaped from the shadow of the past. He had, against all odds, been generous rather than mean, tolerant rather than intolerant, cheerful rather than depressed, modest rather than vain. He was not without faults: domestically, he must have been much of the time quite impossible, with his rigid timetables, his insomnia and dyspepsia, his irritability about the placing of furniture. His attitude towards women, despite the great understanding of them shown in some of his books, was strange. He was not logical, passionately though he praised reason: who, with a fixed dislike of noise, would move into a flat over a railway station? But these are faults quite insignificant when compared with the rest of his nature. It is a pity that the end of his life should have been so sad, though the last scene of a biography can never be cheerful. His death was a tragic and senseless waste. One cannot help feeling that he left the world anxious for the future of Dorothy and Virginia, rather than at a moment of triumph and success. But although his death was a tragedy, his life, as he said himself, was an immense romance. He triumphed over poverty and heredity, and the ending of the story is irrelevant. Respect and affection for him grow with acquaintance, and my sadness at reporting his death is rather like his own feelings about one of his characters – when he had just finished *Lord Raingo*, Dorothy (according to the *Standard*'s 'London Diary', 27 March) said to him that he must be feeling triumphant and he said no, he wasn't, for: 'I had come to like Raingo enormously. I can't help feeling depressed now that the man is dead.'

So I, too, feel depressed, unreasonably enough, by his death. He was a great writer from a stony land, and he was also one of the kindest and most unselfish of men. Many a time, rereading a novel, reading a letter or a piece of his journal, I have wanted to shake his hand, or to thank him, to say well done. I have written this instead.

Source Notes

Chapter 1

1 Gordon Rhodes, report on reclamation, *Guardian* (21 June 1971).

2 *Clayhanger*, Book 1, ch. 14, 'The Architect'.

3 Letter from A.B. to George Moore of 24 December 1920, in *Letters*, ed. Hepburn (London 1968), vol. 3.

4 George Moore, *A Mummer's Wife* (London 1918), ch. 4.

5 Harold Owen, *The Staffordshire Potter* (London 1901), appendix 5, 'Where and How the Workers Live', p. 337.

6 *The Journals of Arnold Bennett* (London 1932), entry for 10 September 1897.

7 *Leonora*, ch. 2, 'Meshach and Hannah'.

8 Owen, *op. cit.*, p. 339.

9 Samuel Scriven, *Report on the Staffordshire Potteries* (London 1843), vol. 14, C 2–5.

10 *Ibid.*, p. C 78.

11 John Wesley, *Journal* (London 1827), entries for 19 March 1760 and 20 June 1763.

12 *These Twain*, Book 1, ch. 3, 'Attack and Repulse'.

13 Robert Peel, quoted by L. Tyerman in *John Wesley* (London 1870), vol. 3, p. 499.

14 Wesley, *op. cit.*

15 William Shaw, *When I Was a Child, Recollections of an Old Potter* (London 1903), ch. 1, 'Education', p. 7.

16 *Ibid.*, ch. 5, 'My Native Town', p. 45.

17 Samuel Bamford, *Autobiography* (London 1849), vol. 1, 'Early Days'.

18 T.R.Roberts, *Arnold Bennett's Five Towns Origins* (Stoke-on-Trent, 1967).

19 Dr Andrew Ure, *The Philosophy of Manufactures* (London 1835), Book 3, ch. 1, p. 301.

20 M.McKendrick, 'Josiah Wedgwood and Factory Discipline', *Historical Journal*, IV, 1 (1961), p. 46.

21 E.P.Thompson, *The Making of the English Working Class* (London 1963), part 2, ch. 11.

22 *The Religious Interregnum.*

23 *Ibid.*

24 Roberts, *op. cit.*

25 *Clayhanger*, Book 2, ch. 12, 'The Top of the Square'.

26 *Ibid.*, Book 2, ch. 12, 'The Oldest Sunday School Teacher'.

27 *The Old Wives' Tale*, Book 1, ch. 5, 'The Traveller'.

28 *These Twain*, Book 3, ch. 18, 'Auntie Hamps Sentenced'.

29 *Anna of the Five Towns.*

30 *Ibid.*

31 *Our Women*, ch. 5, 'Salary Earning Girls'.

32 Shaw, *op. cit.*, ch. 23, 'The Pursuit of Knowledge', p. 225.

33 *The Old Wives' Tale*, Book 1, ch. 4, 'Elephant'.

34 *Leonora*, ch. 6, 'Comic Opera'.

35 *Journals*, entry for 18 July 1910.

36 *Helen With the High Hand*, ch. 1.

37 'Clay in the Hands of the Potter', *Windsor Magazine* (1913).

38 *Journals*, entry for 24 December 1899.

Chapter 2

1 *Journals*, entry for 13 May 1901.

2 'The Making of Me', *Daily Express* (6 June 1928).

3 *Journals*, entry for 26 February 1901.

4 'The Making of Me', *loc. cit.*

5 *Ibid.*

6 *Journals*, entry for 13 May 1901.

7 'The Making of Me', *loc. cit.*

8 *Ibid.*

9 *Clayhanger*, Book 2, ch. 3, 'The New House'.

10 *Ibid.*

11 *Anna of the Five Towns*, ch. 2, 'The Miser's Daughter'.

12 Angus Wilson, *The Wild Garden* (London 1963).

13 *The Truth about an Author* (London 1903), p. 14.

14 Mrs F.Beardmore, *Sunday Chronicle* (22 December 1929).

15 *A Man from the North*, section 15, p. 90.

16 *Clayhanger*, Book 1, ch. 1.

17 *Ibid.*

18 'My Education', *Keele* (22 January 1930).

19 Article in school magazine, *The Median*, 1909.

20 H.K.Hales, *The Autobiography of 'The Card'* (London 1936), p. 14.

21 'The Making of Me', *loc. cit.*
22 *The Truth about an Author*, p. 25.
23 Roberts, *op. cit.*
24 *Leonora*, ch. 1, 'The Household at Hillport'.
25 *Whom God hath Joined*, ch. 2, 'Rogue's Alley', p. 58.
26 *Ibid.*, p. 57.
27 *The Card*, ch. 2, 'Widow Hullins' House'.
28 *Clayhanger*, Book 2, ch. 21, 'The Marriage'.
29 *The Truth about an Author*, pp. 28–30.
30 *Hilda Lessways*, Book 1, ch. 8, 'Hilda's World'.

Chapter 3

1 *A Man from the North*, section 1, p. 1.
2 *Whom God hath Joined*, ch. 6, 'Renée', p. 161.
3 *Clayhanger*, Book 4, ch. 3.
4 Winifred Gerin, *Evolution of Genius*, ch. 7, 'The Drudge's Life'.
5 *Hilda Lessways*, Book 2, ch. 1, 'Sin'.
6 Louis Tillier, *The Sources of Arnold Bennett's Novels* (Paris 1949), p. 17.
7 *The Truth about an Author*, p. 48.
8 Reginald Pound, *Arnold Bennett: A Biography* (London 1952), p. 76.
9 Letter from A.B. to Douglas Baddeley of 8 June 1889, in Hepburn, *op. cit.*, vol. 2.
10 Letter from A.B. to Douglas Baddeley of 9 July 1889, in *ibid.*
11 *The Truth about an Author*, p. 55.
12 *Clayhanger*, Book 1, ch. 14, 'The Architect'.
13 *The Old Wives' Tale*, Book 2, ch. 8, 'The Proudest Mother'.
14 Frederic Marriott, *My Association with Arnold Bennett* (Keele 1967).
15 *These Twain*, Book 1, ch. 9, 'The Week-End'.
16 *The Truth about an Author*, p. 59.
17 *Ibid.*, p. 60.
18 Letter from George Sturt to A.B.
19 *The Truth about an Author*, p. 76.
20 *Ibid.*, p. 55.
21 George Paston, *A Modern Amazon* (London 1894).
22 Letter from A.B. to George Sturt of 11 December 1895, in *Letters*, vol 2.
23 'Fame and Fiction', essay on Silas Hocking (London 1901).
24 George Sturt, *Journals* (Cambridge 1967), vol. 1, pp. 221, 453.
25 Letter from A.B. to George Sturt of 28 January 1896, in *Letters*, vol. 2.
26 Letter from A.B. to George Sturt of 28 October 1894, in *Letters*, vol. 2.
27 Letter from A.B. to George Sturt of 10 May 1895, in *Letters*, vol. 2.
28 Letter from A.B. to George Sturt of 5 January 1899, in *Letters*, vol. 2.

29 Letter from A.B. to George Sturt of 29 May 1896, in *Letters*, vol. 2.

30 Letter from George Sturt to A.B. in *Letters*, vol. 2, p. 53, quoted in footnote.

31 Letter from A.B. to John Rickards of 27 November 1898, in *Letters*, vol. 2.

32 Letter from A.B. to John Rickards of 9 October 1900, in *Letters*, vol. 2.

33 Letter from A.B. to George Sturt of 9 April 1900, in *Letters*, vol. 2.

34 Letter from A.B. to George Sturt of 11 November 1895, in *Letters*, vol. 2.

35 *The Truth about an Author*, p. 97.

36 *Journals*, entry for 15 May 1896.

37 Letter from A.B. to George Sturt of 29 May 1896, in *Letters*, vol. 2.

38 *Journals*, entry for 28 May 1896.

39 Letter from A.B. to George Sturt of 29 May 1896, in *Letters*, vol. 2.

40 *A Man from the North*, section 32, p. 177.

41 *The Truth about an Author*, p. 97.

42 *A Man from the North*, section, 29, p. 167.

43 *King Albert's Book*, Daily Telegraph Belgian Fund (London 1914), p. 37.

44 *Op. cit.*, 'The Return'.

45 *Ibid.*

46 *Journals*, entry for 29 September 1896.

47 Letter from A.B. to George Sturt of 28 September 1896, in *Letters*, vol. 2.

48 *Journals*, entry for 15 October 1896.

49 *Journals*, entry for 18 June 1897.

50 *Journals*, entry for 2 September 1897.

51 *Ibid.*

52 *Journals*, entry for 30 September 1897.

53 *Journals*, entry for 5 October 1897.

54 *Journals*, entry for 19 December 1897.

55 'A Personal Sketch', in *The Art of A. E. Rickards* (London 1920).

56 *Journals*, entry for 23 December 1909.

57 Fragment of a letter from A.B. to A.E.Rickards, autumn 1910, in *Letters*, vol. 2.

58 *Journals*, entry for 22 May 1901.

59 *Journals*, entry for 23 October 1897.

60 Nikolaus Pevsner, *London*, vol. 1. *The Cities of London & Westminster* (London 1957).

61 *The Art of A. E. Rickards.*

62 *Journals*, entry for 29 October 1897.

Chapter 4

1 *Journals*, entry for 25 October 1897.

2 *The Truth about an Author*, p. 112.

3 *Ibid.*

4 *Ibid.*

5 Eden Phillpotts, *The Children of the Mist* (London 1898).
6 *Journals*, entry for 8 November 1898.
7 Letter from A.B. to George Sturt of 10 April 1898, in *Letters*, vol. 2.
8 *Journals*, entry for 22 February 1899.
9 Letter from A.B. to J.B.Pinker of 4 March 1907, in *Letters*, vol. 2.
10 *The Ghost*, ch. 19, 'The Intercession'.
11 *The Truth about an Author*, p. 158.
12 *The Grand Babylon Hotel*, ch. 6, 'In the Gold Room'.
13 *Ibid.*, ch. 10, 'Mr Sampson Levi Bids Prince Eugen Good-Morning'.
14 Letter from A.B. to William Morris Colles of 10 February 1902, in *Letters*, vol. 2.

Chapter 5

1 *Journals*, entry for 18 September 1898.
2 Doris Langley Moore, *E. Nesbit* (London 1933).
3 Letter from A.B. to Mrs H.Penrose of 24 January 1899, in *Letters*, vol. 2.
4 Letter from A.B. to Thomas Humberstone of 17 December 1899, in *Letters*, vol. 2.
5 Letter from A.B. to Emily Phillpotts of 22 January 1900, in *Letters*, vol. 2.
6 Letter from A.B. to George Sturt of 13 February 1900, in *Letters*, vol. 2.
7 *The Truth about an Author*, p. 206.
8 *Journals*, entry for 4 November 1899.
9 *Clayhanger*, Book 3, ch. 1, 'After a Funeral'.
10 *Ibid.*, ch. 2, 'The Conclave'.
11 *Ibid.*, ch. 12, 'Revenge'.
12 *Journals*, entry for 5 January 1900.
13 Letter from A.B. to George Sturt of 13 February 1900, in *Letters*, vol. 2.
14 Letter from A.B. to H.G.Wells of September/October 1897, in *Letters*, vol. 2.
15 Letter from A.B. to H.G.Wells of 2 August 1900, in *Letters*, vol. 2.
16 Letter from A.B. to T.Humberstone of 14 May 1901, in *Letters*, vol. 2.
17 *Clayhanger*, Book 3, ch. 14, 'The Watch'.
18 *Ibid.*
19 Letter from A.B. to George Sturt of 18 February 1896, in *Letters*, vol. 2.
20 *Anna of the Five Towns*, ch. 13, 'The Bazaar'.
21 *Ibid.*, ch. 14, 'End of a Simple Soul'.
22 *Ibid.*, ch. 11, 'The Downfall'.
23 *Ibid.*
24 'The Making of Me'.
25 Letter from George Sturt to A.B. of 15 September 1902, in *Letters*, vol. 2.
26 Letter from A.B. to George Sturt of 4 October 1902, in *Letters*, vol. 2.
27 *A Good Woman*, one of three one-act plays in *Polite Farces*.

28 *A Question of Sex*, in *Polite Farces.*
29 *Journals*, entry for 10 November 1899.
30 *The Truth about an Author*, p. 177.
31 *Ibid.*, p. 165.
32 'The Crisis in the Theatre', *Cupid and Commonsense* (1912), preface.
33 *Journals*, entry for 27 January 1901.
34 *Journals*, entry for 17 May 1901.
35 Letter from A.B. to W.Kennerley of 8 April 1902, in Pound, *op. cit.*, p. 123.

Chapter 6

1 *Journals*, entry for 29 September 1903.
2 *Journals*, entry for 2 December 1903.
3 *Journals*, entry for 23 November 1903.
4 *Journals*, entry for 3 November 1903.
5 *Journals*, entry for 18 November 1903.
6 Roger Shattuck, *The Banquet Years*, ch. 7 (London 1959).
7 Clive Bell, *Old Friends* (London 1956), ch. 9, 'Paris'.
8 D.W.Buchanan, *James Wilson Morrice, a Biography* (Toronto 1936).
9 'Paris Flats', in *Things That Have Interested Me.*
10 Somerset Maugham, *Life and Letters* (June 1931).
11 Arthur Mizener, *The Saddest Story, a Biography of Ford Madox Ford* (London 1972).
12 Violet Hunt, *American Bookman* (August 1932).
13 Articles on marriage in *T.P.'s Weekly* (30 October and 6 November 1903).
14 *Journals*, entry for 27 January 1909.
15 Letter from A.B. to J.B.Pinker of 22 November 1903, in *Letters*, vol. 2.
16 Letter from A.B. to J.B.Pinker of 14 April 1904, in *Letters*, vol. 2.
17 *Journals*, entry for 21 October 1903.
18 *Leonora*, ch. 7, 'The Departure'.
19 *Ibid.*, ch. 10, 'In the Garden'.
20 *Ibid.*
21 *Journals*, entry for 28 September 1903.
22 *A Great Man*, ch. 29, 'The President'.
23 *Ibid.*, ch. 24, 'Cosette'.
24 *Ibid.*
25 *Journals*, entry for 26 January 1904.
26 *Journals*, entry for 30 January 1904.
27 *Journals*, entry for 23 December 1903.
28 *Journals*, entry for 26 November 1904.
29 Letter from A.B. to J.B.Pinker of 8 April 1904, in *Letters*, vol. 2.
30 Frank Swinnerton, *Background with Chorus* (London 1956), p. 128.

31 *Journals*, entry for 18 March 1904.

32 *Hugo*, part 2, ch. 19, 'What the Phonograph Said'.

33 *Journals*, entry for 11 May 1904.

34 *Journals*, entry for 14 May 1904.

35 *Journals*, entry for 27 May 1904.

36 Letter from A.B. to George Sturt of 22 June 1904, in *Letters*, vol. 2.

37 *Journals*, entry for 27 June 1904.

38 *Journals*, entry for 2 January 1905.

39 *Journals*, entry for 29 November 1904.

40 *Journals*, entry for 28 February 1905.

41 *The Athenaeum* (4 March 1905).

42 Letter from A.B. to George Sturt of 22 June 1904, in *Letters*, vol. 2.

43 *Sacred and Profane Love*, part 2, ch. 2, 'Three Human Hearts'.

44 Letter from A.B. to H.G.Wells of 30 September 1905, in *Letters*, vol. 2.

45 *Journals*, entry for 18 October 1910.

46 Letter from A.B. to H.G.Wells of 30 September 1905, in *Letters*, vol. 2.

47 Swinnerton, *An Autobiography* (Hutchinson 1937), ch. 5, p. 121.

48 Letter from A.B. to J.B.Pinker of 5 April 1905, in *Letters*, vol. 2.

49 Paul Bourget, *Divorce* (London 1904).

Chapter 7

1 *Journals*, entry for 6 May 1904.

2 *Journals*, entry for 10 May 1906.

3 Anne Greene, *With Much Love* (London 1949).

4 *Ibid.*

5 Letter from A.B. to Eden Phillpotts of 21 June 1906, in *Letters*, vol. 2.

6 Letter from A.B. to Violet Hunt of 21 June 1906, in *Letters*, vol. 2.

7 *Journals*, entry for 3 August 1906.

8 Letter from A.B. to Violet Hunt of 11 or 18 August 1906, in *Letters*, vol. 2.

9 Pound, *op. cit.*, p. 164.

10 Letter from A.B. to J.B.Pinker of 7 or 14 August 1906, in *Letters*, vol. 2.

11 'Paris Flats'.

12 *Journals*, entry for 3 October 1906.

13 *Journals*, entry for 21 September 1906.

14 *Journals*, entry for 9 January 1907.

15 Agnes Farley, *Ashdod* (London 1907).

16 *Journals*, entry for 21 January 1907.

17 Letter from Lytton Strachey to Dora Carrington of 28 June 1921, quoted by Michael Holroyd in *Lytton Strachey. A Critical Biography* (London 1967).

18 *Journals*, entry for 19 April 1907.

19 *Journals*, entry for 3 May 1907.

20 *Journals*, entry for 11 May 1907.

21 *Journals*, entry for 27 May 1907.

22 Letter from A.B. to Marguerite Bennett of June 1907, in *Arnold Bennett in Love*, ed. George and Jean Beardmore (London 1972).

23 Letter from A.B. to H.G.Wells of 1 July 1907, in *Letters*, vol. 2.

24 Letter from A.B. to J.B.Pinker of 11 July 1907, in *Letters*, vol. 2.

25 Letter from A.B. to J.B.Pinker of 26 November 1904, in *Letters*, vol. 2.

26 *Journals*, entry for 14 May 1907.

27 *Journals*, entry for 27 March 1907.

28 *Journals*, entry for 19 April 1907.

29 *Journals*, entry for 15 November 1903.

30 'The Death of Simon Fuge'.

31 *Ibid.*

32 *Ibid.*

33 *Journals*, entry for 22 December 1907.

34 *Journals*, entry for 15 February 1904.

35 *The Old Wives' Tale*, preface.

36 Francisque Sarcey, *Le Siège de Paris* (Paris 1871).

37 Jules Claretie, *L'Histoire de la Révolution de 1870–1871* (Paris 1872). See particularly plates on pp. 393 and 396, of butchers and elephants.

38 *Journals*, entry for 5 April 1908.

39 Letter from A.B. to George Sturt of 4 November 1907, in *Letters*, vol. 2.

40 Letter from A.B. to Tertia Kennerley, in Mary Kennerley's possession, quoted by Kilner E.Roby in *A Writer at War* (Louisiana 1972), p. 75.

41 *Journals*, entry for 4 May 1908.

42 *Journals*, entry for 29 May 1908.

43 *Ibid.*

44 *Journals*, entry for 25 May 1908.

45 *Ibid.*

46 *Buried Alive*, ch. 6, 'A Putney Morning'.

47 Marguerite Bennett, *Arnold Bennett* (London 1925), pp. 35–6.

48 Pauline Smith, *A.B., A Minor Marginal Note* (London 1933), p. 22.

49 *Journals*, entry for 11 June 1910.

Chapter 8

1 Letter from A.B. to J.B.Pinker of 29 November 1908, in *Letters*, vol. 2.

2 Letter from H.G.Wells to A.B. of October 1908, in *Arnold Bennett and H. G. Wells*, ed. Harris Wilson (London 1960).

3 Letter from H.G.Wells to A.B. of November 1908, in *ibid*.

4 Letter from A.B. to H.G.Wells of 18 November 1908, in *Letters*, vol. 2.

5 Letter from Frank Harris to A.B. of 27 November 1908, in *Letters*, vol. 2.

6 *Ibid.*

7 Letter from A.B. to Frank Harris of 30 November 1908, in *Letters*, vol. 2.

8 Edward Garnett, review in *The Nation* (21 November 1908).

9 Letter from A.B. to J.B.Pinker of 8 November 1908, in *Letters*, vol. 1.

10 *Journals*, entry for 2 March 1909.

11 Hales, *op. cit.*, p. 244.

12 *Buried Alive*, ch. 7, 'Tears'.

13 *Ibid.*, ch. 6, 'Collapse of the Putney System'.

14 *Ibid.*, ch. 24, 'Culmination'.

15 *Ibid.*

16 *The Glimpse*, ch. 15, 'Towards Oblivion'.

17 *Ibid.*, ch. 1, 'The Concert'.

18 *Ibid.*, ch. 23, 'The Palace'.

19 *Ibid.*, ch. 12, 'In the Study'.

20 *New Age* (11 February 1909).

21 *New Age* (1 April 1909).

22 Ford Madox Ford, 'Women and Men', *The Little Review* (May 1918).

23 Swinnerton, *Background with Chorus*.

24 *The Regent*, ch. 9, 'The First Night'.

25 *What the Public Wants*, Act 1.

26 Letter from A.B. to Doris Keane of 4 September 1916, in *Letters*, vol. 2.

27 Max Beerbohm, review in *The Saturday Review* (8 May 1909).

28 J.E.Barton, review in *New Age* (13 May 1909).

29 Letter from A.B. to Lee Matthews of 24 June 1909, in *Letters*, vol. 2.

30 *Journals*, entry for 8 March 1910.

31 *Daily Mail* (7 October 1911).

32 Hector Bolitho, *Marie Tempest* (London 1936).

33 *Ibid.*

34 Pauline Smith, *op. cit.*

35 *Ibid.*, pp. 17–18.

36 *Ibid.*, p. 19.

37 Preface to Pauline Smith, *The Little Karoo* (London 1925).

38 *Journals*, entry for 5 December 1909.

39 *Ibid.*

40 *Journals*, entry for 2 January 1910.

41 *Journals*, entry for 17 December 1908.

42 *Journals*, entry for 21 January 1910.

43 *English Review* (February 1910).

44 Review of Harold Owen's *The Staffordshire Potter* in *Manchester Guardian* (1901), quoted by Shaw, *op. cit.*

45 Shaw, *op. cit.*, ch. 5, 'My Native Town'.

46 *Ibid.*, ch. 6, 'A New Situation'.

47 *Clayhanger*, Book 1, ch. 4, 'The Child Man'.
48 *Ibid.*
49 *Journals*, entry for 23 June 1910.
50 *Florentine Journal*, entry for 1 April 1910.
51 *Ibid.*
52 Pauline Smith, *op. cit.*, p. 178.
53 *Journals*, entry for 7 April 1910.

Chapter 9

1 *Journals*, entry for 16 August 1910.
2 *Journals*, entry for 19 September 1910.
3 *Journals*, entry for 22 September 1910.
4 Ian Dunlop, *The Shock of the New* (London 1972), ch. 4, 'The Post-Impressionists'.
5 William Blunt, *My Diaries*.
6 Letter from A.B. in *The Nation* (10 December 1910).
7 *Journals*, entry for 2 October 1910.
8 *Hilda Lessways*, Book 1, ch. 5, 'Mrs Lessways' Shrewdness'.
9 *Ibid.*, Book 1, ch. 1, 'An Event in Mr Skellorn's Life'.
10 *Ibid.*, Book 1, ch. 3, 'Mr Cannon'.
11 *Ibid.*, Book 5, ch. 2, 'Some Secret History'.
12 Letter from A.B. to *Manchester Guardian* (10 April 1910).
13 André Gide, *Journals* (London 1947–9), entry for February 1912.
14 *Journals*, entry for 21 April 1910.
15 Letter from A.B. to the Duchess of Sutherland of 23 June 1911, in *Letters*, vol. 2.
16 E.Knoblock, *Round the Room* (London 1939).
17 *Ibid.*
18 E. Knoblock
19 Letter from A.B. to Lee Mathews of 24 August 1911, in *Letters*, vol. 2.
20 Letter from A.B. to E.Knoblock of 24 August 1911, *ibid.*
21 Letter from A.B. to F.Marriott of 22 November 1911, *ibid.*
22 *Those United States*, ch. 1, 'The First Night'.
23 *Journals*, entry for 21 October 1911.
24 *Those United States*, ch. 8, 'Human Citizens'.
25 *Journals*, entry for 27 October 1911.
26 *Journals*, entry for 15 November 1911.
27 *Ibid.*
28 *Journals*, entry for 2 December 1911.
29 *Journals*, entry for 23 January 1912.
30 Letter from A.B. to Lee Mathews of 28 February 1912, in *Letters*, vol. 2.

31 *The Times* (6 March 1912).

32 Rupert Hart-Davis, *Hugh Walpole* (London 1952), p. 88.

33 John Gielgud, *Distinguished Company* (London 1972).

34 *Journals*, entry for 4 March 1912.

35 Letter from A.B. to Lee Mathews of 3 April 1912, in *Letters*, vol. 2.

36 André Gide, *Journals*, entry for 8 May 1912.

37 *Journals*, entry for 27 June 1913.

38 *From the Log of the Velsa*, ch. 1, pp. 5–6.

39 *Ibid.*, ch. 6, p. 60.

40 Letter from A.B. to Mrs E.Herzog of 14 December 1912, in *Letters*, vol. 2.

41 *Journals*, entry for 31 December 1912.

42 *Ibid.*

43 Letter from A.B. to Lee Mathews of 3 April 1912, in *Letters*, vol. 2.

44 Letter from A.B. to Cedric Sharpe of 13 September 1913, in *Letters*, vol. 2.

45 Charles Sarolea, in *Everyman* (18 October 1912).

46 Letter from A.B. to *Everyman* (1 November 1912).

47 *Journals*, entry for 31 December 1912.

48 Letter from A.B. to J.B.Pinker of 20 January 1913, in *Letters*, vol. 2.

49 *Journals*, entry for 31 May 1913.

50 *From the Log of the Velsa*, ch. 10, p. 108.

51 *Ibid.*

52 *Ibid.*, ch. 11, p. 115.

53 *Journals*, entry for 31 August 1913.

54 *The Price of Love*, ch. 19, 'Rachel and Mr. Horrocleave'.

55 Letter from J.B.Pinker to A.B. of 2 December 1914, in *Letters*, vol. 1.

56 Letter from A.B. to J.B.Pinker of 16 July 1914, *ibid.*

57 *Journals*, entry of 18 January 1914.

58 *Journals*, entry of 24 November 1913.

59 *Journals*, entry for 21 February 1914.

60 *Journals*, entry for 22 April 1914.

61 Letter from A.B. to Mrs Herzog of 14 April 1912, in *Letters*, vol. 2.

62 Mrs Parnell, review of *Life of Parnell* in *The Times Literary Supplement* (21 May 1914).

63 *Hilda Lessways*, Book 2, ch. 3, 'Journey to Bleakridge'.

64 *Clayhanger*, Book 4, ch. 13, 'Her Heart'.

65 *These Twain*, Book 2, ch. 12, 'Dartmoor'.

66 *Ibid.*

67 *Ibid.*, Book 1, ch. 8, 'The Family at Home'.

68 *Journals*, entry for 20 November 1914.

69 *Journals*, entry for 27 November 1914.

70 Hart-Davis, *op. cit.*, p. 103.

71 *These Twain*, Book 3, ch. 18, 'Auntie Hamps Sentenced'.

Chapter 10

1 *Journals*, entry for 21 August 1914.
2 *Journals*, entry for 8 August 1914.
3 Letter from H.G.Wells to *The Times* (31 October 1914).
4 Letter from A.B. to *The Times* (3 December 1914).
5 Letter from H.G.Wells to *The Times* (5 December 1914).
6 Letter from H.G.Wells to *The Times* (31 October 1914).
7 *Journals*, entry for 6 December 1914.
8 *Journals*, entry for 16 December 1914.
9 Letter from A.B. to Hugh Walpole of 1 April 1915, in *Letters*, vol. 2.
10 *Journals*, entry for 23 March 1915.
11 Letter from A.B. to Mrs Herzog of 27 May 1915, in *Letters*, vol. 2.
12 Roby, *op. cit.*, ch. 3, p. 77.
13 *Journals*, entry for 13 June 1915.
14 *The Lion's Share*, ch. 12, 'Widowhood in the Studio'.
15 *Ibid.*, ch. 21, 'Jane'.
16 *Ibid.*, ch. 12, 'Widowhood in the Studio'.
17 *Ibid.*
18 Letter from A.B. to *New Age* (end of January 1911).
19 *Our Women*, ch. 5, 'Women as Charmers'.
20 *Ibid.*, ch. 4, 'Are Men Superior to Women?'.
21 *Journals*, entry for 23 June 1915.
22 *Journals*, entry for 12 July 1915.
23 *Over There.*
24 *Ibid.*
25 *Ibid.*
26 *Ibid.*
27 *Ibid.*
28 Letter from A.B. to H.G.Wells of 8 July 1916, in *Letters*, vol. 3.
29 *Journals*, entry for 21 August 1915.
30 Articles in *Daily News* (26 August, 9, 15, 30 September, 22 October 1915).
31 *Journals*, entry for 12 October 1915.
32 Letter from A.B. to J.B.Pinker of 12 August 1915, in *Letters*, vol. 2.
33 *Ibid.*
34 *Journals*, entry for 30 December 1915.
35 Letter from A.B. to Mrs Herzog of 23 February 1916, in *Letters*, vol. 3.
36 Letter from A.B. to Mrs Herzog of 25 March 1916, *ibid.*
37 Letter from A.B. to Mrs Herzog of 10 September 1916, *ibid.*
38 *Journals*, entry for 3 November 1916.
39 Letter from A.B. to Marguerite Bennett of 15 June 1917, quoted in *Arnold Bennett in Love*, George and Jean Beardmore.

40 *Journals*, entry for 17 December 1917.

41 *Journals*, entry for 27 October 1918.

42 Letter from A.B. to Hugh Walpole of 1 May 1917, in *Letters*, vol. 3.

43 Letter from A.B. to J.B.Pinker of 24 January 1914, *ibid*.

44 Letter from A.B. to Hugh Walpole of 1 May 1917, *ibid*.

45 *The Roll Call*, ch. 5, 'The Tea'.

46 Review in *The Times Literary Supplement* (23 January 1919).

47 *Journals*, entry for 30 October 1918.

48 Review in the *Sunday Chronicle* (14 April 1918).

49 *Journals*, entry for 14 December 1918.

50 *Journals*, entry for 11 January 1918.

51 F.E.Smith (Lord Birkenhead), *My American Visit* (London 1918).

52 Articles in *Daily News* (8, 12, 15 November 1918).

53 Letter from A.B. to Geoffrey Madan of 3 March 1918, in *Letters*, vol. 3.

54 *Journals*, entry for 15 August 1919.

55 Letter from R.Kenney to H.V.Rhodes of 26 August 1938, INF 4/IA P.R.O.

56 *Lord Raingo*, ch. 26, 'The French National'.

57 *The Tatler* (1914).

58 Diana Cooper, *The Rainbow Comes and Goes* (London 1958).

59 Letter from A.B. to J.C.Squire of 29 September 1918, in *Letters*, vol. 3.

60 Letter from A.B. to Mrs Herzog of 7 September 1918, *ibid*.

61 *Journals*, entry for 21 November 1918.

62 A.J.P.Taylor, *Beaverbrook* (London 1972), ch. 7, p. 156.

63 Letter from Lord Beaverbrook to A.B. of 1918, quoted in Hepburn, *op. cit.*, vol. 3, p. 78.

64 *Journals*, entry for 23 October 1918.

Chapter 11

1 *Journals*, entry for 11 April 1919.

2 *Daily Telegraph* (24 April 1919).

3 *Journals*, entry for 4 May 1919.

4 Dudley Barker, *Writer by Trade* (London 1966).

5 Quoted by Barker, *op. cit.*, p. 197.

6 Letter from Marguerite Bennett to A.B. of 18 September 1917, in *Letters*, vol. 3.

7 Barker, *op. cit.*, p. 200.

8 Letter from A.B. to Marguerite Bennett of 29 July 1917, quoted in *Arnold Bennett in Love*.

9 Robert Graves, *Goodbye to All That* (London 1929), ch. 30.

10 John Rothenstein, *Summer's Lease, an Autobiography* (London 1965), part 1, p. 116.

11 Letter from A.B. to Paul Nash of 16 July 1919, in *Letters*, vol. 3.
12 Note for an Exhibition at the Mansard Gallery, August 1919.
13 Letter from A.B. to Paul Nash of 5 November 1919, *ibid.*
14 Letter from A.B. to Thomas Bodkin of 18 September 1919, *ibid.*
15 Letter from A.B. to Hugh Walpole of 12 December 1919, *ibid.*
16 Letter from A.B. to Richard Bennett of 2 March 1920, *ibid.*
17 Letter from A.B. to Hubert Griffith of 25 February 1925, *ibid.*
18 H.G.Wells, *An Experiment in Autobiography* (London 1934), vol. 2, ch. 8.
19 Letter from A.B. to Harriet Cohen of 21 September 1922, in *Letters*, vol. 3.
20 *The Times* (22 March 1922).
21 *Journals*, entry for 15 May 1920.
22 'A Personal Sketch', in *The Art of A. E. Rickards.*
23 Letter from A.B. to Richard Bennett, October 1920, in *Letters*, vol. 3.
24 Marguerite Bennett, *op. cit.*, pp. 124, 125.
25 *Journals*, entry for 8 December 1920.
26 *Journals*, entry for 30 November 1920.
27 Letter from D.H.Lawrence to A.J.Mcleod of 6 October 1912, in *Letters*, vol. 3.
28 Kate Millett, *Sexual Politics* (London 1971), ch. 5, 'D.H.Lawrence'.
29 Frieda Lawrence, *Not I, but the Wind ...* (New York 1934).
30 Virginia Woolf, *Night and Day* (London 1919).
31 *The Pretty Lady*, ch. 23, 'The Call'.

Chapter 12

1 *Journals*, entry for 23 November 1921.
2 Letter from A.B. to Marguerite Bennett of 31 December 1920, in *Letters*, vol. 3.
3 Letter from A.B. to Marguerite Bennett of 4 April 1921, *ibid.*
4 p. 255.
5 Letter from A.B. to John Galsworthy of 28 August 1921, in *Letters*, vol. 3.
6 'Marriage and the Modern Girl', *Sunday Pictorial.*
7 Letter from A.B. to Lord Beaverbrook of 7 November 1921, in *Letters*, vol. 3.
8 Letter from A.B. to Marie Belloc Lowndes of 16 February 1922, in *Letters*, vol. 3.
9 *Our Women.*
10 *Ibid.*
11 *Ibid.*
12 *Ibid.*
13 *Ibid.*
14 *Journals*, entry for 12 May 1925.
15 *Mr Prohack.*

Chapter 13

1 Letter from A.B. to Dorothy Cheston of 1 November 1922, in *A Portrait Done at Home*, by Dorothy Cheston Bennett (London 1935).
2 Dorothy Cheston Bennett, *op. cit.*, p. 33.
3 *Ibid.*, p. 41.
4 *Riceyman Steps*, ch. 11.
5 John Wain, 'The Qualities of Arnold Bennett', *Twentieth Century* (September 1954).
6 Harriet Cohen, *A Bundle of Time* (London 1969).
7 Letter from A.B. to André Gide of 15 August 1923, in *Letters*, vol. 3.
8 Dorothy Cheston Bennett, *op. cit.*, p. 56
9 *Ibid.*
10 *The Adelphi* (July 1923).
11 Letter from A.B. to John Middleton Murry of 10 September 1923, in *Letters*, vol. 3.
12 J.B.Priestley, article in *London Mercury* (February 1924).
13 *Journals*, entry for 18 October 1924.
14 Letter from A.B. to Frank Swinnerton of 12 February 1924, in *Letters*, vol. 3.
15 *Ibid.*
16 Letter from A.B. to André Gide of 25 February 1924, in *Letters*, vol. 3.
17 'Elsie and the Child', (London 1924)
18 *New Age* (8 December 1910).
19 John Middleton Murry, *The Adelphi* (April 1924).
20 *Journals*, entry for 8 May 1926.
21 Letter from A.B. to John Middleton Murry of 1 May 1923, in *Letters*, vol. 3.
22 Letter from A.B. to J.B.Priestley of 5 September 1924, *ibid.*
23 Letter from D.H.Lawrence to Aldous Huxley of 27 March 1928, *ibid.*
24 Ezra Pound, *Hugh Selwyn Mauberley* 'Mr Nixon'). (London 1920),
25 Wyndham Lewis, *The Roaring Queen*, p. 28.
26 Wyndham Lewis, *Blasting and Bombardiering* (London 1937).
27 Lewis, *The Roaring Queen*, p. 80.
28 *Cassell's Weekly* (28 March 1923).
29 *Journals*, entry for 4 November 1926.
30 Virginia Woolf, *A Writer's Diary* (London 1953), entry for 2 December 1930.
31 *Ibid.*
32 *Ibid.*
33 *Daily Express* (17 November 1924).
34 *Ibid.*
35 Marguerite Bennett, *op. cit.*, p. 63.
36 Letter from A.B. to George Doran of about 3 April 1923, in *Letters*, vol. 3.
37 Quentin Bell, *Virginia Woolf* (London 1972), vol. 2, p. 95.

38 Beverley Nichols, *The Sweet and Twenties* (London 1958), p. 157.
39 Compton Mackenzie, *My Life and Times* (London 1963–71), octave 3, pp. 271–2.
40 Ottoline Morrell, *Early Memoirs* (London 1963).
41 *Ibid.*
42 *Journals*, entry for 3 April 1924.
43 Dorothy Cheston Bennett, *op. cit.*, p. 112.

Chapter 14

1 Letter from A.B. to Dorothy Cheston Bennett of 18 August 1925, quoted in *A Portrait Done at Home.*
2 *Ibid.*
3 Letter from A.B. to Dorothy Cheston Bennett of 29 August 1925, quoted in *A Portrait Done at Home.*
4 Letter from A.B. to Jane Wells, of 17 September 1925, in *Letters*, vol. 3.
5 *Journals*, entry for 8 February 1926.
6 *Ibid.*
7 *The Savour of Life*, ch. 1, 'The Discovery of Calais'.
8 *The Old Wives' Tale*, Book 2, ch. 3, 'Cyril'.
9 Letter from A.B. to Harriet Cohen of 20 April 1926, in *Letters*, vol. 3.
10 *Journals*, entry of 11 May 1926.
11 *New York Herald Tribune* (9 May 1926).
12 *Ibid.*
13 Quoted to me by Dorothy Cheston Bennett.
14 F.A.Hornibrook, *The Culture of the Abdomen* (London 1924).
15 *Journals*, entry for 6 April 1925.
16 *Journals*, entry for 20 October 1926.
17 D.H.Lawrence, review in *Calendar* (October 1926).
18 *Journals*, entry for 10 February 1927.
19 *Daily Mail* (25 November 1926).
20 Letter from Aldous Huxley to his father of 31 December 1926, in *Letters of Aldous Huxley*, ed. Grover Smith (London 1969).
21 *Evening Standard* (25 November 1926).
22 Lewis, *The Roaring Queen*, p. 83.
23 *Journals*, entry for 19 August 1927.
24 *Accident*, ch. 7, 'The Tea Car'.
25 *Journals*, entry for 13 July 1927.
26 *Journals*, entry for 29 July 1927.
27 Letter from A.B. to T.S.Eliot of 3 June 1926, in *Letters*, vol. 3.
28 *Journals*, entry of 21 August 1927.
29 *Journals*, entry of 10 October 1927.
30 *Journals*, entry of 2 January 1928.

31 *Evening Standard* (12 January 1928).

32 Letter from A.B. to Richard Bennett of 23 January 1928, in *Letters*, vol. 3.

33 *Journals*, entry of 4 February 1928.

34 *Journals*, entry for 6 September 1928.

35 *Journal, 1929* (London 1930).

36 *Close Up* (December 1927).

37 Somerset Maugham, article in *Life and Letters* (1931).

38 Letter from A.B. to Dorothy Cheston Bennett of 12 August 1929, quoted in *A Portrait Done at Home*.

39 *Daily Express* (4 September 1929).

40 *Journals*, entry for 25 September 1929.

41 Letter from A.B. to Dorothy Cheston Bennett of 30 May 1930, quoted in *A Portrait Done at Home*.

Chapter 15

1 *Journals*, entry for 20 October 1927.

2 *Journals*, entry for 2 February 1928.

3 Letter from A.B. to Ralph Pinker of 6 December 1928, in *Letters*, vol. 3.

4 *Imperial Palace*, ch. 50, 'In the Rain'.

5 *Ibid.*, ch. 19, 'Powder and Rouge'.

6 *Ibid.*, ch. 66, 'Her Letter'.

7 Letter from A.B. to Dorothy Cheston Bennett of August/September 1929, quoted in *A Portrait Done at Home*.

8 *Ibid.*

9 Letter from A.B. to Harriet Cohen of 22 October 1930, in *Letters*, vol. 3.

10 Dorothy Cheston Bennett, *op. cit.*, p. 154.

11 Dorothy Cheston Bennett, article in *John o'London's Weekly* (24 September 1932).

12 Virginia Woolf, *A Writer's Diary*, entry for 28 March 1931.

13 Hart-Davis, *op. cit.*

14 *Journals*, entry for 22 October 1924.

Bibliography

Principal Published Works

A Man from the North (John Lane 1898)
Journalism for Women. A Practical Guide (John Lane 1898)
Polite Farces for the Drawing Room (Lumley and Co. 1900)
Fame and Fiction (Grant Richards 1901)
Anna of the Five Towns (Chatto and Windus 1902) ·
The Grand Babylon Hotel (Chatto and Windus 1902)
The Gates of Wrath (Chatto and Windus 1903)
Leonora (Chatto and Windus 1903) ·
The Truth about an Author 1903 (reprinted from the Academy, published by
    Methuen in 1914)
How to become an Author (*A Practical Guide*) (C.A.Pearson 1903)
Teresa of Watling Street (Chatto and Windus 1904)
A Great Man (Chatto and Windus 1904)
Sacred and Profane Love (Chatto and Windus 1905)
Tales of the Five Towns (Chatto and Windus 1905)
The Loot of Cities (Alston Rivers 1905)
Whom God hath Joined (A.Nutt 1906) ·
The Sinews of War, a romance by Arnold Bennett and Eden Phillpotts (T.Werner
    Laurie 1906)
Things that have interested me (privately printed, Burslem. 3 series: 1906, 1907,
    1908)
Hugo (Chatto and Windus 1906)
The Ghost (Chatto and Windus 1907)
The City of Pleasure (Chatto and Windus 1907)
The Grim Smile of the Five Towns (Chapman and Hall 1907)
The Reasonable Life (A.C.Fifield 1907)
Buried Alive (Chapman and Hall 1908)
The Statue, with Eden Phillpotts (Cassell and Co. 1908)

The Human Machine (New Age Press 1908)
The Old Wives' Tale (Chapman and Hall 1908)
The Glimpse (Chapman and Hall 1909)
What the Public Wants (a play) (Duckworth and Co. 1909)
Literary Taste: how to form it (New Age Press 1909)
Helen with the High Hand (Chapman and Hall 1910)
Clayhanger (Methuen 1910)
The Feast of St Friend (Hodder and Stoughton 1911)
The Card (Methuen 1911)
Hilda Lessways (Methuen 1911)
The Honeymoon, a Comedy (Methuen 1911)
Cupid and Commonsense (a play) (Frank Palmer 1912)
How to live on 24 Hours a Day (Hodder and Stoughton 1912)
The Matador of the Five Towns (Methuen 1912)
Mental Efficiency (Hodder and Stoughton 1912)
Milestones, a play by A.Bennett and E.Knoblock (Methuen 1912)
Those United States (Martin Secker 1912)
Paris Nights (Hodder and Stoughton 1913)
The Plain Man and his Wife (Hodder and Stoughton 1913)
The Regent (Methuen 1913)
The Great Adventure, a play of fancy (Methuen 1913)
The Author's Craft (Hodder and Stoughton 1914)
The Price of Love (Methuen 1914)
Liberty. A Statement of the British Case (Hodder and Stoughton 1914)
Over There. War Scenes on the Western Front (Methuen 1915)
These Twain (Methuen 1916)
The Lion's Share (Cassell and Co. 1916)
Books and Persons (selections from the New Age 1908–1911) (Chatto and Windus 1917)
The Title, A Comedy (Chatto and Windus 1918)
Self and self-management (Hodder and Stoughton 1918)
The Pretty Lady (Cassell and Co. 1918)
The Roll-Call (Hutchinson and Co. 1918)
Judith (a play) (Chatto and Windus 1919)
Our Women (Cassell and Co. 1920)
The Art of A. E. Rickards, with a personal sketch by Arnold Bennett (Technical Journals 1920)
From the Log of the Velsa (Chatto and Windus 1920)
Things that have interested me (Chatto and Windus 1921)
The Love Match (a play) (Chatto and Windus 1922)
Mr Prohack (Methuen 1922)
Lilian (Cassell and Co. 1922)

Body and Soul (a play) (Chatto and Windus 1922)
Don Juan de Marana (a play) (T.Werner Laurie 1923)
How to make the best of life (Hodder and Stoughton 1923)
Riceyman Steps (Cassell and Co. 1923)
Elsie and the Child (stories) (Cassell and Co. 1924)
The Bright Island (a play) (Bookman's Journal 1924)
A London Life, a play by A.Bennett and E.Knoblock (Chatto and Windus 1924)
Lord Raingo (Cassell and Co. 1926)
The Woman who stole everything (Cassell and Co. 1927)
Mediterranean Scenes (Cassell and Co. 1928)
The Savour of Life (Cassell and Co. 1928)
The Strange Vanguard (Cassell and Co. 1928)
Accident (Cassell and Co. 1929)
The Religious Interregnum (Ernest Benn 1929)
Piccadilly, The Story of the Film (Readers' Library Publishing Co. 1929)
Imperial Palace (Cassell and Co. 1930)
Venus Rising from the Sea (Cassell and Co. 1931)
The Night Visitor and other stories (Cassell and Co. 1931)
A Dream of Destiny (Cassell and Co. 1932)

Journals

Journal 1929 (Cassell and Co. 1930)
Journals, Vol. 1, 1896–1910, edited by Newman Flower (Cassell and Co. 1932)
Journals, Vol. 2, 1911–1920, edited by Newman Flower (Cassell and Co. 1932)
Journals, Vol. 3, 1921–1928, edited by Newman Flower (Cassell and Co. 1933)
Florentine Journal, 1 April–25 May 1910, with illustrations by Arnold Bennett
   (Chatto and Windus 1967)
The Journals, edited and selected by Frank Swinnerton, with the first publication
   of the missing Volume Six (Penguin 1971)

Letters

Arnold Bennett's Letters to his Nephew, edited by Richard Bennett (Harper and
   Bros. 1935)
Arnold Bennett, a Portrait Done at Home, with 150 letters from Arnold Bennett to
   D.C.Bennett (Jonathan Cape 1935)
Arnold Bennett and Frank Harris, 58 letters, 1908-1910. (Privately printed, Merion
   Station 1936)
Arnold Bennett and H. G. Wells, a record of a personal and literary friendship, edited
   by Harris Wilson (Rupert Hart-Davis 1960)
The Letters of Arnold Bennett, 3 volumes, edited by James Hepburn
   Volume 1, Letters to J. B. Pinker (Oxford University Press 1966)

Volume 2, Letters 1889–1915 (Oxford University Press 1968)
Volume 3, Letters 1916–1931 (Oxford University Press 1970)
Arnold Bennet in Love, a previously unpublished correspondence, edited and translated by George and Jean Beardmore (David Bruce and Watson 1972)

Selected Autobiographical Ephemera

'A Visit from Mr Hurley, by Arnold Bennett' (School Magazine, *The Median*, Christmas 1909)
My Education (Keele University, 22 January 1930)
'The Making of Me' (*Daily Express*, 6 June 1930)
'Clay in the Hands of the Potter' (*Windsor Magazine* 1913)
'The Return, an article by Arnold Bennett' (*King Albert's Book*, published by the *Daily Telegraph*, 1914)
'My Religious Experience' (*Century*, vol. 3, p. 540, 1926)

Principal Critical and Background Works Consulted

Allen, Walter, *Arnold Bennett* (Home and Van Thal 1948)
Barker, Dudley, *Writer by Trade, a view of Arnold Bennett* (Allen and Unwin 1966)
Bell, Clive, *Old Friends* (Chatto and Windus 1956)
Bennett, Dorothy Cheston, *Arnold Bennett, a Portrait done at Home* (J.Cape 1935)
Bennett, Marguerite, *Arnold Bennett* (Philpot 1925)
Bennett, Marguerite, *My Arnold Bennett* (Ivor Nicolson and Watson 1931)
Bolitho, Hector, *Marie Tempest* (Cobden Sanderson 1936)
Cohen, Harriet, *A Bundle of Time* (Faber and Faber 1969)
Cooper, Diana, *The Rainbow Comes and Goes* (Rupert Hart-Davis 1958)
Dean, Basil, *Seven Ages* (Hutchinson 1970)
Dickson, Lovat, *H. G. Wells* (Macmillan 1969)
Gide, André, *Journals 1889–1949* (Penguin 1967)
Gielgud, John, *Distinguished Company* (Heinemann 1972)
Greene, Ann, *With Much Love* (Geoffrey Bles 1949)
Gross, John, *The Rise and Fall of the Man of Letters* (Weidenfeld and Nicolson 1969)
Hales, H.K., *The Autobiography of 'The Card'* (Sampson Low 1936)
Hart-Davis, Rupert, *Hugh Walpole* (Macmillan 1952)
Hepburn, James, *The Art of Arnold Bennett* (Indiana University Press)
Hepburn, James, *The Author's Empty Purse and the rise of the Literary Agent* (Oxford University Press)
Holroyd, Michael, *Lytton Strachey* (Heinemann 1967–8)
Hunt, Violet, *My Association with Arnold Bennett* (American Bookman 1932)
Jenkins, J.G. (ed.), *The Victoria History of the County of Stafford*, vol. 8 (Oxford University Press 1963)

Knoblock, Edward, *Round the Room* (Chapman and Hall 1939)

Lewis, Wyndham, *The Roaring Queen* (Secker and Warburg 1973)

Locherbie-Goff, *La Jeunesse d'Arnold Bennett* (Editions de l'Observateur, Avesne-sur-Helpe, France)

Mackenzie, Compton, *My Life and Times* (Chatto and Windus 1963-71)

Mackerness, E.D. (ed.), *The Journals of George Sturt* (Cambridge University Press)

Marriott, F., *My Association with Arnold Bennett* (Keele University 1967)

Martin, Wallace, *The New Age under Orage* (Manchester University Press 1967)

Maugham, Somerset, *Life and Letters, June 1931.*

Mizener, Arthur, *The Saddest Story, a biography of Ford Madox Ford* (The Bodley Head 1972)

Moore, Harry T. (ed.), *Letters. D. H. Lawrence* (Heinemann 1962)

Morrell, Ottoline, *Early Memoirs* (Faber and Faber 1963)

Nichols, Beverley, *The Sweet and Twenties* (Weidenfeld and Nicolson 1958)

Owen, Harold, *The Staffordshire Potter* (Grant Richards 1901)

Pound, Reginald, *Arnold Bennett: a biography* (Heinemann 1952)

Roberts, T.R., *Arnold Bennett's Five Towns Origins* (Museums and Information Committee, Stoke-on-Trent libraries 1967)

Roby, Kilner E., *A Writer at War* (Louisiana State University Press 1972)

Rothenstein, John, *Summer's Lease* (Hamish Hamilton 1965)

Shattuck, Roger, *The Banquet Years* (J.Cape 1969)

Shaw, William, *When I was a Child, by an Old Potter*, with an introduction by Robert Spence Watson (Methuen 1903)

Smith, Grover (ed.), *Letters. Aldous Huxley* (Chatto and Windus 1969)

Smith, Pauline, *Arnold Bennett, a minor marginal note* (J.Cape 1933)

Swinnerton, Frank, *An Autobiography* (Hutchinson 1937)

Swinnerton, Frank, *Background with Chorus* (Hutchinson 1956)

Taylor, A.J.P., *Beaverbrook* (Hamish Hamilton 1972)

Thompson, E.P., *The Making of the English Working Class* (Gollancz 1963)

Tillier, Louis, *Studies in the sources of Arnold Bennett's novels* (Didier, Paris 1949)

Wain, John, *The Qualities of Arnold Bennett* (*Twentieth Century*, September 1954)

Warrilow, E.J.D., *Arnold Bennett and Stoke-on-Trent* (Etruscan Publications 1966)

Wells, H.G., *An Experiment in Autobiography* (Gollancz 1934)

Woolf, Virginia, *Mr Bennett and Mrs Brown* (Hogarth Essays No. 1, 1924)

Woolf, Virginia, *A Writer's Diary* (The Hogarth Press 1953)

Index

INDEX

Bennett, Arnold—*cont.*

tastes, 150; purchases paintings by Edouard Vuillard, 150-1; restlessness and unease apparent regarding sex, 151; liking for independence, 151; differences of opinion and rows with wife, 153-4; established as writer through *The Old Wives' Tale*, 155; first play staged, 155; quarrel with Eden Phillpotts, 157-8; experiences period of acute and difficult reassessment of views on women, 163-4; to England, 164; meets John Galsworthy, 164; regarded as one of England's contacts with Continental tastes, 165; return to France, 168; writes *The Honeymoon*, 168; domestic period of happiness, 170; prospering friendship with Pauline Smith, 170; as mentor to Pauline Smith, 170-1; suffers from lumbago and intense cold, 171; trip to Burslem, 171; to London, 171; meets and likes William Rothenstein, 171; his steadily-growing reputation, 172; at Bournemouth and Brighton, 172; writes part of *Clayhanger* in Brighton, 172; return to France, 173; writes about politics, 173; finishes *Clayhanger*, 177-9; travels extensively, 177; to Italy, 177; joined by Pauline Smith in Florence, 177; stay at Florence *pensione*, 177-8; return to Paris, 178; goes to Brittany, 179; moves to furnished flat in Paris, 180; visits England, 183; to Burslem, 183; views on H.G.Wells's *The New Machieavelli*, 183; activity in London, 184; plans trip to United States, 184-5; goes to Glasgow, 186; to America, 186; in New York, 186-7; visit to Washington and Boston, 187; to Chicago, Indianapolis, Philadelphia, 188; return to Britain, 188; on to Paris, 188; to Cannes, 188-9; bad attack of gastroenteritis, 189; success of play *Milestones*, 189-90; returns to England for good, 190-1; settles in Putney, 191; purchases yacht *Velsa*, 191; further illness, 191; sets off for Holland, 192; purchases country house Comarques, 192; strain on health imposed through being public figure and by constant travel in 1911, 193; collapse of wife with ill-health, 193; rows with editor of *Everyman*, 193-4; to

Paris, 194; move to Comarques, 194; illness of wife, 194; prepares *Velsa* for Baltic cruise, 196; tours with A.E. Rickards, 196-7; return to England, 197; Marguerite joins golf club, 197; to Continent for month, 198; to Brussels and Paris, 198; goes on further yachting trip, 200; sight-seeing in France and Italy, 200-1; death of his mother, 204-5; finishes writing *These Twain*, 201, 210; Marguerite operated on in Paris, 207; as responsible citizen at outbreak of World War I, 207; writes articles for *Daily News*, 208; anti-conscription views, 208; attends meeting of authors, 209; becomes military representative of Thorpe Division Emergency Committee, 209; engaged in committee work, 211; invites Frank Swinnerton to spend weekend on yacht, 211; longer stays in London, 211; as member of many Clubs, 211; agrees to become director of *New Statesman*, 211; returns to Comarques, 212; begins work on *The Lion's Share*, 212; accompanies G.H.Mair on tour of Western Front, 212, 217; asserts women inferior to men, 216; reports on World War I operations, 217-19; an exceptionally law-abiding citizen, 218; with H.G.Wells, plans campaign against 'Yellow Pressism', 218; return to London, 219; finishes *The Lion's Share*, 219, 221; attack on War Office inefficiency and class prejudice, 220; visit to H.G. Wells, 220; to Comarques, 220-1; quarrels with publishers, 221; starts work on *The Roll Call*, 222, 225; takes flat at Royal Yacht Club, 222; sends Richard Bennett to Oundle School, 223; mixes with new people, 223, 230; breakup of marriage, 224, 257-8; low work output in 1916, 224; finishes *The Roll Call*, 225; reactions to *The Pretty Lady*, 227; meets Siegfried Sassoon and F.E. Smith (*later* Lord Birkenhead), 230; elected to Other Club, 230; journey to Ireland, 230-1; sympathizes with Sinn Fein, 231; meets Lord Beaverbrook, 231-2; close friendship with Lord Beaverbrook, 232, 238; common affinity with Lord Beaverbrook, 232; invited by

384